The 1955 modernisation programme involved the development of block train working. One of the earliest such services transported iron ore from Tyne Dock to Consett Steelworks. As such trains were introduced, so more traffic was able to bypass the marshalling yard. British Railways 9F 2-10-0 No. 92065 steps crisply out of South Pelaw with a Consett-bound train.

*M. Dunnett*

Acton Yard — The Great Western yard at Acton saw increased prominence in the late 1970s as the concentration point for wagonload traffic from the Western and Southern Regions. In this August 1983 view, shortly before closure, Class 08 No. 08486 shunts HTV coal hoppers at the west end of the yard.

*P. Shannon*

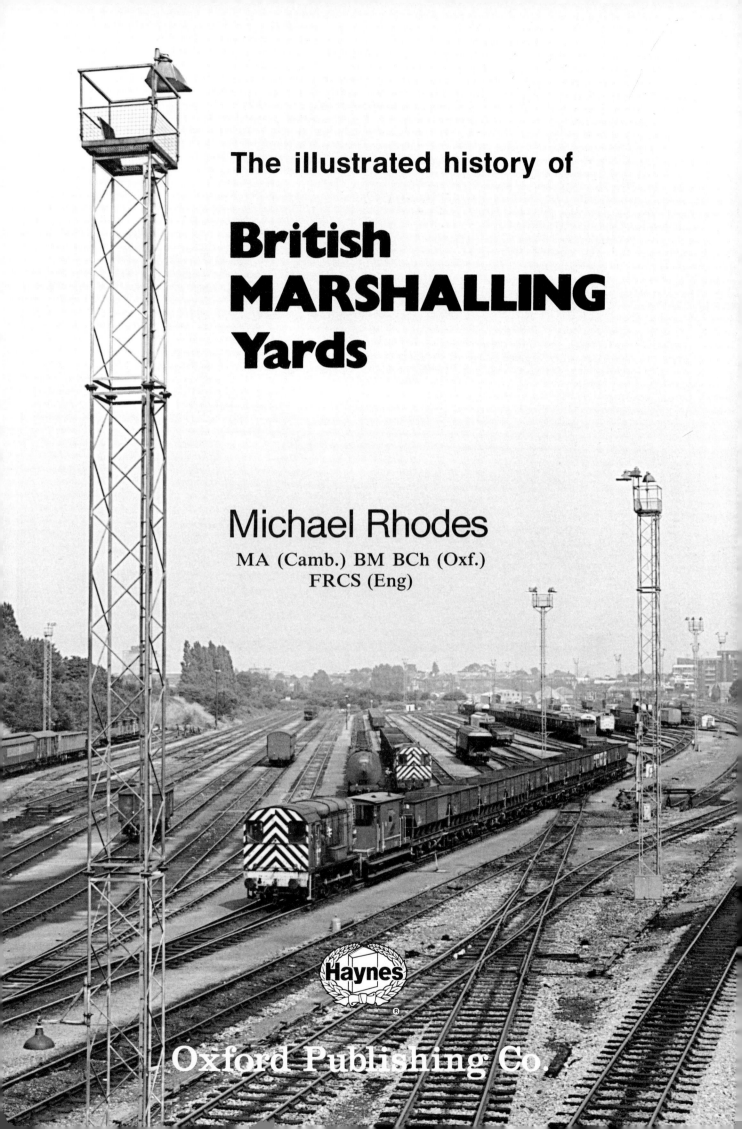

The illustrated history of

# British MARSHALLING Yards

## Michael Rhodes

MA (Camb.) BM BCh (Oxf.)
FRCS (Eng)

Oxford Publishing Co.

# Dedication

To my wife Jenny, daughter Lydia
and son Jonathan.

A view of the 'down' yards at Bescot taken from the No. 5 signal box in the early 1960s. Ivatt 2-6-0 No. 46421 stands in the yard, as an ex-LMS diesel shunter propels a wagon into one of the sorting sidings. On the far right is the New Yard which was replaced, along with the old sidings by the new 'down' hump yard, opened in 1966.

*N. Hazelwood*

A FOULIS-OPC Railway Book

© 1988 M. Rhodes & Haynes Publishing Group

**British Library Cataloguing in Publication Data**
Rhodes, Michael, *1960–*
British marshalling yards.
1.   Great Britain.   Railway freight transport
services
I.   Title
385'.264'0941

ISBN 0-86093-367-9

**Library of Congress catalog card number**
88-83695

Published by:
Haynes Publishing Group,
Sparkford, Near Yeovil, Somerset. BA22 7JJ

Haynes Publications Inc.
861 Lawrence Drive, Newbury Park, California
91320, USA.
Printed by J.H. Haynes & Co. Ltd.

# Contents

# Preface

The demise of the marshalling yard is almost complete. Like so many other facets of railway infrastructure, the hump marshalling yard has all but disappeared from the British Rail network. The first major hump yard to be abolished was Ripple Lane in East London and by 1971 the 'down' side of Kingmoor Yard was closed; this after less than ten years of active service. Since 1970 closures have followed one after another, until in 1988 the only automated hump yard still in operation in the United Kingdom is Scunthorpe New Yard. Here, a Dowty retarder system controls wagons as they descend from the hump.

The first large, purpose-built marshalling yard in Britain was the 'Grid Iron' at Edge Hill near Liverpool. Opened at the turn of the century the yard used a continuously falling gradient to facilitate wagon movement through its sidings. The 'hump' principle, a refinement of the simple falling gradient, was first incorporated in a major yard at Feltham in South London. Once the 'hump' yard was accepted as the most efficient method for sorting large numbers of freight wagons, further development concentrated on automation.

The first retarders, or rail-brakes, were installed in the 1930s at Whitemoor Yard near March. More refined retarders were used in both Scotland and East London in the 1950s. By 1960, at the peak of marshalling yard construction, installations such as Margam and Kingmoor could boast primary and secondary retarders, automatically controlled by means of radar and weigh-bridges. Complex gadgetry compensated for variables such as wind speed, wagon rollability and track curvature. In spite of these complex systems damage to wagons and their cargoes was still a major problem and a more modern type of wagon control was therefore developed. The Dowty system was installed between 1966 and 1971 at three of Britain's most modern yards; Tinsley, Bescot, and Scunthorpe. The damage to wagons decreased but the cost of maintenance to the thousands of small hydraulic rams proved too expensive to justify as wagon throughput at Britain's major yards fell. Increased efficiency and a decrease in freight traffic was the fatal combination which led to the closure of Britain's hump yards.

An introductory chapter is followed by a detailed study of 25 major yards. Important developments that have taken place over the last 60 years are explained. Each chapter concentrates on one or two large installations and describes their planning, construction and operation. The text is complemented with track plans and tables of the freight traffic dealt with by each yard. Illustrations have been gathered from a broad spectrum of photographers and include many official pictures, some taken from the air. It is hoped that the text will prove interesting and informative, both to the serious railway historian and the more casual reader.

# Acknowledgements

This book could not have been produced without the generous help of well over one hundred British Rail employees, many of whom are credited individually at the end of each chapter. Special thanks are also due to Mark Bentley at the BRB for his overall support and the British Rail Staff photographers at York and Waterloo who helped by providing many of the official photographs in the book. Final thanks go to Frank Knaggs, and the secretaries at NEI Parsons in Newcastle who devoted many spare evenings to type the manuscript.

All photographs are by the author unless stated.

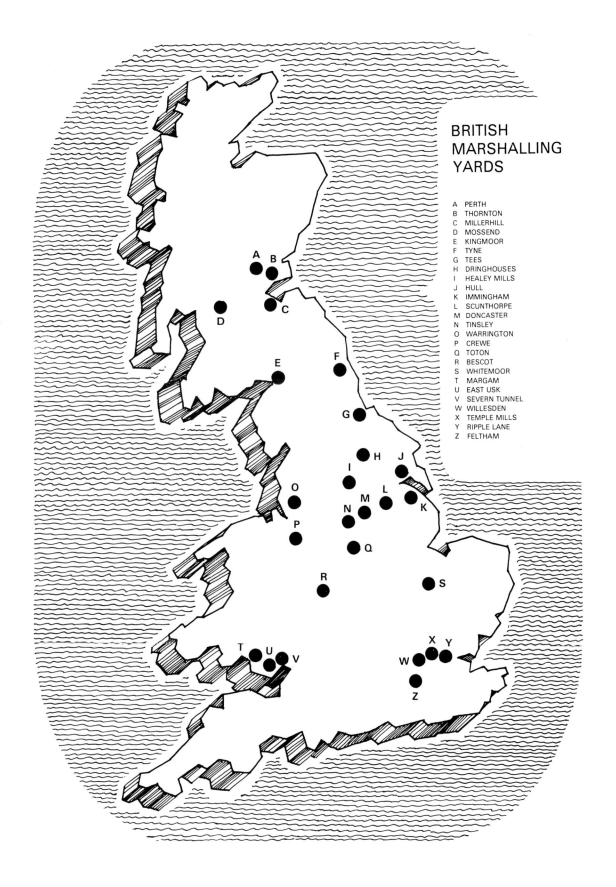

BRITISH
MARSHALLING
YARDS

A PERTH
B THORNTON
C MILLERHILL
D MOSSEND
E KINGMOOR
F TYNE
G TEES
H DRINGHOUSES
I HEALEY MILLS
J HULL
K IMMINGHAM
L SCUNTHORPE
M DONCASTER
N TINSLEY
O WARRINGTON
P CREWE
Q TOTON
R BESCOT
S WHITEMOOR
T MARGAM
U EAST USK
V SEVERN TUNNEL
W WILLESDEN
X TEMPLE MILLS
Y RIPPLE LANE
Z FELTHAM

A Stanier 'Black Five' locomotive is prepared for a day's duty around Workington. Coal can be seen falling into the hopper on its way into the locomotive tender. Scenes such as these have passed, and like many of the major marshalling yards are part of railway history.

Workington no longer has a marshalling yard, just a few sidings to handle local traffic. The locomotive depot has closed and only two or three daily freights serve this previously-busy centre.

*M. Dunnett*

# Chapter 1

# Marshalling Yards — An Introduction

A marshalling yard is defined as a railway yard in which goods trains are assembled (Oxford English Dictionary). This may be regarded as a simplistic understanding of a marshalling yard, but forms a good basic definition from which to elaborate.

From the very beginning of public railways on the Stockton & Darlington system, freight traffic has required marshalling; that is the sorting of wagons bound for different destinations into appropriate train loads. Many railway companies were slow to recognise the profitability of transporting freight and hence did not invest in major marshalling yards until many years after their formation. The Midland Counties Railway is a good example of such a reluctance to invest in freight handling facilities, for it was not until 1871 that a large complex of sidings was built at Toton Yard, although coal had been carried by the Railway for some 30 years prior to the construction of these sidings. Similar sluggish investment in freight handling was the reason for so many small and inadequately equipped marshalling yards scattered around the country.

During the second half of the nineteenth century, however, there was considerable development of the marshalling yard. From three or four parallel single-ended sidings the concept of a purpose-built yard for the

sorting of freight wagons was expanded. The pinnacle of this idea was probably the Grid Iron Yard at Edge Hill, in Liverpool, which was completed by the London & North Western Railway by the late 1800s (*Plan 1*). Here, for the first time, there were reception sidings, passing through a shunting neck to sorting sidings, after which there were North and South Grid Irons where fine shunting of trains could take place.

The Edge Hill Grid Iron was also unique in being the first yard to use the assistance of gravity in sorting freight trains. It was built on a continuously falling gradient and this was used to facilitate the consecutive movement of wagons from the reception lines to the sorting sidings, through the grid irons and into the departure lines. All shunting at the yard was manual in that the control of wagons, as they rolled down the gradient, required a shunter to bring down their brakes. The control of point work in the yard area was also manually executed and the yard was obviously very labour intensive. The Grid Iron, whilst perhaps representing the modern hump marshalling yard 'in-embryo', was by no means typical of the marshalling yards of the late 1800s and early part of the twentieth century. The majority of these were flat-shunted rather than gravity assisted and consisted of

single-ended sorting sidings which obviously lacked the benefit of yards like Edge Hill where wagons flowed through the sidings in an orderly sequence. The less advanced single-ended sorting yards were often ill-equipped to deal with heavy freight flows. Reception roads were often short, inappropriately placed and accessible only through the shunting neck, creating several major operating difficulties.

Britain's first hump marshalling yard was opened on the 4th November 1907 at Wath. The Great Central Railway provided a pair of yards each with nine reception roads and 30 sorting sidings. Shunting was controlled by two signal cabins, 'A' for the 'down' yard and 'B' for the 'up' side. The points from the hump were controlled by compressed air which gave a response time of less than one second for points furthest from the box. Siding layout was unusual with two fans of 15 sidings and it was not until 1920 when Feltham Yard was built that the more conventional hump yard design appeared in the United Kingdom.

The London & South Western Railway freight concentration yard at Feltham was the most modern in the country when it was opened in the early 1920s. Its design was based upon the best of both American and European marshalling yard technology. There were separate yards for 'up' and

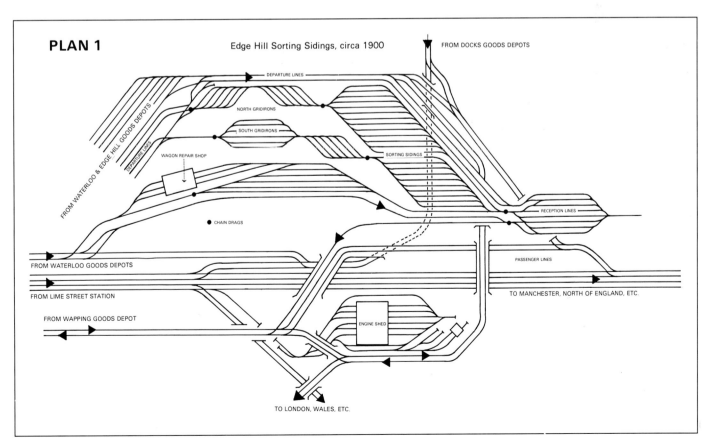

**PLAN 1**     Edge Hill Sorting Sidings, circa 1900     FROM DOCKS GOODS DEPOTS

DEPARTURE LINES

FROM WATERLOO & EDGE HILL GOODS DEPOTS

DEPARTURE LINES

NORTH GRIDIRONS

SOUTH GRIDIRONS

WAGON REPAIR SHOP

SORTING SIDINGS

CHAIN DRAGS

RECEPTION LINES

FROM WATERLOO GOODS DEPOTS

PASSENGER LINES

FROM LIME STREET STATION

TO MANCHESTER, NORTH OF ENGLAND, ETC.

FROM WAPPING GOODS DEPOT

ENGINE SHED

TO LONDON, WALES, ETC.

'down' traffic. The hump shunting system was adopted and the turnouts to the sorting sidings were electrically controlled. Reception sidings and sorting sidings were provided although there were no departure sidings. The hump was manually operated and all wagons had to be retarded by the shunters or chasers working from the hump summit.

Such installations were expensive to construct but where freight flows were heavy enough the justification for modern marshalling facilities was becoming much clearer. Even as the yard at Feltham was being completed, plans were already well underway for the construction of Britain's first mechanised hump shunting yard at Whitemoor, near March. This yard was unique in several ways. It was the first installation where rail-brakes or retarders were incorporated in the marshalling yard. These were of German design and were patented by Dr Fröhlich. A cross-section of the design is shown in *Figure 1*. They were operated by hydraulic pressure which when released into the braking mechanism raised two metal rails either side of the running rail. These two pieces of metal then grasped the running wheel of a wagon passing over them. By increasing the hydraulic pressure, the braking force on a wagon could also be increased. The yard was opened in 1929 and the Fröhlich rail-brakes installed at this time were still in operation in October 1980 when the hump was finally closed. There are examples of exactly the same rail-brake mechanism still operating in many of West Germany's major marshalling yards even in the late 1980s.

Not only was Whitemoor the first yard to incorporate retarders, but it was also the first where the setting of points leading to sorting sidings could be automatically controlled. This was effected by a novel system of concentric drums which are described in more detail in the chapter about Whitemoor. Although only the 'King', 'Queen' and 'Jack' points could be thus controlled, this was the first step towards the automation of sorting siding selection.

The LNER were quick to recognise the benefits of their new yard at March and a similar hump marshalling yard was constructed on the same site for 'down' traffic in 1933. In spite of the success of Whitemoor, it was not until 1948 that another major hump marshalling yard was constructed. The 1930s saw yards like Mottram on the Great Central Railway built on much the same design as the original Grid Iron at Edge Hill. The cost of hump marshalling yards and the necessity for a throughput in excess of 3,000 wagons daily made them hard to justify at many less important freight marshalling centres. Two hump marshalling yards similar to March (Whitemoor) were constructed between 1930 and 1948, at Hull and at Toton 'down' sidings. Neither contained major advances on the Whitemoor complex, and both rail-brakes and marshalling control were of a similar type. In 1948 however, the 'up' sidings at Toton were completely rebuilt and equipped with rail-brakes, automatic point operation throughout the shunting area, and other modern features such as electric lighting and telecommunication.

The perceived benefits of the yards like Toton and Whitemoor were part of the reason for the heavy investment by British Railways in hump marshalling yards when they drew up their 1955 Modernisation Plan.

# The 1955 Modernisation Plan

The 1955 Modernisation Plan tackled not only the needs of the freight traffic network, but also motive power and passenger modernisation. The aim of the plan for freight traffic was:

1. Shorter transit times.
2. Greater reliability.
3. Punctuality of delivery.
4. A reduction in operating costs.

The yards inherited by British Railways, and still in operation in 1955, were largely constructed at the time of individual railway companies and reflected various companies' attempts to keep traffic on their systems for as long as possible. Thus there was a geographical overlap of yards with multiple traffic staging. The majority of these sidings and yards were small, flat-shunted and inefficient. The 1955 plan hinged around the construction and modernisation of 55 yards, allowing the closure of 150 smaller, less well-utilised, marshalling sites. The cost of such a scheme was £80,000,000 and it was aimed to execute the plan over 15 years. Similar modernisation of both goods stations, rolling stock and motive power was also planned for the freight sector. In 1955 there were approximately 1,000 locations where brakes had to be pinned down on unfitted freight trains — this cost 10,000 man hours every week. It was therefore regarded as a priority to introduce fully-fitted freight trains which could travel at higher speeds, saving 2,000 locomotives nationwide and reducing the number of man hours needed for the pinning down of brakes.

The continuous braking of all freights was the single most important step in the 1955 Modernisation Plan and was undertaken at a cost of £75,000,000. The centralisation of goods stations was not successful. British Railways had not appreciated that in decreasing the convenience of small local goods sidings, they would lose customers hand over fist. Other less dramatic changes were the increase of wagon capacity and the rationalisation of wagon stock. The total number of British Railways' owned freight vehicles in 1955 was 1,141,500; the general total was to be reduced to 752,000 by 1974.

In 1956, the first report on the progress of the Modernisation Plan was undertaken by the Traffic Survey Group. The key area highlighted for improvement was provision of efficient terminal facilities with easy road/rail interchange. Such freight transfer depots would decrease railway trip working and increase the distribution of rail-hauled goods by road vehicles. Two solutions were put forward to implement this idea. First, major transfer depots such as the Stratford Freight Terminal were planned and con-

structed; this aided the concentration of large amounts of locally generated traffic. Secondly, ports and steelworks were connected to the main rail network via their own private sidings and freight traffic arriving on the British Railways network was often not ready-marshalled. It was suggested that if a financial inducement could be provided for better organisation of freight train working, then there could be a large scale reduction in marshalling operations by co-operation between private siding owners and British Railways. A third and less clearly emphasised idea was the provision of freight depots adjacent to major marshalling yards. This was not initially pursued, but has come into prominence during the 1980s with striking examples such as the P.D. Stirling Railfreight Depot at Mossend.

By June 1957 the fifth progress report on the modernisation programme was published and in it a review of the major marshalling yards under construction was provided. The Eastern Region had already 70 per cent completed the new yard at Temple Mills, whilst site clearance was underway at Ripple Lane. The London Midland Region were preparing a scheme for a yard at Swanbourne, near Bletchley, to deal with the outer circle route for cross-London freight; Carlisle (Kingmoor) was also being planned. In the north east, plans existed for a new yard at Newport, near Middlesbrough, and the remodelling of Nos 1 and 2 'up' yards at York, as well as the Dringhouses site to the south of York. Meanwhile, further north in Scotland, modernisation was well advanced. Thornton Yard, in Fife, opened in December 1956, and was the first British yard to incorporate both primary and secondary rail-brakes. As well as this increased sophistication in wagon retardation, the rail-brakes themselves were the first to incorporate automatic control by means of radar and a weighbridge. Some difficulties and teething problems were experienced with the automatic equipment at Thornton, but by 1957 it was efficiently sorting up to 2,000 wagons daily.

**Small country goods stations provided the interface for millions of tons of rail-borne freight until their mass closure under Dr Beeching. The goods shed, cattle dock and coal depot are all visible in this view of Penicuik station, taken in March 1967. With the closure of such stations, the number of wagons needing sorting at major yards, such as Millerhill, fell precipitously.**

*G. Turnbull*

A new hump yard was built at Alloa at a cost of £500,000 and reaped a saving of £60,000 per annum by the concentration of marshalling facilities in Clackmannan. Millerhill, near Edinburgh, was already 25 per cent completed, and a scheme for a new yard at Perth, costing £820,000, was approved in October 1956. The Southern Region had made enquiries with design consultants in order to construct new yards at Tonbridge in Kent, and Eastleigh, near Southampton. The Western Region had completed plans for a hump yard at Margam, and invested £90,000 for the provision of ten sorting sidings at Port

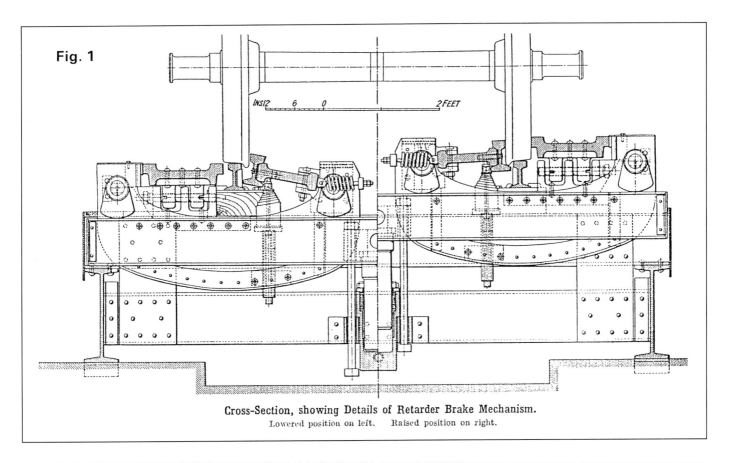

**Fig. 1**

INS 12  6  0  2 FEET

Cross-Section, showing Details of Retarder Brake Mechanism.
Lowered position on left.    Raised position on right.

Talbot as a stop-gap measure. The accommodation in Severn Tunnel Junction 'up' and 'down' yards was increased at a cost of £420,000 and land at Elmbridge, Gloucester, was obtained for £40,000 in preparation for the construction of a £1,500,000 marshalling yard.

Major new goods sheds were planned for 21 big cities and numerous other improvements were underway, including the strengthening of the staithes at West Blyth to accommodate diesel shunting locomotives and 24½ tonne coal hoppers. Reappraisal of the 1957 review in 1959 reported that all projects were still on course and progressing well. The freight tonnage handled by British Railways during that year (excluding coal) was in excess of 85 million tonnes.

In July 1960, Sir Brian Robertson reported for the Select Committee on Nationalised Industries and for the first time highlighted problems and doubts in the original 1955 Modernisation Plan. The

The yardmaster, Warwick Burton, oversees the staff of the 'down' control tower at Tees Yard on 12th September 1980. Tees was the busiest 'hump' yard built under the 1955 Modernisation Plan and had the capacity to sort up to 7,500 wagons daily.

*P. Shannon*

The vice-like grip of the primary retarders at Tees 'up' yard slows three HTO coal hoppers on their descent from the hump.

*P. Shannon*

The steep gradients over the hump can be seen in this view of the 'down' hump at Tees Yard. One of the major expenses of modern hump marshalling yard construction was the necessity to provide such a large hump. The invention of the Dowty Wagon Control System meant that hump earthworks could be considerably reduced, but even this saving did not reduce the cost of major yards sufficiently and as traffic decreased they became increasingly difficult to justify.

*P. Shannon*

initial estimated cost of £1,240 million for the entire re-equipment of British Railways had risen by 1957 to £1,500 million, and again by a similar amount in 1959. Railway earnings were falling and it was decided to speed up the implementation of the Modernisation Plan with increased spending between 1959 and 1963. This allowed the benefits of the plan to be reaped earlier. The aims and priorities of modernisation were somewhat different from those in 1955, and it was reported that the first priority of freight rationalisation should be "To exploit the great natural advantages of railways as bulk transporters of passengers and goods and to revolutionise the character of the services provided for both".

Disappointments in 1960 with regard to the original 1955 plan included the difficulty in decreasing the quantity of wagons because customers liked the cheap storage of stationary wagons. British Railways were still tackling the same problem in 1986 in the Swansea Docks system, where large numbers of unfitted coal wagons lay as storage bunkers for several weeks at a time. It was also found that the decrease in freight depots caused customers to change to road-haulage if there was any inconvenience in the transfer to central freight depots.

Concern was expressed that Great Britain was the only country in the modern world where the majority of freight traffic remained loose-coupled and wagon turnaround times were very poor, averaging 11.9 working days between revenue-earning trips.

The operating view of British Railways' management during the late 1950s and early 1960s was still that the provision of the most modern and efficient marshalling yards was the best way to increase freight revenue and retain the already dwindling tonnages of goods hauled by rail. The London Midland Region marshalling yard plan provided for a reduction in the number of yards from 111 to 42, a very small number of which would be major marshalling yards, with a greater number of satellite yards. This plan, conceived in 1958, was the result of traffic studies initiated by the BTC

and consultation with industry to assess the needs of different areas. The criteria for the construction of a marshalling yard were clearly laid out. 'Such a machine should be of the most modern design, contain every technical aid to achieve speed of throughput, avoidance of damage and minimum detention of engines and wagons. They should be few in number and sited in relation to traffic flows so that trunking over the longest distance is the standard operation.'

A number of alternative types of yard were available. The single bi-directional yards dealing with both 'up' and 'down' traffic over a single hump and through a common set of sorting sidings was the most practical, as long as wagon throughput did not exceed 4,000 per day. Ideally such a yard would lie between 'up' and 'down' running lines, but where this was not possible, or the traffic throughout exceeded 4,000 wagons daily, the provision of separate yards to deal with 'up' and 'down' traffic was deemed a better option. The fundamental requirement of such yards was that wagons be dealt with in a sequential manner. Thus a freight train would arrive in one of the reception roads, where the locomotive was detached and a shunting engine attached at the rear to propel the train over the hump. The wagons were placed into the sorting sidings, from where completed trains could be drawn forward into departure roads. The local requirements of different yards might include the provision of secondary sorting sidings if there were a large number of neighbourhood private sidings requiring fine marshalling of trip freights. There might also be provision of wagon repair workshops and a trans-shipment shed. *Plan 2* shows a schematic drawing of the ideal bi-directional yard dealing with approximately 4,000 wagons daily.

There were limitations to the introduction of this 'ideal' marshalling yard strategy. Sites of sufficient size were hard to find, when an area of approximately three miles in length, and up to half a mile wide, was needed for a single yard. The number of reception sidings was always difficult to

judge. In an ideal world, trains would arrive evenly spaced over twenty four hours, but in many yards their arrivals were bunched, causing congestion in the reception sidings. The reception roads were to be laid out on the basin principle, so that when the incoming train engine was detached, the vehicles could stand without the brakes having to be applied. In the sorting sidings it was recognised that the maximum number of roads should not exceed 50 because of the problems of curvature on the outside of the yard, and the increased length of the point area between the hump and the clearance of the final sets of turnouts. There were also problems in the control of wagons descending from the hump, and whilst the rail-brakes originally introduced at March in 1929 had been refined and automated, it was still difficult to control the variables of wind, rail-resistance and rollability, and damage to cargo was not infrequent.

The evolution of control techniques for wagon movement from the hump to sorting sidings had developed in four stages:

(a) The provision of shunting staff to brake and control the movement of each cut of wagon — for example, Feltham.

(b) The provision of single-stage manually-operated retarders, which took account of weight only, and the success of which was almost entirely dependant upon the skill and judgement of the retarder operator in the control tower — for example, March (Whitemoor).

(c) Partial automation where the primary retarders were equipped with automatic control and the secondary retarders were actuated manually by the operator, selecting the pressure to be applied according to the weight of the cut, speed from the primary retarder and distance to run — for example, Temple Mills.

(d) Full automation in which all the factors (ie weight, acceleration, rolling characteristics and distance to run) were automatically computed so as to provide a final leaving speed from the secondary

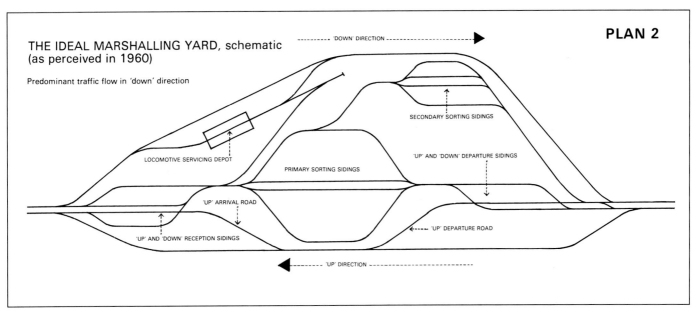

THE IDEAL MARSHALLING YARD, schematic (as perceived in 1960)

PLAN 2

Predominant traffic flow in 'down' direction

'DOWN' DIRECTION

SECONDARY SORTING SIDINGS

LOCOMOTIVE SERVICING DEPOT

'UP' AND 'DOWN' DEPARTURE SIDINGS

PRIMARY SORTING SIDINGS

'UP' ARRIVAL ROAD

'UP' DEPARTURE ROAD

'UP' AND 'DOWN' RECEPTION SIDINGS

'UP' DIRECTION

retarders. This, in theory, would enable all wagons to run as far as required down the individual sorting sidings and buffer up at a speed low enough to avoid damage to their cargoes — for example, Margam.

The options (c) and (d), whilst theoretically great improvements upon the single-stage manually-operated retarders were, in practice, difficult to operate. In 1962, the instance of damage at Toton 'up' sidings, which was manually-operated, had been less than in the more modern and semi-

dangerous cargoes to be marshalled over a hump. Such wagons still needed manual shunting where either the shunter propelled them directly on to the rear of the trains to which they were to be attached, or a shunter pinned down their brakes as they were released into a sorting siding.

In the early 1960s, the problems of the mechanised hump yard became ever more evident, and doubts about the long-term benefits of such installations meant that many of the original plans for marshalling yards were withdrawn. The Reshaping of British Railways' report in 1963 began to highlight other areas for investment and

The Freightliner network was to replace many of the long-haul mixed freight trains of the 1960s. A small number of trains do convey goods at speeds of up to 75mph but the idea has not been as successful as was originally hoped. One of the first Freightliner trains, the 3E22, Aberdeen to King's Cross, is seen leaving the Forth Bridge behind the first Class 47, No. D1100.

*A. Vickers*

automatic yards. Problems such as these were the stimulus to the birth of a new wagon control system using miniature hydraulic rams. These could both retard and accelerate wagons. A pilot study with this Dowty automatic wagon control system was undertaken at Goodmayes Yard in Essex, and such was its success that the new yard at Tinsley, completed in 1966, benefited from the installation of the Dowty system through its sorting sidings. This system was undoubtedly a vast improvement upon the traditional provision of rail-brakes. It was however expensive to install, difficult and costly to maintain, and therefore its justification hard to defend, unless the throughput of wagons at the yard equipped with the Dowty system was in excess of 3,000 daily. Even the Dowty wagon control system was, however, not sufficiently safe to allow fragile or

development. The first target for modernisation was once again the wagon fleet. In 1963, the average time between loads was 11.9 working days, whilst the average loaded transit time was two days with an average journey length of 67 miles. Modernisation was aimed at reducing wagon turn-around time to six days, increasing the average length of journey and decreasing the transit time. In order to achieve this, both new wagons and a reduced network of rail heads were needed.

In 1961, of the 620 collieries nationwide, 600 were rail-connected, and the annual tonnage of coal dealt with by rail was 133 million tonnes. There were 5,031 stations open to coal traffic, 61 per cent of which was wagonload. Of these wayside coal depots, 1,172 received no delivery at all during 1960, whilst 1,790 dealt with only one to five wagons each week, and 2,005 of

Two views of the typical 1960's freight highlight the large volume of freight handled prior to Beeching. Household containers and vans predominate in both pictures. The irony of such views lies in the fact that modernisation of marshalling yards and then freight stock took place in the wrong order. Once freight vehicles and motive power had been modernised, many of the 'new' yards were no longer suitable to sort them! 'Royal Scot' 4-6-0 No. 46115 climbs Shap on its way home to Carlisle Kingmoor on 3rd June 1965. The exhaust from the banking engine can just be seen in the background.

A lengthy van train leaves the loop at Southwaite after an express has passed. 'Black Five' 4-6-0 No. 44780 has the long climb to Shap ahead.

*M. Welch*

the depots handled 74 per cent of the coal traffic. This was obviously an area for rationalisation.

Great hopes were also held for the new Freightliner network and it was predicted that during 1980, 57 million tonnes per annum would be transported an average distance of over 200 miles per container. An estimate that block train load working would increase from 6 million tonnes per annum to 20 million tonnes per annum in 1984 has been more than fully realised. The predictions regarding coal, iron, steel and oil all pointed to increased block train working and were largely correct. One area,

collapse in wagonload rail freight operations, the Speedlink network was introduced, and it is upon the success of this network that the future of Britain's marshalling yards depends.

Many of the planned yards were never constructed. However, large installations at Tees, Tyne, Healey Mills, Carlisle (Kingmoor), Millerhill, Margam, Tinsley and Bescot were built.

As wagonload traffic decreased so too did the workload of these new automated marshalling yards, and as early as 1971 major closures were being undertaken at yards such as Carlisle (Kingmoor). This

**Modernisation suggested that Shrewsbury might benefit from the construction of a major hump marshalling yard. The project was never pursued and Coton Hill Yard remained unchanged. In August 1985, a pair of Class 20 locomotives, Nos 20120 and 20020 depart with the 7G19, 08.00 Speedlink to Bescot. The train is made up of empty timber wagons returning from Welshpool to Scotland, and a few empty oil tanks from the Abbey Oil Terminal.**

*P. Shannon*

however, where the Reshaping report got things seriously wrong, was in the handling of general merchandise. This was deemed an area with very substantial traffic potential and a predicted growth between 1964 and 1984 of 120 per cent was assessed on the basis of a 4 per cent increase in gross national product each year. This prediction totally ignored the large increase in motorways during the 1960s, and the phenomenal success of road haulage companies in competing for much of the general merchandise traffic, previously regarded as the preserve of British Railways.

Between 1968 and 1975 wagonload freight traffic fell from 143 million tonnes per annum to just 39 million tonnes each year. During the same period the tonnage of block trains increased from 67 million tonnes per annum to 136 million tonnes annually. In the face of such a complete

process has continued over the last 15 years, but from being a purely negative exercise aimed at coping with a drastic fall off in wagonload traffic, it has developed into a more positive restructuring and reshaping of the marshalling yard network to cater for a successful and profit-making Railfreight operation. The British Railways Board's corporate plan, 1983 to 1988, pronounced that by May 1984 non-airbrake wagonload mixed freight traffic would have been phased out completely, and the Speedlink network which was born in 1975, would be running at a level of 6 million tonnes per annum. Whilst this might seem small when compared to the wagonload movements of the 1960s, which exceeded 100 million tonnes annually, it is regarded by many as the re-birth of wagonload freight, after an almost disastrous decade, when very little future was seen in this side of British Rail

operations. The national Speedlink network, in contrast to the National Freight Train Plan of 1966, was a network established by customers' demands. The NFTP was purely an operating manoeuvre rather than a business-orientated reorganisation.

The Speedlink network was designed primarily to give a high standard of service based on the backbone of twelve network marshalling yards. These were fed by 17 secondary or supportive yards, and the whole service used a wagon fleet of just 10,000. The nationwide introduction of the TOPS, or Total Operations Processing System, allowed Railfreight to control tightly the distribution of their wagons. This enabled Speedlink to operate with the minimum number of vehicles and therefore with the maximum efficiency.

In 1980, the twelve network yards were: Willesden (Brent) in London, Severn Tunnel Junction in South Wales, Bescot in Birmingham, Whitemoor, as the gateway to East Anglia, Toton in the Midlands, Warrington Yard for the North West, Healey Mills, Doncaster and York (Dringhouses) in Yorkshire, Tyne and Carlisle in the North of England and Mossend in Glasgow for the whole of Scotland. There were, as already mentioned, 17 secondary or supportive yards which fed into this network, these being: Thornton, Grangemouth, Millerhill and Ayr in Scotland, with Ellesmere Port, Manchester (Ashbury), Tees, Scunthorpe and Tinsley in the North of England, whilst London and the south

might be similarly remarshalled after a journey of only 50 miles. Long-distance freights between the twelve major yards already mentioned were sorted in portions such that sections of the train were detached or attached at key calling points along the route between two major centres. This led to a reduction in the number of marshalling yards and a rationalisation of their facilities.

Efficient Speedlink work was not only achieved by the rationalisation of yards, but also by limited investment to update facilities at some yards, making them more suitable for such traffic. The whole

at Toton were Speedlink-based. The further fall in wagon throughput experienced with the loss of the old-style wagonload coal and scrap traffic meant that less than 1,000 wagons each day were marshalled at Toton. Similar reductions in wagon throughput were experienced all over the country and, by 1984, when the conversion to air-braked freight working was complete, traffic at yards like Whitemoor was running at 3,500 wagons per week. In South Wales, at Severn Tunnel Junction, the throughput of 10,000 wagons a week in 1976 had fallen to just 6,000 in 1984. Both Tyne Yard and Carlisle (Kingmoor) had undergone drastic

east was served by yards at Ipswich, Parkston Quay, Temple Mills, Hoo Junction and Dover. The sidings at Cardiff, Exeter and Eastleigh were the final yards classified as secondary or supportive sidings. The traffic feeding into the Speedlink network based upon these yards was generated from 112 Railfreight terminals, which were privately-owned, and a further 115 British Rail-owned loading and unloading points.

By May 1984, all traffic, including household coal and scrap, was transported in air-braked wagons (with the exception of some bulk loads which remained vacuum or unfitted) and the entire wagonload operation of British Rail came under the aegis of the Speedlink system. Because of this transfer to Speedlink, the requirements of British Rail for marshalling yards had completely changed. No longer were complete trains propelled over the hump and separated into dozens of separate cuts before reassembly into new freights, which

Speedlink network resembled most nearly the pattern of fast goods trains that were the pride of the London & North Eastern Railway in the 1930s. Like them, the Speedlink services were usually long-distance trains. Rather than being reformed en-route Speedlinks were allowed several intermediate yard stops of approximately one hour, where limited portion swapping could take place. In the late 1970s and early 1980s, Toton Yard was the hub of the Speedlink network with over 100 Speedlink trains each week. The yard throughput at Toton had fallen from 5,000 wagons daily in the mid-1970s to 1,600 daily by 1980. Of these wagons, a substantial proportion were made up of coal and scrap vehicles which were not incorporated in the Speedlink network. Toton was selected as the focus for the remaining old style wagon movements over the North/South and West Coast/East Coast routes.

By 1985, however, the need for such wagons had disappeared and all operations

**Hamburg Maschen is the largest and most advanced marshalling yard in the world. A Class 291 No. 291 034-7 diesel shunts over the south/north hump into the 64 sorting sidings at the yard. The yard's capacity to handle 11,000 wagons daily has not been reached because of the industrial recession which has afflicted all the nations in Western Europe.**

surgery to reflect their reduced wagon throughput. Meanwhile, small yards like Doncaster (Belmont), which was constructed as part of the Doncaster resignalling during the late 1970s, were the up and coming examples of a Speedlink era yard. The emphasis was on minimum cost yard operation, the abolition of civil engineering stock from the marshalling sidings, a minimum detention of traffic wagons in the yard and an evenly-spaced timetable to guarantee a large throughput even with a small number of sorting sidings.

The 1980s were a period of consolidation on the backbone of this Speedlink network. In all, about 650 private sidings and 150

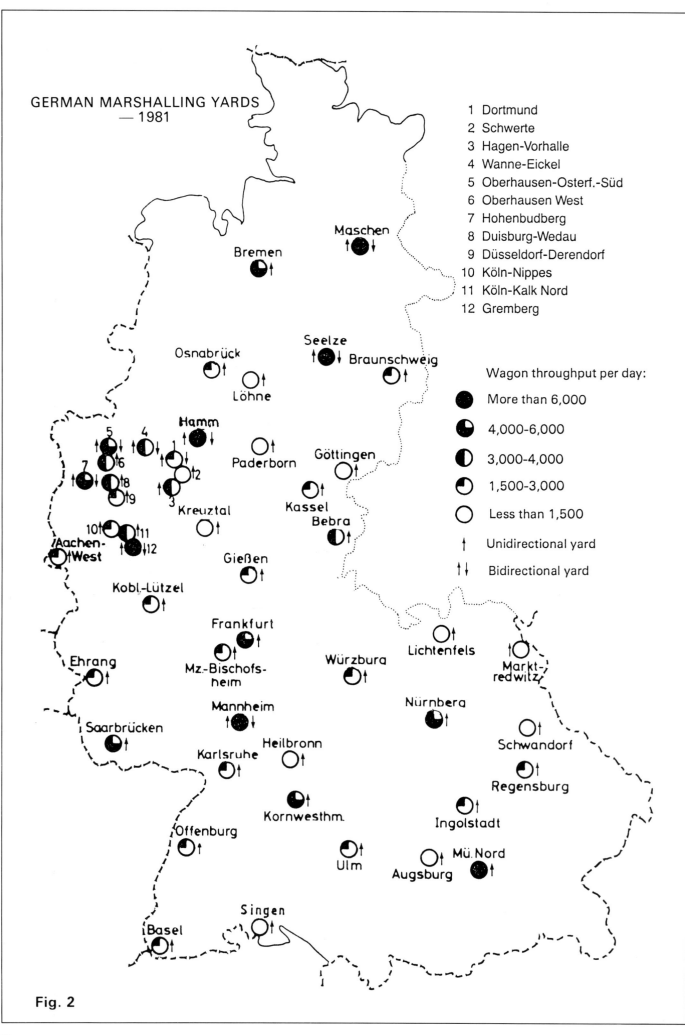

GERMAN MARSHALLING YARDS
— 1981

1 Dortmund
2 Schwerte
3 Hagen-Vorhalle
4 Wanne-Eickel
5 Oberhausen-Osterf.-Süd
6 Oberhausen West
7 Hohenbudberg
8 Duisburg-Wedau
9 Düsseldorf-Derendorf
10 Köln-Nippes
11 Köln-Kalk Nord
12 Gremberg

Wagon throughput per day:

● More than 6,000
◕ 4,000-6,000
◐ 3,000-4,000
◔ 1,500-3,000
○ Less than 1,500

↑ Unidirectional yard
↑↓ Bidirectional yard

Maschen
Bremen
Osnabrück
Löhne
Seelze
Braunschweig
Hamm
Paderborn
Göttingen
Kassel
Bebra
Kreuztal
Gießen
Kobl.-Lützel
Frankfurt
Lichtenfels
Markt-redwitz
Mz.-Bischofs-heim
Würzburg
Ehrang
Mannheim
Nürnberg
Saarbrücken
Heilbronn
Schwandorf
Karlsruhe
Regensburg
Kornwesthm.
Ingolstadt
Offenburg
Ulm
Augsburg
Mü. Nord
Singen
Basel

5  6
7  8  9
4  1  2
3
10  11  12
Aachen-West

Fig. 2

18

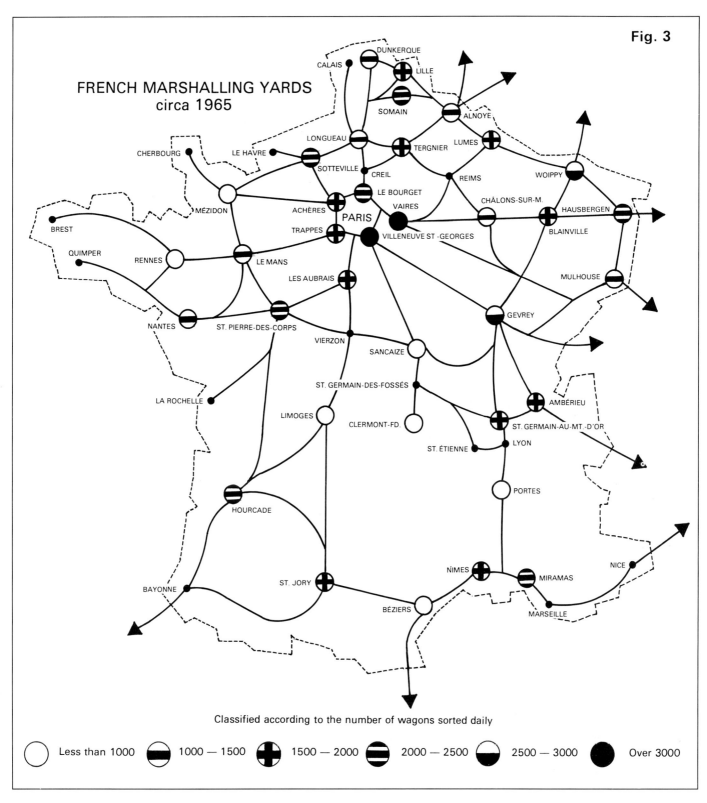

**Fig. 3**

**FRENCH MARSHALLING YARDS**
circa 1965

Classified according to the number of wagons sorted daily

| | | | | | |
|---|---|---|---|---|---|
| ○ Less than 1000 | ⊖ 1000 — 1500 | ✚ 1500 — 2000 | ⊜ 2000 — 2500 | ◗ 2500 — 3000 | ● Over 3000 |

British Rail-owned sidings can be serviced by the Speedlink system. The provision of Section 8 grants for investment in private rail sidings has meant that there has been a steady increase in such facilities, along with an interest in privately-owned terminals offering handling facilities. British Rail is now investing in railway-owned freight depots, sited near major marshalling centres and capable of both distribution and warehousing of rail-borne goods.

## A Brief Comparison with the Continent

*Figures 2 and 3* illustrate the distribution of marshalling yards on both the West German and French railway systems. Both enjoy a considerably higher level of public sector investment, when compared to British Rail, and neither have had to suffer the ravages of Beeching or quite the degree of state-sponsored onslaught by road traffic hauliers. The Deutsche Bundesbahn has long been a byword for an efficient and intensively operated rail network, and the plethora of large marshalling yards are a reflection of a very heavy commitment to rail freight by the German railways.

The optimism of the railway operating staff of the DB is nowhere better reflected than in the Hamburg Maschen marshalling yard. This enormous complex, with a capacity to sort 11,000 wagons daily, was opened in 1981 and has a total of 112 sorting sidings. Marshalling is fully automatic and controlled by a Siemens Computer. Wagon retardation has been pursued to its logical, but extremely expensive end, by the provision of three sets of equipment to deal with wagons descending from the hump. Thyssen jaw-type rail-brakes provide the initial retardation followed by secondary Thyssen rubber beam retarders. As soon as wagons emerge from the secondary retarders, the vehicles are kept moving at a steady rate of 1.25 metres per second by Thyssen rim haulers. These are track-mounted mules, which operate the secondary retarders to the head

of each sorting siding. From here, Halhinko track mounted mules take over to carry the wagon gently along the sorting siding until it reaches the other vehicles in its road. The yard at Maschen is indeed a remarkable piece of engineering, but was planned in pre-recessionary days, and even the Deutsche Bundesbahn whose investment in rail freight has been ten times that of British Rail, have had to rationalise marshalling yards in the light of recent traffic changes, and the tightening of state-controlled purse strings. This has meant that large yards such as Hohenbudberg, which handled up to 6,000 wagons daily, have been closed completely. Increased efficiency in wagon usage, capacity of modern air-braked wagons, and block freight train working, added to an underlying fall in freight traffic, have all conspired to force even this most pro-railway administration to ask for economies to be made by a reduction in marshalling yards. In some areas, such as Duisburg Wedau, traffic has been concentrated on one of two parallel hump yards.

The French railways, whilst heavily subsidised, were never as reliant upon freight traffic for their revenue. The marshalling yard network of the 1960s shown in *Fig. 3* is a reflection of the less industrialised nature of France. Developments since the 1960s have seen the SNCF passenger network flourish. Marshalling yard capacities have, in contrast, been reduced in line with increased block freight train working.

# The Future of British Marshalling Yards

Since 1985 there has been rapid change in the Railfreight network of Great Britain. The twelve major marshalling yards of the early 1980s have already been reduced to just ten. Both Dringhouses and Healey Mills were surplus to operating requirements because of their close proximity to the network yard at Doncaster (Belmont). Speedlink traffic has also fallen at Toton with a redistribution of services to Bescot and Doncaster (Belmont) and this has left a question mark over the future importance of Toton as a Speedlink centre. The number of yards continues to fall but aggressive marketing has meant a steady increase in both the tonnage of traffic and the number of trunk Speedlink trains operated.

The way ahead for marshalling yards may well be indicated by small, intensively used, yards such as Doncaster (Belmont), Warrington (Arpley) and Mossend. In 1986, a clear indication of the future was given by a reshaping report directed at the Railfreight infrastructure in South Wales. In it, the closure of both Margam and Severn Tunnel, in favour of a new yard at East Usk, was proposed. This move to the twelve sorting sidings at East Usk indicated the considerable spare capacity contained in the large arrays of sorting sidings at Britain's hump marshalling yards. This radical scheme may well be the first of several, which will be aimed at providing a network of marshalling yards, more suited to the expanded Speedlink network. Plans to concentrate marshalling at Bescot on a

In 1982 Wath Yard was nearing closure and very little traffic was marshalled at this site. Closure of the Woodhead route in 1981 was the final act which precipitated the disappearance of Great Central marshalling yards from the country. Here, Class 08 0-6-0 diesel-electric No. 08434 shunts empty wagons on 6th March 1982, which will form the 8T21 service to Healey Mills. Class 31 No. 31220 is parked in the background, awaiting departure of the train. The unusual layout of the sorting sidings is well seen in this view looking north over the 'up' sorting sidings. The 'B' hump signal box can just be seen in the distance.

new yard, on the 'down' side of the main line, have a similar aim; the provision of a small number of long, parallel sorting sidings, through which a large number of Speedlink wagons can be sorted. The plans for a new Speedlink yard at Willesden, with sidings of capacities in excess of 100 Standard Wagon Lengths (SWL), is perhaps the clearest indication of what the distant future may hold if Speedlink traffic continues to expand as it has done over the last ten years.

The following 14 chapters cover the major British marshalling yards from Feltham, constructed in the 1920s, through to more modern yards such as Doncaster and Scunthorpe. Many of the yards mentioned have been conceived, built, heavily utilized, rationalised and disappeared all within the period covered by this book. The rapidly changing Railfreight network of today is an example of how railway infrastructure must continually adapt to industrial and technological progress in order to provide an efficient service.

# Chapter 2

# The London Yards

Each major English railway company built its own railway terminus in London. In a similar way, each company constructed a major marshalling yard or yards for freight services to the Capital. This proliferation of marshalling yards meant that cross-London traffic was invariably delayed by marshalling at two yards within the city. The LSWR built their new yard at Feltham. The other Southern Railway companies had yards at Norwood Junction, Hoo Junction and Hither Green. The Great Western Railway built a large yard at Acton, the Great Central at Neasden, the Midland at Brent, and the Great Northern at Ferme Park. The Eastern Region followed this pattern by modernising both the Great Eastern yards at Temple Mills and the London, Tilbury & Southend yard at Ripple Lane. In the early 1960s, the pattern of freight operation around the capital was virtually unchanged from that of pre-Grouping days. Whilst the 1955 Modernisation Plan had brought about mechanisation at Temple Mills and Ripple Lane, it had done nothing to streamline the freight network in London as a whole.

The National Freight Train Plan of the mid-1960s took the first steps towards the concentration of freight marshalling at a few major centres. The traffic along the East Coast Main Line (ECML) was diverted to the Joint line south of Doncaster, and from here via Whitemoor to Temple Mills. This allowed the closure of the yard at Ferme Park. A similar transfer of LSWR traffic to Acton brought about the closure of Feltham Yard. The close proximity of Ripple Lane to Temple Mills meant its early closure, further reducing the major marshalling yards in London. The 1960s also saw the demise of the former Great Central Railway London Extension and with it Neasden Yard. Heavy coal traffic from Yorkshire and the Midlands was transferred to the Midland Main Line and marshalled at Brent Yard.

During the 1970s, seven yards handled the capital's freight. Temple Mills for the Eastern Section of the city, Brent for the heavy coal from the Midlands, and Sudbury (Willesden) for West Coast Main Line (WCML) traffic. Acton handled the Western Region freights as well as some from the South Western Division of the Southern Region. Norwood Junction Yard dealt with traffic from the Central Division of the Southern Region and Hoo Junction the South Eastern Division. The seventh centre was at Hither Green where much Continental traffic was staged on its way to and from Dover. The 1970s were a time of further rationalisation.

Trains from Toton to Brent were transferred to Acton at the end of the 1970s leaving just a few stabling sidings at the old Midland Railway yards. A similar redirection of traffic occurred on the Southern Region. Ferry trains from Dover were routed through to Acton as were many local freights from Southern Region metals. Acton became an important centre for traffic from a wide area. During the same decade a gradual decline occurred at the two remaining London yards of Temple Mills and Willesden.

Further change was, however, still to come. In 1982, Temple Mills was partially closed and 1984 saw the closure of Acton Yard to Speedlink freight. All trains from Dover and the Southern Region were routed round the North London line to Willesden Brent Yard. Additional long-haul trains were introduced from Severn Tunnel and Toton to Willesden and the ex LNWR yard effectively became London's only major marshalling facility. The transfer of freight marshalling to Willesden (Brent) meant the partial closure or 'moth-balling' of Sudbury Yard. Thus, at the time of writing, the major Speedlink yard for London was Willesden (Brent) Yard, with a secondary yard still in use at Temple Mills.

The future is not clear. Whilst the electrification of the North London line from Stratford will undoubtedly bring yet more traffic to Willesden, there is still a possible future role for Temple Mills as a smaller marshalling centre. The Brent Yard at Willesden is operating at near capacity and any increase in traffic would force changes to the current layout at Willesden. Staff at the yard see the current importance of Brent sidings as short-lived, and just a holding operation until British Rail build a new yard on the site of the old Sudbury yards. Plans do exist for a brand new Speedlink yard at Willesden. The yard would cater for trains up to a length of 100 Standard Length Units (SLUs) and would be flat-shunted. It is envisaged that some Channel Tunnel traffic may terminate at this new 'super yard'.

If such plans come to fruition, then Willesden (Brent) may also close or be handed over to the Civil Engineer's Department. Whether, after such major investment, there would be any future for Temple Mills remains to be seen. It is, however, clear that the main yard to serve London in the next decade will be at Willesden. Twenty years ago the freight marshalling around the capital was handled in ten major yards. Today a long rationalisation programme has left just one major yard, Willesden (Brent).

## Feltham Yard

Designed in 1919 and completed in 1923, Feltham Yard was heralded as the first modern hump marshalling yard in the United Kingdom. The yard provided marshalling facilities for traffic between the London & South Western Railway and the rest of the country *(Plan 3)*. The operational advantages of the new yard were fivefold:

1.  The main line between Weybridge and Clapham Junction was relieved of goods trains.
2.  All traffic from the South West to Brent, Willesden, Neasden and Nine Elms travelled in single trainloads to Feltham avoiding a duplication of services from major centres such as Southampton.
3.  The average loading of freight trains from the South West was increased.
4.  Time was saved at smaller goods stations by the dispatch of traffic "rough" to Feltham.
5.  Economies in both locomotive and rolling stock utilization were achieved.

Even in 1920 there was considerable concern about the inability of marshalling yards to function efficiently when the flow of traffic through them was high (greater than 2,000 wagons daily). A document published in 1920 states; "most of the greater marshalling yards in the British Isles have developed from relatively small beginnings; they are often subject to operating inefficiency due to that reason alone". In the light of such problems the construction of a yard like Feltham was a new and radical approach to the freight operating difficulties of the day.

## Planning and Layout

Painstaking research was undertaken before the final plan of Feltham Concentration Yard was drafted. A daily capacity of 3,500 wagons was envisaged, the largest of any yard in Britain in 1920. A committee was formed from the higher echelons of the traffic and engineering departments of the London & South Western Railway Company.

This group of engineers and operating staff studied the major yards in Great Britain and visited the more notable freight concentration yards in Europe and the USA. The result of their deliberations was Feltham, "probably the highest development in this class of yard in operation" (1920).

Two similar yards were constructed next to each other *(Plan 3)*. The 'up' yard

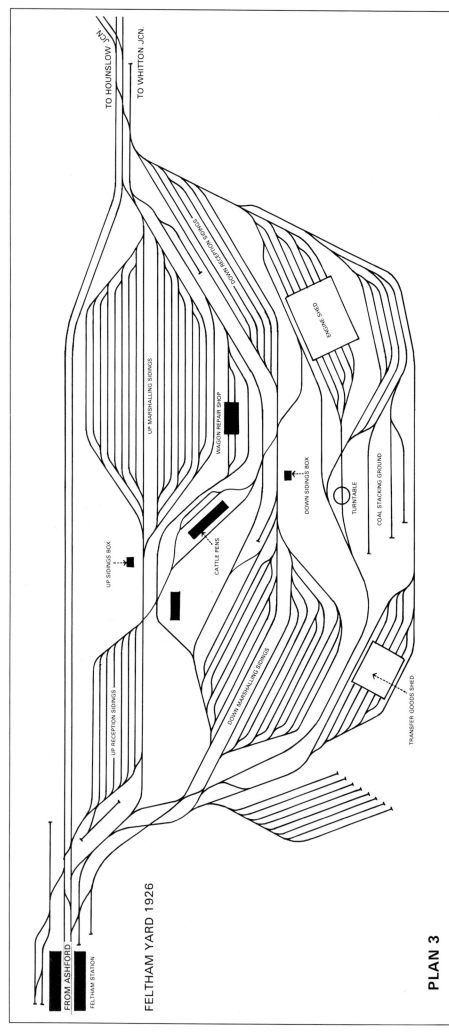

FELTHAM YARD 1926

PLAN 3

contained eight reception sidings leading to eighteen sorting sidings, whereas the 'down' yard had twenty sorting sidings from its array of eight reception roads. In addition to the two main yards, a nest of eight sidings was provided at the east end of the yard for re-sorting traffic into 'station order'. Between the two main yards was a large wagon repair shop. A central site was chosen for this as a separate workshop for both 'up' and 'down' yards could not be justified. Next to the wagon shops were the cattle pens. These facilities for feeding and watering cattle in transit were provided because of the large amount of livestock handled at Feltham. Both an engine shed

**Feltham Yard — Three views of the yard taken in the 1920s showing both ends of the complex and the 'down' hump.**
*Railway Gazette International*

and goods shed were constructed on the outer boundary of the yard. The goods shed enabled the cargoes of several lightly-loaded wagons bound for the same destination to be transferred into one wagon. Thus traffic from the northern lines to Southampton could be added to traffic from Nine Elms to the coast and a more efficient use of wagons was achieved. The engine shed had a capacity for 42 tender locomotives and a coal stacking ground for 12,000 tons of coal. The new shed provided 'on site' servicing for freight locomotives and allowed the closure of nearby Strawberry Hill Depot. Operations at the yard were managed from an impressive two-storey office building, topped by a large clock tower. Such was the prestige of the yard that a lawn and shrubbery were laid out in front of the main office, in the centre of the yard!

## Operation

Entrance to the east end of the yard was controlled by Feltham signal box. The west end was paradoxically controlled by Feltham East box. Both boxes were manual, lever-operated, cabins with electric track diagrams. In addition to these two boxes there were two 'hump' signal cabins. Each cabin contained a diagrammatic operating board with two press buttons adjacent to each set of points. All points were electrically-operated, and suitable manipulation of the point buttons allowed easy access into the sorting sidings. The 'up' and 'down' humps were similar, although the slope of the yard site, a falling gradient of 1 in 653 from Feltham station, accounts for their slightly different gradient profiles.

An approach of 130ft at 1 in 40 was followed by a fall of 1 in 50 for 170ft on the 'up' hump. A further 580ft at 1 in 150 saw the wagons into their respective sidings. These gradients are very small compared to modern yards, (cf. Kingmoor 1 in 16 off the hump), but allowed a 70 wagon test train, with 50 cuts, to be sorted in twelve minutes.

Urie's 4-8-0 tank engines were used to bank trains over the hump. As the train was propelled at a speed of 1 mph, an ingenious system of chalking the wagons was used to sort them into the correct sidings. The first

wagon had chalked on it the number of the road into which it had to run. This was observed by the signalman who duly set the points. On the rear of the first wagon was the siding for the second wagon. By observing the number chalked on the rear of each shunt the signalman could thus set the points appropriately. The introduction of rail-brakes or retarders had not yet taken place, and it was therefore necessary to employ three 'brake chasers' to follow the wagons down into the yard. A total of ten staff were employed at each hump with two assistant shunters responsible for the despatch of trains from each yard. The yard as a whole was under the control of the yardmaster who had further clerical, technical and maintenance staff at his disposal. The addition of freight guards to the staff provided employment for well over one hundred people at Feltham marshalling yard.

Traffic through the yard was heavy. In 1924, 50 'down' trains arrived each day as compared to 26 arrivals on the 'up'. A total of 46 departures left in the 'up' direction whilst 18 were timetabled to head west. Most local freights were handled by the Urie 4-6-2 tank locomotives. These trains brought a total of 2,500 wagons to the yard each day, 1,200 to the 'down' hump and 1,300 to the 'up' hump. *Table 1* shows the road allocation of the sidings at Feltham, whilst *Table 2* lists the 'down' departures recorded on 17th March 1924.

As one of Britain's early marshalling yards, Feltham closed relatively early in the 1970s. Much traffic from the south west to London travelled by road. Freight from Exeter and further west ran along the Great Western routes to London whilst trains from Eastleigh and Southampton were diverted to a variety of different yards including Norwood, Acton and Willesden. As modernisation progressed, much traffic from Southampton was containerised and the extensive Freightliner depot at Millbrook was constructed. Closure of many small goods stations was inevitable; Windsor, Feltham station, Kingston upon Thames, Staines, Twickenham and Bracknell have all disappeared from the freight map.

Today, wagonload traffic from the South West to London travels to Willesden Yard. Much traffic for northern England travels directly from Southampton and Eastleigh, via Severn Tunnel or Oxford. This avoids marshalling in London and accounts for the considerable reduction in freight yards around the Capital. Feltham was London's first major hump marshalling yard and, as its most primitive, was the first to close. It led the way for several later developments such as the massive Great Eastern yard at Whitemoor, but changes in the economy and transport policies brought about its early demise.

# Temple Mills Yard

The first marshalling yard at Temple Mills was constructed in 1880. Subsequent developments in East London were haphazard, and by the early 1900s there were ten separate yards at Temple Mills. Satellite

## Table 1
### Road Allocation of Sidings at Feltham

#### Down side
#### Reception Roads

| No. | Length Feet | Wagon Capacity | No. | Length Feet | Wagon Capacity |
|---|---|---|---|---|---|
| 1 | Not yet provided | — | 6 | 1,125 | 56 |
| 2 | Not yet provided | — | 7 | 1,056 | 52 |
| 3 | 1,205 | 60 | 8 | 1,211 | 60 |
| 4 | 1,169 | 58 | | | 340 |
| 5 | 1,090 | 54 | | | |

#### Marshalling Sidings

| No. | Length Feet | Wagon Capacity | Allocation |
|---|---|---|---|
| 1 | 1,564 | 78 | Southampton Docks |
| 2 | Not yet provided | | |
| 3 | 1,435 | 71 | Southampton Town. |
| 4 | 1,435 | 71 | Basingstoke. |
| 5 | 1,448 | 72 | Portsmouth via Eastleigh |
| 6 | 1,448 | 72 | Eastleigh |
| 7 | 1,555 | 77 | Dorset line. |
| 8 | 1,555 | 77 | Andover and Salisbury line. |
| 9 | 1,639 | 82 | Transfer wagons for Up side. |
| 10 | 1,635 | 81 | Wimbledon. |
| 11 | 1,545 | 77 | Chertsey to Surbiton. |
| 12 | 1,545 | 77 | Woking. |
| 13 | 1,487 | 74 | Guildford. |
| 14 | 1,487 | 74 | Reading. |
| 15 | 1,435 | 71 | Windsor and Reading line. |
| 16 | 1,435 | 71 | Twickenham, Richmond and Thames Valley. |
| 17 | 1,435 | 71 | Kingston. |
| 18 | Not yet provided. | | |
| 19 | Not yet provided. | | |
| 20 | 1,435 | 71 | Stock, wait orders and cripple traffic. |
| | | 1,267 | |

#### Up side
#### Reception Roads

| No. | Length Feet | Wagon Capacity | No. | Length Feet | Wagon Capacity |
|---|---|---|---|---|---|
| 1 | 1,376 | 64 | 6 | 1,426 | 67 |
| 2 | 1,288 | 60 | 7 | 1,375 | 64 |
| 3 | 1,367 | 64 | 8 | 1,477 | 70 |
| 4 | 1,350 | 63 | | | 515 |
| 5 | 1,350 | 63 | | | |

#### Marshalling Sidings

| No. | Length Feet | Wagon Capacity | Allocation |
|---|---|---|---|
| 1 | Not yet provided | | |
| 2 | | | |
| 3 | | | |
| 4 | | | |
| 5 | 1,600 | 76 | G.C.R. |
| 6 | 1,600 | 76 | Brentford to Point Pleasant. |
| 7 | 1,495 | 70 | Common users. |
| 8 | 1,495 | 70 | Common users. |
| 9 | 1,725 | 82 | N.L.R. |
| 10 | 1,662 | 79 | L. & N.W.R. |
| 11 | 1,547 | 73 | Hounslow. |
| 12 | 1,493 | 70 | Nine Elms loaded. |
| 13 | 1,520 | 72 | Nine Elms empties. |
| 14 | 1,531 | 72 | Nine Elms loaded. |
| 15 | 1,542 | 73 | G.N.R. |
| 16 | 1,531 | 72 | Midland Railway |
| 17 | 1,481 | 70 | Transfer wagons to Down yard. |
| 18 | Not yet provided. | | |
| 19 | 1,331 | 62 | Cripples, stock, etc. |
| | | 1,017 | |

The capacity of the various lines in the sortings sidings at the Feltham station end of the yard is as follows:-

### Marshalling Grid

| No. | Length Feet | Wagon Capacity | No. | Length Feet | Wagon Capacity |
|---|---|---|---|---|---|
| 21 | 1,800 | 90* | 5 | 600 | 30 |
| Shed road | 1,056 | 52* | 6 | 600 | 30 |
| 1 | 600 | 30 | 7 | 600 | 30 |
| 2 | 600 | 30 | 8 | 400 | 20 |
| 3 | 600 | 30* | *Temporary capacity* | | |
| 4 | 600 | 30 | 372 | | |

### Table 2
### West End Departures—Feltham Marshalling Yard

From 12.01 am to 11.59 pm 17th March 1924

| Train | | Load |
|---|---|---|
| 1.45 am | Feltham to Twickenham. | 49. |
| 2.45 am | Feltham to Exeter. | 61. |
| 3.05 am | Feltham to Woking. | 69. |
| 3.50 am | Feltham to Eastleigh. | 64. |
| 4.15 am | Feltham to Reading. | 44. |
| 5.10 am | Feltham to Reading. | 58. |
| 5.40 am | Feltham to Southampton. | 67. |
| 6.05 am | Feltham to Windsor. | 49. |
| 8.00 am | Feltham to Feltham Station. | 59. |
| 9.30 am | Feltham to Woking. | 62. |
| 10.00 am | Feltham to Eastleigh. | 69. |
| 10.40 am | Feltham to Southampton. | 69. |
| 11.00 am | Feltham to Reading. | 70. |
| 12 noon | Feltham to Kingston. | 45. |
| 12.40 pm | Feltham to Alton. | 50. |
| 1.15 pm | Feltham to Staines. | 46. |
| 1.30 pm | Feltham to Twickenham. | 40. |
| 1.40 pm | Feltham to Southampton. | 70. |
| 2.20 pm | Feltham to Bracknell. | 36. |
| 3.10 pm | Feltham to Surbiton. | 63. |
| 5.40 pm | Feltham to Southampton. | 70. |
| 6.40 pm | Feltham to Eastleigh. | 61. |
| 7.00 pm | Feltham to Woking. | 35. |
| 8.00 pm | Feltham to Surbiton. | 41. |
| 9.00 pm | Feltham to Woking. | 64. |
| 9.25 pm | Feltham to Wimbledon. | 50. |
| 9.33 pm | Feltham to Kingston. | 41. |
| 10.25 pm | Feltham to Southampton. | 63. |
| 11.05 pm | Feltham to Wimbledon. | 62. |
| 11.50 pm | Feltham to Exeter | 67. |
| 50 trains | Total | 1694 |

Average 56 wagons per train

yards at Goodmayes, Broxbourne, Thames Wharf, Mile End and Northumberland Park also handled traffic passing through the eastern side of London. Extensive trip working and complex interconnections greatly delayed the shunting and dispatch of wagons from this area, and a new yard was therefore needed. In February 1954, the Temple Mills project was authorised. The £3 million scheme envisaged a large new yard at Temple Mills, capable of dealing with over 4,000 wagons each day.

Rail connections from Temple Mills were convenient. To the north was Copper Mill Junction, on the Cambridge main line, whilst, to the south, access was possible to the Norwich main line as well as the North London line and the London Docks. The site for the yard was already occupied by ten smaller yards and construction of the new sidings was therefore slow and carefully planned. The piecemeal construction lasted four years and was completed in September 1958. During this time other marshalling yards at Whitemoor, Goodmayes, Thames Wharf, Mile End and Northumberland Park undertook extra marshalling to reduce the burden on the sidings at Temple Mills. It was possible to divert 20 per cent of traffic from Temple Mills, but even during the disruption of reconstruction, the balance of traffic continued to be handled at the London yard. For twelve months prior to the completion of the new marshalling yard, all train movements in the area were controlled by hand signalling. Instructions to the signalmen and train crews changed on an almost daily basis to reflect the rapidly changing layout of sidings. In spite of such operating difficulties no major accidents occurred during this twelve month span, a tribute to the staff at Temple Mills.

## Layout of the Yard
### (Plan 4)

As Britain's second automated hump marshalling yard, Temple Mills had a conventional layout. Twelve reception sidings led to 47 sorting sidings in eight groups. To the east of the sorting sidings lay eight departure roads. In addition to the main hump yard there were two smaller yards for local traffic; the West Yard and the East Yard. The main yard was designed for two directional working. 'Down' arrivals had access into seven of the reception roads and 'down' departures could leave directly from the sorting sidings in groups A and B. Shunting in these two fans could be conducted from the south end over a secondary hump called the Manor hump.

The sorting sidings varied in length from 51 to 82 SLUs, with the exception of one single-ended road in fan A. This 'short brake siding' was for the storage of brake vans and was equipped with a special 24in stroke hydro-pneumatic buffer stop. This was capable of halting a brake van travelling at up to 12¹/₂mph; an innovation in 1958! The sorting sidings had the capacity to hold up to 3,044 wagons as compared to the reception sidings standage of 680 wagons. The longest reception road held 75 wagons with engine and van, the shortest just 47.

To the north of the hump and retarders was the newly-constructed West Yard. It handled traffic for the western side of the Great Eastern (GE) network. This was mostly bound for stations along the Cambridge route. The East Yard was built on the site of the old Loughton Yard and undertook further marshalling of local traffic for the stations, along the lines to Southend and Ipswich.

## Operation of the Yard

Shunting of the main yard was under the dual control of staff in both the hump cabin and the yard control tower. After arrival in the reception sidings, each train was inspected by one of the cutters on the hump. The wagon dockets were checked and each vehicle was chalked with a code indicating the siding into which it should be sorted. 'A3' denoted the No. 3 road in the A fan and 'B5' the fifth siding in the B fan. Meanwhile the train locomotive was released to be serviced in a purpose-built depot in the yard or sent direct to Stratford. Four standard 350hp diesel-electric shunters from Stratford depot were used in pairs to shunt the hump. This practice continued until the closure of the hump in 1981 even though early planning had suggested the development of a single 500hp machine. This planned 'super-shunter' was never built, but the Class 13 units used at Tinsley were a partial answer to the need for more powerful shunters.

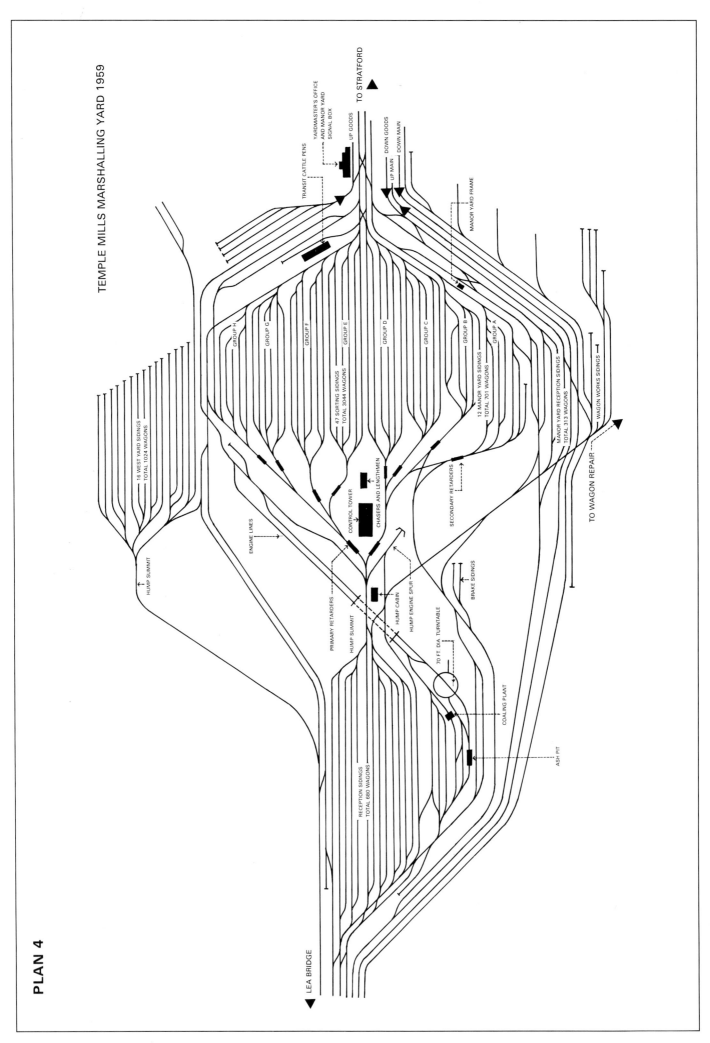

TEMPLE MILLS MARSHALLING YARD 1959

Temple Mills Yard — Taken in 1972, this view shows a pair of Class 08 shunting locomotives propelling a mixed rake of wagons over the hump. On the left are vans stored in the West Yard Sorting Sidings which were only used during the sugar beet season.

*British Rail*

The operator in the yard control tower at Temple Mills guides a rake of VVV vans into their appropriate sorting siding in 1972.

*British Rail*

Control of wagon sorting was not as sophisticated as that at Thornton Yard in Scotland. A unique three-position semaphore signal stood at the hump top. A vertical position indicated to the shunter that he should propel his train briskly to the hump; 45 degrees inclination meant shunt slowly over the hump, and horizontal meant stop. This signal was under the control of the hump cabin operator. As the train crawled over the hump, the signalman in the hump cabin read the siding number chalked on each wagon and set the route appropriately. It was possible to set up to three routes in advance; this was usually as far as the signalman could read along the approaching wagons. Below the panel for route setting were six buttons to indicate the number of wagons in a cut. These transmitted the information to the control tower where the operation of the secondary retarders was based. The hump cabin was therefore in control of route setting and transmission of cut size to the yard control tower.

After the wagons had passed the hump cabin they were arrested by one of two primary retarders. These were entirely automatic although fitted with a manual override. They operated on the basis of information collected in the short run from the hump apex towards the retarder. The speed of the wagons was measured using a radar device and their weight taken by a weighbridge installed as part of the permanent way. A combination of the mass

27

The Old Temple Mills Yards — LMS English Electric shunter No. 12134 shunts a wagon of livestock, whose horns are clearly visible, 10th April 1954.

*B. Morrison*

In January 1971, Class 31 No. 5518 leaves the south end of Temple Mills Yard with the 8J88 freight to Norwich.

*J. Cooper-Smith*

In December 1980, hump shunting was still in progress at Temple Mills. A cut containing six MXV scrap wagons is caught in the grip of the primary retarders after their arrival on a trip freight from Stratford Market.

and velocity of each cut allowed computation of its momentum and therefore the correct retardation could be applied. The function of the primary retarders was to maintain an even interval between each cut at the approach to the secondary retarder, in order to prevent malfunction of the route-setting apparatus through premature occupation of the controlling track circuits.

The control tower stood abreast of the eight secondary retarders, one for each group of sorting sidings. The top floor of the control tower housed two control desks, one for each retarder operator. Above each desk was a large mirror in which the signalmen could see the cuts rolling off the hump behind him. For the vital information on what was happening over his shoulder however, each of the control tower operators watched display panels on his desk. Most of the desk was occupied by a diagrammatic representation of the sidings under the operator's control. Indicator lights recorded track circuit occupation, thumb-switches for manual operation of pointwork were provided, and an emergency control to lower the hump signal was also installed.

Below this main panel was a smaller illuminated panel unique to the yard at Temple Mills. Owing to the split control of shunting at the yard, it was necessary to develop a code to inform the retarder operator about the approaching cut of wagons. A readout denoting the siding for which the cut was destined, the number of wagons in the cut, the weight of the wagons and their rollability was provided. Thus 'A52', 'H', 'B', meant the cut was bound for Siding 5 in Fan A, it contained two wagons which were heavy and had bad rollability. Weight was assessed as heavy, 'H', medium, 'HL' and light, 'L'. Rollability was scored in a similar fashion with codes of 'G', 'GB' and 'B' for good, medium and bad. This data enabled the control operator to apply one of five brake gradings with the secondary retarders. This hopefully brought the wagons gently to rest in their appropriate siding. Whilst this system was theoretically operable in poor visibility, much weight was placed on the 'eyeball' assessment of a cut's progress over the hump. In addition to some difficulties in poor weather the relatively crude choice of five pre-set brake pressures made it difficult to bring wagons together gently into a train. Often cuts fell short of the wagons already in the siding or met them with considerable force, causing damage to both cargoes and rolling stock.

At the time of its construction there was much criticism of Temple Mills, not because it was deemed a 'white elephant', but rather

because of the anachronistic juxtaposition of 'chalk' and complex electronic wagon retardation equipment! Justification for the chalking of wagons is hard to understand today, but a combination of factors made it the best option at Temple Mills at the time. The equipment chosen for the yard could not set more than three route settings in sequence, thus a cut card with an entire train consist could not be fully read at the start of a shunt. The consist of a train was not available at the yard until the shunter had recorded it, after the train's arrival in the reception sidings. It was quicker for a cutter to chalk the wagons of a newly-arrived freight than record them on a cut card and return the card to the hump cabin where routes could only be set piecemeal for the shunt.

An overview of Temple Mills Yard in 1980 shows the eastern half of the yard closed and littered with condemned LNER coal hoppers.

In spite of this antiquated system and the needless separation of signalling and retarder control, Temple Mills handled 250 arrivals and departures each day in 1959. Many connections were tight, none more so than those for the 2.49pm freight to Acton, which conveyed traffic for the Western Region. The express freight from Parkeston carried regular consignments of Danish Bacon and arrived at Temple Mills at 1pm. This allowed only just over one and a half hours for resorting of the whole train and the connection of the bacon wagons to the Acton freight. Temple Mills was thus a very busy marshalling yard but not particularly sophisticated, even by the standards of the late 1950s.

## Traffic at Temple Mills

In 1955, before Temple Mills was built, the freight flows in the area were analysed. The largest tonnage of goods to arrive at Temple Mills (old yards) was from Whitemoor and Cambridge. Much traffic from the north of England and the Midlands reached London via this route. The second most important flow was from the Ipswich main line, and this included much traffic from the ports of Harwich and Felixstowe. Third in the ratings came the North London line which

By 1986 all Speedlink traffic was handled in the Manor Yard at Temple Mills, whilst the hump and most of the sorting sidings lay derelict. Class 31 No. 31262 leaves the south end of the yard with a trip freight to Silvertown made up of seven POA scrap wagons to be filled by the scrap merchant at this site.

carried trains from Feltham, Acton and Willesden yards. Further cross-London freights ran via Tottenham and Hampstead from the yards at Brent and Neasden. A substantial stream of freights arrived from the Tilbury line, via Forest Gate Junction, whilst there were six trains daily from London's docks. In addition to all these trains, Temple Mills also sorted traffic for the important City goods depots at Spitalfields and Bishopsgate. These services were the reason for the 47 sorting sidings and the

capacity to sort 4,500 wagons each day. In 1959 an average 3,000 wagons passed the hump each day, a warning sign of the decline to come.

By January 1967, the yard had rendered seven years of service to the Eastern Region of British Railways. Eighty seven daily arrivals brought a total of 3,400 wagons to the hump. The eight fans of sorting sidings (A-H) were allocated to be used by specific traffic. Fans A and B were for traffic leaving for the Southern and London Midland regions, via Tottenham. Also, all northerly departures to the Lea Valley, Bishops Stortford, Hertford, Cambridge and Whitemoor used these two fans. Fans C to H were used by departures to the east, Southend, Chelmsford, Colchester, Ipswich and Norwich, plus of course the local services to London Docks. Cross-London freights to Ferme Park, Feltham, Willesden and Acton also used these fans. The heavy freight traffic to Whitemoor was worked on an out and back basis. Seven turns each day were booked from Temple Mills to Whitemoor and back, a remarkable frequency of services for a freight route. There were four services each way between Parkeston Quay and the yard, augmented by seasonal extras.

In addition to the Main Yard there were the two subsidiary yards, East and West. These both received approximately ten trains each day bringing 300 wagons to each yard. These trains carried local traffic as well as coal for West Ham Power Station and the gasworks at Lea Bridge and Bow. A large seasonal flow was sugar beet from East Anglia to the Tate & Lyle factory at Silvertown. This was dealt with by a large pool of mineral wagons working in a circuit from October to February. A pool of vanfits carried the seasonal flow of processed sugar beet from East Anglia to London destinations. The staff at Temple Mills totalled 300, of whom 150 were guards and 85 shunters, the remaining 65 filled positions ranging from number takers to telex operators. Indeed, by 1967, an Advance Traffic Information System had been installed at the yard, and this was manned by a telex operator. This would inform the yard staff of wagons from other major yards en route to Temple Mills and list their number, contents and final destination. The archaic chalking technique was still used to sort wagons until the introduction of TOPS in the late 1970s.

## The 1970s

A considerable amount of old-fashioned mixed freight persisted at Temple Mills throughout the 1970s. As the main lines from the north into Euston, St Pancras and King's Cross each restricted the passage of slow-moving freights, there was a concomitant increase in the flow of traffic from Toton, Tinsley, Tyne and Millerhill to March (Whitemoor). From here, daily departures to Temple Mills brought traffic to the Capital. In 1970 these were seven in number. By 1980, four trains were timetabled along this route; a reduction far less severe than those experienced elsewhere in the country. Whilst long-haul vacuum-

fitted trains continued to arrive from the north, much was changing in and around Temple Mills itself. Natural gas rendered the local gasworks obsolete. Older coal-fired power stations were superseded by large coastal power stations, or major inland sites such as Didcot. The docks in London declined; a once thriving industry lost much of its traffic to the new South Coast container ports. As each facet of the local economy changed so too did the rail traffic served by Temple Mills. Local freight working was drastically reduced.

In parallel with this steady decline, modernisation was underway. The London, Tilbury & Southend system became one of the first networks to be served almost entirely by block trains and freightliners. Air-braked Speedlink trains from Harwich were increasingly routed away from the Capital whilst new Freightliner services from Harwich and Felixstowe bypassed Temple Mills on their way to Stratford Freightliner Terminal. By 1980, the yard had been reduced to half its original capacity. The hump remained open, but only on the southern side of the yard. Fans A to D were used for traffic whilst Fans E to H held stored and condemned wagons. In 1979, 1,000 wagons were sorted over the hump each day. By December 1980, a further fall in wagons hump shunted to 600 brought about the decision to close the hump and flat-shunt the yard from the south end.

## The 1980s

The National Freight Train Plan of the 1960s made Temple Mills the only London yard on the Eastern Region. Ferme Park Yard was closed and all ECML freights diverted south via Whitemoor. As mentioned above, this kept the throughput at Temple Mills high during the 1970s, but by 1980 it was clear that the yard was becoming an operating luxury. At one stage in 1980 it was thought that Temple Mills could be closed completely. This would, however, have involved investment in expansion at Willesden which could not be justified. A three stage rationalisation programme was implemented instead. This was completed in 1982, the year in which the hump closed at Temple Mills (Plan 5). The West Yard was closed along with Fans G and H in the Main Yard. The East Yard was taken over by the Civil Engineer's Department, and the departure roads used for both arrivals and departures. Speedlink marshalling was concentrated on the Manor Yard; all shunting taking place over the small hump at the south end of the yard.

Rationalisation at Temple Mills catered for Speedlink and the dwindling vacuum-fitted freight traffic as well as the engineering trains from the area. A unique additional feature at Temple Mills was the marshalling of Freightliner trains. Services arrived from Stratford, Dagenham, Tilbury and the North Sea ports of Harwich and Felixstowe. Sections were exchanged between these services before their departure for the North. The new track layout and timetable constituted a great blow to staff morale and punctuality was as low as 40 per

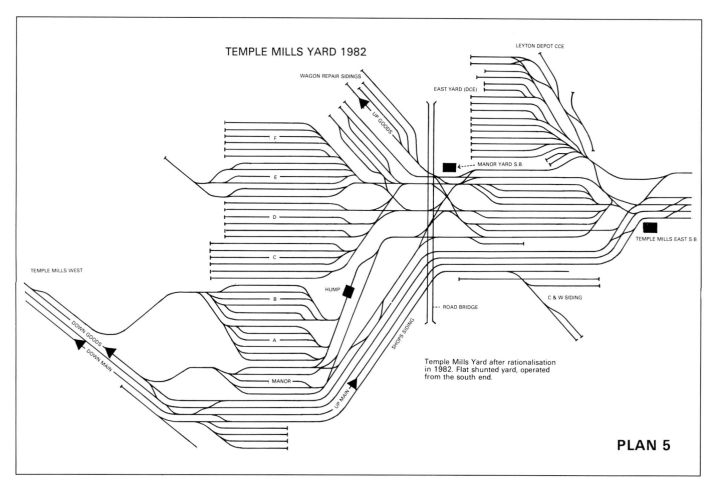

TEMPLE MILLS YARD 1982

Temple Mills Yard after rationalisation in 1982. Flat shunted yard, operated from the south end.

PLAN 5

cent. The daily throughput of wagons had fallen from 4,000 in 1970 to 250 in 1982. These were carried on 20 daily Speedlink arrivals and departures. Morale and freight punctuality rallied in the next two years. April 1985 saw 90 per cent of Speedlink trains running on time.

Another body blow was dealt to the yard in December 1985. Freightliner services from the North Sea ports were concentrated at Felixstowe. With the withdrawal of services from Parkeston, the need to exchange portions at Temple Mills disappeared. Freightliners Limited therefore decided to remove their operations from the yard. This meant the loss of ten arrivals and nine departures each night, a considerable reduction in traffic at the yard. The start of 1986 saw further questions raised regarding the viability of the yard.

## The Future

The first and most important question about the future at Temple Mills is the recurrent suggestion of closure. Any closure would mean a transfer of present services (*Table 3*) to Willesden Yard. This would mean extensive trip working along an already congested North London line. The capacity of Willesden Brent Sidings is not capable of absorbing this extra traffic without investment and modernisation at the Willesden Yard. In addition to operating problems there is the theoretical objection that it is unwise to put 'all one's eggs in the same basket', ie Willesden (Brent) Yard.

Since the closure of the freight line from Stratford to Bow Junction, all freight from

| ARRIVALS | Table 3 Temple Mills Freight | | |
|---|---|---|---|
| **Train** | **From** 1985 | **Arrive** | **Days** |
| 7C81 | Parkeston | 06.43 | MO |
| 7E73 | Crewe | 06.45 | ThO |
| 7E80 | Willesden | 07.11 | SX |
| TRIP | Stratford TMD | 07.00 | SX |
| 9C71 | Whitemoor | 11.18 | SX |
| 7C68 | Bow Depot | 11.50 | SX |
| 7000 | Stanstead | 11.55 | MO |
| 6C79 | Gidea Park | 12.30 | SX |
| 6C17 | Ilford | 14.03 | MWO |
| 8C30 | Mile End | 14.17 | ThO |
| 8C32 | Thornton Flds | 14.17 | TFO |
| 6C99 | Southend | 14.32 | SX |
| 6C88 | Palace Gates | 14.37 | SX |
| 9C83 | Stratford Mkt | 15.17 | SX |
| 6C93 | Shoeburyness | 15.30 | MWFO |
| 7V72 | Marks Tey | 15.56 | TThFO |
| 6C87 | Gidea Park | 16.03 | SX |
| 6C11 | Bishops Stort | 16.07 | SX |
| 7C73 | Southminster | 16.25 | ThO |
| 6C97 | Silvertown | 16.33 | SX |
| 6C84 | Bow Depot | 16.48 | SX |
| 6E53 | Dover | 17.14 | SX |
| 9C97 | LIFT | 18.19 | SX |
| 6E64 | Wolverton | 18.27 | WO |
| 4M75 | Ripple Lane | 19.09 | SX |
| 4S83 | Tilbury FLT | 19.45 | SX |
| 7E86 | Willesden | 20.10 | SX |
| 4C66 | Stratford FLT | 20.22 | SX |
| 7C71 | Leiston | 20.31 | ThO |
| 7C83 | Thames Haven | 20.36 | SX |
| 4M87 | Parkeston | 21.17 | SX |
| 6C95 | Ipswich | 21.47 | SX |
| 4C85 | Tilbury FLT | 21.51 | SX |
| 6R82 | Tyne | 22.06 | SX |
| 4M67 | Felixstowe | 23.03 | SX |
| 6090 | Whitemoor | 23.14 | SX |

| | | | |
|---|---|---|---|
| 4E69 | Birmingham | 23.52 | SX |
| 4M53 | Felixstowe | 00.02 | MX |
| 7E92 | Dover | 00.13 | MX |
| 6E94 | Eastleigh | 00.29 | MX |
| 7E41 | Paddington | 00.58 | TThFO |
| 4E83 | Trafford Park | 01.19 | MX |
| 6044 | Tyne | 01.24 | SX |
| 4E73 | Birmingham | 02.12 | MX |
| 7061 | Rye House | 02.22 | MX |
| 4E72 | Nottingham | 02.34 | MX |
| 7E24 | Woking | 02.41 | MX |
| 6C89 | Ripple Lane | 02.53 | MX |
| 4C62 | Leeds | 03.25 | MX |
| 6E38 | Hoo Junction | 04.27 | WO |
| 7C81 | Parkeston | 04.48 | SX |
| 9C89 | Thames Haven/ Parkeston/ Ipswich | 05.37 | MX |

DEPARTURES

| Train | Time | Days | To |
|---|---|---|---|
| 6C83 | 06.05 | MSX | Bow Depot |
| 6C86 | 06.31 | MSX | LIFT |
| 9C86 | 06.45 | MO | LIFT |
| 6C90 | 07.08 | SX | Stratford Mkt |
| 6C83 | 07.20 | MO | Bow Depot |
| 7E80 | 07.40 | SX | LIFT |
| TRIP | | SX | Tender Shops |
| 6C96 | 09.07 | SX | Silvertown |
| 6C10 | 09.19 | SX | Bishops Stortford |
| 7Y70 | 09.36 | THO | Leiston |
| 6R92 | 09.46 | MWFO | Shoeburyness |
| 6C80 | 10.06 | SX | Gidea Park |
| 6C81 | 10.20 | SX | Bow Depot |
| 6C98 | 10.27 | SX | Southend |
| 7C72 | 10.49 | THO | Southminster |
| 6B69 | 11.35 | SX | Palace Gates |
| 9H86 | 12.14 | SX | Whitemoor |
| 7000 | 12.28 | WO | Hoo Junction |
| 6C16 | 12.35 | MWO | Ilford |
| 8C29 | 12.35 | THO | Mile End |
| 8C31 | 12.35 | TFO | Thornton Fields |
| 9H38 | 14.32 | MTO | Chesterton |
| 7R80 | 15.08 | SX | Shell Haven |
| 7M82 | 17.35 | SX | Willesden |
| 6091 | 19.17 | SX | Hoo Junction |
| 4M75 | 19.49 | SX | Nottingham |
| 7V72 | 19.58 | TTHF | Paddington |
| 7F84 | 20.03 | SX | Parkeston |
| 6E64 | 20.31 | WO | Parkeston |
| 4S83 | 20.36 | SX | Glasgow |
| 6V95 | 20.59 | SX | Severn Tunnel |
| 6E53 | 21.48 | SX | Tyne |
| 9F86 | 21.53 | SX | Parkeston |
| 9F86 | 21.53 | SX | Colchester |
| 9F88 | 22.23 | SX Y | Parkeston |
| 9R88 | 22.23 | SX Y | Thames Haven |
| 9Y88 | 22.23 | SX Y | Ipswich |
| 4M87 | 22.48 | SX | Birmingham |
| 6R82 | 23.00 | SX | Ripple Lane |
| 7M74 | 23.48 | THO | Crewe |
| 4M67 | 23.59 | SX | Garston |
| 9F72 | 00.18 | MO | Parkeston |
| 9F72 | 00.18 | MO | Colchester |
| 4M53 | 00.48 | MX | Trafford Park |
| 9F72 | 00.55 | MX | Parkeston |
| 6090 | 02.00 | MSX | Southampton |
| 6090 | 02.00 | SO | Eastleigh |
| 6E94 | 02.08 | MX | Whitemoor |
| 4C63 | 02.14 | MX | Stratford FLT |
| 4E83 | 02.24 | MX | Felixstowe |
| 6044 | 02.30 | MSX | Paddock Wood |
| 6044 | 02.30 | SO | Hoo Junction |
| 7Y84 | 02.39 | MX | Ipswich |
| 8M58 | 02.43 | SX | Croft |
| 4E72 | 03.08 | MX | Ripple Lane |
| 7E24 | 03.22 | MX | Rye House |
| 7061 | 03.30 | MX | Woking |
| 7M10 | 03.36 | MX | Willesden |
| 7R86 | 04.00 | MSX | Grays |
| 7R86 | 04.00 | SO | Ripple Lane |
| 4E69 | 04.20 | MX | Felixstowe |
| 7F38 | 04.57 | TTHF | Marks Tey |
| 4R54 | 05.12 | MX | Tilbury |
| 4R54 | 05.12 | SO | Tilbury |
| 4E73 | 05.16 | MX | Parkeston |
| 6E38 | 05.25 | WO | Stansted |

Dagenham to Ipswich and Norwich must reverse at Temple Mills. This so-called 'Docklands Run-Round' means that at least a run-round loop must be maintained at Temple Mills. In addition some train storage capacity may be useful during peak periods on the congested North London line. Further freight expansion in the London area may occur in response to the Channel Tunnel; any closure decision must therefore keep in mind the possibility of an upturn in the wagonload traffic passing through London in the mid-1990s. The case for a low-cost freight facility at Temple Mills is a persuasive one. Management planning envisages several alterations to bring this to fruition. Speedlink traffic would be transferred from the Manor Yard to Fans C, D and E in the Main Yard. This would avoid the troublesome 'knuckle' in Manor Yard and bring benefit from the straighter and longer roads in the centre of the old yard. It may then be possible to reduce activities to Fans C and D only.

This small yard, with only twelve roads, would then require only a small staff to function efficiently. The permanent way yard at Leyton could be transferred to the redundant sidings in Fans E to H. This would leave the Leyton site clear for the London extension of the M11 Motorway. The Manor Yard and Fans A and B could then be closed. The yard would have the capacity to deal with both engineering and Speedlink traffic with a small staff and very simple layout. All arrivals and departures would be from the south end of the new yard. The site of the old departure roads would include at least three sidings, a departure line and two arrival sidings. The old 'down' goods line could be converted to a new Docklands run-round loop, with the capacity to hold a 30-set Freightliner train. Such plans were still under discussion at the time of writing.

From 13th April 1987 it was proposed that all trunk Speedlink marshalling should be re-routed from Temple Mills to Ripple Lane or Willesden, Sparc capacity became available at Willesden after the introduction of the Discrete Coal Network (DCN) in 1987, when Didcot Yard took over the marshalling of household coal for London and the South East. The requirement at Temple Mills was for a single 100 SLU run-round loop and nine sidings to cater for local Speedlink traffic and emergency recessing of freights.

Whatever the outcome of the deliberations of London's railway managers a run-round facility at Temple Mills is bound to remain. Whether the yard continues to play an important role in freight marshalling or hands on this responsibility to new yards elsewhere in the Capital remains to be seen. Whatever the decisions taken, Temple Mills has already rendered over 100 years of good service to the railway; may it continue to marshal freight trains for another century!

**Following page:**

**In February 1986, the northern end of Temple Mills had been completely closed for two years and was rapidly returning to nature. Compare this sight with that on page 27, photographed from about the same spot 14 years earlier.**

# Ripple Lane

Construction of a new automated hump marshalling yard at Ripple Lane began in January 1957. The yard was the first of its type to be placed between the two running lines and cater for a bi-directional traffic flow from a single yard. The hump led to 41 sorting sidings in eight groups. The sidings had a capacity to hold 2,271 wagons, 1,280

**Ripple Lane — This picture of the east end of the yard, taken in 1958, shows the temporary operation of the yard from the non-hump end before it was fully completed later the same year.**

*Railway Gazette International*

in the southern half of the yard and 991 in the northern part. Whilst somewhat smaller than Temple Mills, Ripple Lane was more modern than its important neighbour. The primary retarders were automatically controlled by radar and weight-measuring devices. In addition, the secondary retarders were fitted with a device to measure the track occupation in the sorting sidings automatically. This was a new feature and one not used at Temple Mills.

In June 1958, the yard was partially opened and shunting started at the flat end of the yard. This allowed the closure of smaller yards at Little Ilford, Plaistow and Ripple Lane Down. These closures in turn allowed electrification to progress along the London to Tilbury line, and a new carriage shed to be built at East Ham.

The yard at Ripple Lane was the most short-lived major development of the 1955 modernisation programme. By December 1965 the contraction and closure of Ripple

Lane was in hand. A life span of only seven years is clearly far too short for such an expensive installation. Why then did such a modern marshalling yard disappear so quickly? As with all yards, the factors that determined the demise of Ripple Lane were both local and national. The authors of the 1955 Modernisation Plan had made the assumption that traditional rail freight methods would be pursued indefinitely and had designed new yards accordingly. This presupposition was, however, shattered by the policies of Dr Beeching. The advent of block train working on the London, Tilbury & Southend system came relatively early in the 1960s. Traffic fell at Ripple Lane and the yard became hard to justify. The close proximity to Temple Mills also

made the survival of Ripple Lane much more unlikely. The two yards were only five miles apart and it was inevitable that one would close, the more remote Ripple Lane being the casualty.

By 1988 however, the ten double ended and two single ended sidings that remained at Ripple Lane had witnessed a renaissance. Fourteen trunk Speedlink Freights were diverted to the yard as Temple Mills closed to Speedlink traffic; the wheel had turned full circle!

**Ripple Lane — As one of the earliest major yards to close, there was very little sign of the old hump yard left in April 1984 when this view was taken of Class 08 No. 08541 shunting oil tanks at Ripple Lane.**

*P. Shannon*

Stonebridge Park Yard — In the 1950s this yard was an important London yard and, as can be seen from the large number of shunters at the hump, was manually shunted. This view looks north towards the reception sidings.

*British Rail*

The sorting sidings at Stonebridge Park are here viewed from the top of one of the shunting signals controlling egress from the reception sidings.

*British Rail*

# Willesden

There were several separate marshalling yards along the main line between Willesden and Wembley. The main freight yard was at Sudbury, near Stonebridge Park. Here most of the traffic from the LNWR was sorted before continuing its journey across London. The yard was not equipped with retarders or automatic points and represented the older design of hump marshalling yard. All points were changed by hand, and wagons were guided into the sidings by a shunter who pinned down their brakes whilst they rolled off the hump. Seven reception roads led to a fan of 20 sorting sidings, and a brake van siding.

The 1980s saw the transfer of wagonload traffic to the flat-shunted yard at Willesden (Brent). Trains arrive either directly from the South along the 'down' slow or via the

**Opposite:**
Willesden Brent Yard — The major wagon-load yard for London in the 1980s was Brent Yard at Willesden. In March 1986, Class 86 No. 86420 stands at the head of the 6S73 Dover to Mossend Speedlink, whilst Class 08 No. 08533 shunts the newly-arrived 6M88 trip from Redhill. The consist of the Mossend train was as follows:

| | |
|---|---|
| VGA | — Park Royal to Deanside (Guinness). |
| 2 VDA | — Northfleet to Uddingston (bagged cement). |
| YRX | — Slade Green — Dundee. |
| 2 VGA | — Wolverton to Corpach. |
| 2 VTG | — Neuves (France) to Aberdeen (unimetal). |
| VTG | — Dover to Warrington (bonded goods). |
| VTG | — Meznau (Switzerland) to Blackburn. |
| CARGO | — La Bathie (France) to Manchester (bonded goods). |
| VTG | — Chiarlia (Italy) to Warrington (bonded goods). |
| SNCF | — St. Perdou (France) to Ditton (timber). |
| SNCF | — Rivesaltes (France) to Crewe. |
| YLA | — Wolverton to Mossend. |
| TEA | — Willesden to Ditton (empty oxygen tank). |
| CARGO | — Park Royal to Spekeland Goods (Guinness). |

**Below:**
Two BTH diesel-electric locomotives, Nos D8217 and D8406, enter Temple Mills Yard 14th June 1967 with a trip freight from the Cambridge direction. The train is made up mainly of Covhops which were used to transport large amounts of sugar in the 1960s.
*P. Groom*

**Above:**
BTH diesel No. D8209 shunts the coal depot at Ilford in September 1969. Many such trip freights of unfitted coal wagons plied the network providing a substantial proportion of the wagon throughput at major yards such as Temple Mills.
*J. Cooper-Smith*

Class 71 No. E5022 arrives at Hither Green Yard with pantograph raised in May 1968. The multiplicity of London yards generated a wide range of inter-yard trips such as this train from Kent.

*J. Cooper-Smith*

By 1976, much of the freight traffic from the Southern Region made its connection with the national freight network at Acton. Here a cross-London freight from Norwood Yard to Acton passes through Kensington Olympia on 24th March 1976 behind Class 52 No. D1021 *Western Cavalier*.

*B. Morrison*

'down' low-level line. Arrival via the low-level line involves running north as far as Sudbury Yard (*Plan 6*) and then a lengthy reversal along the 'up' reception line. This complex manoeuvre takes about 15 minutes during which time a considerable backlog of freights may start to build up. The Brent Yard itself has 26 roads, five of which are single-ended, the rest are through sidings. The longest siding is 622yds long, however, many of the roads are under 400yds in length and not suitable for trunk Speedlink

trains. The majority of freights arrive and depart from the northern end of the yard and there is considerable congestion here because shunting movements, of which there are many, conflict with these arrivals and departures.

Trackwork, and particularly pointwork, on the two northern entrance lines is very worn, and has caused several derailments. In spite of these problems, the yard is one of Britain's busiest. *Table 4* shows the daily Speedlink services using the yard. There is a

total of 23 trunk Speedlinks which use the yard each twenty four hours. These trains are supplemented by 20 daily departures which run as Speedlink trip and feeder services. A similar total of 20 such trains arrive each day bringing a guaranteed throughput of at least 60 freights over the twenty four hour period. In addition to Speedlink work there are numerous Freightliners and block loads which pause for remanning in the two 'down through sidings' at Willesden.

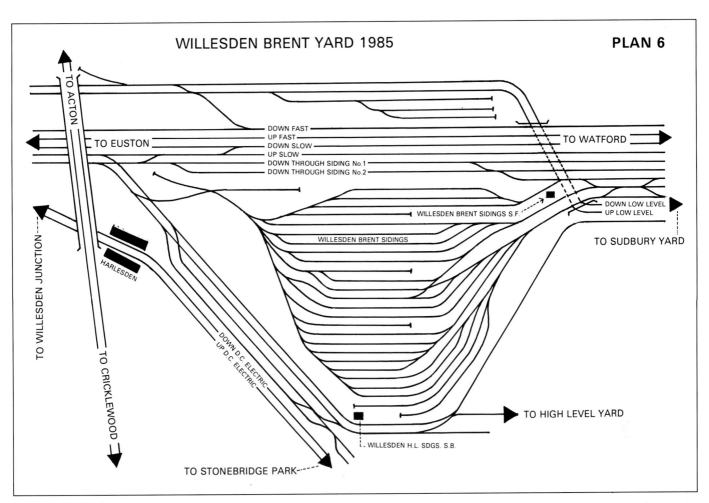

WILLESDEN BRENT YARD 1985

PLAN 6

TO ACTON

TO EUSTON

TO WATFORD

DOWN FAST
UP FAST
DOWN SLOW
UP SLOW
DOWN THROUGH SIDING No.1
DOWN THROUGH SIDING No.2

WILLESDEN BRENT SIDINGS S.F.

WILLESDEN BRENT SIDINGS

DOWN LOW LEVEL
UP LOW LEVEL

TO SUDBURY YARD

TO WILLESDEN JUNCTION

HARLESDEN

TO CRICKLEWOOD

DOWN D.C. ELECTRIC
UP D.C. ELECTRIC

TO HIGH LEVEL YARD

WILLESDEN H.L. SDGS. S.B.

TO STONEBRIDGE PARK

## Table 4
## Willesden Freight—September 1985

### Speedlink services

| Code | From | To | Arr. | Dep. |
|------|------|-----|------|------|
| 6A21 | Bescot | Willesden | 00.01 | |
| 6M92 | Severn Tun. | Willesden | 00.03 | |
| 6M48 | Dagenham | Garston | 00.57 | 02.03 |
| 4M64 | Bathgate | Willesden | 01.32 | |
| 6V02 | Willesden | Severn Tun. | | 01.56 |
| 6A83 | Toton | Willesden | 03.25 | |
| 6O38 | Workington | Dover | 03.33 | 05.26 |
| 4M38 | Mossend | Willesden | 04.37 | |
| 6O48 | Willesden | Dover | | 05.23 |
| 6O56 | Dundee | Dover | 05.56 | 09.01 |
| 6O57 | Willesden | Southampton | | 06.51 |
| 6M61 | Dover | Willesden | 07.16 | |
| 6F86 | Willesden | Warrington | | 09.10 |
| 7A84 | Toton | Willesden | 10.51 | |
| 7A80 | Warrington | Willesden | 11.10 | |
| 7E02 | Willesden | Worksop | | 17.45 |
| 6S73 | Dover | Mossend | 14.22 | 16.20 |
| 6V45 | Willesden | Severn Tun. | | 17.53 |
| 6M93 | Southampton | Willesden | 19.04 | |
| 6S57 | Sheerness | Mossend | 19.23 | 20.22 |
| 6M94 | Dover | Bescot | 19.32 | 22.25 |
| 6O88 | Willesden | Dover | | 20.43 |
| 6E75 | Willesden | Leeds | | 21.24 |
| 4S48 | Willesden | Bathgate | | 21.57 |
| 6P85 | Willesden | Workington | | 22.15 |
| 6E85 | Halewood | Dagenham | 23.39 | 02.55 |

There are now plans to build a new yard at Willesden. Such a yard would probably occupy the site of Sudbury sorting sidings and have the capacity to deal with considerably more traffic than Willesden (Brent) Yard. With the Channel Tunnel project very much in mind, the siding length has been set at 100 SLUs to cater for potential long-haul traffic from the Continent. The yard will be the most important new development of its kind since the construction of Tinsley Yard in the mid-1960s, and as such should be awaited with interest!

My sincere thanks to Mr R.C. Phillips, the Area Freight Manager for North Thameside, whose help was invaluable in producing this chapter.

**Left:**
Class 74 No. 74010 passes through Eastleigh station, en route to Southampton from Acton in West London on 3rd May 1976.

*B. Morrison*

**Right:**
The 6V47 Willesden to Reading freight is seen here in Brent Yard behind Class 31 No. 31113. The train carries coal from Linby Colliery in Nottinghamshire and Deep Navigation pit in South Wales to Aldermaston, as well as two tankers of fuel oil from Fawley to Reading depot. Most of the traffic has been subject to a considerable detour because of the need for freight flows to fit into the Speedlink network.

**Left:**
The North London line also carries a large volume of freight traffic. Here, Class 50 No. 50049 *Defiance* descends into Acton with the 9V81 trip fom Temple Mills, on 8th August 1983.

*P. Shannon*

An empty nuclear flask leaves the south end of Willesden (Brent) Yard on its way to Dungeness Power Station in Kent on 21st February 1986. Class 73 No. 73124 is in charge of the freight.

Much freight traffic from the area served by the Ripple Lane Yard is now marshalled into block loads or handled by Freightliners Ltd. Here the 4M30, 13.42, Dagenham Dock to Garston pauses at Willesden to change to electric haulage, freeing Class 37 Nos 37038 and 37141 to return to Essex. When the electrification of the North London line is completed, such locomotive changes will be unnecessary, speeding up freight trains through London and saving motive power.

This view of Willesden (Brent) Yard emphasises the wide area from which traffic is collected. Southern Region Class 33 No. 33018 arrives, on the left with the 6M88 trip from Redhill. In earlier days traffic from the Redhill area would have been marshalled at Norwood before being tripped across the Capital to Willesden or Acton.

## Table 5
## Willesden Trip Freights
## September 1985

| Willesden | | Arr. | | | | |
|---|---|---|---|---|---|---|
| 6V63 | 00.56 T-S W'den – West Drayton | (01.47) | 6A33 | 22.55 M-F Tring Cutting – Willesden | (23.47) |
| 6048 | 01.16 M-F Willesden – Eastleigh | (03.45) | 6M39 | 02.50 T-S West Drayton – Willesden | (04.05) |
| 7T33 | 02.40 M-F W'den Brent – Watford CCD | (03.15) | 7M10 | 03.36 T-S T Mills – W'den Brent | (04.27) |
| 6A23 | 02.52 T-S W'den Brent – Tring Cutting (RR at Bletchley Detach) | (04.32) | 6M89 | 00.10 MO Dover – W'den Brent (Calls Hoo Jn 01.46/03.00) | (04.31) |
| 6V57 | 04.59 T-S W'den Brent – Southall W. Jn | (05.50) | 7T33 | 02.25 M-F Watford CCD – W'den Brent | (03.00) |
| 6B50 | 08.00 M-F Bletchley – Aylesbury | (09.25) | 6M61 | 04.25 MO Dover – W'den Brent | (07.16) |
| 6054 | 03.20 T-F W'den Brent – Hoo Jcn | (04.45) | 7T33 | 09.20 M-F Neasden CCD – W'den Brent | (10.00) |
| 6048 | 05.23 MO W'den Brent – Dover (Calls Plumstead 06.37 – 07.33 Hoo Jn. 08.05 – 08.25) | (09.59) | 6R50 | 15.17 M-F Chessington CCD – Tolworth NCB | (15.23) |
| 7C60 | 06.10 M-F W'den Brent – Lutcon C Rd | (08.42) | 6M45 | 10.23 M-F Tolworth NCB – W'den Brent | (11.20) |
| 6T82 | 09.12 M-F Luton C Rd – Luton Lin Rd | (09.22) | 6M88 | 15.20 M-F Redhill – W'den Brent (Calls Purley 10.55 – 11.45) | (16.37) |
| 6049 | 06.07 T-F W'den Brent – Sheerness (Calls Plumstead 07.07 – 08.05 Hoo Jn 08.35 – 09.23) Queenboro 10.08 – 10.53) | (11.03) | 7M62 | 11.30 TTHO W. Ruislip LTE – W'den Brent | (12.40) |
| | | | 6M91 | 09.25 M-F Sheerness – W'den Brent (Calls Hoo Jn 10.25/11.25) | (15.14) |
| 7E80 | 06.25 M-F W'den Brent SSE/LIFT (Calls T Mills 07.14 – 07.40) | (07.50) | 6A74 | 14.54 M-F Wolverton – W'den Brent | (16.14) |
| 6V15 | 07.20 M-F W'den Brent – Park Royal | (08.03) | 6B74 | 12.25 M-F Aylesbury – Wolverton | (13.55) |
| 7E82 | 06.44 M-F W'den Brent SSE – Tilbury R'side (Calls R Lane 07.35 – 08.08 W. Thurrock Jn 08.33 – 08.57 Grays 09.02 – 09.25) | (09.33) | 4M34 | 13.18 M-F Hayes – W'den Brent | (14.09) |
| | | | 6M85 | 13.57 M-F Hayes & H-W'den Brent | (16.14) |
| | | | 7M52 | 15.13 M-F Grays – W'den Brent (Calls Ripple Lane 15.37/16.11) | (17.04) |
| 6057 | 06.48 M-F W'den B – Southampton Dn Yd (Calls Woking 08.21 – 08.36 B'stoke 09.10 – 09.34 Eastleigh 10.10 – 10.33 Sthampton Up Yd 10.47 – 11.08) | (11.13) | 6M80 | 14.37 M-F Reading – W'den Brent (Calls Park Royal 15.46/16.15) | (17.04) |
| | | | 7M82 | 17.35 M-F T Mills – W'den Brent | (18.15) |
| | | | 6T82 | 14.00 M-F Wellingboro – Luton C. Rd (Calls Limbury Rd 15.28/15.58) | (16.05) |
| 7T34 | 07.30 M-F W'den Brent – Neasden CCD | (08.05) | 7A40 | 16.57 M-F Luton C. Rd – Willesden Brent (R.R at West Hampstead and Acton Canal Wharf) | (19.01) |
| 6B43 | 07.27 M-F W'den Brent – Wolverton | (08.37) | | | |
| 6E28 | 08.38 W'den Brent – | (09.35) | 6M93 | 14.28 M-F Southampton Up Yd – W'den Brent (Calls Eastleigh 14.42/15.58 and Woking 17.06 – 17.20) | (19.04) |
| 7E84 | 09.17 W'den Brent SSE – Ripple Lane | (10.13) | | | |
| 4V20 | 09.38 M-F W'den Brent – Maidenhead | (11.25) | | | |
| 7M61 | 10.08 TTHO W'den Brent – W. Ruislip LTE | (11.00) | 7M81 | 15.51 M-F Thames Haven – W'den B (Calls W Thurock 16.20u 16.47 Purfleet 16.54u 17.17 R Lane 17.36 – 18.14) | (19.18) |
| 7066 | 12.35 M-F W'den Brent – Chessington CCD (Calls Tolworth NCB 13.48/14.15) | (14.22) | | | |
| 6063 | 09.17 M-F W'den Brent – Redhill | (11.00) | 6M57 | 22.20 SUN H. Green – W'den Brent | (23.15) |
| 6V47 | 13.45 M-F W'den SW – Reading | (15.53) | 6V67 | 10.26 M-F Willesden – O.O.Common (Calls Action 10.54/11.10 Park Royal 11.40/12.20) | |
| 7E86 | 19.24 M-F W'den Brent SSE – T Mills | (20.10) | | | |
| 6088 | 20.43 M-F W'den Brent – Dover (Calls Hoo Jn 22.36/23.05) | (00.38) | 6M27 | 14.15 M-F O.O.Common – Willesden (Calls Park Royal 14.35 – 15.13) | (16.08) |
| 6B28 | 09.48 M-F Kings Cross FT – Bounds Green | (11.12) | | | |
| 6T82 | 10.12 M-F Luton C Rd – Wellingboro (Via Luton Bute St & Dunstable) | (13.02) | 6M49 | 20.55 M-F Eastleigh – Willesden | (23.23) |

Class 25 No. 25086 shunts at Princes Risborough on 19th January 1983. The train is the 8T21 arrival from Aylesbury and conveys empty HTV and HEA hoppers returning to South Wales via Acton Yard as well as empty wine wagons returning to Yugoslavia.

# Chapter 3

# Bescot

## The Old Bescot Yards

The LNWR yards at Bescot were just one of several marshalling centres that dealt with considerable freight traffic from the Black Country. The yards grew up piecemeal over the years and by 1960 (*Plan 7*), when it was decided to modernise the site, there were three separate hump yards at Bescot. On the 'up' side of the main line

The locomotive depot at Bescot is host to a cross-section of London Midland Region steam power — all freight types. The shed was replaced by a modern diesel maintenance depot when the yard was modernised in 1966.
*N. Hazelwood*

were the 'up' sorting sidings. Here, four reception sidings led over a hump to a total of twelve sorting sidings. These were supplemented at the south end by several small secondary sorting sidings and three roads used as a cripple dock. Control of this yard was under Bescot No. 4 signal box. The hump was completely manually-operated with chasers employed to pin down wagon brakes as wagons rolled from the hump summit.

In 1965, the construction of the new yards was well under way. On the left are the 'down' recessing sidings, to their right the 'down' reception roads and next, the secondary sorting sidings, packed with freight traffic.
*British Rail*

On the 'down' side of the main line, the first set of sidings was the Old Yard. Leaving the main line at Newton Junction access was gained into a total of eleven reception roads. These converged on a traditional manual hump from where nine sorting sidings radiated. This layout had limited capacity and a new yard had been added to the west of the old yards. This had seven reception sidings and eleven lengthy sorting sidings. Departure from the old 'down' yard was effected under the control of Bescot No. 5 box, whereas departure from the New Yard was controlled by Bescot No. 3 signal cabin.

## Bescot Hump Yards

On 18th April 1966, the remodelled Bescot Marshalling Yard, near Walsall came into full operation (*Plan 8*). It was selected as the concentration point for traffic to and from the industrial area between Birmingham, Wolverhampton and Walsall. Of the several yards previously servicing this area, Bescot was the choice for modernisation, largely because some of the biggest concerns in the Black Country were located nearby and produced a heavy volume of private siding traffic. On the same date as the yard was opened, the freight services to the North were taken over by 25kV ac electric traction.

Both 'up' and 'down' yards were re-modelled, but because the 'down' yard handled the heaviest traffic it was also comprehensively mechanised. The re-modelled yard covered approximately 72 acres, and lay eight miles from Birmingham astride the old Grand Junction line to Wolverhampton at the point where the route to Walsall and Dudley diverged.

The 'down' yard consisted of four interconnected siding groups:

1) Reception sidings, 6 roads.
2) Sorting sidings, 21 roads.
3) Local sorting sidings, 10 roads.
4) Storage sidings, 7 roads.

The 'down' side was also equipped with an engine release line and an engine run-round line in the reception sidings. In contrast, the modernised 'up' side of the marshalling yard was less well equipped, with four reception sidings which lead to 18 sorting sidings with the addition of six roads for local sorting on the eastern fringe of the yard. Both sides of the yard were equipped with brake van and wagon repair sidings. The yard was designed to deal with 4,000 wagons daily.

The 'down' yard was equipped with Dowty automatic wagon control below the hump. This equipment was first used by British Railways on a large scale at Tinsley Yard. The advantage of such a wagon retardation system was that the hump earthworks could be considerably reduced and control of wagons moving along the sorting sidings greatly refined. At Bescot some 4,300 Dowty retarder and booster/retarder units were laid and these controlled the speed of wagons descending from the small hump, and kept them moving until

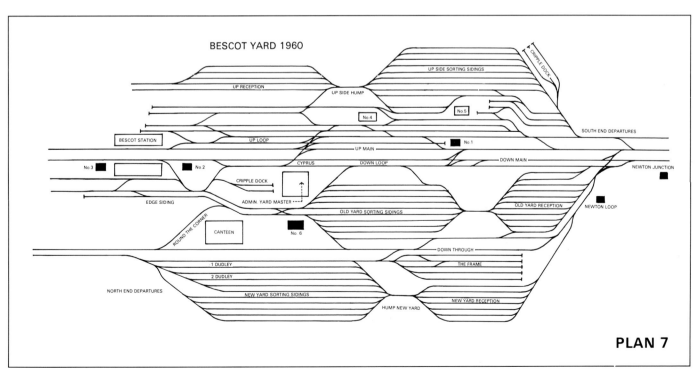

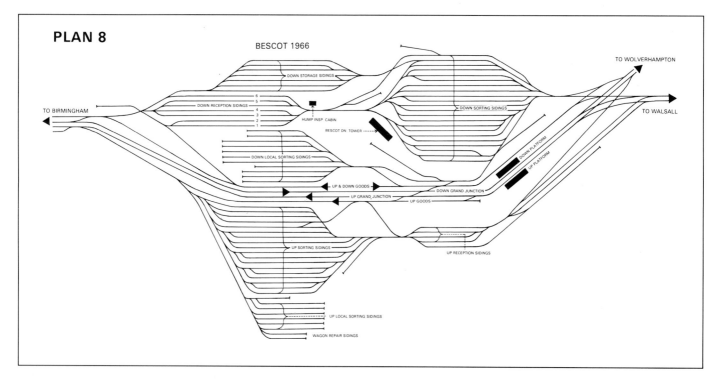

PLAN 8

BESCOT 1966

they buffered up with wagons already occupying the sidings to which they were destined. The shunting consul in the 'down' control tower showed diagramatically the entire track layout. Press buttons and thumb switches were provided in the corresponding positions of all signals and points control tower showed diagrammically the the signalling and Dowty equipment failure indicators. Loudspeaker and radio telephone apparatus was also available. On an adjacent desk were the keyboard, tape perforator and tape reader used in association with the route setting apparatus to sort an arrival.

The staff at Bescot in 1961 and 1985. Remarkably one man appears in both pictures. In 1961 on the right, is Foreman/Head Shunter Mr N. Hakesley, and in April 1985, still patrolling his old patch is Mr Hakesley, now Yard Supervisor!

*N. Hazelwood and author*

**Opposite:**
Again two pictures taken from the same spot, but 20 years apart. In the early 1960s, the new reception sidings for the modernised 'up' yard were just being laid as 'Jubilee' class No. 45567 *South Australia* drifted by. By 1985, the sidings had already been lifted for a couple of years. Electric multiple unit No. 304015 passes with a Walsall-bound passenger train.

*J. Haddock and author*

46

Once a freight service had arrived in the reception sidings, a cut list was compiled by the shunter. These lists were sent by pneumatic tube to the Hump Inspector's office where they were checked, then on to the control tower. Here the wagon and siding destination details were transferred to a punched tape in the traditional manner. This tape was then fed into a reader to transfer the information to the automatic route-setting system. After the panel had set up the relevant route from the reception sidings to the hump, and signalled humping to commence, the automatic route setting system took over switching and the Dowty apparatus controlled the wagons speed as they descended into the sorting sidings. A panel operator kept in contact with the hump locomotive's driver by radiotelephone. The mechanised yard at Bescot was staffed by a total of 12 supervisors and 77 other railway employees, many of whom were transferred from smaller yards such as Norton Junction and Bushby, which closed when the New Yard at Bescot was opened.

# Rationalisation at Bescot

Only three British yards were equipped with the Dowty wagon control system — those at Tinsley, Bescot and Scunthorpe. All of these were constructed after the boom of the later 1950s and early 1960s. In spite of its relatively recent modernisation, Bescot did not escape the ravages of rationalisation which have greatly reduced the capacity of all of Britain's marshalling yards. In response to the inception of Speedlink and TOPS computer control in the mid-1970s and the gradual transfer away from unfitted wagons, the 'up' reception sidings were closed and all Speedlink traffic concentrated on the 'down' yard, by the end of the 1970s.

Bescot was chosen as one of the twelve network yards to marshal the high-speed air-braked freight rolling stock of the new Speedlink network. This ensured that a heavy flow of traffic would be maintained in the Midlands yard at the expense of many smaller yards such as Washwood Heath, which have virtually closed. From serving local industry in an area of approximately ten miles radius, the catchment area for Bescot considerably increased in the 1980s. The yard serviced the needs of sidings and goods depots in an area extending west as far as Welshpool, in Mid-Wales, and encompassing the large industrial areas which lie between Stoke-on-Trent to the north, and Oxford to the south. In many ways, Bescot became a less 'glamorous' freight counterpart to the nearby Birmingham New Street passenger station.

In October 1984 the expensive Dowty retardation equipment was removed from the 'down' hump and all marshalling conducted by the old-fashioned manual methods; the hump was closed between 6 am and 10 am each morning. Problems were experienced using a hump yard to conduct what was effectively flat-shunting and perhaps, because of this, the seven parallel sidings known as the 'down' storage yard became an important marshalling

point for Speedlink traffic.

A visit to the yard during 1985, revealed a large variety of both wagonload and block freight train working. The 'up' yard, on the east side of the main line, was not part of the Speedlink network. It contained a total of 27 sidings shunted from the south end, 19 of these having connections to the closed 'up' hump. The other eight were split into two groups; six entitled 'up local sorting sidings' and the remaining two for wagon repairs. The main traffic using this yard was engineering and permanent way workings. This traffic was non-revenue producing for British Railways. It was, however, an essential service needed to maintain the fabric of the rail network. The 'up' yard was also used to stable merry-go-round trains on their journey south to Didcot Power Station. Trainloads of HAA hoppers arrived from Littleton Colliery, near Stafford, and waited for several hours before departure to ensure the even distribution of trains unloading at Didcot Power Station.

Any crippled wagon found in the area was also stabled in the 'up' yard. Immediately a cripple was discovered, a red label was allocated to it and it was left where it lay until the Carriage & Wagon Examiner had checked it. He decided whether it was safe to move the wagon across the main line. Once it was cleared to be transported to the 'up' yard, a green label was attached and a more detailed assessment of its viability then made in the 'up' yard by the Cripple Grader. This Grader decided whether the repairs to the wagon would be cheap enough to justify the retention of the vehicle. If the damage was more serious, then the wagon's future was decided by higher authority. Cost effective wagon repairs were dealt with in either the 'up' yard or at the nearby Vauxhall & Duddeston Wagon Works.

The old 'up' reception sidings had been converted into engine holding sidings, better known as Bescot Stabling Point. Entry into the sidings was from the south and was controlled by Walsall power signal box. The driver paused on the entry road and 'phoned the panel for information about where to place his locomotive, before proceeding into the sidings. There were five sidings, four of which were electrified. Overhead catenary had also been installed in the south end of roads 4 to 14 in the 'up' yard sorting sidings.

Transferring to the 'down' side of the main line, the first group of sidings were the 'down' local sorting sidings, which were ten single-ended roads placed between the reception sidings for the 'down' yard and the main line. These were the site of the old locomotive stabling point, but in 1985 were used for the storage of surplus wagons. These consisted of a selection of coal hoppers (HTV) and vacuum-braked cement wagons (CPV), which were not needed to carry traffic during certain periods of the year. To the west of the 'down' local yard were the 'down' reception sidings. There were six of these electrified throughout; the seventh and most westerly road was, in fact, the entrance to another group of sidings called the 'down' storage yard. Although there were only seven sidings in this group, this was a very important area of Bescot

Yard from which there were 15 Speedlink departures every day. The No. 1 road was electrified throughout, whilst its neighbour, the No. 2 road, was the only other siding with catenary at its south end, this to allow the Willesden Speedlink to depart from here. The rest of this yard had overhead wires at the north end of each siding.

The last main group of sidings was the 'down' yard. There were 21 roads radiating from the 'down' hump, each one of these sidings being the recipient of traffic heading for a specific destination (Table 6). The tracks in the 'down' yard varied in length from 43 in No. 8 road to 54 SWL in roads 12 to 16. This was rather short and was a major operating poblem faced by BR at Bescot Yard. As in the 'up' yard, several of the sidings were electrified at one end, these were Nos 4 to 14.

By 1966, the yard was completed as this print shows. Looking south from Bescot station, the 'up' reception sidings are on the left whilst the 'down' sorting sidings stretch out to the right.

*British Rail*

As already mentioned, the yard was busy with both wagonload and block train working. A total of 45 local trip freights arrived and departed each twenty four hours (Table 7). These brought traffic from the immediate area which fed into the Speedlink network. Steel and steel products formed a major section of the freight handled with trip workings to Wednesbury, Wolverhampton, Bloxwich and Brierley Hill. Rolled steel and steel wire were brought to Bescot from South Wales and Scunthorpe and then forwarded to the steel termini mentioned above. The future of such traffic seemed secure with BR having invested in a large new steel terminal for the West Midlands on the site of the old Round Oak Steelworks. Scrap metal from Midlands' merchants at Bilston travelled to

This picture was taken from the control tower as it was under construction, and shows the finishing touches being applied to the trackwork of the 'down' sorting sidings.

*N. Hazelwood*

Bescot. This enabled some trip freights to carry revenue-earning traffic on both legs of their journey. Coal from collieries at Littleton, Three Spires and Lea Hall was also tripped to Bescot where it joined the main freight network. Block trains of HAA merry-go-round coal hoppers departed each evening to Didcot, whilst individual HEA hoppers joined Speedlink trains on their journeys to industrial and domestic customers all over the country. Miscellaneous traffic carried on other trip freights included chemicals to Albright & Wilson at Langley Green, and Ministry of Defence traffic to Donnington, near Wellington, Shropshire.

The long-distance freights to and from the yard (Tables 7 & 8) were divided into two groups. First there were those which were part of the national Speedlink net-

## Table 6
### Bescot Siding Allocation – 1985

| Road No. | Destinations |
|---|---|
| 1 | cripples |
| 2 | Nuneaton, Four Ashes, Bloxwich, Stour valley, Anglesea |
| 3 | Littleton, Rugeley (non-MGR) |
| 4 | Wellington, Stoke (vacuum) |
| 5 | Northampton, Rugby |
| 6 | Stoke |
| 7 | Rough feed |
| 8 | Wedensfield (coal) |
| 9 | Wolverhampton (steel), Ashburys |
| 10 | Crewe, Stafford |
| 11 | Washwood Heath |
| 12 | Toton (45mph) |
| 13 | Gloucester (45mph) |
| 14 | Severn Tunnel Junction |
| 15* | transfer to "up" side |
| 16 | Whitemoor, Parkeston, Brierley Hill |
| 17 | Brierley Hill, Pensnett, Kidderminster, Hartlebury |
| 18 | Wednesbury, Coton Hill |
| 19 | Coton Hill |
| 20 | Hunslet |
| 21 | head-shunt for "down" storage yard |

*– north end has been removed because of three derailments of "Tiger" china clay wagons at this point

## Table 7
### Bescot Trip Workings – 1985

| Arrivals | | | | | Departures | | | |
|---|---|---|---|---|---|---|---|---|
| Trip | From | Arr | | | Trip | Destination | Dep | |
| T44 | Wednesbury | | SX | | T50 | Coleshill | 04.14 | SO |
| T43 | Wolverhampton | 10.00 | SX | | T51 | Tyseley | 05.15 | SX |
| T48 | Langley green | 10.45 | SX | | T50 | Lawley St | 05.16 | SX |
| | | | | | T51 | W.W. Heath/ Bordesley | 05.40 | SX |
| T50 | W. Heath | 11.25 | SX | | T60 | Littleton Colly | 05.55 | SX |
| T44 | Bloxwich | 11.45 | SX | | T43 | Wolves S.T. | 06.00 | SX |
| T43 | Wednesfield Rd | 13.00 | SX | | T42 | Brierley Hill | 06.25 | SX |
| T44 | Bloomfield | 14.35 | SX | | T49 | Curzon St | 06.45 | SX |
| T41 | Wellington | 14.40 | SX | | T48 | Langley Green | 06.50 | SX |
| T40 | Support Service | 15.15 | SX | | T44 | Wednesbury | 06.45 | SX |
| T59 | Littleton Colly | 15.25 | SX | | T44 | Wednesbury | 08.20 | SX |
| T43 | Wednesbury | 17.00 | SX | | T41 | Wellington | 08.30 | SX |
| T59 | Littleton Colly | 17.15 | SX | | | | | |
| T42 | Brierley Hill | 17.45 | SX | | T40 | Support Service | 08.45 | SX |
| | | | | | T59 | Littleton Colly | 09.25 | SX |
| T44 | Duddeston | 17.55 | SX | | T44 | Bloxwich | 10.30 | SX |
| T48 | Langley Green | 18.10 | SX | | T43 | Wednesfield Rd | 10.50 | SX |
| T51 | Three Spires | 18.37 | SX | | T48 | Langley Green | 11.35 | SX |
| | | | | | T59 | Littleton Colly | 11.55 | SX |
| T50 | Lawley St | 18.45 | SX | | T50 | Kingsbury | 12.15 | SX |
| T59 | Littleton Colly | 19.50 | SX | | T44 | Bloomfield | 11.50 | SX |
| T43 | Wolverhampton | 21.10 | SX | | T51 | Daw Mill | 11.40 | SX |
| 58 | Lea Hall Colly | 20.10 | SX | | T43 | Wednesbury | 13.50 | SX |
| | | | | | T50 | Lea Hall Colly | 14.00 | SX |
| | | | | | T44 | Duddeston | 15.55 | SX |
| | | | | | T45 | Wolverhampton ST | 17.50 | SX |

work, linking Britain's twelve major yards every day. Then there were a group of air-brake freights which took traffic to, and brought traffic from, satellite yards at Burton, Cotton Hill, Banbury, Longport, Northampton, Oxford and Gloucester. These Speedlink feeder services were similar to secondary passenger services, which have connections with the main Inter-City network at most of Britain's major passenger stations. With over 40 such long-haul freights arriving and departing each day, Bescot was handling between 750 and 1,000 wagons during each twenty four hour period.

Since 1985, alterations to freight services on the Speedlink network, particularly within the Midlands, have placed a further burden on yards like Bescot. The reduction of Speedlink activity at the nearby Toton Yard has meant that several Speedlink trains have been re-routed via Bescot, and it has become increasingly clear that the old 'down' hump yard is no longer suitable for Speedlink traffic. Two major problems have become evident. The 'down' sorting sidings, ranging as they do from 43 SWL to 54 SWL, are too short for the heavy Speedlink freights and, secondly, much Speedlink traffic cannot be hump-shunted because of the risk of damage to the produce being carried. Thus, the presence of a hump albeit redundant, renders the 'down' yard unsuitable for much freight traffic. It is a combination of these problems and the increased importance of Bescot as a national Speedlink yard that have forced the railway management to consider modernisation of the existing facilities.

## Re-modernisation of Bescot

The current plans for concentrating freight facilities on a modernised 'up' yard at Bescot are the result of a cost-cutting exercise. It became clear that not only could a large tract of land on the 'down' side of the main line be sold, but that the 'up' yard,

## Table 8
### Bescot Speedlink Arrivals – 1985
### Bescot Yard Arrivals Comm. 1st October 1984

| Train Run | From | DN Yard | DN Storage | Up side | Days Run | Remarks |
|---|---|---|---|---|---|---|
| 6O49 | Haverton Hill | | 0009 | | MX | ABS |
| 6G69 | Warrington | | 0100 | | MX | ABS |
| 4M52 | Tilbury | | 0105 | | MO | F.Liner |
| 6M94 | Dover | 0108 | | | MX | ABS |
| 6V14 | Whitemoor | | 0124 | | MX | ABS via Walsall |
| 7M80 | Doncaster | 0154 | | | MX | ABS via Walsall |
| 6M83 | Severn Tul Jcn | 0200 | | | MX | ABS via Galton |
| 4E86 | Holyhead | | 0313 | | MO | F/Liner |
| 6M85 | Tees | 0329 | | | MX | ABS via Walsall |
| 6M88 | Parkeston Quay | 0341 | | | MX | ABS via Walsall |
| 6M79 | Mossend | 0350 | | | MX | ABS via P'bello |
| 4M51 | Glasgow | 0351 | | | SO | F/Liner |
| 6G36 | Burton | 0353 | | | FO | MGR |
| 6M20 | Didcot | 0440 | | | MX | MGR |
| 6A80 | Warrington | | | 0636 | MSX | ABS via P'bello |
| 6M72 | Severn Tunnel | 0727 | | | SX | ABS |
| 7G19 | Coton Hill | 1000 | | | SX | ABS |

| Train Run | From | DN Yard | DN Storage | Up side | Days Run | Remarks |
|---|---|---|---|---|---|---|
| 6F86 | Willesden | 1223 | | | SX | ABS |
| 4090 | Lawley St | | | 1311 | SO | F/Liner |
| 6G55 | Banbury | 1330 | | | SX | ABS |
| 7M14 | Severn Tunnel | 1340 | | | SX | ABS via Dudley |
| 7G13 | Blodwell Quarry | | | 1355 | SX | CCE |
| 8G12 | Ashburys | | | 1410 | SX | CCE |
| 4M78 | Leeds | | | 1440 | SO | F/Liner |
| 7G80 | Crewe | 1558 | | | SX | ABS via P'Bello |
| 6V70 | Cliffe Vale | 1654 | | | SX | ABS via Soho |
| 7G50 | Longport | 1753 | | | SX | ABS via Soho |
| 6G81 | Northampton | 1814 | | | SX | ABS |
| 7G01 | 1625 Bardon Hill | | | 1828 | SX | CCE |
| 7G25 | Blodwell | | | 1835 | SX | CCE |
| 6M93 | Morris Cowley | 1856 | | | SX | ABS |
| 6M65 | Dover | 2021 | | | SUN | ABS |
| 6E82 | Severn Tunnel | 2206 | | | SX | ABS via Soho |
| 6M73 | Parkeston Quay | 2345 | | | SUN | ABS |

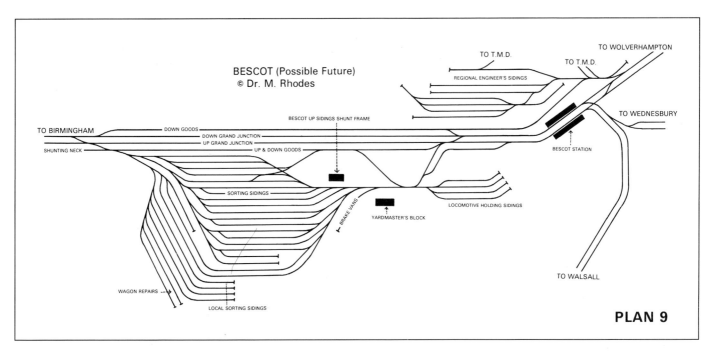

BESCOT (Possible Future)
© Dr. M. Rhodes

PLAN 9

with its longer sidings, (up to 73 SWL long) was eminently more suitable for modern Speedlink freight marshalling. The probable layout for the new Bescot yards is shown in *Plan 9*. It entails the removal of the 'down' reception sidings, the 'down' local sorting sidings, and the 'down' storage yard, along with most of the 'down' sorting sidings. Six of these may be retained for use by the Civil Engineer, who will then be banned from the 'up' yard. This will be utilised only by revenue-earning freight traffic. New connections at the north end of the sorting sidings will allow both arrival and departure from the north end of the 'up' yard.

Shunting could potentially be conducted from either end of the 'up' sorting sidings, but the majority of marshalling is likely to take place from the south end. Sidings numbered 1 to 5 would act as arrival lines with departures possible from any of the through roads provided. Slight reorganisation on the eastern fringe of the yard would make roads 19 and 20 through sidings at the expense of the old No. 17 and 18 sidings. This is an important move, providing two long sidings at the expense of creating two single-ended roads in the middle of the yards. These would be ideal for long-haul Speedlinks, which may exceed 60 SWL in the future. Four 'up' local sorting sidings would be retained for local trip freights and a wagon repair facility would be left on the eastern fringe of the yard. The possible future design of Bescot Yard is an important pointer for those interested in the new breed of marshalling yard which Speedlink traffic requires.

The salient features of such yards are long, parallel sidings with easy access to both 'up' and 'down' main lines from a single yard. The presupposition that each destination needs a separate siding has been abolished by the efficient control of wagons under the TOPS system. This has meant that wagons are delayed for much shorter periods in marshalling yards and the throughput of a small number of sidings can therefore be increased to match that of previously more expansive layouts.

Traffic for the West Midlands DCN has been marshalled at Washwood Heath since July 1987, creating some spare capacity at

In 1985 the trackwork over the 'up' hump was still intact although not utilised. The sidings themselves were full of engineering wagons as at this time all Speedlink traffic was concentrated on the 'down' sidings.

A key area of Bescot Yard is the 'down' storage sidings where a large proportion of Speedlink departures are assembled or altered. In April 1985, Class 08 No. 08901 shunts in this past of the yard to assemble the 6S74 to Mossend.

Above right:
Wagons are propelled over the 'down' hump by Class 08 No. 08603 on 2nd April 1985. This view from the control tower shows the shunter travelling with the train before leaping off to pin down the brakes of the ballast wagon upon which he rides. With no retarders, the hump has become a hindrance rather than a help.

Right:
On 11th September 1980, Class 25 No. 25257 passes through Bescot station with a morning freight to Toton via the freight only line to Wichnor Junction.

The short sharp drop over the 'down' hump at Bescot is typical of a yard where Dowty wagon control was utilised. Because of the ability to both accelerate and retard wagons, there was no longer the necessity to provide large humps to guarantee that a wagon would travel the distance to its allocated sorting siding. In 1985, the hump remains, although the Dowty equipment has long-since been removed.

Again in 1980, a trip freight from the Wolverhampton Steel Terminal arrives at Bescot behind Class 25 No. 25158. The line of empty BCV bogie-bolsters will return to South Wales later in the day; here they will pick up more steel for distribution in the Midlands.

Bescot. The 'down' hump was levelled and the sorting sidings of the 'down' yard lengthened, this for use "for the forseeable future".

The untidy collection of yards at Bescot constructed by the LNWR over 50 years ago was modernised somewhat later than other major yards in the country. It

The 9T50 transfer freight rounds the corner from Walsall on the last leg of its journey from Washwood Heath Yard. Class 46 No. 46030 brings coal from the collieries at Daw Mill and Kingsbury to the network yard at Bescot.

The 8G80 mixed freight from Crewe (Basford Hall) trundles into Bescot under the shadow of the M6 Motorway. Class 85 No. 85010 brings a mixture of predominantly vacuum-fitted rolling stock into the Midlands yard.

*P. Hawkins*

benefited from the most modern wagon control equipment available, the Dowty system. The key geographical situation of Bescot has guaranteed a continued role in freight marshalling, which with centralisation has expanded over the last ten years. Modern freight handling methods are now placing demands upon Bescot, which in its current guise the yard finds difficult to fulfil. Remodelling was inevitable and the 'down' yard has been altered to handle all Speedlink traffic. This should lead to Bescot becoming one of the three busiest yards in the country and remaining a focal point for both Speedlink and block load freight services.

In concluding this chapter I would like to thank the Area Manager of Bescot, Mr Hook and Mr N. D. Hakesley the Yard Supervisor who kindly spent an afternoon showing me around the yard in 1985.

Block loads also pass the yards at Bescot, although not as frequently as at other yards in the country. Here a northbound oil train storms past the diesel depot at Bescot behind Class 47 No. 47192 on 9th July 1985.

An express freight in the pre-Speedlink era winds its way north out of the 'down' sorting sidings at Bescot. On 21st August 1975, Class 86 No. 86037 heads a uniform snake of VVV vanfits.

*P. Hawkins*

# Table 9
## Bescot Speedlink Departures – 1985

### Bescot Yard Departures
Comm. 1st October 1984

| Train | Destination | DN Yard | DN Storage | Up side | Day run | Remarks |
|---|---|---|---|---|---|---|
| 6F71 | Warrington | | 0055 | | MX | ABS |
| 6049 | Eastleigh | | 0124 | | MX | ABS |
| 6F81 | Edge Hill | | 0210 | | MO | ABS |
| 6V14 | Severn Tunnel | | 0235 | | MX | ABS |
| 4E74 | Leeds | | 0300 | | MO | F/Liner |
| 6H61 | Trafford Park | | 0320 | | MO | ABS |
| 4E86 | Stratford | | 0358 | | MO | F/Liner |
| 7K87 | Longport | 0445 | | | SX | ABS |
| 6B83 | Northampton | 0453 | | | SX | ABS |
| 7J36 | Coton Hill | 0500 | | | SX | ABS |
| 6G80 | Banbury | | 0523 | | SX | ABS |
| 7K88 | Crewe | 0530 | | | SX | ABS |
| 6V19 | Didcot | | 0605 | | SX | ABS D/Recps. |
| 4G51 | Dudley | 0620 | | | MO | F/Liner |
| 7J27 | Blodwell | | | 0637 | SX | CCE |
| 7V66 | Gloucester | 0730 | | | SX | ABS |
| 7D56 | Toton W.Yd | 0744 | | | SX | ABS |
| 6A80 | Willesden | | | 0745 | MSX | ABS |
| 7J02 | Blodwell | | | 1015 | SX | CCE |
| 6M72 | Cliffe Vale | 1030 | | | SX | ABS |
| 7F01 | Bardon Hill | | | 1132 | SX | CCE |
| 6F86 | Warrington | 1313 | | | SX | ABS |
| 4090 | Southampton | | | 1356 | SO | F/Liner |
| 8M45 | Ashburys | | | 1507 | SX | CCE |
| 4M78 | Rugby | | | 1508 | SO | F/Liner |
| 6V70 | Severn Tunnel | 1724 | | | SX | ABS |
| 6E83 | Whitemoor | 1954 | | | SX | ABS |
| 6D81 | Toton | | 2008 | | SX | ABS |
| 6V80 | Severn Tunnel | 2020 | | | SX | ABS |
| 6S74 | Mossend | | | 2102 | SX | ABS |
| 6A21 | Willesden | | | 2130 | SX | ABS |
| 7P36 | Burton | | | 2140 | THO | MGR |
| 7V95 | Didcot | | | 2153 | SX | MGR |
| 6E82 | Whitemoor | | 2254 | | SX | ABS |
| 6E38 | Doncaster | | | 2133 | SX | ABS |

Class 85 No. 85001 arrives at the south end of Bescot Yard on 9th July 1985 with the 7G80 freight from Crewe. The train must reverse across the 'down' main line and into the 'down' arrival sidings, the entrance to which can be seen in the left foreground.

# Chapter 4
# South Wales

The railway network along the southern fringe of the Principality has grown up around the coal mining and steel industries. Both the geography of the railway lines and the marshalling yards had been built in response to the demands of local industry. The two main marshalling yards in South Wales were Margam, near Port Talbot, and Severn Tunnel Junction, to the east of Newport.

Margam Yard was opened in 1960 and was the most fully-automated marshalling yard in Europe at the time of its completion *(Plan 10)*. In contrast, the yards at Severn Tunnel Junction were traditional hump yards without the sophistication of wagon retarders and automatic shunting control. Severn Tunnel was an ideal focus for the marshalling of traffic entering or leaving South Wales, and continued in this role until November 1987. As well as the two major installations at Margam and Severn Tunnel, there were many smaller yards in South Wales. Radyr, to the north of Cardiff, was an important point for the marshalling of coal traffic, and the Tidal Sidings in Cardiff Docks dealt mainly with steel produced by the East Moors Steelworks. Both East Usk and Alexandra Dock Yards, near Newport, dealt with a variety of traffic, with a predominance of coal. A further major yard in South Wales was sited at Llandeilo Junction, to the east of Llanelli. Here, traffic from the local Duports Steelworks was sorted before distribution to the rest of the country. Many other small groups of sidings were scattered throughout the Principality at places such as Pantyffynnon, Swansea Burrows, Aberbeeg and Briton Ferry. These were not so much marshalling yards as concentration points for locally-generated rail traffic.

## Freight traffic in South Wales

As already mentioned the rail network of South Wales has grown up in response to the development of many heavy industries in the area. The Cardiff Division of British Rail has always been one of the most dependent upon rail freight and, in 1966, 80 per cent of its revenue accrued from freight traffic. The largest single commodity carried by rail was coal, accounting for 49 per cent of the total revenue of the Cardiff Division, and 66 per cent of the gross tonnage carried annually. During the 50 years prior to 1966, the output of the South Wales and Monmouthshire Coalfield had fallen from 56 to 20 million tons a year, and consequently the raison d'etre for much of the rail network in the area had disappeared. There were still 127 separate forwarding points, 65 per cent of which dispatched fewer than 1,000 wagons a month. Added to these statistics, 74 per cent of coal was for distribution within the Cardiff Division itself and the number of depots receiving house coal in 1963 was 344; freight movements were consequently complex. By 1966, the number of coal depots had been reduced to 66 with the ultimate objective of rationalising facilities still further to 39 coal depots. It is interesting to note that by 1986 there were only two coal depots left in South Wales, one at Newport and the other at Swansea Docks.

As early as 1966, questions were being asked about the old-fashioned methods of transporting coal, still used by British Rail. Where else in Europe would one find traffic grossing many millions of tons a year conveyed in little rusty boxes with an average loading of $15^{1}/_{2}$ tons? This meant that something like 4,000 wagons were required in 1965 to cope with coal shipments of around 2.3 million tons. The average turn-around time for a $16^{1}/_{2}$ ton mineral wagon was ten days, a gross inefficiency. It would have taken only 60 to 70 high-capacity 32.5 ton merry-go-round wagons doing three round trips a day to export 1.5 million tons annually. Even though these figures were put forward in 1966, there is still no sign of rationalisation at South Wales's major coal exporting centre, Swansea Docks.

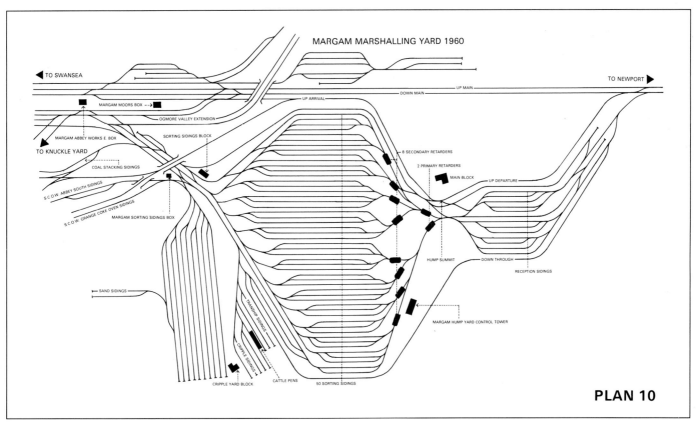

PLAN 10

One of the many smaller yards in South Wales is Ebbw Junction. From a major freight yard in 1972, when this photograph of the Marshfield milk train was taken, the yard declined until virtual closure in 1984. It may, however, play a role in the future Railfreight strategy for South Wales as the major civil engineering yard for the Principality. Class 35 No. D7096 winds out of the western end of the yard on 7th July 1972.

*J. Cooper-Smith*

The mid-1970s saw a 36 per cent decline in coal traffic over the 1965 tonnages, but this was offset by parallel gains in steel and sundries traffic within the South Wales region. The introduction of a full TOPS system by the end of 1975, meant that considerable efficiencies were wrought in coal and other freight carriage. The forwarding points for mined coal were reduced to only 64 and the major destinations were the five power stations along the South Wales coast, along with three major steelworks, two docks, and a variety of washeries and blending plants. Further centralisation of both forwarding points and destinations was, however, in hand.

By 1978, forwarding points had reduced to only 50, whilst the rationalisation of the steel industry in 1980/1 meant that only Llanwern and Margam steelworks remained. The power stations along the South Wales coast were ill-equipped to receive coal in modern air-braked wagons, with only the large Aberthaw Power Station suited to such traffic. The move by both British Rail and British Coal to concentrate on high-capacity merry-go-round coal trains meant the gradual decline in the power stations at Uskmouth, Camarthen Bay and Rogerstone, whilst the consumption at Aberthaw Power Station climbed ever higher, reaching 50,000 tons of coal each week.

The arrival of the steel industry in South Wales was directly related to the lighting of Britain's first blast furnace at Dowlais, near Merthyr Tydfil, in 1750. By the early 1960s, there were four major steel producing works in South Wales, at Margam, East Moors (Cardiff), Llanwern (Newport) and

Ebbw Vale. As well as these four large plants there was a plethora of smaller steel company sites involved in the processing of semi-finished steel. In 1979, 5.9 million tons of steel products were carried by rail in the Cardiff Division, and it was anticipated that a steady growth in this area of rail freight would continue. In 1980, however, the rationalising arm of Sir Charles Villiers and the resultant steel strike caused a catastrophic fall in steel output throughout the country. As a result of these industrial changes, only 2.1 million tons of steel were carried in the Cardiff Division during 1980 as compared with the anticipated figure of 6

Severn Tunnel. The introduction of air-braked wagons for all types of freight traffic allowed the area management team to concentrate freight marshalling for the whole of South Wales at Severn Tunnel Junction. Coal from Pantyffynnon had been taken to Margam for sorting, but the high maximum speed of air-braked wagons allowed the dispatch of train loads direct to Severn Tunnel Junction. Just as the industry of South Wales has a direct and marked effect on rail freight in the area, so modernisation of the wagon fleet has led to changes in the operation of freight services in the Principality. Recent proposals by

expansion of the Margam Abbey Works, owned by the Steel Company of Wales Limited (SCOW). The yard was the most up to date in Europe and was the first to be fully-automated. It was capable of sorting 4,500 wagons daily and could deal with a total of 220 trains in and out each twenty four hours.

The marshalling yard was situated between Bridgend and Port Talbot approximately $3\frac{1}{2}$ miles to the east of the latter. It was on the 'down' side of the main line, and occupied an area of 178 acres. It stretched for over $1\frac{3}{4}$ miles and comprised 33 miles of track and 240 points. There were twelve reception sidings with an engine release line and hump engine return road, together with 50 double-ended sorting sidings, ten single-ended holding sidings, and seven single-ended tranship and cripple sidings, with tranship platform and cattle pens. The capacity of the reception sidings varied from 63 to 95 SLU, plus room for locomotive and van. The shortest sorting siding held 43 wagons, whilst the longest had a capacity to store 101 wagons. All twelve of the reception sidings were availa-

It is 1959 and Margam is nearing completion as this view of the sorting sidings shows.
*British Rail*

Margam 'Knuckle' yard — The small 'Knuckle' yard is seen in this 1962 photograph. To the left are the SCoW Abbey South sidings.
*British Rail*

million tons. This short-fall cost British Rail £28 million nationally, and is a clear example of the close inter-dependence between heavy industry and the health of the Railfreight network.

During the same year as the slump in steel carriage, the South Wales area saw a number of Speedlink workings into and out of the region. There were nine outgoing and eight incoming trains daily. Part of Speedlink's success in South Wales was due to depots such as the Cory Link Depot at Cardiff. This was aided by a Section 8 grant and one of two such depots operating in South Wales. Other growth areas for the wagonload business were the new Ford's engine factory at Bridgend, the BP Chemical Plant at Baglan Bay, and the carriage of coal to industrial users such as the Aberthaw Blue Circle Cement Works on the Vale of Glamorgan line.

During the early 1980s, a review was made of the rail infrastructure in South Wales and near the top of the list for alteration were the large marshalling yards. A planned disengagement from the traditional wagonload movements was drawn up and it was hoped that all wagonload freight could be transferred to the Speedlink network by the end of 1983. This obviously led to an increase in the number of Speedlink trains working to and from the South Wales railhead at Severn Tunnel Junction. By 1986 there were twelve inward and twelve outward trunk trains from Severn Tunnel. In addition to the trunk services there were a further 80 trip freights and Speedlink feeder services based at

British Rail (Western Region) have taken these changes to their logical end, but these changes will be discussed towards the end of this chapter.

# Margam

The British Rail modernisation proposals for speeding up freight trains on the Western Region, envisaged three new yards; Margam (Port Talbot), Gloucester and Shrewsbury (Walcote). The first of these was the only one to be constructed, and the decision of the British Transport Commission to provide a large marshalling yard at Margam was influenced by the

ble for 'down' trains and were accessible over a new junction from the main line at Water Street. Five of the reception sidings were also available for 'up' trains, access being via a new 'up' arrival line linked to the 'up' goods line from Margam Moors signal box and the Steel Company of Wales sidings by means of two new flyover bridges at the west end of the yard. Departures to the west were possible from all the sorting sidings, and facilities were available for eastbound or 'up', departures from the two most northerly fans of sidings.

The sub-soil in the area consisted of sand and peat to a considerable depth, and it was therefore necessary to infill a large amount of the area by levelling off the existing irregularities and excavating a nearby borrow pit. In all, approximately 750,000 cubic yards of sand were moved, using seven diesel tractors, and during the peak period of construction as much as 2,000 tons of ballast per day were delivered to the site by specially-programmed shuttle services. The River Kenfig flowed across the site and a diversion was carried out in two straight cuts, one each side of the yard.

The twelve reception sidings converged to a single track over the hump which had a vertical curvature of eleven chains radius. The gradient fell sharply to 1 in 18 towards the sorting sidings, flattening out to 1 in 80 through the two 72ft long primary retarders and the eight 36ft secondary retarders. All track joints in the yard, with the exception of insulated joints, were site-welded by the Thermit process. The sorting sidings were allocated to three main uses, and sidings numbered 1 to 15 were for the exclusive use of the South Wales steel company. Sidings 16 to 38 were for 'down' line traffic and Nos 39 to 50 for 'up' line destinations. A complete list of siding allocations is shown in *Table 10*.

Lighting for the whole yard was provided by 99 55ft high steel lighting towers, each capable of holding four 1,000 watt flood-lights. These were all controlled by one consul in the control tower. The control tower itself had three floors. The first floor contained relay and battery rooms, the second an air conditioning plant, and the third, or top floor, the control room, from where operations in the marshalling yard were directed. Provision was made for a future depot to service diesel locomotives, and this was completed some two years after the main yard.

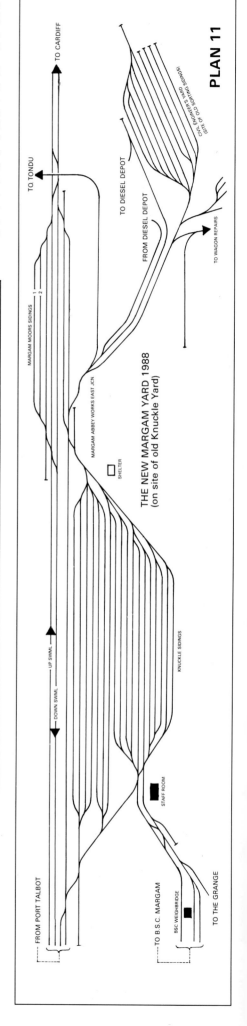

**PLAN 11**

**THE NEW MARGAM YARD 1988**
(on site of old Knuckle Yard)

### Table 10
### Margam Siding Allocation — 1961

| Siding | Capacity (Wagons) | Traffic |
|---|---|---|
| 1 | 43 | S.C.O.W. Abbey Works Scrap |
| 2 | 43 | S.C.O.W. Abbey Works Miscellaneous |
| 3 | 61 | S.C.O.W. Grange Coke Ovens Coal |
| 4 | 50 | S.C.O.W. Low Volatile Raw Coal |
| 5 | 50 | S.C.O.W. Medium Volatile Raw Coal |
| 6 | 60 | S.C.O.W. High Volatile Raw Coal |
| 7 | 57 | S.C.O.W. Low Volatile Washed Coal for Margam Tipplers |
| 8 | 62 | S.C.O.W. Medium Volatile Washed Coal for Margam Tipplers |
| 9 | 67 | S.C.O.W. High Volatile Washed Coal for Margam Tipplers |
| 10 | 63 | S.C.O.W. Low and Medium Volatile Large Coal |
| 11 | 63 | S.C.O.W. High Volatile Large Coal |
| 12 | 75 | S.C.O.W. Abbey Works Empties |
| 13 | 65 | S.C.O.W. Margam Works Scrap |
| 14 | 65 | S.C.O.W. Margam Works Miscellaneous |
| 15 | 70 | S.C.O.W. Port Talbot Steelworks Scrap and Miscellaneous |
| 16 | 67 | Port Talbot Goods and Mileage |
| 17 | 74 | Port Talbot Docks |
| 18 | 82 | B.I.S. Factory, Kenfig |
| 19 | 73 | Duffryn Yard; P.T. line; R & SB. line; O.V.E. line and Tondu |
| 20 | 73 | Swansea High Street Goods |
| 21 | 81 | Landore Steel Works; Landore; Cockett; Gowerton; Loughor |
| 22 | 72 | Swansea Valley Junction |
| 23 | 72 | Neath; Neath Junction including N. & B. and Vale of Neath; Skewen |
| 24 | 79 | Briton Ferry |
| 25 | 76 | Swansea Docks including Swansea Eastern Depot |
| 26 | 80 | Cripples |
| 27 | 93 | Hybars and Shock Opens |
| 28 | 80 | Shock Vans |
| 29 | 80 | Steel Carrying Wagons (Hytwins, Bolsters etc.) |
| 30 | 87 | Whitland and beyond excluding Fishguard Harbour Branch |
| 31 | 82 | Fishguard Harbour Branch |
| 32 | 88 | Carmathen Junction and branches |
| 33 | 93 | Miscellaneous empties waiting orders |
| 34 | 89 | Felin Fran including Clydach North and Llangyfelach; Pontardulais and Central Wales line |
| 35 | 89 | Llandarcy |
| 36 | 101 | Llandilo Junction including Llanelly, Bynea, Pembrey, Kidwelly and Ferryside |
| 37 | 89 | Urgents to connect with vacuum services |
| 38 | 89 | Spare |
| 39 | 77 | Maintenance by day. Swansea and Neath Goods at night |
| 40 | 77 | Opens |
| 41 | 84 | Pools |
| 42 | 71 | Vans |
| 43 | 74 | Vanfits |
| 44 | 74 | Shrewsbury and Saltney |
| 45 | 70 | Severn Tunnel Junction |
| 46 | 60 | Cardiff |
| 47 | 57 | Newport A.D. Junction and East Usk Junction |
| 48 | 49 | Banbury and Leamington |
| 49 | 47 | Cardiff District Shorts |
| 50 | 50 | Brake Vans |

The parallel metal rail brakes of the primary retarders at Margam are clearly seen along with the hydraulic rams used to apply braking pressure in this September 1959 picture. It appears that the retarders are being tested, as several wagons are rolling down the hump.

*M. Welch*

## Operation of the Yard

A train arriving at Margam from the east, via Pyle, left the main line on a turnout controlled by Pyle West signal box. From this turnout the train ran into one of twelve reception roads, seven exclusively for westbound traffic and the remainder bi-directional. On either side of the reception sidings were two through roads, 'up' departures could bypass reception roads on the northern side whilst through block trains for the Steel Company of Wales could circle the southern side of the whole yard on the 'down' through line. Once a train was deposited in the reception roads the engine set off 'light', via the locomotive link line, to the other end of the yard for its next job. Diesel engines were permitted to travel over the hump whilst most steam engines, including Western Region eight-coupled tanks, Stanier 2-8-0s, Class 5 4-6-0s, British Railways Standard 4-6-0s and 2-10-0s, had to make a double shunt to reach the locomotive link line.

A shunter and a tallyman walked the length of the newly-arrived train, the shunter uncoupled the wagons into cuts for the sorting sidings, and the tallyman read details off the trains into his portable radio transmitter, his account of the cuts destinations, and the number of wagons in each cut was picked up in the traffic office on the ground floor of the control tower. Here a traffic clerk transcribed his readout as a teleprint. As he typed, the teleprint was reproduced on receivers in the offices of the Sorting Sidings Inspector, the office of the SCOW checker and on the top floor of the control tower. Simultaneously, the traffic office teleprinter made a copy of the cut list in code on a perforated tape. When the traffic office decided that it was ready for the train to be humped, the advice was broadcast over the loudspeaker telephone network to all concerned, and the relevant perforated tape was fed into the tape reader in the traffic office. It was the tape reader, which during normal automatic operation of the yard initiated the route-setting below the hump. It read off the first four routes selected, stored them until humping began, then waited for the first one to be used, before reading off further routes in step with activity over the hump, but always four cuts ahead. The coded tape, being fed into the traffic office tape reader, also caused illuminated panels on the operating consul of the control tower to display the numbers of the first four sorting sidings to be used. The control tower operator could thus check these sidings against the teleprint, which he had previously received for

the same train. If the tape reader had made a mistake, the signalman in the control tower could correct this by using a push button below the illuminated display to cancel the incorrect route and interpose the correct one.

In preparation for humping, one of the two operators who manned the consul in the control tower summoned a diesel shunter on to the rear of the train to be humped. Three 400hp diesel-electric shunters, numbered D3436 to D3438, and allocated to Duffryn Yard Depot, were equipped with two-way radio telephones specifically for use at Margam Hump Yard. In this way, easy communication with the Sorting Sidings Inspector, as well as the control tower operators, was possible. In addition, every diesel cab was fitted with a replica of the position light humping signal. This was done by superimposing ac sonic frequency over the normal dc track circuits and mounting inductor coils on each corner of the locomotive to detect the alternating current. The induced current was amplified on the locomotive where it operated the humping signal repeater. Shunting was commenced when the consul operator depressed the start tape button on his panel and instructed the diesel shunter to propel his train at the required speed towards the hump summit. From this point onwards, in normal conditions, the controller merely watched the complex electronic equipment function properly. He was, however, able to intervene at any time to take personal control of the retarders or route-setting, if this was required.

Both primary and secondary retarders were controlled by devices that aimed to buffer a cut up to the wagons already standing in its appointed siding at not more than 4mph. Margam was claimed to be the first yard in Europe whose retarders all functioned automatically with such precision. This automatic control required the input of information about the cut's weight, its rollability, the curvature of its route, and how far it had to run. Rollability was assessed by successive pairs of inductive wheel detectors which measured the acceleration of each cut over the known gradient down from the hump. Each siding had a potentiometer, which took account of the occupation of each siding and produced a voltage proportional to the amount of free space left in that road. As wagons entered the sidings during humping, the potentiometer voltage was stepped up by an amount corresponding to the length of each cut. As at Temple Mills and Thornton, radar assessed the speed of wagons as they approached each retarder, and ahead of the primary retarders was a weight detector which was essential to calculate the momentum of each cut. Finally, the control tower operator had consul switches which he set according to the strength and direction of the wind, and whether conditions were wet or dry. These factors also affected the speed of wagons and the efficiency of the rail brakes.

The chief function of the primary retarders was to maintain a safe interval between cuts and to insure that the cuts reached the secondary retarders at a controllable speed. The secondary retarders were then used to apply braking pressure, such that a cut reached the other wagons in its siding at no greater than 4mph. The consul operators could override the computers at any moment. For each retarder there were two multi-position switches on the consul. One switch, marked A, O, L, M and H, allowed the following settings: retarders on automatic, retarders open, and then three manual brake pressures of low, medium and high. When the first switch was set for automatic working, 'A', another switch marked 'C', and labelled 1, 2, 3, 4 and 5, was brought into play. Left on position 'C', this second switch allowed the retarders to obey the computer implicitly, but if the operator found it desirable to override the computer he then turned the switch to one of its other positions. This caused the retarders to apply a braking pressure appropriate to an exit speed from 8mph to 12mph. Such overriding control might be appropriate when a cut of 30 wagons came over the hump in one piece.

In May 1960, the yard at Margam was humping some 30 to 35 trains a day, or approximately 1,000 wagons. It was decided to operate the first phase of the new yard — well below capacity in order to iron out any teething troubles with the complex electronic gadgetry. Initially, Margam 'down', Duffryn Yard and Bryndu on the Ogmore Valley extension were closed. However, by 1961, the yard came into full operation leading to the closure of several smaller marshalling yards in the Port Talbot and Swansea areas.

In 1961, Margam was dealing with an average of 2,250 wagons a day, and inward traffic, terminating in the reception sidings, amounted to 70 trains daily. Points of origin ranged from Old Oak Common and Acton to Swindon, Stourbridge Junction, Cotton Yard in Shrewsbury, and Saltney in Chester. Almost one third of the trains came from Cardiff, Newport and Severn Tunnel Junction yards, and over half from points in the surrounding area. Departures ran to various destinations to the west of Margam, mainly in the Swansea and Llanelli areas. Long-distance through services left for Acton, Didcot, Salisbury, Swindon, Bristol and Saltney. In addition there were several trains to Severn Tunnel Junction Yard.

The design capacity of the yard, 4,500 wagons daily, was never approached, and even the 1960 estimate of 3,000 wagons daily was rarely reached. About 30 per cent of the 2,250 wagons handled were for the adjacent Steel Company of Wales and carried mainly coal, iron ore, pig iron and scrap metals. Outgoing freight traffic was of steel products, including hot strip coil and steel slabs. All classes of Western Region freight and mixed traffic steam locomotives worked to the yard, but the internal yard work was handled entirely by standard 350hp diesel-electric shunting locomotives. The yard was still being expanded in 1961, even in the face of the already very clear, short-fall in traffic.

On 3rd July 1961, a 'Knuckle' yard was opened on the site of the former Abbey Sidings. This dealt with secondary sorting and refining of wagons for 'up' and 'down' line trains scheduled to start from Margam. A total of 15 freights were timetabled to leave the yard each day and facilities were available for through express freights to call in at one of the three reception sidings where they could attach or detach traffic without becoming enmeshed in the nearby Margam Hump Yard. The three reception sidings were complemented by a further 16 sorting sidings, and on the western extremity of the yard were three departure roads. The British Rail 'Knuckle' yard was constructed on the site of the SCOW Abbey Sidings, and these were therefore relocated to the west and stand today as the British Steel Corporation Abbey Yard.

The new hump marshalling yard at Margam was not without its problems. In relation to industrial centres, ports, and railway geography, the site was excellent, but the disadvantages of proximity to sand dunes only became apparent during the first year of operation. Marram grass was planted in an attempt to reduce the large volume of wind-blown sand encroaching on the yard. The wind, when westerly, impeded wagons running from the hump, even when the primary and secondary retarders were left open, and it appeared that the possible strength of the wind had been seriously underestimated. If, however, the wind blew from the direction of the SCOW, it brought smoke from the industrial plant over the yard, hampering, and even causing suspension of working, because of bad visibility.

In general, the layout of the yard was satisfactory, although more reception sidings were needed. Also a slight westward 'down' slope from the reception sidings caused uncoupled wagons to gravitate towards, or even on to, the hump. The small radius of curvature on the hump profile limited the classes of wagons that could pass over it. One final quirk of the automatic wagon retardation system was found when an empty or lightly-loaded tank wagon was shunted in the same cut as a fully loaded tanker. The pressure exerted by the retarders, as a result of the rollability of the heavier wagon, sometimes led to the wheels of the lighter wagon being forced off the rails!

It was clear that not only was Margam far too large for the volume of traffic passing through Port Talbot, but its sophistication and automation had as many disadvantages as the potential advantages of a modern yard. The two further Western Region enterprises at Gloucester and Shrewsbury, for which Margam was the model, were never constructed. This verdict of 'no confidence' in the modern Margam Yard has been proved correct during the last 20 years.

The peak throughput of 2,500 wagons at Margam began to decline by the 1970s, and even though Margam was made into the empty wagon supply yard for the whole of Port Talbot, Swansea and Llanelli areas, its throughput fell to 1,800 wagons per annum by 1975. Further concentration in the Railfreight handling of coal led to a drop in the wagon throughput at Margam to 1,000 wagons each day by 1978, and in 1980 the hump at the yard was closed, as were the sidings in the nearby 'Knuckle' yard. These closures were just the start of a rationalisation programme, which reflects the change in coal carriage in South Wales discussed at the beginning of the chapter, and the modernisation of the Speedlink wagon fleet.

# Rationalisation at Margam

By December 1985 the Railfreight facilities at Margam had been reduced to 32 single-ended sorting sidings shunted from the western end of the complex. The stepwise alteration in the track plan was complex, involving four stages, each of which requires a full page diagram to explain, and they are therefore beyond the scope of this book. The road allocation of the sidings, as it stood in 1986, is shown in *Table 11*. As well as the sorting sidings, two loops and two mileage roads at the west end of the yard adjacent to the 'down' through line saw large amounts of traffic. So too did the single-ended holding sidings used predominantly for crippled wagons.

At any one time the yard at Margam contained 700 to 800 wagons and 50 per cent of these were either crippled or in departmental use. A further one hundred vehicles were stationed in the carriage &

Stored and condemned wagons fill the eastern end of Margam Yard on Christmas Day in 1983. The hump has been closed and several sections of track in the hump area taken up.

## Table 11
### Margam Yard Siding Allocation — 1986

| | | | |
|---|---|---|---|
| No. 1-2 | Condemned wagons | No. 36 | MDO |
| No. 3-22 | Out of use | No. 37 | HTV |
| No. 23 | Spare, vans, cripples | No. 38 | MDV |
| No. 24-26 | Run-round roads | No. 39-41 | Removed |
| No. 27 | Cripples | No. 42 | Permanent Way stock |
| No. 28 | Llandarcy | No. 43 | Radyr |
| No. 29 | Cripples | No. 44 | Severn Tunnel |
| No. 30 | West Wales | No. 45-50 | All other outward traffic |
| No. 31-35 | Permanent Way stock | No. 51 | 'Up' through road |

## Table 12
### Margam Freight — January 1986

**Departures**

| | | | | | | | |
|---|---|---|---|---|---|---|---|
| 7C20 | 01.25 | MX (Y) | Llanwern or Severn Tunnel | 9C27 | 12.10 | SX | Felin Fran |
| 6C30 | 02.40 | MSX | Port Talbot Docks | 6C14 | 12.28 | SX | Llandarcy |
| 6C10 | 02.45 | MX | Radyr | 6B99 | 13.00 | SX (Y) | Llantrisant |
| 6C49 | 03.15 | SX | Trostre | 6B61 | 13.20 | SX | Radyr |
| 7C15 | 03.25 | MSX | Carmarthen | 6B81 | 14.00 | SX | Llantrisant |
| 9C72 | 03.50 | MX (Y) | Pantyffynnon | 6C59 | 14.35 | SX (Y) | Llanwern or Severn Tunnel |
| 9B91 | 04.00 | MX | Llandeilo Junction | 6C36 | 14.40 | SX (Y) | Velindre or Trostre |
| 6C16 | 04.00 | MSX | Fishguard | 6B70 | 15.00 | SX | Onllwyn |
| 6C51 | 04.25 | SX (Y) | Port Talbot Docks | 6C01 | 15.05 | SX | Severn Tunnel |
| 6B96 | 05.55 | SX | Onllwyn | 4A85 | 15.55 | SX (Y) | Llanwern or Severn Tunnel |
| 6C65 | 06.15 | SX | Blaengarw | 6C44 | 18.45 | FSX | Trostre or Velindre |
| 9C21 | 06.15 | SX | Felin Fran | 9B89 | 19.30 | SX (Y) | Cynheidre |
| 6B68 | 06.30 | SX | Llynfi | 9C95 | 19.45 | SX (Y) | Coedbach |
| 6C34 | 07.00 | MWFO | Swansea (High Street) | 7C10 | 20.15 | SX | Llanwern or Severn Tunnel |
| 6B60 | 07.05 | SX | Mill Pit | 6B93 | 20.40 | SX | Llantrisant |
| 6C21 | 07.15 | SX (Y) | Velindre or Trostre | 7B06 | 20.50 | SX | Barry |
| 6A60 | 07.30 | MSX | Swansea Burrows | 9B28 | 21.00 | TTho | Gloucester |
| 6B21 | 08.10 | SX | Radyr | 6B82 | 21.05 | SX | Onllwyn |
| 9C23 | 09.10 | SX | Felin Fran | 6C55 | 21.35 | SX | Llanwern |
| 7C54 | 09.25 | SX | Haverfordwest | 6E88 | 21.35 | SX | Whitemoor |
| 9B94 | 10.40 | SX | Swansea Docks | 9C08 | 22.25 | MO | Severn Tunnel |
| 9B94 | 11.55 | SX | Onllwyn | 9B88 | 22.55 | SX (Y) | Cynheidre |
| 9C28 | 11.20 | WFO | Llandeilo Junction | 4A86 | 23.05 | SX (Y) | Llanwern or Severn Tunnel |

wagon repair sidings, and a similar number were to be found on British Steel Corporation (BSC) metals. The yard was effectively out of the Speedlink network and operated purely to attach and detach traffic from Speedlink feeder services bound for Severn Tunnel as well as dealing with through block trains which required re-manning or change of locomotive.

The existence of Margam reflects the outdated parts of the railway system in its immediate vicinity. Coal from Onllwyn, as well as Pantyffynnon, was still carried in traditional unbraked mineral wagons, even at the end of 1985. The large siding capacity was also of use to the Civil Engineer, who could store large volumes of crippled wagons and civil engineering vehicles on the site. In February 1986, a radical rethink regarding the Railfreight infrastructure in South Wales was put forward by the regional management team. It was suggested that Margam Sorting Sidings would close completely, except for a few roads retained for the Civil Engineer. All British Rail activity was to be transferred to the existing set of BSC-owned sidings known as Abbey South Yard. Unfortunately BSC agreement for this plan was not forthcoming and it was decided to rebuild the old Knuckle Yard as a new marshalling facility. This has functioned well since closure of Margam Hump Yard in November 1987. New access tracks would be constructed to enable this transfer to take

The author's camera bag lies next to the derelict hump crest at Margam, under the old humping signal in May 1986. The southern half of the yard is disused although the cost of track removal has meant that the rails are still in situ. The northern half of the sidings are shunted from the west end and contain mainly unfitted coal wagons used in West Wales to transport shipment coal.

place. Changes in local industry only confirmed the correctness of the management decision to streamline siding capacity in the area. The start of 1986 saw the closure of the Llandarcy Oil Refinery with a concomitant decrease in oil trains needing staging at Margam. In 1985, Blaengarw Colliery closed, leaving a question mark over the future of Ogmore Washery. Coal trains from Maerdy were contracted to run twice a day until 1987 in order to clear a stock pile of 1.5 million tons of coal. By 1988, 2 million tons had been moved, and there was still in excess of a further 2 million tons at the washery! When this work is completed there is a possibility that everything north of Tondu may close, further decreasing the wagonload freight needing marshalling in the Margam area.

Steel production too was in decline. Increased production of finished steel in the 'Third World' has meant that the output of western furnaces has declined steadily for the last 15 years. Altered materials used in the packaging of food and other manufactured goods also seriously effect the tin-plating works at Trostre, Velindre and Ebbw Vale, where all of the United Kingdom's tin-plating is done.

There are some optimistic signs for the future however, and it is hoped that several

new customers could be won by the railways in West Wales. Coke to Imperial Smelting in Avonmouth was due to return to rail haulage from January 1986. The local North British Wharfage Company at Briton Ferry had regular consignments of steel with trains dispatched to Brierley Hill and Ebbw Vale. Other potential areas for growth included the carriage of eggs from Carmarthen, which was amounting to two VDA vans daily, and the expansion of a Railfreight-based depot at Danygraig, linked to the Gower Chemicals Company. Baglan Bay Chemical Works at Briton Ferry also dispatched regular loads to Partington three times a week and daily consignments of Speedlink wagons to Saltend in Hull. There were also two trains a week to Dow Chemicals in Barry.

Whatever the growth in Speedlink traffic around Port Talbot and Swansea, the current daily freight train total of 60, dealing with approximately 600 wagons, is not likely to be exceeded. Only 60 per cent of this traffic passed through Margam and a yet smaller percentage actually required marshalling in the yard. The proposals to centre all British Rail traffic on a new Margam Yard on the site of the old Knuckle Yard should more than adequately

cater for Speedlink traffic in the area. In addition, three 'up' sidings at Margam Moors deal with the recessing of a daily merry-go-round service from Mill Pit to Didcot. This is run as two trains to Margam Moors before departing east in the evening. Oil and chemical trains are also staged at Margam Moors as is coal from Tondu.

Further rationalisation in the area is also proposed. The sidings at Swansea Burrows should ideally contain just five roads, four for traffic and one for crippled wagons. To the west lies the rambling network of lines in Swansea Docks. Here British Rail employs 27 staff, more than the rest of the Swansea freight staff put together. Five hundred unfitted wagons are used to bring coal from Onllwyn and Pantyffynnon, each wagon averaging one load per fortnight. Up to 200 of these wagons may lie idle as output from the local collieries exceeds speed of export from the docks, and they thus form a mobile storage bunker. This is convenient for British Coal, but expensive and inefficient for British Rail to run. Modernisation of the freight facilities at Swansea is essential if the export of Welsh coal is to continue from this point. Either investment at Swansea or a transfer of coal exports to another point must be undertaken if British Rail is not to abandon this previously prosperous carriage of coal.

The freight rationalisation plans for South Wales affect not only Margam but also several other sites in West Wales. Wagon servicing and locomotive stabling will be retained at Margam, as will the train crew depot. There will, however, be increased staff allocated to Port Talbot station, and Briton Ferry Yard could see increased Speedlink usage. This depends on the capacity of Margam Knuckle Yard, now called Margam Traffic Centre. The remnant at Llandeilo Junction Yard in Llanelli will remain a centre for civil engineering activity in West Wales. The train crew depot at Llanelli will probably close with work being transferred to Port Talbot or Pantyffynnon. Obviously, the planning of such major reorganisation will take some time, and many of the decisions have not yet been finalised. It is, however, certain that the British Rail policy of the 1990s will concentrate on two or three small groups of sidings, utilised efficiently by Speedlink trains, and encourage private users of the railway such as the BSC to invest more heavily in the railway infrastructure, which they have for so long taken for granted.

# Severn Tunnel Junction

The sidings at Severn Tunnel Junction have never had the sophistication or glamour of large modern yards like Margam, but because of their geographical situation at the entrance to South Wales, they have always been an important freight marshalling centre. In the 1920s a modest provision of sorting sidings dealt with large volumes of freight traffic. On the 'down' side of the main line three reception sidings were laid in parallel to twelve single-ended sorting sidings. There were several freight recessing loops on the 'up' side of the main line at the junction as well as twelve single-ended sorting sidings divided into two equal groups, called the Bristol Yard and the West Sidings.

In 1931, a new 'up' yard was constructed with three reception sidings, from which trains were drawn westward on to a headshunt before being propelled over a new hump into an array of 16 sorting sidings. Similar improvements were made on the 'down' side of the main line, with a new 'down' yard opening in 1939. Further expansion during World War II and the early 1950s led to the extension of the 'up' yard to include 21 sorting sidings. The 'down' yard was somewhat larger than its counterpart on the 'up' side of the main line. Four reception sidings had a direct access into 19 sorting sidings, with the provision of four loops off the main line, for the recessing of 'down' traffic and the addition of carriage and wagon servicing facilities on the southern extremity of the yard. Further expansion was yet to come, and in 1960 a new 'up' hump was constructed with eleven new reception sidings which were collectively known as "Undy Yard" *(Plan 12)*. These led to the 'up' hump from which 21 sorting sidings radi-

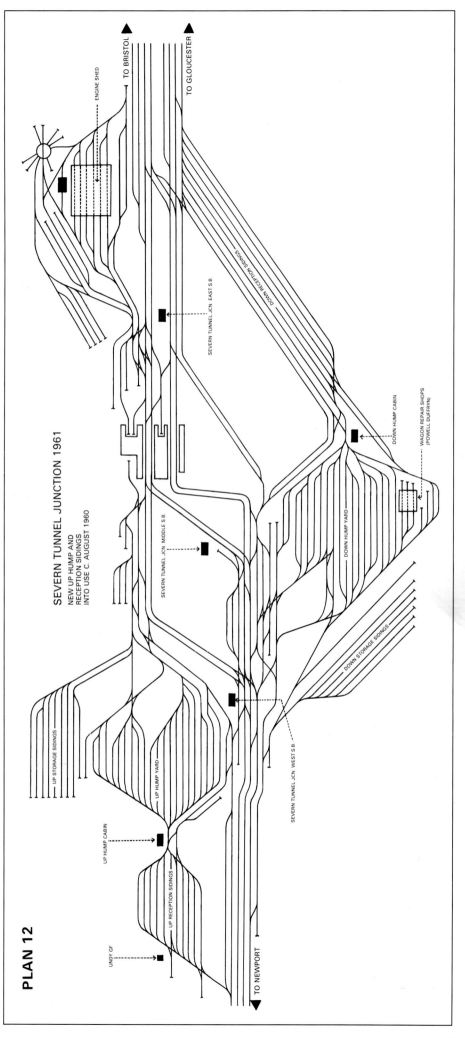

**PLAN 12**

SEVERN TUNNEL JUNCTION 1961
NEW UP HUMP AND
RECEPTION SIDINGS
INTO USE C. AUGUST 1960

ated. Ten single-ended 'up' storage sidings were added to the northern perimeter of the sorting sidings already mentioned. Similar expansion took place at the 'down' yard and a new 'down' hump cabin was opened in 1962 with the addition of three further reception sidings. This remained the basic pattern of the yard at Severn Tunnel until the closure of the 'down' hump in 1978. Both of the humps were operated by the manual method, whereby chasers were employed to pin down the brakes of wagons as they rolled off the hump summit. The points controlling access to the sorting sidings were automatically changed via a switching panel in the hump control cabin, and the site looking down from the hump, displays the absence of point levers, but a very strong presence of shunting staff.

Even after the closure of the 'down' hump, the traffic passing through Severn Tunnel continued to increase. Speedlink traffic, long wheelbased wagons and fragile cargoes were dealt with at the newly truncated 'down' yard and all shunting was conducted from the west end. The 'up' yard continued to utilise the hump shunting method and subsequently dealt with unfitted and vacuum-braked wagons, predominantly carrying coal. By the early 1980s, however, the decrease in vacuum and unfitted wagons meant that such an installment was hard to justify, and the 'up' yard was similarly converted into a flat-shunted group of sidings, marshalled from the east end. By the end of 1983 all but coal traffic was dealt with in air-braked Speedlink wagons, and the introduction of HEA coal hoppers meant the speedy conversion of even coal traffic into modern Speedlink vehicles. As the maximum speed of wagons has been standardised at 60mph, so the size of the area served by a major yard, like Severn Tunnel, has increased.

In the 1960s and early 1970s, long-haul freight from throughout the country arrived at Severn Tunnel, and traffic was sorted for distribution in South Wales. Similarly, trains with West Wales traffic from Margam arrived at Severn Tunnel, where wagons could be incorporated in long-haul freights bound for further afield. Local trips brought wagons from Newport and Cardiff and these too were marshalled into long-distance freights. As marshalling facilities around the country were rationalised and wagonload traffic decreased in volume, so trip freights to Severn Tunnel began to run from further afield. By the early 1980s, traffic from the most westerly point of the rail network in South Wales, Fishguard Harbour, was tripped directly to Severn Tunnel without stopping at any intermediate yards. This was also true for coal traffic from washeries such as Coed Bach, near Kidwelly, and the group of sidings at Pantyffynnon.

A general view of the 'up' sorting sidings at Severn Tunnel Junction in 1960.

*British Rail*

Modernisation of Severn Tunnel Junction Yard in 1960 included the provision of ten reception sidings for the 'up' yard, viewed here shortly after their construction. Following the closure of the 'up' hump in 1981, the reception roads, or Undy Yard, were used exclusively for Speedlink traffic for a couple of years before their limited capacity meant the transfer of Speedlink back into the main yards at Severn Tunnel in 1983.

*British Rail*

The hump signal cabin at Severn Tunnel 'up' yard contained switches to control the points leading to the sorting sidings, whereas the descent of wagons from the hump was manually executed by shunters who pinned down their brakes.

*British Rail*

Here the shunters examine wagons as they separate into cuts at the 'up' hump; Severn Tunnel, circa 1950.

*British Rail*

Right:
An overview of the 'down' yard shows clearly the absence of retarders at Severn Tunnel. To the left of the picture, beyond the overbridge stands the Powell Duffryn wagon repair shop, which finally closed in 1972.

*British Rail*

A line of shunters with their poles can be seen standing between the 'Queen' and 'Jack' points waiting for wagons to descend from the 'down' hump at Severn Tunnel in 1960.

*British Rail*

Right:
Great Western steam locomotives cross with rakes of coal empties as a Class 08 shunter propels a freight along the 'down' reception sidings at Severn Tunnel in about 1960. The reception sidings and hump closed in this yard in 1978.

*British Rail*

In June 1978, shortly before the closure of the 'down' hump, Class 08 No. 08940 shunts empty mineral wagons at the 'Tunnel'.

Speedlink traffic from the Swansea and Port Talbot areas also travelled directly to Severn Tunnel. Not only did trip freights run from South Wales to Severn Tunnel, but a redirection of services from the South and south west of England made the yard a collection point for the whole of the south west of the British Isles. Speedlink feeder services from St. Blazey in Cornwall, and Exeter brought heavy loads of China Clay and related traffic to the South Wales yard. Connections from the south coast, notably Southampton and Eastleigh, were also effected through Severn Tunnel Junction and even though one through Speedlink service was retained from Eastleigh to Tyne Yard, a much heavier flow of traffic was directed via Severn Tunnel Junction. The zenith of this concentration of traffic at the 'Tunnel' is reflected by the timetable for January 1985 shown in *Table 13*. During this year the 'down' yard was utilised as follows:

## Table 13
## Severn Tunnel Freight
## 1985

### 'DOWN' ARRIVALS

| Train | From | Arrive | Days |
|-------|------|--------|------|
| 6V89 | Redhill | 06.05 | SO |
| 6V88 | Ripple Lane | 06.28 | MX |
| 7C45 | East Depot | 08.56 | MO |
| 6C29 | Swindon | 09.38 | SX |
| 8C45 | Tidenham | 11.22 | SX |
| 7C34 | Stoke Gifford | 12.15 | SX |
| 6V60 | Scunthorpe | 16.00 | SX |
| 6C44 | Bridgwater | 16.18 | SX |
| 6C36 | Swindon | 16.43 | SX |
| 8C47 | Tidenham | 16.46 | SX |
| 6C39 | St Blazey | 16.55 | SX |
| 6C42 | Cardiff | 17.32 | SX |
| 7C12 | Gloucester | 17.55 | SX |
| 6V39 | Mossend | 19.00 | SX |
| 8C01 | Exeter | 22.10 | SX |
| 8C50 | Gloucester | 22.30 | SX |
| 6V45 | Willesden | 23.03 | SX |
| 6V80 | Bescot | 23.16 | SX |
| 6V06 | Healey Mills | 01.10 | SX |
| 6V30 | Dagenham | 01.39 | SX |
| 6V03 | Scunthorpe | 01.40 | SX |
| 6V85 | Whitemoor | 02.42 | SX |
| 7C50 | Reading | 04.25 | MX |
| 9C28 | Gloucester | 05.28 | WFO |
| 6V14 | Whitemoor | 05.33 | SX |

### 'UP' ARRIVALS

| Train | From | Arrive | Days |
|-------|------|--------|------|
| 6C07 | Margam | 06.10 | SX Y |
| 7B87 | Radyr | 06.20 | MSX |
| 6B79 | Abercwmboi | 08.45 | MO |
| 4A84 | Waunllwyd | 09.05 | MSX Y |
| 6B13 | Llandarcy | 09.28 | MWFO |
| 6A04 | Pantyffynnon | 10.12 | SX |
| 6A71 | Bedwas | 10.18 | SX Y |
| 6A62 | Coed Bach | 10.33 | SX |
| 7C59 | Radyr | 10.45 | SX |
| 7A66 | Oakdale | 10.58 | SX |
| 6A25 | Glascoed | 11.41 | SX |
| 6B44 | Llanwern | 12.00 | SX |
| 7C09 | South Quay | 12.15 | SX |
| 8A61 | Machen | 13.00 | SX |
| 4A85 | Waunllwyd | 14.55 | SX Y |
| 9C07 | Moreton on Lugg | 15.35 | SX |
| 6A90 | Oakdale | 15.50 | SX Y |
| 6C17 | Hallen Marsh | 16.04 | SX |
| 6C59 | Margam | 16.25 | SX |
| 6C01 | Fishguard | 16.50 | SX |
| 6C42 | Cardiff | 16.58 | SX |
| 6C19 | Baglan Bay | 17.05 | SX |
| 6C24 | Barry | 17.18 | SX |
| 7V79 | Eastleigh | 17.20 | SX |
| 9B92 | Radyr | 17.28 | SX |
| 8A63 | Machen | 18.15 | SX |
| 6C73 | Abercwmboi | 19.20 | SX |
| 6C78 | Radyr | 19.55 | SX |
| 6C09 | Cardiff | 20.38 | SX |
| 6V83 | Eastleigh | 20.38 | SX |
| 6V32 | Ellesmere Port | 21.12 | SX |
| 6A78 | Llanwern | 21.35 | SX |
| 6C43 | St Blazey | 22.00 | SX |

| Train | From | Arrive | Days |
|-------|------|--------|------|
| 6V93 | Mossend | 22.00 | SX |
| 8A65 | Machen | 22.10 | SX |
| 4A80 | Waunllwyd | 22.20 | SX |
| 6V70 | Cliffe Vale | 22.33 | SX |
| 7C10 | Margam | 22.35 | SX |
| 9B14 | Barry | 22.40 | SX |
| 6E46 | Swansea | 22.57 | SX |
| 6E88 | Trostre | 23.10 | SX |
| 6V91 | Garston | 23.55 | SX |
| 6C26 | Bridgend | 00.02 | SX |
| 9C08 | Margam | 00.20 | MO |
| 6C58 | St Blazey | 00.25 | SX |
| 6V95 | Ripple Lane | 01.03 | SX |
| 9B28 | Llandeilo Junc. | 01.40 | TThO |
| 7B92 | Llantrisant | 01.50 | MX |
| 4A86 | Waunllwyd | 02.10 | MX Y |
| 6V81 | Doncaster | 02.30 | SX |
| 6V92 | Mossend | 02.40 | SX |
| 7C17 | Radyr | 02.50 | MSX |
| 6V86 | Warrington Arp. | 03.02 | SX |
| 7C20 | Margam | 03.10 | MX |
| 6A07 | Pantyffynnon | 03.37 | MX |
| 6A98 | Waunllwyd | 04.30 | MX Y |
| 6V02 | Willesden | 05.22 | MX |

### 'DOWN' DEPARTURES

| Train | To | Time | Days |
|-------|------|------|------|
| 7A70 | Machen | 06.05 | SX |
| 9C28 | Llandeilo Junc. | 06.15 | WFO |
| 6C22 | Baglan Bay | 07.05 | SX |
| 7C04 | Llanwern | 07.25 | SX |
| 6C06 | Barry | 07.35 | SX |
| 9C02 | Cardiff | 07.45 | SX |
| 6A15 | Glascoed | 07.55 | SX |
| 9C06 | Moreton on Lugg | 08.15 | SX |
| 7C43 | Margam | 09.30 | SX |
| 6A60 | Bedwas | 09.40 | SX |
| 6C29 | Llanwern | 09.58 | SX |
| 6A85 | Waunllwyd | 10.30 | SX Y |
| 6A05 | Pantyffynnon | 11.35 | SX |
| 6C14 | Llandarcy | 11.55 | FO |
| 6A63 | Margam | 12.15 | SX |
| 6S75 | Mossend | 12.55 | SX |
| 9A95 | Dock Street | 13.00 | SX |
| 7A62 | Machen | 15.20 | SX |
| 7C05 | Llandeilo Junc. | 16.20 | MO |
| 6M54 | Ince | 17.30 | SO |
| 6A80 | Waunllwyd | 17.45 | SX Y |
| 6S78 | Mossend | 18.10 | SX |
| 8C41 | Cardiff | 18.35 | SX |
| 7A64 | Machen | 19.20 | SX |
| 6A06 | Pantyffynnon | 20.20 | SX |
| 6S82 | Mossend | 20.30 | SX |
| 9C57 | Margam | 20.40 | SX |
| 6C74 | Abercwmboi | 20.50 | SX |
| 6M22 | Ince | 21.05 | WO |
| 6C04 | Margam | 21.15 | SX Y |
| 6A86 | Waunllwyd | 21.45 | SX Y |
| 7B67 | Radyr | 22.30 | SX |
| 6A97 | Waunllwyd | 00.05 | SX Y |
| 6C18 | Margam | 00.30 | MX |

| Train | To | Time | Days | | Train | To | Time | Days |
|---|---|---|---|---|---|---|---|---|
| 9C04 | Barry | 02.00 | MX | | 6E92 | Ripple Lane | 10.50 | SX |
| 6M73 | Blackburn | 02.10 | MSX | | 7C07 | Tidenham | 12.05 | SX |
| 6M81 | Crewe | 02.10 | SO | | 6B44 | Swindon | 12.20 | SX |
| 6V30 | Swansea | 02.35 | MX | | 7C08 | Chepstow | 12.35 | SX |
| 6M78 | Aintree | 03.00 | MSX | | 7B12 | Gloucester | 17.15 | SX |
| 6M78 | Edge Hill | 03.00 | SO | | 6E82 | Whitemoor | 18.20 | SX |
| 6C25 | Bridgend | 03.50 | MX | | 6E91 | Ripple Lane | 19.55 | SX |
| 7B93 | Llantrisant | 04.15 | MX | | 6M92 | Willesden | 20.10 | SX |
| 6A84 | Waunllwyd | 04.25 | MSX Y | | 7A50 | Reading | 21.30 | SX |
| 7C26 | Llandarcy | 05.00 | MO | | 6M83 | Bescot | 22.40 | SX |
| 6C05 | Cardiff | 05.10 | MSX | | 7E95 | Scunthorpe | 22.45 | SX |
| 6C05 | Pengam | 05.30 | SO | | 8B14 | Exeter | 23.10 | SX |
| 6A66 | Oakdale | 05.30 | SX | | 6B42 | St Blazey | 23.45 | SX |
| 9A99 | Radyr | 05.40 | MSX | | 6E88 | Whitemoor | 00.35 | MX |
| | | | | | 6E94 | Doncaster | 01.25 | MX |
| | | | | | 6050 | Dover | 01.50 | MX |
| | | | | | 9B28 | Gloucester | 02.15 | WFO |
| | | | | | 6E46 | Dagenham | 02.55 | MX |
| | | | | | 6M72 | Cliffe Vale | 03.15 | SX |
| | | | | | 7068 | Eastleigh | 03.35 | MSX |
| | | | | | 7B38 | Westbury | 03.35 | SO |

**'UP' DEPARTURES**

| Train | To | Time | Days | | Train | To | Time | Days |
|---|---|---|---|---|---|---|---|---|
| 6B46 | Bridgwater | 06.30 | SX | | 6B19 | Exeter | 03.45 | SX |
| 7C06 | Tidenham | 06.40 | SX | | 6B30 | Gloucester | 04.50 | MSX |
| 6B18 | Stoke Gifford | 07.35 | SX | | 6B36 | Swindon | 04.55 | SX |
| 7E16 | Scunthorpe | 08.00 | SX | | 6B16 | Lawrence Hill | 05.10 | SX |
| 6B32 | Gloucester | 08.10 | MO | | 6B39 | St Blazey | 05.50 | MSX |
| 7042 | Eastleigh | 08.30 | SX | | 6B39 | Tiverton Junc. | 05.50 | SO |
| 7M14 | Bescot | 09.45 | SX | | | | | |
| 6B13 | Bath Road | 10.00 | MWO | | | | | |

The six 'down' storage sidings were used to stable empty coal wagons bound for East Usk and merry-go-round coal sets used between Oakdale and Llanwern, as well as the train allocated to work Welsh coal to Scunthorpe. New air-braked HEA coal hoppers with coal bound for local coal depots were also shunted into these six sidings. The main yard contained two reception roads labelled 'A' and 'B' and then 21 sorting sidings. Nos 1 to 9 were used for Speedlink traffic, 10 to 19 for vacuum braked traffic and the final six sidings were allocated to the Civil Engineer. On the 'up' side of the main line the Bristol yard contained 31 lines. The three adjacent to the main running lines were allocated as reception sidings and labelled 'A', 'B' and 'C'. The next nine roads were exclusively used by Speedlink traffic, whereas sidings 10 to 18 were used mainly for Speedlink traffic. The final ten roads, numbered 19 to 28, were used to sort vacuum-fitted traffic. The Undy Yard, which had previously been the reception sidings for the Bristol Yard, was used exclusively by ballast traffic. Two trains left each weekday with additional weekend working making the yard most busy on Saturdays and Sundays. Some arrivals and transfers from the 'down' side of the main line were also routed into the Undy Yard prior to marshalling in the Bristol Yard.

Traditional freight operation in the 1960s and 1970s operated on the simple principle that the siding allocated to traffic bound for Bescot was filled as wagons rolled off the hump, and when full a train would depart. With the advent of Speedlink in 1974, a new era of freight train marshalling began. Each train had to be marshalled in a specific order. Traffic had a guaranteed transit and, because of this, any internal engineer's traffic on the Speedlink train could often be squeezed out. A forecast of traffic from the hinterland is received at 17.30 each day, and the yardmaster at Severn Tunnel may have to select the most important loads for forwarding. Each morning there is an audit on the previous twenty four hours performance, and any delays are explained over the telephone to Swindon. From here the Western Region Speedlinks are fed to the British Railways Board, and a national audit is compiled. Such planning is greatly aided by the TOPS computer which allows the efficient use of wagons and an immediate explanation when a wagon appears to have gone missing.

Traffic at Severn Tunnel has been heavy for the first half of the 1980s. A typical week in January 1984 saw the yard receive 3,494 wagons and dispatch 3,661, making a total of 529 trains. The 'up' yard, or Bristol yard, received only 769 wagons as compared to an output of 1,514. Similarly, the Undy Yard, which was operating at this as a Speedlink reception yard, accepted 1,645 vehicles, whilst dispatching only 816. The 'down' side of the yard was somewhat less busy with 1,080 arriving and 1,331 departing wagons. The daily throughput averaged 750 wagons with a peak throughput of 1,000 wagons during busy periods.

Just as the concentration of all rail freight in South Wales on Severn Tunnel Junction Yard seemed inevitable, it was becoming clear that the old yards were not only labour intensive, but inappropriate for the lengthy long-haul Speedlink trains in which British Rail was investing. It was therefore of no surprise when, in 1986, the document 'Railfreight a future in South Wales' was published. It proposed the complete closure of the Severn Tunnel marshalling and locomotive stabling complex, along with the closure of the wagon repair sidings at the junction. There were some reservations about this plan because of the necessity to maintain a rescue train for the nearby Severn Tunnel.

In spite of this objection to restructuring, the yards at Severn Tunnel closed in November 1987. A completely new freight service was introduced overnight. Speedlink traffic, not needing to pass through Wales, is dealt with at Gloucester. Thus trains from the south west and south coast are marshalled into long-haul Speedlink services at Gloucester New Yard. Here, on the avoiding line for Gloucester station, there is a group of long parallel reception sidings which are ideal for such traffic. Block loads, currently stabled at Severn Tunnel, are either stabled elsewhere within South Wales, or at locations outside the Western Region. Civil engineering traffic has been reallocated to use Newport (Alexandra Dock) Junction where recent contraction has rendered many sidings vacant. Wagon servicing is an area for which a new facility has not yet been decided upon.

It may be noteworthy that the 'For Sale' signs which have hung from Ebbw Junction diesel depot for so long, have been removed and this might provide an ideal centralised site for wagon maintenance. At present, coal wagons are serviced at Barry, whilst the steel fleet is repaired at Margam. Severn Tunnel Junction train crew depot has closed with staff being redeployed to other depots. The majority have moved to Newport (High Street), where the Godfrey Road Stabling Sidings have been turned into a small locomotive stabling point.

South Wales Speedlink is marshalled at the Newport (East Usk) Sidings *(Plan 14)*. These have been used for many years to marshal coal from the Eastern and Western Valleys to both Llanwern Steelworks and Uskmouth Power Station. The presence of twelve long parallel sidings with good access to the 'up' and 'down' goods lines, along with two reception sidings make this site the ideal choice for a modern Speedlink yard. Minor alterations to the yard and the removal of No. 7 siding to install high power lighting, have completed its transformation to a modern Speedlink yard. The wagon repairs which were conducted at East Usk on old vacuum-fitted coal wagons have been transferred to Radyr, near Cardiff. The closure of Severn Tunnel has also placed an increased workload on the railway amenities in Cardiff. Cardiff (Canton) locomotive servicing depot has an increased throughput because of the closure of the depot at Severn Tunnel, and there is also additional work for train crews based at Canton.

**SEVERN TUNNEL JUNCTION — JANUARY 1985**

X Normally clipped for No.1 Reception

**PLAN 13**

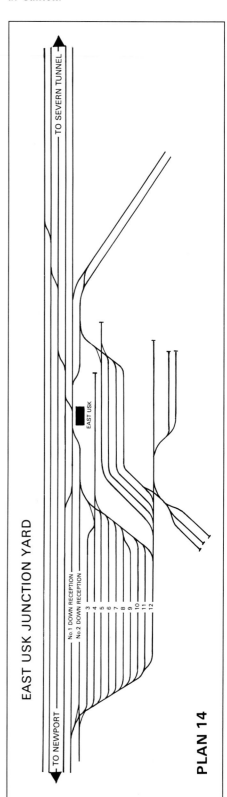

**EAST USK JUNCTION YARD**

**PLAN 14**

Views of the 'down' yard taken in 1960 and 1985 show a similar contrast. In the 1985 view, Class 45 No. 45069 leaves for Llanwern to pick up steel coil bound for the British Leyland plant at Swindon. The steel was conveyed in ex-GWR steel wagons dating back to the 1940s.

*British Rail and Author*

This view of the 'up' yard in 1960 shows it full of loaded wagons, a stark contrast to the view taken in January 1985. In 1985, on a very dull morning, the 6E91, 10.50, Severn Tunnel to Ripple Lane awaits departure behind Class 47 No. 47202, whilst Class 08 No. 08848 awaits its next shunt. The miles of empty sidings were not only a mark of Speedlink's efficiency but also heralded the fate of Severn Tunnel announced just twelve months later.

*British Rail and Author*

## South Wales Freight

Class 45 No. 45076 departs from Severn Tunnel with vacuum-fitted freight, to Exeter (Riverside) Yard. On 2nd October 1980, the train contained a single CXV explosives van as well as thirteen loaded mineral wagons.

Cardiff Tidal Sidings concentrates almost exclusively on steel sector traffic. In addition to servicing the adjacent Allied Steel & Wire Factories, it marshalls trains from South Wales to the North West, with services to Warrington, Dee Marsh and Mossend. This avoids separate marshalling of steel wagons in the new East Usk site. The marshalling yard at Radyr has taken on increased wagon maintenance, but the traditional marshalling of coal wagons to and from the valleys has been gradually phased out as the use of modern merry-go-round block trains increases. Both Barry and Aberdare remain as train crew depots and there has been some increased activity at Aberdare.

It is remarkable to reflect that within one year the base from which Railfreight conducts its South Wales business has been so radically altered. After minor teething problems, particularly at Gloucester, the service has settled to the satisfaction of both Railfreight customers and British Rail. A new level of efficiency has been reached, yet retaining a degree of flexibility to cope with the changing demands of the coal and steel industries in the Principality. No longer will railway men and enthusiasts talk of Margam and Severn Tunnel, but rather East Usk and Cardiff Tidal.

On 28th May 1984, the sun sets on the departing 6M92, 20.20, Severn Tunnel to Willesden Speedlink service headed by Class 47 No. 47337. In the background a block load of steel from Hamworthy Docks, in Poole, accelerates towards Cardiff.

Class 47 No. 47314 winds its way east past the stabling point at Severn Tunnel Junction in July 1986. Its varied load of air-braked wagons includes BDA bogie-bolsters carrying steel from the Allied Steel & Wire Company in Cardiff, and POA wagons loaded with scrap; together they constitute the 6E64, Severn Tunnel to Haverton Hill Speedlink.

Another lengthy Speedlink freight, the 6S82, 20.30, Severn Tunnel to Mossend, departs west from Severn Tunnel on 2nd July 1986. Class 47 No. 47229 hauls 30 wagons totalling 60 SLU, the maximum length for such a service.

**Left:**
Class 37 No. D6856 crosses the main line at Margam Moors to gain access to the reception sidings at the then newly-opened Margam Yard. Its load of unfitted mineral wagons (MCO) render the train a Class 9 because of the absence of any train braking.
*British Rail*

**Right:**
On 30th December 1985, a special block freight, the 6Z56 Ditton to Margam, arrives in one of the recessing roads at Margam, Class 47 No. 47231 has brought ten tankers of liquid oxygen for the nearby BSC Works.

A freight from Gloucester stands on the old 'down' hump avoiding line at Severn Tunnel Junction in 1983. The train, hauled by Class 25 No. 25262, is made up predominantly of

vacuum-fitted wagons. An air-braked ferry van at the rear must travel unbraked because of its incompatibility with British Rail's outdated vacuum-fitted stock.

**Right:**
Class 08 No. 08361 winds its way across the exit from Margam Yard with the tankers pictured previously. On the left, another Class 08 stands in the sorting sidings whilst the large number of wagons to the right of the train are standing in the numerous wagon repair roads provided at the yard.

**Left:**
A Margam to Severn Tunnel freight leaves the yard at Margam on 27th May 1983, passing the derelict reception sidings. Class 37 No. 37020 hauls a load of chemical tankers and coal hoppers.

My sincere thanks to Mr P. Musselwhite, Freight Operations Manager, Swansea, Mr S. Sharp, Area Manager's Customers Office, Cardiff, Mr J. Lewis, Traffic Assistant, Margam, the Freight Manager at Severn Tunnel Junction, Mr Goldson from the Regional Freight Office at Swindon, and finally Andrew Nock, the Western Region Freight Manager, all of whom helped and contributed to this chapter.

On 31st December 1976, the 'down' yard at Severn Tunnel is almost filled with vacuum and unfitted rolling stock. Class 08 No. 08657 hauls a transfer freight from the 'up' yard on its way to the 'down' reception sidings.

The yards at Cardiff and East Usk have taken over much of the marshalling undertaken at Severn Tunnel until its closure in November

1987. The preponderance of steel and coal traffic can be seen in the wagons at Cardiff Tidal Yard in this view taken on 29th May 1988.

An aerial view of Margam shows the new yard laid on the site of the old Knuckle Yard. On the left are the disused BSC Abbey Yard sidings. In the centre Class 37 No. 37255 is at the head of the 6B28 to Cardiff Tidal Yard, whilst 08 Nos 08769 and 08897 shunt the yard. On the right is the disused Margam Moors East signal cabin. In the background is BSC Margam; the lines in the foreground divide to Margam diesel depot to the left and the main line to the right.

# Chapter 5

# Warrington and Crewe

The first passenger station at Crewe was opened in 1838 under the name Monks Coppenhall. This rather small, two-platformed, station was replaced in 1860 by a large station which forms the backbone of today's 137 acre site. It was not until 1890, however, that a major marshalling yard was planned for the town. The new complex of staging sidings was called Basford Hall and opened in 1901. The yard remained virtually unchanged until the modernisation of the West Coast Main Line (WCML) in 1960. The opportunity was taken to rebuild the 'down' yard at Basford Hall and a hump was added to the layout. Within a decade, the entire complex was closed and traffic transferred to the yards at Bescot and Warrington.

In contrast, Warrington has never had the illustrious reputation of its southerly neighbour. The first mention of a marshalling yard in the town occurs in 1851 when, "The LNWR were holding other Company's wagons for Manchester at Walton Junction for all sorts of absurd excuses!" Developments in the town created yards at eight sites; the largest at Arpley had a capacity to hold 1,232 wagons. The evolution of the rail network in the north west has seen the increase in importance of Warrington as a freight centre. As yards like Basford Hall have closed, so the workload at Speedlink yards like Warrington has grown. Today Warrington is one of the busiest marshalling yards in the country, with a daily throughput approaching 900 wagons.

## Crewe Basford Hall
### (Plan 15)

The town of Crewe evolved in the second half of the 19th century from a group of small villages in Cheshire and took its name from Lord Crewe, who owned much of the land now covered by railway lines and workshops. The phenomenal increase in the population of the town was due entirely to its importance as a railway junction. Such was the expansion of local industry connected with the new 'iron road', that serious delays were inevitable for freight trains passing through Crewe. In the 1880s all freight trains had to pass through the main station and queues of trains often stretched as far north as Weaver Junction and south to Stafford. A radical rethink in freight traffic policy of the day brought about the construction of Basford Hall Sidings.

The scheme entailed the construction of staging sidings between Basford Wood and Gresty Road. These sidings were divided into two groups, 'up' and 'down', and had the capacity to hold a total of 2,350 wagons. The yard included reception roads, a shunting neck and departure lines, but not a hump, and was therefore flat-shunted. Access to the site was greatly improved by a complete set of connections, which avoided the bottleneck of Crewe station. Trains from Liverpool and the north left the main line at Coal Yard Junction, whilst trains from Manchester left at Sydney Bridge Junction. The goods lines tunnelled south to emerge just north of Salop Goods Junction to the west of Crewe Station. A total of 50 miles of double track was laid and one million cubic yards of earth was excavated in order to create these new connections; a vast engineering operation.

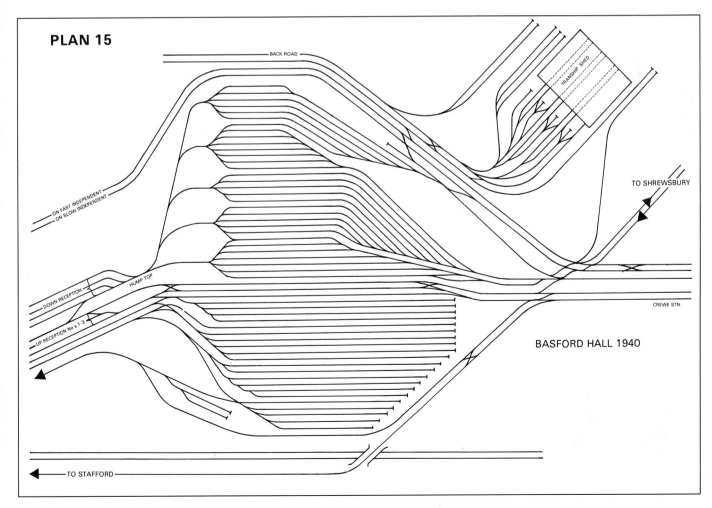

PLAN 15

BACK ROAD

TRANSHIP SHED

TO SHREWSBURY

ON FAST INDEPENDENT
ON SLOW INDEPENDENT

HUMP TOP

CREWE STN

DOWN RECEPTION

UP RECEPTION No.s 1-3

BASFORD HALL 1940

TO STAFFORD

Class 08 No. 08916 shunts stock for the 6V93 Mossend to Severn Tunnel Speedlink freight. Most of the trackwork at Arpley Yard is electrified and very cramped in layout, as seen by this picture taken on 23rd June 1986.

The main marshalling yard was opened in 1901 and took over the work of yards at Gresty Green, North Staffordshire Junction and Gresty Lane.

The early days of the yard are not well documented, but an average throughput of 28,000 wagons each week was recorded for the early 1920s. A record workrate of 36,000 wagons in a week makes today's 'busy' yards pale into insignificance! The main yard was equipped with a goods transhipment shed from where 300 wagons each day were attached to trunk freights. The connections to the rest of the country were widespread. Some destinations remain unchanged, such as South Wales, Holy-

British Railways Standard Class 9F 2-10-0 No. 92160 passes Walton Old Junction signal box as it arrives from Stanlow with a train of fuel oil carried in a variety of tank wagons. In 1986, 20 years later, the same spot has been transformed by modernisation in all areas of railway operation. Class 47 No. 47279 passes Walton Old Junction with the 6T78, Stanlow to Walton, conveying fuel oil for diesel depots in the north east. A pair of Class 20 locomotives complete their first run-round on the way from Bickershaw Colliery to Fiddler's Ferry Power Station, whilst the yard pilot at Walton Yard awaits its next shunt.

*D. Lennon and Author*

head, Carlisle and Chester. Others such as Stour Valley, Trent Valley, Carnforth and Manchester Oldham Road have disappeared after the rationalisations and re-organisations of the last 85 years.

The yard was controlled by three signal boxes, Sorting Sidings North, Middle and South. Locomotives for the freights from Basford Hall came predominantly from Crewe South depot, whilst GWR interlopers were serviced at Gresty Lane Shed. The marshalling yard was particularly busy during the two world wars. In World War I a large volume of local armaments from the Royal Ordnance Factory were transported via Basford Hall to ports around the country. By 1937, the weekly throughput of about 47,000 wagons made Basford Hall the busiest marshalling yard complex in Europe. Two hundred daily arrivals provided an average of 7,000 wagons to be detached for local customers. The number of trip freights generated by this traffic was enormous, not to mention the shunting movements involved in placing 420 wagons of sundries into the tranship shed each day. The busiest part of Basford Hall was the 'down' yard which contained 30 through sidings. The 'up' yard, in contrast, had '20' single-ended roads which handled 1,500 wagons daily. Even the smaller satellite yards such as the GWR sidings at Gresty Lane marshalled over 1,000 wagons each twenty-four hours!

The year 1937 was not only one of the busiest times at Basford Hall, but also the first year in which shunting was undertaken by diesels. The first batch of LMS-designed diesel-mechanical shunting locomotives had their initial trials at the yard, and by 1939 only diesels were to be found shunting at Basford Hall. World War II saw a great deal of freight traffic marshalled south of Crewe, and a phenomenal throughput of up to 10,000 wagons daily was achieved. After the war, Crewe continued as the main WCML freight yard between Willesden and Carlisle, and by the mid-1950s the decision was taken to modernise the yard.

The LMR electrification between London and Liverpool was the ideal opportu-

In 1966 a 9F class 2-10-0, No. 92102, winds out of Arpley Yard with a special freight. In 1983, the Class 08 diesel-electric shunters remain, and the track layout is unchanged. Class 85 No. 85035 departs with all air-braked 6V93 Speedlink from Mossend to Severn Tunnel Junction, meanwhile Class 08 No. 08337 shunts modern high capacity rolling stock for the next departure.

*A. Chester and Author*

A general view of Walton Old Junction Yard shows a selection of Speedlink wagons awaiting departure on the evening freights.

nity for modernisation of Basford Hall Yard. New connections from the Alsager line at Crewe North Stafford 'Down' Sidings and the Stoke to Market Drayton line at Madeley allowed all northbound traffic direct access to the Basford Hall 'Down' Sidings. The new layout made it possible to close the yards at Chatterley, Alsager and Crewe North Stafford 'Down' Sidings. The 'down' sidings at Basford Hall were remodelled to cope with the increased traffic, and a hump was built to facilitate easy marshalling of incoming trains. There were no retarders at the yard, and wagons were guided into their sidings by 'chasers' who had to pin down the handbrakes on each wagon. Even though the yard was old-fashioned in its operation, it was the first to be fully electrified, and in May 1961 a restricted freight service to Manchester was introduced. By June 1962 the 110 miles of catenary in and around the yard was fully energised and a full commercial freight service started to run at the end of the month. A total of 66 main freights were booked to call at Basford Hall. In addition to these, there were numerous local trip freights from the sidings.

When the yard closed in May 1972, 34 of these trains disappeared from the timetable. Eight services were transferred to Warrington (Arpley) Yard and six to Bescot Yard, near Birmingham. Ten trains were marshalled at the now-closed yards at Stoke and Cockshute, and several other trains were redirected to other smaller yards around the North West. Within ten years the need for a major marshalling yard at Crewe had disappeared and now only lines

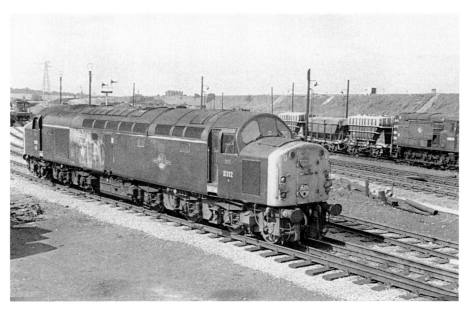

of rusty sidings are to be found at what was once Europe's busiest yard.

# Warrington Arpley and Walton Yards

Once a Lancashire town, Warrington now finds itself in the north of Cheshire. It lies on the WCML, 182 miles from London Euston and midway between Liverpool and Manchester on the east/west axis. In 1968 the population of Warrington was 72,400. Since then its growth as a 'New Town' has brought an increase in the number of inhabitants within its boundaries to

The Manchester Ship Canal Sidings are currently used for the run-round of mgr services. Back in 1969, Class 40 No. D312 reverses on to a freight train in these sidings while Class 11 No. 12073 shunts cement wagons in Walton Old Junction Yard.

*D. Lennon*

Basford Hall marshalling yard by night, taken in the mid-1960s. Looking north, the 8K16, Cockshute to Crewe can be seen behind a Class 47 locomotive. The yard was one of the main marshalling points along the WCML until its closure in May 1972.

*BR/LMR, Ken Groundwater Collection*

The German influence on yard design is evident in the signal box at Mottram. The yard is viewed in July 1935, shortly before opening.

*British Rail*

## North-West Freight

British Railways Class 9F 2-10-0 No. 92082 passes Walton Old Junction with a southbound freight from the nearby Arpley Yard. The semaphore signals and old lighting stands have been replaced by overhead catenary as can be seen in the following picture.

*D. Lennon*

168,000. The town is a major crossroads for both rail and road transport, and now contains one of the busiest freight marshalling yards in the country.

In 1960 the town contained eight separate groups of sidings. The largest of these at Arpley remains as the backbone of the current Speedlink yard. Warrington's second largest yard, at Dallam, has long-since closed but recent developments have brought the railway back to this site with the construction of a new freight depot. Much steel traffic formerly dealt with at Warrington Central is now handled at Dallam. In addition to regular consignments of steel it is hoped that aggressive marketing will attract many new customers to the terminal. The main 'down' yards at Warrington were Froghall and Walton. It is Walton yard that survives today, and is used by the majority of northbound Speedlink traffic. Warrington (Arpley)

Yard consists of 19 sidings and four shunting necks, whereas the smaller Walton Old Junction Sidings have just 13 roads. There are four further sidings at Walton called the Manchester Ship Canal Sidings; these are used almost exclusively for the run-round of local merry-go-round services.

## Traffic at Warrington

The Warrington yard of the 1980s has inherited all the traffic previously marshalled along the WCML from Crewe to Wigan. The various yards at Springs Branch and Basford Hall are all now closed, and the nearest Speedlink marshalling centres are Bescot, in Birmingham, and Carlisle's Kingmoor Yard. Since the closure of Crewe (Basford Hall), all freight traffic from North Wales must join the Speedlink

**Opposite top:**
The same location as seen previously, but photographed from the other side of the line. Here, in 1986, Class 87 No. 87034 heads south from Arpley Yard with the 6V93, Mossend to Severn Tunnel Junction Speedlink service.

The 6A81 from Carlisle Kingmoor to Stonebridge Park Yard passes Euxton Junction in july 1972. Class 25 No. 5255 will call at Warrington and Bescot on its way south.

*T. Heavyside*

network at Warrington, and three trip services run each day from the northern part of the Principality. Goods traffic from the two northern conurbations of Liverpool and Manchester is also routed through Warrington. Speke Yard, in Liverpool, handles all the city's Speedlink freight and sends a daily trip to Arpley Yard. In addition there are three daily trips from Ditton and one from Edge Hill which also

make their connections with long-haul freights at Warrington.

Industrial development along the Wirral Peninsula began in 1793 with the construction of a canal to Ellesmere Port, but it was not until 1924 that the first oil refinery was opened by the Shell-Mex company. In 1949, construction of a large refinery and chemical complex was started at Stanlow and this now covers a 2,000 acre site and employs 6,000 people. Other industries have been attracted to the area and these include Vauxhall motors, United Kingdom Fertilizers and Associated Octel. The rail traffic from these large industrial complexes is mainly in the form of block trains; there are 38 such arrivals and departures from Stanlow each day. The UKF plant at Ince & Elton has twelve booked block freights each twenty four hours, whereas the yard at Ellesmere Port is mainly served by trip freights. It collects traffic from neighbouring companies and sends three daily departures to Arpley Yard in Warrington. There are two further trip freights from the Wirral to Warrington, and these may run from either Ince & Elton or Stanlow. As with the industrial areas on the Wirral Peninsula, so at Northwich most freight trains are marshalled as block loads. Salt is distributed from the town on a seasonal basis whereas traffic flows related to the ICI Mond Chemical Works are more regular. A total of 28 daily block freights arrive and depart from Oakleigh Sidings and nearby Northwich Yard. There are a further six daily departures classified as trip freights and two of these convey Speedlink wagons to Warrington.

Manchester has never had a modern marshalling yard. The largest group of sidings in the city was at Mottram on the old Woodhead route. The yard at Mottram was opened in October 1935 and contained eight reception roads leading to 20 sorting sidings. It was not equipped with retarders, and hump shunting over a 1 in 30 gradient was conducted by the manual method using 'chasers'. Mottram was, however, unique in that the reception sidings were on a falling gradient of 1 in 85, therefore trains could be brought to the hump simply by releasing

their brakes, thus avoiding the use of shunting engines. This meant that shunting was relatively silent.

Mottram was one of the cheapest yards to operate on the LNER and also very efficient with 1,000 wagons sorted each shift; it was, however, not only a 'fast' yard but also very dangerous. With the closure of Mottram in the early 1970s most freight from the Manchester area was marshalled at Dewsnap Sidings, near Guide Bridge. The start of the 1980s saw the closure of the Woodhead route and, with it, the demise of Dewsnap Yard. A collection of ten or so sorting sidings at Ashburys then became the main marshalling centre for Manchester. In November 1985 further rationalisation brought about the closure of most of the sidings at Ashburys leaving only the East Yard in operation. This received three daily engineer's trains at the start of 1986 and all Speedlink trip freights were transferred to Warrington (Arpley) Yard. There are five daily trips to the Manchester area and these service the coal depot at Middleton Junction, the mineral sidings at Peak Forest, and sidings at Newton Heath, Trafford Park, Horwich and Chorley.

By 1986, the yards at Warrington were acting as the concentration point for Speedlink traffic from as far north as the Cumbrian Coast, west to Holyhead, east to Peak Forest and south to Northwich and Crewe. A total of over 100 daily freights ran to and from the yard making it one of the busiest in the country. These trains could be allocated into three categories. Thirty were trunk Speedlink services to other major yards, a further 30 were Speedlink feeder trains from secondary yards around the north west, whilst the remaining 40 were classified 'T' or trip freights and ran from yards or sidings within the Warrington area, (Table 14).

In addition to the large number of freight trains marshalled at Warrington there were 140 daily block trains passing through the Warrington TOPS area in 1986. As at Doncaster (Belmont) Yard, these services are an important factor in the efficiency of both Arpley and Walton Old Junction yards. *Plan 16* shows the layout of the

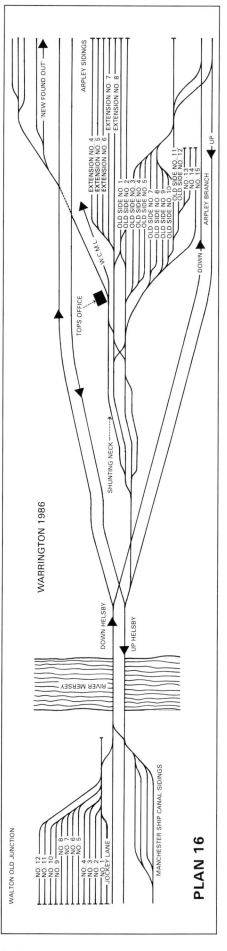

**WARRINGTON 1986**

**PLAN 16**

In August 1973, Class 24 No. 5036 passes through Helsby station with an evening freight from Chester to Warrington. North Wales continued to link with the Speedlink network at Warrington in 1986.

*T. Heavyside*

# Table 14
## Warrington Freight March 1986

ARPLEY AND WALTON TRAINS — AS FROM 17/03/86

| REP NBR | TIME | DAYS RUN ORIGIN | FROM | TO | ARR | DEP | |
|---|---|---|---|---|---|---|---|
| 7H14 | 0600 | MX | ARPLEY | PEAK FRST | — | 0600 | |
| 7T72 | 0615 | MSX | ARPLEY | SP BRCH | — | 0615 | |
| 9D26 | 0625 | SX | ARPLEY | DEE MARSH | — | 0625 | |
| 7T72 | 0630 | MO | ARPLEY | SP BRCH | — | 0630 | |
| 7H15 | 0636 | SX | WALTON | MDDLTN JN | — | 0636 | |
| 7P36 | 0642 | MSX | WALTON | CARLISLE | — | 0642 | |
| 6T68 | 0655 | SX | ARPLEY | OAKLEIGH | — | 0655 | |
| 7T74 | 0700 | SX | ARPLEY | RUNCORN | — | 0700 | |
| 6P80 | 0700 | SX | WALTON | DEEPDALE | — | 0700 | |
| 6P73 | 0609 | MO | CREWE | BLACKBURN | 0647 | 0730 | |
| 6M73 | 0210 | MSX | SEVN TNL | BLACKBURN | 0647 | 0730 | |
| 6T69 | 0740 | SX | ARPLEY | INCE&E | — | 0740 | |
| 7T71 | 0745 | SX | AY/WOJ | DALLAM | — | 0745 | |
| 6P82 | 0755 | SX | WALTON | CHORLEY | — | 0755 | |
| 7P36 | 0809 | MO | WALTON | CARLISLE | — | 0809 | |
| 7P13 | 0815 | SX | WALTON | HORWICH | — | 0815 | |
| 7T71 | 0815 | SX | DALLAM | AY/WOJ | 0830 | | |
| 6S97 | 0853 | SX | WALTON | MOSSEND | — | 0853 | DOO 1 |
| 6T68 | 0845 | SX | OAKLEIGH | WALTON | 0920 | | |
| 7T74 | 0830 | SX | DITTON | ARPLEY | 0930 | | |
| 7T68 | 1020 | SX | ARPLEY | O&WHARTON | — | 1020 | |
| 6F80 | 0900 | SX | DEEPDALE | WALTON | 1028 | | |
| 7T69 | 0950 | SX | E HILL | ARPLEY | 1040 | | |
| 7P87 | 1043 | SX | WALTON | BRN NAZE | — | 1043 | |
| 8F12 | 0811 | TTHO | BESCOT | ARPLEY | 1056 | | |
| 7T74 | 1100 | SX | ARPLEY | A | — | 1100 | |
| 6P81 | 1138 | SX | WALTON | DEEPDALE | — | 1138 | |
| 7T69 | 1140 | SX | ARPLEY | GARSTON | — | 1140 | |
| 8G12 | 1155 | TTHO | ARPLEY | BESCOT | — | 1155 | |
| 6T72 | 1125 | SX | GATHURST | ARPLEY | 1210 | | |
| 6T72 | 1230 | SX | ARPLEY | SP BRCH | | 1230 | |
| 7T68 | 1200 | SX | O&WHARTON | WALTON | 1245 | | |
| 7T74 | 1200 | SX | A | ARPLEY | 1300 | | |
| 7F12 | 1148 | SX | CSTLTN JN | WOJ | 1302 | | |
| 6T71 | 1315 | SX | AY/WOJ | PRESCOT | — | 1315 | |
| 7T74 | 1330 | SX | ARPLEY | STANLOW | — | 1330 | |
| 7F13 | 1209 | SX | HORWICH | ARPLEY | 1357 | | |
| 6F82 | 1226 | SX | CHORLEY | ARPLEY | 1406 | | |
| 7T69 | 1310 | SX | GARSTON | ARPLEY | 1410 | | |
| 6H13 | 1413 | SX | WALTON | NTN HTH | — | 1413 | |
| 6F81 | 1338 | SX | DEEPDALE | WALTON | 1446 | | |
| 6T71 | 1430 | SX | PRESCOT | ARPLEY | 1505 | | |
| 7T74 | 1445 | SX | E PORT | ARPLEY | 1520 | | |
| 7F86 | 0910 | MSX | WILLESDEN | ARPLEY | 1603 | | |
| 7F86 | 0910 | MO | BESCOT | ARPLEY | 1603 | | |
| 6U93 | 0748 | SX | MOSSEND | SUN TNL | 1500 | 1605 | DOO |
| 7T68 | 1545 | SX | E PORT | ARPLEY | 1620$ | 1630 | |
| 7F87 | 1448 | SX | BURN NAZE | WALTON | 1635 | | |
| 6F84 | 1542 | SX | BLACKBURN | WALTON | 1653 | | DOO |
| 6T74 | 1730 | SX | ARPLEY | INCE&E | — | 1730 | |
| 7F10 | 1538 | SX | LLAN JN | WALTON | 1731 | | |
| 6T68 | 1740 | SX | ARPLEY | E PORT | — | 1740 | |
| 6T66 | 1700 | SX | NORTHWICH | WALTON | 1740 | | |
| 6T69 | 1700 | SX | DITTON | WALTON | 1745 | | |
| 6T65 | 1715 | SX | DITTON | ARPLEY | 1755 | | |

| REP NBR | TIME | DAYS RUN ORIGIN | FROM | TO | ARR | DEP | |
|---|---|---|---|---|---|---|---|
| 7F17 | 1537 | SX | PK FRST | WALTON | 1811 | — | |
| 6F14 | 1605 | SX | NTN HTH | WALTON | 1820 | — | |
| 9F81 | 1625 | SX | CROES NWD | ARPLEY | 1845 | — | |
| 6F32 | 1705 | SX | TRAF PARK | ARPLEY | 1853 | 1913 | |
| 7E77 | 1905 | SX | WALTON | H MILLS | — | 1905 | |
| 6F32 | 1705 | SX | TFRD. PARK | WALTON | 1918 | — | |
| 6T68 | 1845 | SX | E PORT | WALTON | 1920 | — | |
| 7T72 | 1715 | SX | SPR BRCH | WALTON | 1930 | — | |
| 6T74 | 1900 | SX | INCE& E | ARPLEY | 1930$ | 1940 | |
| 6T74 | 1900 | SX | INCE& E | ARPLEY | 1950 | — | |
| 6T65 | 1925 | SX | DITTON | ARPLEY | 1955 | — | |
| 6S80 | 1955 | SX | WALTON | MOSSEND | — | 1955 | DOO |
| 6T69 | 1930 | SX | SPEKE | ARPLEY | 2000 | — | |
| 6E95 | 2012 | SX | ARPLEY | PARKESTON | — | 2012 | |
| 4M64 | 1140 | SX | BATHGATE | WILLSDEN | 2049 | 2135 | DOO 2 |
| 6E81 | 2058 | SX | WALTON | HAV HILL | — | 2058 | |
| 6S73 | 1118 | SX | DOVER | MOSSEND | 2102 | 2145 | DOO |
| 6V86 | 2155 | SX | ARPLEY | SEVN TNL | — | 2155 | |
| 6E26 | 2155 | SX | WALTON | DONCSTER | — | 2155 | |
| 6G69 | 2210 | SX | ARPLEY | BESCOT | — | 2210 | |
| 6O38 | 1658 | SX | WRKGTON | DOVER | 2227 | 2333 | |
| 6S74 | 2102 | SX | BESCOT | MOSSEND | 2244 | 2345 | DOO |
| 6F69 | 2055 | SX | DEE MARSH | WALTON | 2248 | | |
| 6F87 | 2035 | SX | CARLISLE | ARPLEY | 2338 | — | DOO |
| 6O56 | 1510 | SX | DUNDEE | DOVER | 0036 | 0151 | DOO |
| 6M72 | 1828 | SX | WORKSOP | WALTON | — | 0048 | |
| 6M86 | 1439 | SX | P QUAY | ARPLEY | — | 0119 | |
| 6S82 | 2030.. | SX | SVN TNL | MOSSEND | 0132 | 0213 | |
| 6M84 | 2120 | MX | DONCASTER | ARPLEY | — | 0156 | |
| 7T68 | 0215 | MSX | ARPLEY | STANLOW | — | 0215 | |
| 6T68 | 0215 | SO | ARPLEY | STANLOW | — | 0215 | |
| 6E63 | 0223 | MX | WALTON | WORKSOP | — | 0223 | |
| 6T69 | 0230 | MX | ARPLEY | HALEWOOD | — | 0230 | |
| 6P85 | 2215 | SX | WILLESDEN | WORKGTON | 0217 | 0357 | DOO |
| 6M64 | 1852 | SX | HAV HILL | ARPLEY | 0303 | — | |
| 6F71 | 0055 | MX | BESCOT | WALTON | 0307 | — | |
| 6K68 | 0325 | SO | ARPLEY | CREWE | — | 0325 | |
| 6T68 | 0400 | SO | WALTON | DITTON | — | O400 | |
| 7A80 | 0406 | MSX | ARPLEY | WILLSDEN | — | 0406 | |
| 7M95 | 0150 | SX | H MILLS | WALTON | 0422 | — | |
| 7D14 | 0428 | MX | ARPLEY | LUDO JN | — | 0428 | |
| 7T69 | 0500 | MSX | WALTON | E HILL | — | 0500 | |
| 6H21 | 0504 | MX | WALTON | TRAFF PK | — | 0504 | |
| 6M28 | 2233 | SX | MOSS END | ARPLEY | 0512 | — | DOO |
| 6T69 | 0530 | SO | ARPLEY | INCE$ E | — | 0530 | |
| 6F24 | 0545 | MX | ARPLEY | E PORT | — | 0545 | |

| A | Ellesmere Port, Ravenhead, Northwich or Garston |
|---|---|
| S | This entry includes SN or other amendment |
| $ | Times at Walton |
| * | Times at Arpley |
| Q | Runs when required (will be shown on SN). |
| 1 | Ex Preston |
| 2 | CL6 Forward |

various sidings south of Warrington. It can be seen that a potential 'bottleneck' exists where the 'up' and 'down' Helsby lines cross the River Mersey. Not only must all southbound departures from Arpley Sidings, and all northbound departures from Walton Yard, pass along this track but most shunting at Walton Old Junction takes place on the 'down' Helsby because of the short headshunt at the yard. Since the closure, in July 1985, of the direct line from Arpley to Manchester, via Latchford, all merry-go-round (mgr) coal trains from Healey Mills to Fiddler's Ferry Power Station must run-round twice at Warrington. Arrival at Warrington is along the 'up' Helsby line from where trains are routed into the Ship Canal Sidings. They then run north along the 'down' Helsby and 'down' Arpley lines to a second run-round at Latchford loops. A total of 23 paths exist for trains to Fiddler's Ferry, but only 17 of these were in use in May 1986.

Seven trains from Healey Mills were joined in their double run-round by eight services from the Lancashire pits of Bickershaw and Parkside. An allowance of 20 minutes is given for the two reversals, although they may often take twice as long. If an average time of 30 minutes is taken by each train, then the 13 mgrs arriving from the north will occupy tracks within the yard perimeter for over six hours of each day. There are additional arrivals from pits in the south at Trentham, Bersham and Point of Ayr as well as occasional coal flows from **Bidston, Maryport and Knochshinnock.** Together, these block coal trains greatly reduce the capacity of Arpley and Walton yards. As at Doncaster, there are attempts to circumvent these operational difficulties; the scope for re-routing trains is, however, very limited since the closure of the Latchford line. Minor timetable adjustments may create a more even flow of freights through Warrington, and a ban on engineer's traffic at Arpley avoids sidings being blocked by non revenue-earning wagons. The possibility of future expansion at Arpley is discussed later in the chapter.

## Traffic Statistics

During 1985, the Area Manager's Office at Warrington conducted a detailed survey of the performance at Arpley and Walton Old Junction yards. The timetable revealed 51 daily arrivals and 45 departures, of which 40 were classified Speedlink trains. The Speedlink services were handled equally by Arpley and Walton yards; 20 apiece. Of the remaining 56 feeder services and trip freights 68 per cent were marshalled at Arpley Yard. The larger number of freights at Arpley was reflected by a wider range of shunting 'tags' or destinations at the sidings. Sixty separate 'sorts' were made each twenty four hours at Arpley as compared to only 42 at Walton Old Junction. The various wagon portions were shunted to form the trains listed in Table 14. As can be seen from this list, traffic for the north and east was dispatched from Walton Yard, and that for the south and west left from Arpley Sidings.

The total number of wagons detached at Arpley during the week ending 19th October 1986 was 1,777. In the same week, 1,233 wagons were removed from trains at Walton, giving a total of 3,010 wagons detached at Warrington Yards. The total throughout of wagons during the same time span was 4,102; this included wagons in the

forward portions of through trains and exchange trips. Of these vehicles, 94 per cent were air-braked and the average length of each wagon was 1.7 SLUs. Sixty four per cent of wagons could not be loose-shunted; 15 per cent conveyed dangerous goods. Many of these wagons contained cargoes which were not planned for by the railway but a substantial number carried 'mandated' traffic. Mandated Speedlink traffic is traffic booked on a regular basis to travel over a set route. Thus two PWA wagons of fertilizer may be 'mandated' to Bletchley each day, or five HEA hoppers of coal may be 'mandated' from Tinsley to Deepdale on three days each week. In 1985, 21 per cent of wagons marshalled at Warrington were carrying such traffic.

A merry-go-round train of Yorkshire coal approaches Walton Old Junction on 23rd June 1986. Class 56 No. 56097 must run around its train twice before departure from Warrington to Fiddler's Ferry Power Station.

Punctuality at Warrington was mediocre with only 70 per cent of services departing within five minutes of their booked time. Problems with punctuality have been difficult to resolve because of the increasing burden placed on the limited facilities at Arpley and Walton. By 1986, wagon throughput had increased to 4,250 each week. Shunting problems were exacerbated

Bales of scrap metal pass under the main line at Warrington on their way from the Ford Motor Company in Halewood to Tinsley. Class 40 No. 40135 heads its load of MXV wagons on the special working on 17th September 1984.

by the increase in mgr run-round activity, and the yard was operating at near breaking-point.

## The Future

British Rail has placed a large responsibility on the staff and facilities at Warrington. The yard is one of the most important in the country and is well situated next to the WCML. The staff and train crews are freight-orientated and have spent most of their lives operating the less glamorous side of the railway business. There are undoubtedly disadvantages with the cramped layout and short sidings in the yard. What then can be done in the short-term to alleviate congestion in the area? The simplest suggestion is to create more activity during the lull from 08.00 to 14.00. Re-timetabling of certain trains may ease congestion at peak periods. Minor alterations to the layout of both Arpley and Walton may similarly increase the capacity at Warrington. Four sidings recently removed at Arpley Yard could be put back and the yard at Walton could be lengthened to take 70 SLU freights. The provision of direct access into Walton Old Junction Yard from the 'up' Helsby line together with an engine release road at the south of this yard would greatly speed the handling of 'up' arrivals. The addition of a second pilot at Arpley would allow the two sides of the yard to be shunted independently and thus further increase its marshalling capacity. All of these measures are 'tinkering' with the basic layout; what of the more distant future.

Whole scale rebuilding at Warrington is

out of the question. The site is a restricted one with very little adjacent land for development. The question of a new yard for Warrington was put in the early 1960s and at this stage the best solution was felt to be a new yard at Cross Tetleys. As with many such projects, the fall in freight traffic during the 1960s led to its abandonment and the old yards at Arpley and Walton remained unchanged. Today they operate at near capacity and the minor alterations mentioned above can only increase their throughput by about 20 per cent. Several people have suggested that further increases in freight tonnage would force the railway to 'drop' back into Basford Hall Sidings, thus spreading the load of WCML freights between two major yards. This irony may not come to pass, but whatever the decisions of the future, British Rail have certainly had their 'pound of flesh' from the antiquated sidings around Warrington!

My thanks go to Mr T. Rotheram (Area Operations Manager, Warrington), Mr Graham Darbyshire the A.F.A, who kindly accompanied me on a tour of Arpley and Walton, and Mr D. Lennon (Relief Supervisor) for his information and photographs. Acknowledgement is also made to K. Groundwater for his writings about Basford Hall which were essential source material for this chapter.

Class 20 No. 20174 passes through Wigan North Western station on 19th September 1984. It has a load made up mainly of SPA steel wagons and VEA vans being the 6F83, 13.52 Blackburn to Warrington Arpley Yard.

# Chapter 6
# Carlisle

Carlisle, just south of the Scottish border, was a remarkable railway town. Here, seven main lines converged to cross the River Eden north of the impressive Carlisle Citadel station, *(Fig. 5)*. Each of these seven routes was owned by a different railway company. Consequently each line had its own marshalling yard or yards in the border city. In 1923, the railway Grouping considerably simplified the ownership of these varied routes. It did not, however, ease the operating difficulties caused by the complex network of sidings and yards around the city of Carlisle. In order to improve the handling of freight at Carlisle, a new marshalling yard was built north of the city, at Kingmoor. Opened in 1963, it was the largest yard constructed under the British Railway Modernisation Plan.

**Kingmoor 'down' Yard was the smaller of the two sets of sidings at Carlisle. Here in 1966, the 36 sorting sidings are shown from the hump summit as several wagons roll northwards.**

*British Rail*

Although very busy in its early days, the yard has seen a gradual decrease in importance over the last 20 years.

It is remarkable that today all but one of the main lines into Carlisle still survive, but none of the small pre-Grouping marshalling yards are left. Even the expansive Kingmoor Yard, built in 1962, has all but disappeared. This chapter traces the planning and construction of Kingmoor Yard and follows its subsequent rationalisation into a modern 'Speedlink' yard.

## The Old Carlisle

In the 1950s, Carlisle was one of the largest railway centres in the country. The former Caledonian and Glasgow & South Western Railway lines converged from the North, at Gretna. These were joined a few miles further south by the ex-North British

**Another aerial view of the 'down' yard taken in 1966 shows a wide selection of freight rolling stock including well over one hundred vanfits.**

*British Rail*

Railway line from Edinburgh. To the south of the city, lines radiated to Newcastle (North Eastern Railway), Leeds (Midland Railway), Preston (London & North Western Railway) and Workington (Maryport & Carlisle Railway). In addition to these main lines there was a branch line to the port of Silloth, an important point for the export of produce to Northern Ireland.

At the turn of the decade, in 1960, there were nine major yards in operation around

Carlisle. Such a plethora of sidings had posed a great operating problem over the previous ten years. An extensive timetable of trip workings and pilot engines had evolved to make the best of a far from ideal railway infrastructure. The functions of these trip freights were threefold. Firstly they might perform a particular job, eg shunt to various local coal depots, and

secondly a major task was to replace train engines on incoming freights. This was done to avoid main line engines being delayed unduly by congestion in one of the marshalling yards. It was not unknown for trains to wait for several hours before being accepted at Viaduct or Upperby yards. The third type of trip freight was of a more conventional nature. These trains hauled

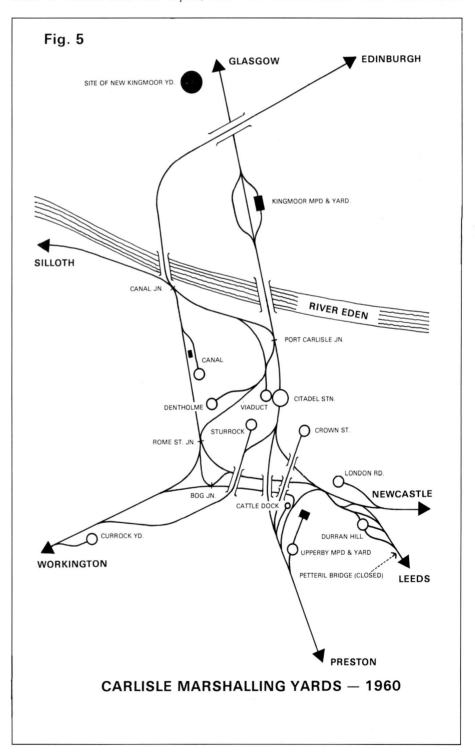

**Fig. 5**

**CARLISLE MARSHALLING YARDS — 1960**

traffic, sorted at an arrival yard, to an appropriate departure point. Such trips were difficult to predict and so most were run on a 'moment-to-moment' basis.

Several dozen engines were designated for trip working around Carlisle, and often their whole day was spent shuttling between the city's yards. Engines were remanned during their trips rather than making the time-consuming trek back to their parent depot. The sheds at Upperby and Kingmoor supplied Class 5 4-6-0s or Class 3 "Jinty" 0-6-0Ts for trip working, whilst Canal depot used ex-NBR 0-6-0T engines.

**A Stanier 'Black Five' storms south from Kingmoor Yard past the new Kingmoor power signal box. The mid-1960s saw the unusual combination of ultra modern marshalling yards, antiquated locomotives and un-fitted freight rolling stock.**
*P.W. Robinson*

The details of every arrival and departure from Carlisle during 1960 are far too extensive to be recounted in full. It is, however, clear that the complex freight operation around this border city was both time-consuming and expensive. 'Down' trains from Preston arrived at Viaduct Yard except for some which terminated at Dentonholme or Kingmoor 'Down' Yard. Arrivals from Leeds could end their journeys at any one of five yards, although most were booked into London Road Yard. Trains from the Cumbrian Coast were dealt with predominantly at Currock Yard, whilst trains from Silloth arrived at Canal Yard. The traffic from an arrival was marshalled at each yard into trips for the despatching yards or made up into main line departures. 'Down' departures were far less complex. Those bound for Silloth or the Waverley route left from Canal Yard. Trains to Glasgow and other points north departed from either Viaduct Yard or Kingmoor 'Down' Yard.

**With regulator open, British Railways ex-Crosti-boilered 9F No. 92026 storms south out of Kingmoor Yard in 1966.**
*P.W. Robinson*

In the 'up' direction most trains from Scotland were received at Kingmoor Exchange Sidings. Some, however, were extended to Upperby or Durranhill Yards during the night shift. 'Up' departures operated on a 'one yard to one line' basis. Trains to Preston used Upperby, and those to Workington used Currock, etc.

# Viaduct Yard

In view of this intricate pattern of freight arrivals and departures, it is hardly surprising that there were considerable delays to freight traffic forced to negotiate the 'spaghetti junction' that was Carlisle. Each yard had its own problems. At Viaduct Yard there were no reception roads, thus any arrival had to be drawn forward and backed into the yard. This could take up to 15 minutes during which time shunting was precluded by the fact that all arrivals and departures crossed the shunting neck (cf. Doncaster today). Shunt-

The asymmetrical wheel arrangement of the Metro-Vick Co-Bo class is highlighted in this view of a freight from Workington to Kingmoor. The train is seen on the old NER canal branch at Dalston Road Crossing in 1966.

*P.W. Robinson*

The windows of the old Kingmoor power signal box have been boarded up in this view of the southern approaches to Kingmoor Yard, taken on 27th September 1985. Class 81 No. 81009 arrives with the 7S68, Hardendale to Ravenscraig train. The ex-iron ore tipplers convey limestone to the BSC plant at Ravenscraig and, although a block load, the train pauses at Kingmoor for a crew change.

ing was further complicated because the yard was divided into two sections joined by a common exchange siding (called Pincher). In addition to the marshalling of main-line freights, the pilot engines at Viaduct Yard had to place traffic into the private sidings in the area. Any lengthy delay of an arrival from the South could lead to a queue of freights as far back as passing loops on the main lines from Leeds and Preston.

## Upperby Yard

At Upperby Yard, the entrance to the sorting sidings was similarly congested. The Carlisle No. 12 signal box controlled the entrance to the yard. As well as the yard, the main line from Preston, the entrances to the locomotive depot and carriage sidings, the goods lines to Bog Junction, and through sidings to London Road Junction, all converged at No. 12 box and Upperby New Junction. Any arrival from the north reversed into the yard, blocking southbound departures. The yard itself was broken up into several groups of sidings. Passing east from the main line were: sidings for Crown Street Goods and southbound departures, through lines to the locomotive depot, sidings for St. Nicholas cattle dock, and then the goods lines to Bog Junction. Next were a group of sidings called Wapping which were used for wagon storage, then followed roads leading to the lower yard which was used for local traffic. Beyond these were two through sidings to London Road Junction, and finally four 'arrival lines'. These four roads were connected to the first main marshalling group which was in turn linked, via an exchange siding, to the second main group of sidings. If such a complex list makes difficult reading, imagine the operational problems at this, Carlisle's major 'up' yard!

## London Road Yard

The ex-North Eastern Railway yards at London Road were the largest and busiest in Carlisle. Traffic to and from Newcastle and the north east was processed here. Crews would arrive from Newcastle with trainloads of steel and coal. After a 90 minute break to service their engine they would return with a train of empties. As most traffic was worked in 'block loads', shunting was generally less complex. Coal from Northumberland and County Durham was dispatched to Carlisle's locomotive depots and the Cumberland iron plant at Workington. Most steel traffic ran between the north east and Scotland and, as with coal, was conveyed in unfitted wagons. The only operational problem at London Road Yard was the co-ordination of the three sections of the sidings to avoid congestion at peak periods.

In the middle distance, the twelve 'up' departure sidings can be seen, beyond them the remnants of the 'up' yard proper. Class 37 No. 37252 departs with the 6E96, Stranraer to Tyne Yard Speedlink in May 1986. The first three wagons in the train are VGA vans and convey 'Cook-in-sauce' from Brunthill to Wisbech!

On 27th September 1985, the 6S82, 20.30, Severn Tunnel Junction to Mossend was delayed at Kingmoor because there was no guard for the train. Class 86 No. 86030 stands in the 'up' departure sidings which form the hub of the Speedlink yard at Carlisle. The varied cargo of the Glasgow-bound freight included three polybulk grain wagons from Oxford (Banbury Road) to Leith South, and five BDA bogie bolsters from Lackenby to the slab dressing bay at Dalzell.

A brace of Class 87s, Nos 87035 and 87013, stand at the head of the 6S97, Warrington Arpley Yard to Mossend, seen at Kingmoor on 8th May 1986. The consist of this long-distance Speedlink freight was as follows:
   8 PRA, china clay, Pontsmill to Corpach.
   1 VGA, light fittings, Truro to Edinburgh.
   1 TTB, china clay, Burngullow to Stirling.
   3 PBA, china clay, Marsh Mills to Mossend.
   4 PAA, china clay, Goonbarrow to Markinch.
   2 TTA, empty, Carlisle to Grangemouth.
   1 BBA, empty, Shotton to Mossend.

The northern end of the 'up' sorting sidings at Kingmoor have been truncated. In 1985 most of the roads were still present, albeit severed from the erstwhile 'up' hump.

A trip freight from Dumfries to Carlisle arrives at Kingmoor on 8th May 1986. Class 27 No. 27003 heads the 6M80, which is made up almost entirely of empty wagons.

The signal box stands derelict in 1985. After a working life of less than 20 years, the massive investment of modernisation is left to dereliction.

## Canal Yard

Canal Yard, as the name suggests, was built on the site of a canal basin. The constraints of such a site led to a chronic shortage of siding space. Added to the problem of a limited siding capacity was the slow access to the yard. Like most of the other pre-Grouping yards in Carlisle, trains had to reverse into the sidings. In spite of these problems the yard handled a large volume of long-haul and short-haul traffic in its two main groups of sorting sidings.

## Freight Traffic in 1960

The yards at Carlisle were far from the quiet derelict sidings which one might picture today. In spite of the large number of separate marshalling installations, each could claim the status of a modern day 'Network' yard. The night shift at Denton-holme started with arrivals from Edge Hill, Broad Street and Camden. This was immediately followed by a departure to Glasgow (Buchanan Street) and one to Greenock. A trip engine also arrived to take traffic to Canal Yard for the 1.10am Dundee and 1.35am Perth freights. All this activity took place between 10pm and midnight. The yards at Upperby, King-moor Exchange and Canal were equally busy. Upperby had a string of fully-fitted

departures to Manchester, Liverpool, Willesden, Warrington and Severn Tunnel Junction; all within the three hours around midnight. Durranhill South Sidings boasted a similar string of southbound departures. Starting with the 9.35pm and 10.20pm, both to London, there followed an 11.32pm to Birmingham, a 12.10am to Leicester. Derby and Nottingham, a 1.10am to Manchester (Ancoats) and a 1.37am to Bradford. Continuing on through the night hours, a stream of fitted freights radiated to the whole country from the hub of Carlisle's nine marshalling yards.

It was in the face of hourly departures from each of these marshalling yards that the new yard at Carlisle (Kingmoor) was suggested. In the 1959 Freight Traffic Plan, the London Midland Region highlighted the need for a fully-automated marshalling yard at Carlisle in order to improve the operation of Anglo-Scottish freights. Not only were the multiple trip workings between the old yards at Carlisle expensive, but also very time consuming. The old yards were also a nuisance because of their short sidings. Most long-distance freights had to be marshalled in two separate portions which were joined just before departure. The new yard was to be sited three miles north of Carlisle near the village of Rockcliffe. Its capacity to sort 5,000 wagons each day and its lengthy sidings were seen as the panacea for Carlisle's considerable congestion.

### Carlisle Freight

**A striking contrast at Kingmoor. On 4th June 1965, Class 40 No. D221 heads south from Kingmoor Yard. The flood lights of the yard are visible in the distance whilst the Kingmoor steam depot is seen to the east of the main line. In May 1977, another Class 40, No. 40176, winds past the same spot with another mixed freight train. The yard lights are still visible, whereas the depot has been moved to the west side of the main line and overhead catenary has been added to the scene.**

*M. Welch and T. Heavyside*

## Kingmoor Yard

At a cost of £4$\frac{1}{2}$ million (1960 price), Kingmoor New Yard was one of the largest and most ambitious projects undertaken during the modernisation of British Railways. This investment was put forward in the hope that £1,000 each day would be saved in the operating costs at Carlisle. This saving was to be made by the drastic reduction in trip working within the city. Upperby depot alone furnished eight pilot engines, triple-shifted, each day. A total of three dozen trips were made daily to service the local carriage and wagon repair shops as well as the two local goods depots at Dentonholme and Crown Street. By reduc-

ing the number of yards servicing these depots from nine to one, the number of trips was reduced from thirty six to two! The total saving of 7,300 engine hours each week was a far more radical reduction in operating hours than had previously been achieved by modernisation projects.

## Planning and Construction

The site chosen for the new Kingmoor Yard was a strip of land alongside the old Caledonian main line to Glasgow. An area of undulating and poorly-drained pasture measuring $2^3/4$ miles by one mile was purchased in 1956. Construction work began three years later in 1959, and in June 1963 the yard was brought into full operation. The construction of the yard was unique in a number of ways. Many precautions were taken to ensure the trouble-

free operation of the complex with a minimum of maintenance. After the farmland at Rockcliffe had been levelled and drained it was covered in 750,000 tons of ironworks slag from West Cumberland and Scotland. The 'blanketing' or bottom ballast was then topped with over 100,000 tons of stone ballast. The yard was thus stone-ballasted throughout, a luxury unheard of in British Railways' older marshalling yards. Manganese steel trackwork was laid over the hump down into the sorting sidings and all open trackwork was 'continuously welded'. Sections of rail to be laid from the hump, through 'King', 'Queen' and 'Jack' points, had to be within $^1/_8$in of specification for the track circuits to function correctly.

Not only were the materials used at Kingmoor of a very high quality, but the innovations to reduce maintenance were considerable. The 381 sets of points were fitted with propane gas heaters, and retarders were fitted with automatic greasing apparatus which obviated the need for a two-man greasing crew. Oilers were installed on sharp curves within the yard, and in the 'down' yard graphite paint was applied to all points in an attempt to reduce the need for lubrication. In addition to these measures, a total of 22 miles of 6in drainage pipe were laid beneath the yard to keep the area dry. These measures were successful in reducing the maintenance gang at Kingmoor to eight men—a remarkable achievement!

**Another set of contrasting views taken on the same days and by the same photographers show the view towards Carlisle. In 1965, Stanier Class 8F No. 48542 crosses the river Eden at Etterby with a Kingmoor freight. In May 1977, a similar mixed freight passes Etterby behind Class 40 No. 40135.**
*M. Welch and T. Heavyside*

# Layout and Operation
## (Plan 17)

Kingmoor and its approaches occupied six miles of land along the main line from Kingmoor to Gretna Junction. Whilst the yard itself was only $2^1/_2$ miles long, considerable land was used to build new access from the goods lines into the main yard. From the north, a third track from Gretna Junction was constructed. This 'up' goods line passed over the main line just north of the yard to enter the 'up' reception sidings on the west side of the passenger route. In conjunction with this new approach, the aged viaduct over the River Esk was rebuilt and enlarged to carry three tracks. A connection from the Waverley route to the new 'up' goods was also built. This chord line from the Longtown branch to the WCML was unusual in that it was signalled for trains in the 'up' direction only. The arrival of trains from Scotland was thus possible without conflicting with the paths of express passenger services on the adjacent main line.

Departures from Carlisle to Scotland were however more complex. The volume of traffic in the 'down' direction was

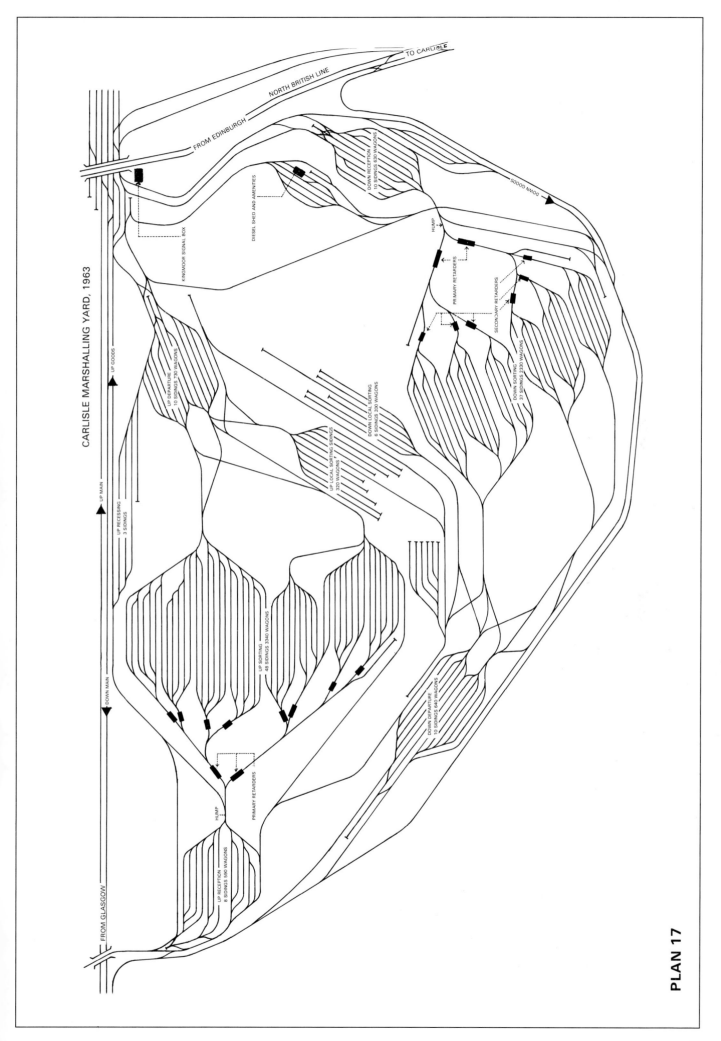

CARLISLE MARSHALLING YARD, 1963

TO CARLISLE

NORTH BRITISH LINE

FROM EDINBURGH

DOWN GOODS

KINGMOOR SIGNAL BOX

DIESEL SHED AND AMENITIES

DOWN RECEPTION
10 SIDINGS 630 WAGONS

HUMP

PRIMARY RETARDERS

SECONDARY RETARDERS

DOWN SORTING
37 SIDINGS 2330 WAGONS

UP GOODS

UP DEPARTURE
10 SIDINGS 730 WAGONS

DOWN LOCAL SORTING
6 SIDINGS 200 WAGONS

UP LOCAL SORTING SIDINGS
320 WAGONS

UP MAIN

UP RECESSING
3 SIDINGS

DOWN MAIN

UP SORTING
48 SIDINGS 3340 WAGONS

DOWN DEPARTURE
10 SIDINGS 640 WAGONS

FROM GLASGOW

HUMP

PRIMARY RETARDERS

UP RECEPTION
8 SIDINGS 590 WAGONS

**PLAN 17**

99

considerably less than the reverse 'up' flow from Scotland. It was therefore thought that a fourth track over the River Esk could not be justified. The 'down' goods line was forced to join the 'down' main line south of the River Esk. In view of this bottleneck for northbound departures it was decided that trains bound for Edinburgh should leave by way of a new spur alongside the Waverley route to the south of the yard. This operation included a lengthy reversal from the 'down' departure sidings, alongside the yard for nearly two miles to the new piece of track installed alongside the old North British line. From here trains would proceed north to Hawick and Edinburgh.

The yard itself was designed along traditional lines with arrival, sorting and departure sidings laid out in sequence. The 'up' side of the yard was larger than the 'down' side with a total of 48 sorting sidings as compared to only 37 in the 'down' yard. Each half of the yard had a separate signal box, the 'up' and the 'down' towers. These installations controlled both the yard itself and the 'up' and 'down' goods line from Gretna Junction to Kingmoor, and each employed three signalmen. Two men were absorbed at the main control desk, overlooking the hump and retarders. From here sorting of wagons was directed. The third man in the panel was responsible for the arrival of trains in the reception sidings and their eventual departure from the other end of the yard. In addition to the two yard boxes a new panel was constructed at Kingmoor. This controlled the main line from Carlisle No. 3 box in the south, to Gretna Junction in the north. It replaced the manual signal cabins at Etterby Junction, Rockcliffe and Floriston.

Marshalling of trains was controlled by means of a 'cut card'. The card was compiled in the reception sidings and then transmitted by pneumatic tube up into the control tower. Here the details on the card were converted into a code on punched tape. This then programmed the Westinghouse-made equipment to execute a fixed sequence of route settings which would ensure that each wagon was shunted into the correct siding. Both the primary and secondary retarders were automatically controlled. The degree of braking pressure was computed taking account of the speed, weight and rollability of each wagon, as well as the length of siding remaining unoccupied. The siding occupation was automatically transmitted to the control tower from axle counters situated at track level. Once a train had departed from the yard, however, the axle counter had to be reset manually, based on information from the shunters in the yard. As with all automatic systems, manual override was possible at any stage in the marshalling process.

The hump was a steep one with a maximum gradient of 1 in 16. The approach to the hump was controlled by visual signalling with an additional radio telephone linkage which was used in bad weather or in the event of an emergency. The layout was designed for a headway of seven seconds between each 'cut', and shunting and route-setting were matched in order to achieve maximum throughput of

wagons. In the 'up' yard there were 96 classes of traffic sorted into the 48 sorting sidings. Much of this traffic was bound for local destinations and had to be re-sorted in a small group of secondary sorting sidings. These were to the west of the main sorting sidings and had a capacity for 320 wagons, many of which were destined for the goods depots at Dentonholme and Crown Street.

Unfortunately, the poor road access to Kingmoor had precluded the inclusion of a goods depot within the yard, thus all freight traffic for Carlisle had to be tripped into the city. The combination of local and long-distance freights should have brought 1,000 wagons to the 'up' yard during each shift, an average of three trains every hour throughout the day. The planned workload in the 'down' yard was somewhat less, and a maximum of 700 wagons per eight hour shift were expected over the 'down' hump. The combined capacity of the two yards allowed 5,000 wagons to be sorted at Kingmoor each day. This vast operation was under the control of the yard master. There were 464 men under the authority of the yard master, and this included 186 goods guards and 126 shunters of all grades. The yard was manned on a three shift basis and, during each shift, a staff of 65 was employed at the yard in addition to the large number of goods guards based at Kingmoor.

Kingmoor was provided with a diesel servicing depot. This contained a single-track inspection shed and fuelling facilities. The easy access from both 'up' and 'down' yards into the shed meant that locomotive crews could work 'out and back' from Glasgow within one shift. This small locomotive stabling point was extremely busy during the early years of Kingmoor. The sidings had a capacity to hold 18 locomotives and the turnover of motive power was very rapid. An average day would see 95 locomotives pass through the depot. The peak of activity was during the night shift, when 45–50 locomotives received attention at the fuelling point.

## 1963 to 1973 at Kingmoor

In the mid-1960s, Kingmoor Yard was very busy. The peak number of trains handled in one day was 134, whilst the largest number of wagons sorted was 4,050. Even with this healthy flow of traffic, the yard's generous capacity was never stretched. During the late 1960s the fall in wagon-load freight began seriously to reduce the workload at Carlisle's new yard. Block train working and Freightliners undoubtedly played their part in this fall in traffic, as did the early closure of the Silloth branch. It was, however, the opening of the M6 Motorway from Birmingham to Carlisle which put the nail in the coffin of many wagonload cargoes from Scotland to the south. The short wheelbased vanfits (VVV) seen filling the yard in 1963 could not compete with long-haul lorries travelling through the northern fells at speeds up to 70mph.

January 1970 saw the closure of the 'Waverley' route and the concomitant loss of several Anglo-Scottish freight services. As a response to this rapid decline in traffic,

the 'down' yard was closed at the end of 1973. *Plan 18* shows the altered layout of the yard in January 1974. 'Down' traffic passed to the 'up' reception sidings where access was gained into road Nos 10, 11 and 12. From here the traffic was hump shunted over the 'up' hump and drawn forwards to the old 'down' arrival sidings. Four of these roads, Nos 7–10, were reallocated for 'down' departures, and it was from here that northbound traffic left Kingmoor Yard.

## 1974 to 1984: Further Rationalisation

The decline in wagonload traffic continued throughout the 1970s in spite of modernisation in the freight sector. In addition to a fall in traffic, much remaining freight along the WCML was organised into block trainloads. The partial closure in 1980 of the West Cumberland Steelworks at Workington meant a decrease in freight trains from the Cumbrian Coast line. The Settle & Carlisle line also had problems, and freight services were withdrawn from this route in May 1983. This meant the abolition of several freight services, including the thrice-daily Healey Mills to Carlisle trains and a daily service from Tinsley. Several trains from Bescot and South Wales were also lost from the timetable, reducing yet further the importance of Kingmoor as a marshalling centre.

The predominant cargo from Yorkshire to Carlisle was household coal bound for Scotland from the pits around Healey Mills Yard. This traffic would have been lost to rail but for the intervention of J.G. Russell Limited. This company's investment in air-braked container wagons (FPA) and rail distribution depots in Scotland has led to an increase in the amount of Anglo-Scottish household coal travelling by rail. In 1986 there were two trains from Doncaster Yard to Mossend via Newcastle and Edinburgh, a faster route than the old one via Carlisle. Prior to 1983, vacuum-fitted, low-capacity wagons (MCV and HTV) travelled over the Settle & Carlisle route to Kingmoor Yard. Here they were remarshalled and dispatched to Scotland via the old Glasgow & South Western Railway route to Ayr. Much vacuum-fitted freight traffic was diverted via this route because of the limited capacity of the WCML. After remarshalling at Ayr, the wagons would be taken to Mossend and again shunted before departure to their Scottish destinations. A similar lengthy journey was undertaken by coal from South Wales. Here, trains from Severn Tunnel Junction to Carlisle brought coal to the border where it was carried north via Ayr and Mossend. The introduction of air-braked hoppers (HEA) has revolutionised this service; not only do trains travel directly from Severn Tunnel Junction to Mossend but a Sundays only service has been instituted from the coke works at Abercwmboi, deep in the Welsh valleys, direct to Mossend Yard. A journey which took two days in 1980 now takes 9 hours and 45 minutes!

The combination of lost traffic and the

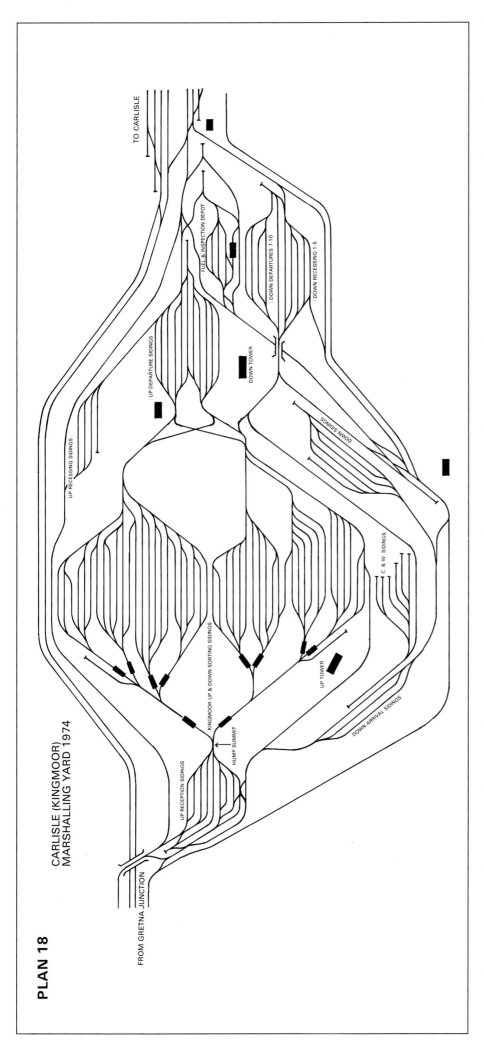

**PLAN 18**

CARLISLE (KINGMOOR)
MARSHALLING YARD 1974

TO CARLISLE

FUEL & INSPECTION DEPOT

DOWN DEPARTURES 7-10

DOWN RECESSING 1-5

UP DEPARTURE SIDINGS

DOWN TOWER

UP RECESSING SIDINGS

DOWN SIDINGS

C & W SIDINGS

KINGMOOR UP & DOWN SORTING SIDINGS

UP TOWER

HUMP SUMMIT

DOWN ARRIVAL SIDINGS

UP RECEPTION SIDINGS

FROM GRETNA JUNCTION

diversion of freight services to other routes has severely affected Kingmoor Yard. In 1981 hump shunting ceased and the 'up' hump was removed leaving a vestigial 'up' yard to handle all traffic. In spite of several suggestions that Kingmoor should be closed altogether, the yard continues to function as a Speedlink network yard.

# Kingmoor 1986

*Plan 19* shows the yard layout in September 1985. Subsequent reduction in facilities has meant that only fans 'B', 'C' and 'D' remain in the sorting sidings, and the remaining yard is essentially unchanged, although further simplification of the layout is planned for the future. The yard is open for traffic from 06.00 on Mondays until 13.00 on Saturdays, whilst the TOPS office at Kingmoor remains open continuously. The staff at Kingmoor totals an average of ten men on each shift; this includes a supervisor, shunters, train preparers and wagon examiners. Even though the reductions in siding capacity and manpower have been so drastic, Kingmoor remains a main 'Network' yard for Speedlink traffic. It lies at the intersection of Speedlink route 4, which is based on the WCML and route 6 which carries traffic from Stranraer to the north east of England.

*Table 15* lists the Speedlink freights to pass through the yard each day; a total of 27 trains on an average weekday. Each one of these trains may be shunted in the yard. Arrivals from the north enter the yard along one of the three 'up' recessing roads. From here they pass forwards before reversing into one of the eleven sidings which were used as 'up' departure roads. This is the main marshalling area at Kingmoor. With the train locomotive still in position, the yard pilot may remove and attach portions at the rear of the train. If two trains arrive together then portions may be exchanged between them. Thus 'marshalling' has changed its meaning over the last 20 years. No longer is the train locomotive removed and the entire consist of a freight propelled over a hump. Shunting in a carefully planned and limited fashion is undertaken where once a whole scale reconstruction of freights was necessary. Its load appropriately altered, the train departs south along the 'up' goods line. Northbound trains have a simpler passage through the yard without the need for the reversal. Departure from the yard is via the old 'hump avoiding line' which is electrified throughout its course.

The sorting sidings to the north of the eleven reception roads are used by traffic from the Carlisle area. The freight trips listed in *Table 16* convey a wide variety of commodities from dog food to timber. Wagons from Dumfries, Appleby, Workington and Carlisle may be sorted in these 18 sidings. The traffic is placed into these roads according to the direction of its departure from Carlisle *(Table 17)*. Thus traffic from No 8 road is brought into the reception sidings as the 6V93 to Severn Tunnel is approaching Kingmoor Yard. A similar pattern of shunting is repeated for

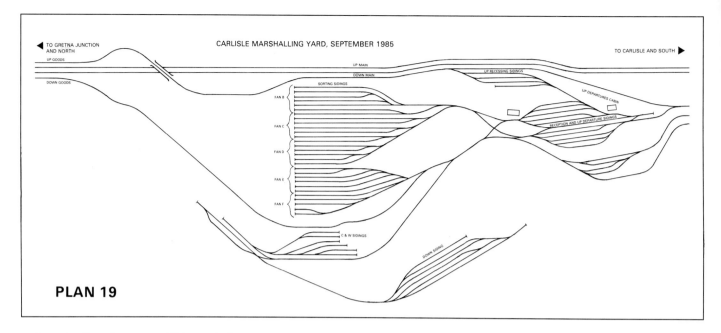

**PLAN 19**

CARLISLE MARSHALLING YARD, SEPTEMBER 1985

each main line departure. This work is undertaken by a single Class 08 shunter from 06.00 to 22.00, whilst an extra pilot is available for the night shift from 22.00 to 06.00. In addition to Speedlink freights and local trip workings, there are numerous block trains which call at the yard. A crew or locomotive change may be undertaken at Kingmoor even though no actual shunting of the train occurs. Fifteen such trains use the yard each weekday; their loads include steel coil, limestone, nuclear waste, oil, parcels and fertilizers.

## The Future of Kingmoor

Many have predicted the complete disappearance of Kingmoor Yard from the rail map. This seems unlikely whilst the city remains at the junction of so many main railway lines. The routes from Glasgow via Dumfries and via Lockerbie converge from the north. To the south, lines from Newcastle, Leeds, Preston and Workington all meet. Indeed it is remarkable that the only main line to have closed at Carlisle is the Waverley route from Edinburgh. The WCML continues to thrive as a Speedlink route and cross-country traffic to the Stockton haulage depot at Stranraer has increased steadily in the last five years. It may be possible to reduce or even abolish the sorting sidings at Kingmoor to leave a very simple Speedlink yard using the eleven 'up' departure sidings. This rests on the presumption that there is no increase in traffic at the yard. If, however, Speedlink continues to expand and Stranraer remains an important Anglo-Irish seaport then the yard may, like many other severely rationalised installations, fail to cope with the demands imposed on it. Only time will tell what will happen at Kingmoor, but the future looks promising.

Thanks to the Area Manager at Carlisle and particularly Peter Kyrsta, the Area Freight Assistant at Kingmoor whose detailed records were of great help. In addition, acknowledgement must be made to K.D. Peel and G. Freeman Allen whose writings were essential source material for this chapter.

### Table 15
#### Trains which undergo marshalling at Kingmoor Yard, January 1986

| Train | Time | | From | To | Arr. | Dep. |
|---|---|---|---|---|---|---|
| 6S59 | 00.20 | MX | Tees | Stranraer | 06.26 | 07.15 |
| 6S56 | 07.15 | MO | Carlisle | Dumfries | | 07.15 |
| 7M27 | 07.30 | MO | Mossend | Crewe CMD | 10.05 | 11.19 |
| 6S97 | 08.53 | SX | Warrington | Mossend | 11.49 | 12.54 |
| 6V93 | 07.48 | SX | Mossend | Severn Tunnel | 10.22 | 13.00 |
| 6S87 | 13.20 | SX | Carlisle | Eastriggs | | 13.20 |
| | | | | | | |
| 7E13 | 14.54 | SX | Carlisle | Tyne | | 14.54 |
| 6M91 | 15.30 | SX | Eastriggs | Carlisle | 15.53 | |
| 6M80 | 16.42 | SX | Dumfries | Carlisle | 17.29 | |
| 6E96 | 11.45 | SX | Stranraer | Tyne | 17.12 | 18.04 |
| 6S31 | 12.40 | TO | Crewe | Mossend | 17.38 | 18.10 |
| 4M64 | 11.40 | SX | Bathgate | Willesden | 16.55 | 18.28 |
| 6V92 | 15.50 | SX | Mossend | Severn Tunnel | 17.42 | 19.15 |
| 7P36 | 06.42 | MSX | Warrington | Carlisle | 19.03 | |
| 7P36 | 08.15 | MO | Warrington | Carlisle | 19.03 | |
| 6F87 | 20.35 | SX | Carlisle | Warrington | | 20.35 |
| 6E86 | 19.20 | SX | Mossend | Parkeston | 21.11 | 21.33 |
| 6M75 | 12.55 | SX | Severn Tunnel | Carlisle | 21.24 | |
| | | | | | | |
| 6M81 | 15.25 | SX | Stranraer | Carlisle | 21.48 | |
| 4M38 | 20.55 | SX | Mossend | Willesden | 22.31 | 23.06 |
| 6S80 | 19.55 | SX | Warrington | Mossend | 22.37 | 23.50 |
| 6S66 | 17.50 | SX | Tees | Stranraer | 00.04 | 00.42 |
| 6E95 | 18.45 | SX | Stranraer | Tyne | 00.25 | 01.26 |
| 6M87 | 18.10 | SX | Severn Tunnel | Carlisle | 01.34 | |
| 4S70 | 23.20 | FSX | Warrington | Bathgate | 01.40 | 02.15 |
| 4S70 | 23.20 | FO | Warrington | Millerhill | 01.40 | 02.15 |
| 6M28 | 22.33 | SX | Mossend | Warrington | 00.23 | 02.32 |
| 6S74 | 21.02 | SX | Bescot | Mossend | 03.10 | 04.17 |
| 4S48 | 21.57 | FSX | Willesden | Bathgate | 04.08 | 04.44 |
| 4S48 | 21.57 | FO | Willesden | Millerhill | 04.08 | 04.44 |
| 6S45 | 05.09 | MX | Carlisle | Stranraer | | 05.09 |
| 6S56 | 05.14 | MSX | Carlisle | Dumfries | | 05.14 |
| 6S96 | 13.50 | SX | Parkeston | Mossend | 03.58 | 05.30 |

### Table 16
#### Kingmoor Yard Trip Freights

| | | | | Class |
|---|---|---|---|---|
| T04 | 06.00 | SX | London Road, Esso Depot, Longtown, Brunthill | 08 |
| T05 | 05.50 | SX | Citadel, Longtown, Upperby, TMD | 08 |
| T06 | 06.50 | SUX | Citadel, Blue Circle cement | 08 |
| T07 | 06.25 | SX | TMD, Brunthill, Currock | 08 |
| T57 | 08.30 | SX | Appleby, Warcop, McGhies | 37 |
| T59 | 04.10 | MX | Wigton, Workington | 47 |

**Note:** The four Class 08 pilots all trip back to the yard from each destination and end their days work at about 18.00

**Table 17**
**Siding Allocation in Kingmoor Yard, September 1985**

| Road | Allocation |
|---|---|
| 7 | Carriage and Wagon shops (Currock) |
| 8 | Severn Tunnel |
| 9 | Warrington |
| 10 | Bescot |
| 11 | Tyne |
| 12 | Tyne (spare) |
| 13 | TMD, fuel oil for Kingmoor diesel depot |
| 14 | Eastriggs |
| 15 | Dumfries |
| 16 | Stranraer and Falkland Junction |
| 17 | Mossend |
| 18 | Longtown (air-brakes) |
| 19 | Tyne (vacuum) |
| 20 | Workington (air-brakes) |
| 21 | Spare |
| 22 | Upperby |
| 23 | London Road |
| 24 | Appleby and Warcop |
| 25-35 | Engineer's traffic and the storage of explosives wagons pending their allocation. This section of the yard was closed in 1986. |

A Kingmoor to Mossend freight passes Beattock behind Class 20 No. D8114, whilst Stanier 'Black Fives' Nos 44787 and 45192 shunt in the sidings.

*M. Welch*

A block load of coal arrives at Kingmoor on its way from Knockshinnock Colliery to Fiddler's Ferry Power Station. Class 20s Nos 20009 and 20035 will be replaced by a Class 47 diesel-electric locomotive before the train can proceed south.

The freight avoiding lines at Carlisle were closed after damage caused by a runaway Freightliner vehicle. In March 1981, all freights still travelled along the lines to the west of Citadel station. Class 40 No. 40019 heads the 7V00, 12.05, Kingmoor to Severn Tunnel Junction.

An 'up' cement train approaches Kingmoor Yard from the south on 10th July 1978. Class 40 No. 40112 has just under a mile to go as it passes Kingmoor diesel depot.

# Chapter 7

# Millerhill and Mossend

The contrast between the freight yards of the 1950s and 1960s and British Rail's modern Speedlink yards is nowhere more clearly illustrated than in Southern Scotland. British Railways have two major yards, one for Glasgow and one for Edinburgh. Mossend Yard between Glasgow and Motherwell is one of twelve Speedlink Network yards and a thriving Railfreight centre. Its compact layout is largely unchanged from the 1930s and copes well with over 1,000 wagons each day. Forty miles to the east in Edinburgh is Millerhill Yard, which was constructed as part of the 1955 Modernisation Plan. Here a bi-directional automated hump marshalling yard was built and its 100 sorting sidings had the capacity to deal with up to 5,000 wagons daily.

Millerhill 'up' yard was opened in June 1962 and handled 2,000 wagons each day. This view shows the sorting sidings and the distinctive design of control tower built there.

*Railway Gazette International*

By 1986, the remnant of Millerhill Yard had been relegated to a secondary marshalling point and saw considerably less traffic than its prosperous neighbour in Glasgow. The introduction of the TOPS wagon control system along with the abolition of whole scale marshalling of long-haul freights has led to a renaissance for the more simple pre-modernisation marshalling yards. The frenzied building programme of the late 1950s and early 1960s has made way for a more measured approach to marshalling yard construction. The emphasis in Railfreight planning has been rapid transit time with a minimum of marshalling. This has led in turn to the overall simplification of all marshalling yards.

## Millerhill

The first stages of Millerhill Yard were brought into operation during May 1962 *(Plan 20)*. By April 1963, both 'up' and 'down' yards were fully commissioned, leading to a simplification of freight marshalling in the Edinburgh area. Like many major cities, the rail network in Edinburgh was complex and the various shunting yards and sidings diffuse. Six separate yards were scattered throughout the eastern outskirts of the Capital. The largest of these were at Niddrie North and

South. Niddrie North Yard had formerly dealt with fitted wagons for the ECML and Carlisle. Niddrie South, in contrast, dealt with traffic flowing in the opposite direction, ie that arriving from the east coast and Carlisle routes for distribution further north and west in Scotland. A smaller yard at Joppa dealt with unfitted wagons and empty coaching stock for the ECML. Portabello Yard formed a focus for the empty mineral wagons which required reallocation to the various Lothian collieries. Leith South was also predominantly involved in the marshalling of coal traffic bound for the west of Scotland. The final group of sidings in the area were at Hardengreen Junction and they processed varied traffic for the numerous branches and collieries in the vicinity.

Class 40 No. D394 arrives at Millerhill with a freight from the ECML in 1966. Wisps of steam can be seen in the 'up' yard, in the background.

*A. Vickers*

In June 1962, the 'up' yard at Millerhill became operational leading to the closure of Niddrie North Yard. In July of the same year further alterations led to the closure of Joppa and Hardengreen yards as well as the diversion of the 'up' traffic using Portabello. In April 1963, the 'down' hump yard at Millerhill was opened and Portabello consequently closed completely. Niddrie South Yard was also closed and Leith South Yard had a reduction in its workload.

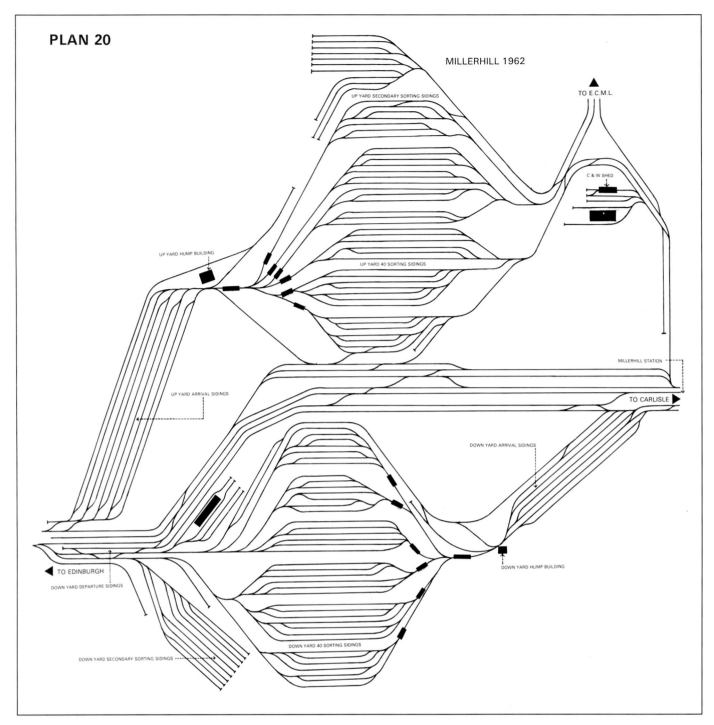

## PLAN 20

MILLERHILL 1962

TO E.C.M.L.

UP YARD SECONDARY SORTING SIDINGS

C & W SHED

UP YARD HUMP BUILDING

UP YARD 40 SORTING SIDINGS

MILLERHILL STATION

UP YARD ARRIVAL SIDINGS

TO CARLISLE

DOWN YARD ARRIVAL SIDINGS

DOWN YARD HUMP BUILDING

TO EDINBURGH

DOWN YARD DEPARTURE SIDINGS

DOWN YARD 40 SORTING SIDINGS

DOWN YARD SECONDARY SORTING SIDINGS

A splendid overall view of the 'down' arrival sidings at Millerhill. A 'Clayton' class diesel-electric arrives, right, with a local trip freight, whilst Class 40 No. D394 heads north to the locomotive refuelling depot. A Class 08 propels one freight over the 'down' hump before shunting the freight illustrated in the previous picture, which stands in the most westerly reception road. In the background the surface buildings of the new Monktonhall pit are nearing completion.

*A. Vickers*

The new yard at Millerhill was constructed over a seven year period at a cost of £3 million. It straddled the Waverley route to Carlisle between Niddrie and the junction with the Loanhead branch. 'Up' and 'down' yards were almost identical, but for the fact that the 'down' yard had an additional set of reception sidings designed to accommodate trains from the ECML. These were routed via a new connection from Monktonhall Junction to the Niddrie to Glenesk line. The hump shunting at the yard was fully automatic and both primary and secondary retarders were equipped with radar and weight-sensing equipment. The method for controlling a shunt was the then standard one of a cut card compiled for each incoming train. This was transferred onto a punch tape in the control tower from which a computer was able to set the routes required for sorting the separate cuts. Both 'up' and 'down' yards were provided with secondary sorting sidings. However, unlike other major yards, these were not used for the detailed segregation of local traffic. Class 4 freights, similar to

**To the right are the secondary sorting sidings belonging to the 'down' yard at Millerhill. A Class 08 shunts at the north end of the sorting sidings as Class 40 No. D260, passes on its way to the diesel depot.**

*A. Vickers*

today's Speedlink services arrived at Millerhill and were shunted into the secondary sorting sidings avoiding the hump. They were then sorted in a similar fashion to the modern Speedlink trains - that is, portions were exchanged between express freights without the remarshalling of the entire consist.

The 'up' yard was concerned mainly with marshalling traffic for the east coast route and the Waverley route to Carlisle. In addition, empty mineral wagons were sorted for the various collieries in the Lothians. The 'down' yard conversely dealt with traffic arriving from the south and bound for destinations in and around Edinburgh. Trunk trains were made up for more distant destinations such as the yards at Gunnie, Cadder, Perth, Slateford and Dundee. The new yards had a radical impact on freight services in the Edinburgh area, and almost all trains were re-routed via Millerhill. There were, however, one or two block services which then, as now, were not affected by the new marshalling arrangements. Block trains of cement between Cliffe and Uddingston and Oxwellmains and Grangemouth bypassed the yard. The Bathgate car trains from Morris Cowley in Oxford also arrived at their destination in Central Scotland without being remarshalled at Millerhill. The yard was initially a great success with a consider-

able reduction in tripping between yards and, therefore, in staff and locomotives required to marshal Edinburgh's freights. There were, however, disadvantages, subsidence at the yard being the biggest problem. This, along with the isolation of those working at the yard, were small prices to pay for the great benefits in operating efficiency which accrued from the new yard.

A new signal box was built at Millerhill to replace three manual signal boxes situated at Niddrie South Junction, Millerhill Junction and Glenesk Junction. It controlled 13 1/2 route miles by a new NX type route-interlocking panel. Services on the Edinburgh to Carlisle main line, as well as all trains entering and leaving the yards, were under its supervision. It contained a total of 328 different route settings and was operated by three signalmen.

The yard itself was a traditional design of the day. Both 'up' and 'down' yards contained 40 main sorting sidings. In addition, the 'up' yard was provided with ten secondary sorting sidings together with eight reception sidings. There were also two goods loop lines, a through engine line, a departure line, and connections. At the southern extremity of the yard there were carriage and wagon facilities as well as a cattle dock to feed and water animals in transit. The 'down' yard had the addition of nine secondary sorting sidings and eleven

The same site as shown previously remained largely unchanged 15 years later in March 1981. Class 26 No. 26003 departs with the J41 trip to Leith South, the train conveying a single wagon of grain from Newmarket at the front. In the background, Class 26 No. 26040 shunts the J25 trip for Bathgate and Ratho coal depot.

Just four years later, in September 1985, the 'down' yard had been completely lifted. This picture, taken from the hump crest, shows the control tower, derelict lighting masts and the remains of the hump shunting signal.

reception sidings. These were divided into five Carlisle arrival sidings, which paradoxically accepted traffic from the East Coast Main Line via the Monktonhall Curve. The second group of six arrival roads were to the north of Millerhill Station and converged on the 'down' hump.

The steepest gradient of the hump was 1 in 16 and both 'up' and 'down' yards contained one primary and six secondary, or group, retarders supplied by the Westinghouse Brake & Signal Company. The primary retarders measured 75ft long, whilst the secondary were shorter at 55ft. The computer control of the retarders utilised information about the weight, rolling resistance and length of each cut, together with the number of wagons already in each siding . By November 1963,

the number of wagons handled in the 'up' yard each week was between 9,000 and 10,000. A similar throughput was recorded for the 'down' yard, although there were seasonal variations in traffic. During the seed potato peak, the throughput in the 'up' yard rose to 11,600 wagons in a $5^{1}/_{2}$ day working week. The average throughput of wagons at both Millerhill 'up' and 'down' totalled approximately 4,000 per day.

A new diesel depot was provided and this avoided the tripping of diesel locomotives to main servicing depots for refuelling and minor examination. They continued to visit the major workshops for maintenance once each week. Steam locomotives were also catered for at the yard and four 3,000 gallon water storage tanks were erected. Two of these were new and purchased from the

firm Cowans Sheldon, whereas two others were simply transferred from the old yard at Portabello. The yard flourished in the early years and began to pay back the heavy investment that had been made in its construction. As in the rest of the country, however, the rail freight scene was changing rapidly, and in 1969 a severe blow was dealt to the yard by the closure of the Waverley route to Carlisle.

## 1969 to 1979

Prior to the closure of the Waverley route in 1970, there had been a steady decline in wagonload freight traffic passing through Millerhill. The added loss of all through freight services from Carlisle was the final

A merry-go-round service from Monktonhall Colliery to Cockenzie Power Station on 11th September 1985 passes the site of the old Millerhill station. Behind the train, hauled by Class 20 No. 20203, lies the track-bed of the Waverley route and on the right are the old Carlisle arrival lines.

On 24th April 1986 the alterations at Millerhill were almost complete. The diesel servicing point remained unchanged, all traffic used the southern half of the old 'up' sorting sidings, and the northern approaches had been singled. Class 20s Nos 20175 and 20171 depart with an empty coal train, returning from Cockenzie to a new opencast site at Roughcastle near Grangemouth.

straw that led to the closure of the 'up' arrival sidings and the 'up' hump. This left an asymmetrical Millerhill Yard. The 'up' sidings were flat-shunted from the south, whilst the 'down' yard continued to operate as originally planned. Wagonload traffic continued to dwindle and the reduced layout was never stretched. In June 1975, TOPS computer wagon control equipment was installed at Millerhill. At the same time some of the sidings on the 'up' side were used to store civil engineering materials and the rest retained as departure roads. All revenue-earning freight traffic was concentrated on the 'down' hump which, in 1975, saw a daily throughput of 1,500 wagons. The daily departure list contained 26 separate freights to ten destinations in Scotland as well as Carlisle, Tyne Yard, Dringhouses, Whitemoor and Parkeston Quay.

Even after the retreat to the 'down' yard, wagonload traffic continued to decline. The reasons for this were, general loss of traffic, especially coal, and much greater use of block trains. In 1979, a review of rail freight in the Lothians highlighted promising growth areas, none of which were in wagonload traffic.

Most of the railway's share of freight in the 1970s was in bulk traffic. The largest flow in the Lothians in terms of volume was coal to the local power stations. There were eight daily merry-go-round services from Monktonhall to Cockenzie and a further

three from Bilston Glen Colliery, in addition, Monktonhall sent two trains daily to Longannet, in Fife. A total of 2½ million tonnes of coal were consigned to rail from Lothian pits. This compared favourably with only 800,000 tonnes transported by road. A further two million tonnes of coal was received by rail annually from collieries outside the Lothians. Domestic coal arrived from Brodsworth Colliery in Doncaster and about 100,000 tonnes of industrial coal was transported annually from Shilbottle in Northumberland to Oxwellmains cement works at Dunbar. After block loads of coal, cement and limestone from Oxwellmains were the most important traffic for British Railways in the area. Daily block cement trains were dispatched to Aberdeen, Dundee, Grangemouth, Inverness, Irving and Uddingston. None of these services required marshalling or routing via the yard at Millerhill. Other railway contracts included the removal of 600,000 tonnes of spoil from Deans to Cambuslang. Petroleum products totalling 130,000 tonnes were forwarded annually by rail from Grangemouth Refinery to storage tanks at Granton.

Anhydrous ammonia was brought from Haverton Hill on Teesside to the fertilizer factory at Leith dock. This traffic amounted to 80,000 tonnes annually and again, was transported in block loads from the south. Cars brought by rail to Bathgate for distribution to motor dealers throughout

Scotland were also an important source of revenue for the Edinburgh region. These were transported in trainloads of up to six four-wagon cartic sets, and travelled direct to Bathgate.

In contrast with such encouraging bulk flows the traffic utilizing Millerhill was very small. Grain and cereal transport has been a recent success area for Speedlink. However, in 1978, the tonnage of grain transported to Leith Docks via Millerhill was only 14,000 tonnes. As distribution depots and general goods depots closed in their tens and hundreds, so the traffic passing through Millerhill dwindled. Some customers undoubtedly transferred to the nearby Freightliner depot in Portabello. From here, daily services were afforded to Stratford and Willesden in London, Newcastle and Cardiff were supplied via the ECML, and Dudley and Nottingham by the West Coast route. By 1979 the throughput at Millerhill 'down' yard had fallen to well below 1,000 wagons daily, and the closure of the installation was therefore inevitable.

## The 1980s

It was not until November 1983 that the 'down' yard was completely closed. Freight marshalling continued at Millerhill with all services being sorted in the 'up' sidings which were shunted from the south end.

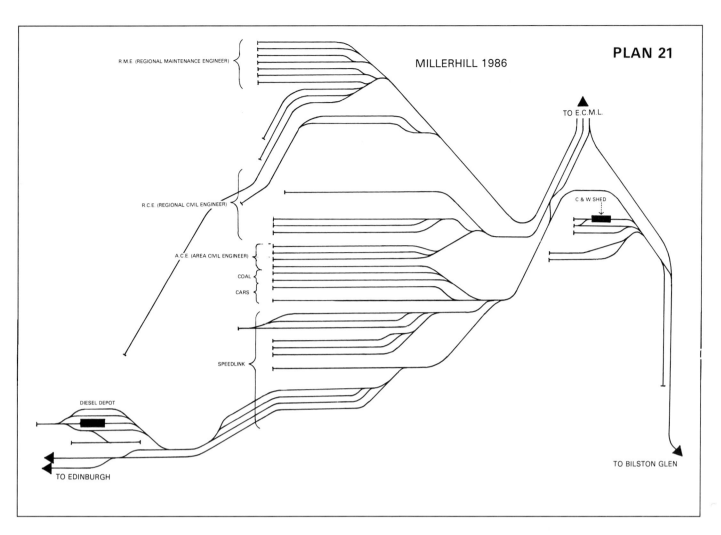

MILLERHILL 1986

R.M.E. (REGIONAL MAINTENANCE ENGINEER)

TO E.C.M.L.

C & W SHED

R.C.E. (REGIONAL CIVIL ENGINEER)

A.C.E. (AREA CIVIL ENGINEER)

COAL

CARS

SPEEDLINK

DIESEL DEPOT

TO EDINBURGH

TO BILSTON GLEN

The layout used was far from ideal, and marshalling at Millerhill seemed to have a very poor future.

The possible abolition of all freight facilities at Millerhill was examined. This would have meant the concentration of all

**Class 37 No. 37051 backs the 6E97 Speedlink freight into Millerhill Yard on 11th September 1985. The train is made up of several VGA vans from Paisley to Wisbech, but will pick up more traffic before its departure south to Ripple Lane.**

Speedlink trains at Mossend Yard and extensive trip working from Glasgow to Edinburgh. This was not financially viable and British Rail have acknowledged the necessity for a marshalling yard in Edinburgh. There are several advantages in this decision and these will be discussed later. By the end of 1985 several minor alterations were in hand to facilitate the rapid and efficient sorting of Speedlink traffic at the remnant of Millerhill hump yard. *Plan 21* shows the layout of the sidings as they stood in January 1986. The secondary sorting sidings on the eastern fringe of the yard were used by the Area Maintenance Engineer for the sorting and grading of crippled wagons which were then transferred to the carriage and wagon shops, just

**The 6E97 from Mossend to Ripple Lane has just arrived and deposited a rake of tank wagons for Class 08 No. 08564 to allocate to the appropriate siding. The diesel fuel comes from Grangemouth Oil Refinery and is bound for Haymarket Diesel Depot.**

south of the sorting sidings. Only three sidings remained in fans A and B of the original sorting sidings, and these were used for track reclamation and the processing of spent ballast. Next in the array of sorting sidings is fan C, and this has been allocated to the Regional Civil Engineer's Department. The final twelve single-ended sidings are used by Speedlink traffic. These have an average capacity of just over 60 SLUs, and can accommodate all but the longest freight services. The most westerly roads in the old

fan area have been converted into arrival and departure loops.

When the 'down' yard was closed in November 1983, the track layout at Millerhill meant that 'down' arrivals still had to traverse the south curve from the Monkton-hall extension and pause in the old Waverley line reception sidings before reversing back northwards to the 'up' yard. This manoeuvre was time-consuming and expensive, and it was therefore decided to construct a new arrival line for trains from

the East Coast Main Line. This having been completed, arrivals from the south would be accepted in either the four loops produced from the old F sorting sidings or three roads in fan E which were joined at their northern end to allow the run-round of locomotives.

The southern curve from the Monktonhall line was still in use during 1986 by the mgr coal trains from Monktonhall and Bilston Glen collieries. Twelve trains daily were afforded direct access on to the East Coast Main Line by the retention of this curve.

Thus, in 1986, the basic layout at Millerhill contained four arrival/departure roads and twelve sorting sidings. The traffic handled by this new compact Speedlink yard is shown in *Table 18*. Eleven trunk Speedlink trains call at the yard each weekday. Traffic for these trains is collected from local destinations by a selection of 14 trip freights and feeder services. The number of wagons shunted at Millerhill is small; usually less than 300 in twenty four hours, but the yard is essential to Speedlink's bid to gain local customers in and around Edinburgh.

As in the late 1960s and early 1970s, considerable tonnages of rail freight bypasses Millerhill in block trains. There are up to 15 daily mgr trains to Cockenzie Power Station, whilst three trains of cars travel direct to the Bathgate distribution terminal. Both the Blyth to Fort William alumina train and the return empty workings call at Millerhill for a crew change as do several of the block cement trains from Oxwellmains. In 1986 an average of four trains ran each day to Aberdeen, Inverness, Dundee. Uddingston or Grange-

**Table 18**
**Millerhill Freight — May 1986**

**Speedlink**

| Code | From | To | Arr. | Dep. |
|------|------|-----|------|------|
| 6S92 | Dringhouses | Craiginches | 02.39 | 03.12 |
| 6E60 | Mossend | Doncaster | 05.05 | 06.10 |
| 4S39 | Dagenham | Millerhill | 06.22 | |
| 4S48 | Willesden | Millerhill | 08.43 | |
| 6S67 | Doncaster | Mossend | 10.35 | 11.07 |
| 4M64 | Bathgate | Willesden | 12.24 | 14.27 |
| 6E97 | Mossend | Ripple Lane | 16.02 | 17.07 |
| 6E61 | Mossend | Doncaster | 17.33 | 18.41 |
| 6E87 | Millerhill | Parkeston | | 17.50 |
| 6E89 | Aberdeen | Immingham | 19.03 | 19.37 |
| 6S46 | Doncaster | Mossend | 23.31 | 23.47 |
| 6S63 | Scunthorpe | Aberdeen | 23.48 | 00.20 |

**Trip Freight**

| Code | From | To | Arr. | Dep. |
|------|------|-----|------|------|
| 6H25 | Millerhill | Inverness | | 03.45 |
| 4B61 | Millerhill | Bathgate | | 05.57 |
| 8B11 | Millerhill | Leith South | | 06.20* |
| 6B07 | Millerhill | Leith South | | 06.30° |
| 6B02 | Millerhill | Oxwellmains | | 08.15 |
| 6B03 | Millerhill | Bathgate | | 08.28 |
| 6B64 | Mossend | Millerhill | 09.28 | |
| 4B62 | Bathgate | Millerhill | 11.53 | |
| 6B83 | Oxwellmains | Millerhill | 11.59 | |
| 6B02 | Oxwellmains | Millerhill | 12.28 | |
| 6B03 | Bathgate | Millerhill | 15.19 | |
| 7B06 | Leith South | Millerhill | 17.00 | |
| 6D48 | Millerhill | Mossend | | 17.39 |
| 6B68 | Inverness | Millerhill | 22.45 | |

\* Makes two trips.
° One return trip.

mouth. Traffic from both Bathgate and Oxwellmains is tripped to Millerhill where its inclusion in Speedlink trains has facilitated connections to customers not normally served by block trains. Similarly, wagons with goods from the extensive rail service depot at Leith South are tripped four times each day to the yard at Millerhill.

## The Future

As has already been mentioned, the yard at Millerhill has been severely rationalised over the last 15 years. In the early 1980s its closure was a strong possibility. Several important considerations have led to its retention and possible future modernisation at the site. The East Coast Main Line electrification programme should bring electrically-hauled express passenger trains to the capital of Scotland by 1991. The eastern approaches to Edinburgh navigate several lengthy tunnels. The detailed costing of the electrification programme has suggested that considerable savings

could be made by electrifying only two tracks at the eastern end of Edinburgh. The Monktonhall Curve could then be electrified into Millerhill Yard, as could the northern departure line on to the Edinburgh district or suburban line. This could be simplified into a single track main line provided that two or three refuge loops were installed at the western end of the city. All freight traffic would be routed round the suburban line and the future of Millerhill Yard under these arrangements would be secure.

The yard itself is approaching the end of its operating life and considerable investment is needed in new trackwork. This, along with electrification, would provide a yard capable of dealing with electrically-hauled East Coast Main Line Speedlink traffic. Longer trains, of an increased tonnage, could circumnavigate the suburban line on which there are no loading restrictions. The present layout can cater adequately with 60 SWL trains, and there is potential for expansion on the present site to cope with much longer freights. The

Mossend Yard (See later in this chapter). Such a distribution depot would cater for local customers without direct rail access and could also be developed to provide warehousing facilities for goods in transit. It may well be possible to build such a depot in Leith Docks from where a considerable tonnage of cereals and other commodities are exported.

The northern approaches to Millerhill Yard have been altered beyond recognition since the construction of a new Edinburgh bypass. The multiple approach routes have been reduced to a single main line which, whilst functional, bears very little resemblance to the previous collection of railway sidings. The Millerhill of the future is likely to contain a similar number of sidings, that is, four reception and departure roads with twelve Speedlink sorting sidings, all of which will be electrified. The arrival and departure roads will receive catenary throughout, whilst the sorting sidings are likely to have the overhead equipment installed at their southern extremity. Electrification of the approaches to the yard

Two pictures of Mossend taken in 1980 and 1986 demonstrate the radical changes that have taken place in just six years. In 1980, both 'up' and 'down' yards are full of a variety of vacuum-fitted wagons. By 1986 the 'down' yards have been completely closed, the 'up' or Speedlink yard contains only air-braked rolling stock and five new through sidings have been added to the eastern border of the yard. This necessitated the removal of a large lighting pylon seen on the left border of the earlier picture.

requirements of the different engineering departments are met by the sidings on the eastern side of the Millerhill complex and the diesel servicing depot has a secure future, particularly as most trip freight workings will remain diesel hauled even after the 1991 'switch on'.

The waste ground on the site of the old 'down' hump yard has not yet been developed. Several possibilites have been suggested including the construction of a Speedlink goods distribution and storage depot. A similar facility has been developed by P.D. Stirling Enterprises adjacent to

along with the Edinburgh suburban line will guarantee electric freight haulage to the capital of Scotland. Because of the small workload at Millerhill in 1986, considerable increases in traffic can be catered for by the current yard, simply by careful timetabling. *Plan 21*, therefore, represents the layout of Millerhill as it is likely to remain into the twenty first century.

My thanks to Mr Simpson, the Area Freight Manager, without whose help and kind accompaniment on a visit to Millerhill this section of the chapter would not have been possible.

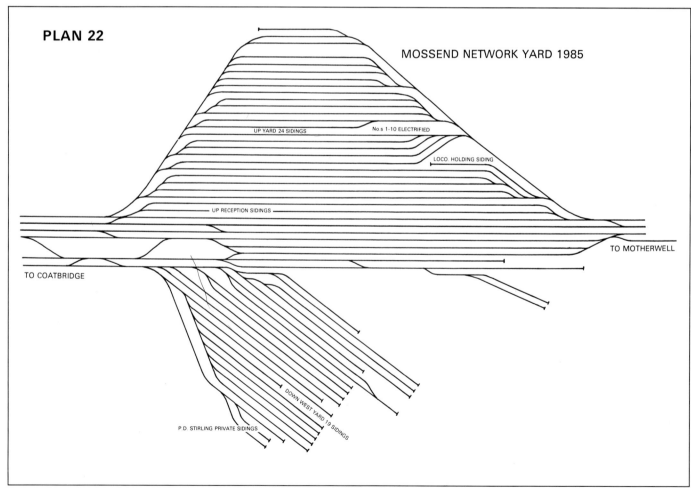

PLAN 22

MOSSEND NETWORK YARD 1985

UP YARD 24 SIDINGS

No.s 1-10 ELECTRIFIED

LOCO. HOLDING SIDING

UP RECEPTION SIDINGS

TO MOTHERWELL

TO COATBRIDGE

DOWN WEST YARD 19 SIDINGS

P.D. STIRLING PRIVATE SIDINGS

# Mossend

The sidings at Mossend grew to serve the steel and iron making industry to the south of Glasgow. By 1943, a daily throughput of 2,000 to 3,000 wagons made them an important and busy marshalling yard. The Ravenscraig steel plant was opened in 1956. This ensured the continuation of heavy freight flows in the Motherwell area, and subsequent concentration of steel making at Ravenscraig, as one of Britain's five major steel plants, has guaranteed the preservation of major marshalling facilities at Mossend. With the introduction of a national Speedlink Network, formed of eleven routes connecting twelve main yards,

Opposite:
A trip freight from Glasgow St. Rollox Works to Mossend arrives at the yard behind Class 27 No. 27047. The six ZRA vans are returning empty to Crewe Works where they will be loaded with more spares.

Mossend became a Network yard. The long parallel sidings, suitable for flat-shunting, were ideal for modern Speedlink traffic, and it was therefore decided to designate Mossend as the major Scottish marshalling yard in favour of the more modern but less suitable and less well-sited Millerhill Yard. In 1980, the network yard at Mossend contained an 'up' and a 'down' half. The 'up' side comprised three loops and 18 through sorting sidings. There were an additional five short single-ended sidings on

In September 1986, the West Yard on the 'down' side of the main line still dealt with a small amount of non air-braked traffic. Here, just such a trip, the 9T22 to Gartcosh, departs behind Class 20 No. 20138.

the eastern fringe of the yard. The 'down' side was more old-fashioned in its layout and contained a mixture of 46 single-ended sorting sidings, many of which were very short by modern standards. The contrasting layouts of 'up' and 'down' sidings meant that concentration of freight working on the 'up' yard was inevitable.

By 1985 the 'down' yard retained only 19 of its original 46 roads *(Plan 22)*. These were in the old West Yard and part of the Steel Yard. The old Goods and Mineral Yards, which were further south, had been closed and, by the end of 1985, it was decided to completely close the 'down'

The P.D. Stirling freight depot lies adjacent to Mossend Yard and it is therefore possible to trip wagons to the depot using the yard pilot rather than a separate trip engine. Here Class 08 No. 08561 shunts an SPA wagon which has travelled north from Cardiff with wire from the Allied Steel & Wire Company.

yard. As the closure of these sidings was being undertaken, so new and exciting developments were underway on the 'down' side of the main line. P.D. Stirling Ltd, a company established in 1870, were developing their Mossend railhead.

The management of the company knew that rail-served terminals would have to be nearer to marshalling yards. This would reduce greatly the cost of trip freights to the terminals and guarantee rapid connections with the new Speedlink network. In the light of these realisations, P.D. Stirling Ltd opened their new rail terminal. Products from china clay to rock salt, coal to limestone, and even oxygen or palatised fertilizer, have been dealt with at the terminal. A turn-round time of less than twelve hours is guaranteed for wagons, and the additional service of repositioning loads for British Railways can be offered within one shift. A rapid turn-round time is essential when one considers that BOC 100 tonne cryogenic tankers cost £125,000 each and convey a pay load of 55 tonnes of oxygen. It is crucial that such a wagon be unloaded and returned to BOC Runcorn within a single shift, as delay means that considerable investment is standing idle

when it should be earning revenue.

A visit to the goods depot in September 1985 revealed a remarkable array of wagons in the company's sidings. HEA 32.5 tonne hoppers were unloading coal from Kellingley Colliery in Yorkshire to be distributed by lorry to various local coal merchants. Two Tiger Leasing PBA china clay wagons had arrived with consignments from St. Blazey in Cornwall for the local paper mills. Two SPA and one SKA wagon were unloading cargoes from Allied Steel and Wire in Cardiff, bound for Newhouse where the steel would be incorporated in reinforced concrete. Two PAA hoppers from Hindlow in the Peak District conveyed limestone which would be unloaded at the Mossend railhead. A single BDA bogie-bolster had brought steel from British Steel Corporation's Skinningrove Works for Clydeside Shipbuilders, Govan, who used the sheets for the ribbing in a new ship. Several other air-braked wagons were to be found in the sidings, and this all in an average weekday afternoon shift. Such versatile terminals in close proximity to modern network marshalling yards are seen as a potential growth area for Speedlink. Indeed, not only bulk handling, but also

warehousing may be possible in such depots.

The railway administration at Mossend controls not only the Network Yard which from the end of 1985 was concentrated in the old 'up' sidings, but also an extensive Traffic Responsibility Area or TRA, A brief description of this area will enable the reader to assess the relative importance of Speedlink traffic and non-Speedlink or block load traffic in the Mossend area. The TRA stretches from Quintinshill, just north of Carlisle, to Coatbridge Freightliner Terminal, a total distance of 90 miles. In the east, it abuts onto the Millerhill AFC, and in the north-west the Rutherglen AFC takes over. There are a total of 70 Railfreight locations and upwards of 2,000 vehicles are under responsibility of the Mossend office at any one time. The majority of these are constantly being moved through the Mossend Network Yard.

The most important location within the Mossend area is of course British Steel's complex at Ravenscraig. Here, steel is produced and sent to various locations throughout the British Rail network. The four separate yards at Ravenscraig are numbered from one to four. Ravenscraig

The overhead catenary of the WCML stretches from Motherwell to Mossend and then on to Coatbridge Freightliner Terminal. The Southampton to Coatbridge liner service pauses at Mossend for a crew change on 11th September 1985. It is hauled by Class 86 locomotives Nos 86323 and 86325.

Crippled wagons from BSC Clydesdale arrive at Mossend West Yard where they will be 'graded'. Class 20s Nos 20123 and 20126 ease the rake of MCV and MDV wagons into the reception sidings before departing on another trip, this time to BSC Ravenscraig.

**Opposite:**

In June 1980, a load of scrap metal heads south from Mossend behind Class 20 No. 20137. The train is the 9T12 from Mossend to Shieldmuir.

## Millerhill Freight

A typical branch line scene at Currie, on the Balerno branch. Class 08 diesel shunter No. D3730 shunts the daily goods train from Millerhill in September 1967.

*G. Turnbull*

No.1 deals with incoming scrap, and lime from quarries at Hardendale. This yard is the oldest in the complex and was constructed in 1956. The No.2 yard receives incoming coal. This was produced by the pit at Polkemmet, but since its closure in 1985 all coal has been supplied from the modern loading terminal at Hunterston. The No.3 yard dispatches trains of finished steel, whereas the No.4 yard, on the eastern fringes of the complex, deals with incoming iron ore from Hunterston and also occasional trains of limestone, again from the quarries around Shap Summit. Finished steel was tripped to the British Steel Corporation site at Gartcosh until its closure in March 1986. Rolled coil is now worked predominantly to Shotton in North Wales and three 1,000 tonne trains are run daily. An additional block load works through to South Wales for eventual processing at Ebbw Vale tin plate works. Occasional trains are also worked to other British Steel Corporation plants at Lackenby, Corby, Scunthorpe and South Wales.

Westbound freights from Millerhill circumnavigated the city of Edinburgh along the district line. In 1963, an unidentified Class 40 locomotive heads a mixed freight past Blackford Hill.

*A. Vickers*

Two pictures taken of the northern approaches to Millerhill Yard show how little changed between 1966 and 1981. In 1966 the E13 trip freight arrives behind 'Clayton' Class diesel-electric No. D8579; the train is made up of engineering stock. To the right are the reception roads to the 'up' yard, and a useful reference point is the water tower in the background. By 1981, the 'up' reception sidings have been removed but the water tower and white hut remain. Class 40 No. 40152 arrives with the 6B85 cement train from Craiginches to Oxwellmains. The freight will be re-engined and re-manned at Millerhill.

*A. Vickers and Author*

A trip freight from Millerhill to Leith South departs from the north end of Millerhill Yard. Class 25 No. 25059 leads a rake of bogie bolsters specifically designed to carry pipes for various North Sea oil and gas projects.

## Table 19
## Mossend Trip Freights
## 1985

| Trip | Loco | To | Depart | Days |
|------|------|----|--------|------|
| TO7 | 37 | Law Junction | 15.30 | SX |
| TO8 | 2 x 20 | Polkemmet | 08.25 | SX |
| | | | 12.37 | |
| T10 | 27 | Bishopton, Greenock & Ladyburn | 06.55 | SX |
| T11 | 26 | Greenock, Ladyburn & Bishopton | 12.50 | SX |
| T12 | 20 | Coltness | 08.00 | SX |
| T14 | 27 | Clydesdale & Imperial | 08.30 | SX |
| | | | 12.15 | SX |
| T19 | 47 | Salkend, Shields & Corkerhill | 08.20 | SX |
| T22 | 26 | Hamilton | 08.35 | SX |
| | | Gartcosh | 12.15 | SX |
| T24 | 26 | Gartcosh | 07.00 | SX |
| | | Shieldmuir | 10.15 | SX |
| | | Ravenscraig No. 1 | 12.20 | SX |
| T30 | 20 | Whifflet | 08.00 | SX |
| | | | 12.34 | SX |
| T31 | 27 | Polkemmet | 08.20 | SX |
| T55 | 47 | Deanside | 10.30 | SX |
| | | | 14.10 | SX |
| T56 | 37 | Deanside | 07.08 | SX |
| T74 | 27 | Russell's & Sighthill | 07.55 | SX |
| | | Russell's | 10.37 | SX |
| T76 | 2 x 20 | Glen Douglas | 06.35 | SX Y |
| T77 | 26 | Shettleston | 08.30 | SX |
| T82 | 37 | Bowling | 09.00 | Sx |
| T83 | 20 | Bowling | 12.57 | SX |
| | | Russell's | 16.25 | SX |
| T86 | 20 | Dumbarton & Dalmuir Riverside | 06.10 | SX |

## Mossend Freight 1988

| Code | From | To | Arr | Dep | Pass | Traffic | Days |
|------|------|----|-----|-----|------|---------|------|
| 6M61 | Gunnie | Clitheroe | 0010 | 0012 | | Cement | MO |
| 6S79 | Oakleigh | Larbert | 0026 | 0030 | | Chemicals | TThO |
| 6DO2 | Inverness | Mossend | 0040 | | | Speedlink | MX |
| 6S43 | Grimethorpe | Mossend | 0043 | | | Speedlink Coal | MO |
| 7D10 | Corpach | Mossend | 0044 | | | Speedlink | MX |
| 7N53 | Mossend | Grangemouth | | 0050 | | Speedlink | MX |
| 6S47 | Dee Marsh | Mossend | 0102 | | | Steel | MX |
| 6S67 | Healey Mills | Gartcosh | 0109 | 0135 | | Speedlink Coal | MX |
| 7D12 | Hunterston | Ravenscraig | 0116 | 0133 | | Coal* | MX |
| 6S58 | Ellesmere Port | Mossend | 0129 | | | Speedlink | MX |
| 6M25 | Mossend | Dee Marsh | | 0137 | | Steel | SX |
| 6S80 | Warrington WOJ | Mossend | 0153 | | | Speedlink | MX |
| 9D37 | Millerhill | Mossend | 0212 | | | Departmental | MX |
| 6S73 | Dover | Mossend | 0224 | | | Speedlink | MX |
| 6S53 | Carlisle NY | Grangemouth | | | 0248 | Oil | MThX |
| 4S52 | Willesden | Coatbridge | | | 0257 | Freightliner | MX |
| 9B78 | Mossend | Millerhill | | 0303 | | Departmental | MX |
| 7E34 | Gartcosh | Healey Mills | 0328 | 0410 | | Speedlink Coal | MX |
| 6D30 | Hunterston | Ravenscraig | 0347 | 0404 | | Iron Ore* | MX |
| 6D49 | Grangemouth | Mossend | 0403 | | | Speedlink | MX |
| 6S81 | Tyne | Mossend | 0410 | | | Speedlink | MX |
| 4S81 | Pengam | Coatbridge | | | 0446 | Freightliner | MX |
| 6D03 | Craiginches | Mossend | 0453 | | | Speedlink | MX |
| 4S83 | Tilbury | Coatbridge | | | 0455 | Freightliner | MX |
| 6D32 | Hunterston | Ravenscraig | 0509 | 0528 | | Iron Ore* | MX |
| 6M24 | Mossend | Dee Marsh | | 0525 | | Steel | SX |
| 7N51 | Mossend | Grangemouth | | 0530 | | Speedlink | MX |
| 6S57 | Sheerness | Mossend | 0534 | | | Speedlink | MX |
| 6M34 | Grangemouth | Dalston | | | 0540 | Oil | WSX |
| 6S74 | Cardiff Tidal | Mossend | 0605 | | | Speedlink | MX |
| 6S82 | Bescot | Mossend | 0620 | | | Speedlink | MX |
| 6V75 | Mossend | Cardiff Tidal | | 0635 | | Steel | MX |
| 6D03 | Fort William | Mossend | 0729 | | | Alumina | MX |
| 6S71 | Whitemoor | Mossend | 0729 | | | Speedlink | MX |
| 7V93 | Mossend | Stoke Gifford | | 0730 | | Speedlink | SX |
| 6V39 | Mossend | Margam | | 0736 | | Steel | SO |
| 6M27 | Larbert | Oakleigh | 0700 | 0740 | | Chemicals | SO |
| 4D45 | Coatbridge | Motherwell | | | 0748 | Freightliner | MSX |
| 7D07 | Hunterston | Ravenscraig | 0743 | 0759 | | Coal* | SO |
| 4D46 | Coatbridge | Mossend | 0750 | | | Freightliner | SO |
| 4S80 | Felixstowe | Coatbridge | | | 0759 | Freightliner | MX |
| 6B64 | Mossend | Millerhill | | 0805 | | Speedlink | MX |
| 6A19 | Mossend | Aberdeen | | 0805 | | Speedlink | MX |
| 4O81 | Coatbridge | Southampton | 0805 | 0810 | | Freightliner | SO |
| 6D27 | Grangemouth | Wishaw | | | 0817 | Oil | TO |
| 6E46 | Mossend | Blyth Dock | | 0840 | | Alumina | SX |
| 6S96 | Parkeston | Mossend | 0844 | | | Speedlink | MX |
| 4D47 | Mossend | Motherwell | | 0859 | | Freightliner | MO |

The Freightliner Terminal at Coatbridge has nine daily departures with a corresponding number of arrivals, and is one of the biggest such terminals on the railway network. Block trains of cement are worked from Clitheroe to Gunnie; block loads of oil are worked to Wishaw Oil Depot from the Teesport and Grangemouth refineries. Speedlink has an important role to play in the distribution of cement, steel products, and general goods traffic. The network yard at Mossend receives up to 400 wagons during each shift and these are marshalled into trunk trains. *Table 19* shows Mossend is one of the busiest yards in the country. The throughput of wagons is regularly in excess of 1,000 and this does not include the various block loads which are stabled or re-manned in the vicinity of the yard.

In September 1985, during the author's visit to the complex, a survey of wagons standing at various major terminals revealed the following:

1. Coatbridge Freightliner Terminal. A total of 90 FGA and FFA Freightliner wagons were standing at this site. This is an indication of the importance of Coatbridge to the Freightliner network and represents a heavy tonnage of traffic transported from the area in Freightliner containers.

2. Gartcosh. A total of 71 wagons were standing in the yard here. Thirty of these were BAA steel bogie-bolsters used in the transport of rolled coil from Ravenscraig, whilst the remainder were a variety of MCV, MDV and MXV scrap-carrying mineral wagons. These were used to transport scrap from Gartcosh to the various other steel processing plants around Glasgow.

3. Gunnie. Here a total of 23 wagons were made up by a selection of PDA and PBA cement-carrying vehicles. The majority of these had arrived from the Ribble Cement Works at Clitheroe.

4. Clydesdale. This location boasted a total of 99 wagons, more than half of which were BDA bogie-bolsters used to carry steel tubes to the BSC plant at Imperial where they were coated prior to their dispatch to Aberdeen. Here they were used in the oil industry.

5. Whifflet. Only five wagons were present at this site. Four of which were used by the Engineering Department.

6. BSC Imperial. A homogeneous population of 32 BDA bogie-bolsters were present in the sidings. All of these conveyed tube for eventual dispatch to Aberdeen.

| Code | From | To | Arr | Dep | Pass | Traffic | Days |
|------|------|------|-----|-----|------|---------|------|
| 6V39 | Mossend | Cardiff Tidal | | 0910 | | Steel | MSX |
| 7Y39 | Mossend | Oban | | 0945 | | Speedlink | MWFo Y |
| 7Y41 | Mossend | Arrochar | | 0945 | | Speedlink | TTho Y |
| 7N67 | Mossend | Stirling | | 1002 | | Speedlink | SX |
| 6D08 | Hunterston | Ravenscraig | 1006 | 1021 | | Iron Ore* | SuX |
| 6M23 | Mossend | Dee Marsh | | 1120 | | Steel | SX |
| 6S75 | Warrington WOJ | Mossend | 1121 | | | Speedlink | MX |
| 7S53 | Hardendale | Mossend | 1145 | | | Limestone | SX |
| 4S89 | Willesden | Coatbridge | 1150 | 1152 | | Freightliner | SO |
| 7Y37 | Mossend | Mallaig Junc. | | 1152 | | Speedlink | SX |
| 7D09 | Hunterston | Ravenscraig | 1208 | 1223 | | Coal* | SuX |
| 6M63 | Mossend | Carlisle | | 1236 | | Limestone | SuX |
| 6S56 | Blyth | Mossend | 1247 | | | Alumina | SX |
| 6D11 | Hunterston | Ravenscraig | 1254 | 1309 | | Iron Ore* | SuX |
| 6D26 | Grangemouth | Mossend | 1345 | | | Speedlink | SX |
| 6S42 | Dee Marsh | Mossend | 1408 | | | Steel | SX |
| 6N59 | Wishaw | Grangemouth | 1402 | 1407 | | Oil | TO Y |
| 6L97 | Mossend | Ripple Lane | | 1440 | | Speedlink | SX |
| 6S51 | Llandarcy | Grangemouth | 1517 | 1519 | | Oil | WFO |
| 7S97 | Gloucester | Mossend | 1559 | | | Speedlink | MSX |
| 7S97 | Bescot | Mossend | 1559 | | | Speedlink | MO |
| 6M27 | Larbert | Oakleigh | 1550 | 1635 | | Chemicals | TO |
| 7D23 | Oban | Mossend | 1607 | | | Speedlink | MWFO Y |
| 7D23 | Arrochar | Mossend | 1607 | | | Speedlink | TTho Y |
| 6V92 | Mossend | Tavistock Junc. | | 1610 | | Speedlink | SX |
| 6L80 | Deanside | Wisbech | | | 1650 | Speedlink | SX |
| 7D13 | Hunterston | Ravenscraig | 1643 | 1703 | | Coal* | SX |
| 6S36 | Dalston | Grangemouth | 1644 | 1653 | | Oil | WSX |
| 4D44 | Motherwell | Coatbridge | | | 1727 | Freightliner | SX |
| 6D14 | Hunterston | Ravenscraig | 1757 | 1817 | | Iron Ore* | SX |
| 4V63 | Coatbridge | Pengam | | | 1815 | Freightliner | SX |
| 6M64 | Craiginches | Willesden | 1821 | 2000 | | Speedlink | SX |
| 7D19 | Corpach | Mossend | 1830 | | | Speedlink | SX |
| 6D20 | Falkland Junc. | Mossend | 1839 | | | Speedlink | SX |
| 6D48 | Millerhill | Mossend | 1854 | | | Speedlink | SX |
| 6B68 | Inverness | Millerhill | 1856 | 2020 | | Speedlink | SX |
| 6S50 | Dee Marsh | Mossend | 1857 | | | Steel | SX |
| 6L86 | Mossend | Whitemoor | | 1920 | | Speedlink | SX |
| 6D21 | Grangemouth | Mossend | 1928 | | | Speedlink | SX |
| 4L81 | Coatbridge | Stratford | | | 1950 | Freightliner | SX |
| 7Y31 | Mossend | Mallaig Junc. | | 1950 | | Speedlink | SX |
| 6V53 | Grangemouth | Llandarcy | | | 1957 | Oil | MWO |
| 6M79 | Mossend | Bescot | | 2025 | | Speedlink | SX |
| 6M38 | Grangemouth | Carlisle NY | | | 2028 | Oil | WSX |
| 6D24 | Hunterston | Ravenscraig | 2013 | 2132 | | Iron Ore* | SX |
| 6S83 | Clitheroe | Gunnie | 2011 | 2030 | | Cement | SX |
| 6S60 | Coedbach | Mossend | 2037 | | | Speedlink Coal | SO |
| 4L95 | Coatbridge | Felixstowe | | | 2046 | Freightliner | SX |
| 6H31 | Mossend | Inverness | | 2059 | | Speedlink | SX |
| 4L97 | Coatbridge | Felixstowe | 2107 | 2109 | | Freightliner | SX |
| 7N69 | Mossend | Grangemouth | | 2112 | | Speedlink | SX |
| 6M28 | Mossend | Willesden | | 2115 | | Speedlink | SX |
| 6R43 | Mossend | Falkland Junc. | | 2202 | | Speedlink | SX |
| 6M83 | Mossend | Warrington Arp. | | 2205 | | Speedlink | SX |
| 6D25 | Hunterston | Ravenscraig | 2222 | 2242 | | Iron Ore* | SX |
| 6M61 | Mossend | Clitheroe | | 2310 | | Cement | FSX |
| 6Y35 | Mossend | Fort William | | 2318 | | Alumina | SX |
| 4S59 | Southampton | Coatbridge | | | 2324 | Freightliner | FO |
| 6A17 | Mossend | Craiginches | | 2334 | | Speedlink | SX |
| 6D22 | Grangemouth | Mossend | 2353 | | | Speedlink | SX |

\* These services pause at Mossend to attach banking assistance for the climb to Ravenscraig

7. P.D. Stirling. A total of 19 revenue-earning wagons were supplemented by twelve ballast wagons at work in the sidings.

Even allowing for a further 300 to 400 wagons standing in Mossend Yard, and 200 to 300 wagons scattered around the Ravenscraig site, only 50 per cent of the wagons under the Mossend TRA were stationary on this particular day in September 1985. Thus over 50 per cent of the TRA's rolling stock was actively involved in revenue-earning service. This remarkably high percentage is a mark of the efficiency of modern Railfreight organisation as epitomised by the new Network Yard at Mossend.

My thanks to the AFA, Mr Hector Leith, and ATA Mr H. McParland whose help was essential with this part of the chapter, and also to Mr McGuigan whose time and company on my visit were of great assistance.

Diesel motive power for freights from Mossend Yard is provided by Motherwell depot. Here, on 8th July 1978 Class 25s Nos 25090, 25064 and 25244 await their next duties.

The daily trip form Millerhill to Haddington is seen at Haddington behind Clayton Type 1 diesel locomotive No. D8583 on 18th September 1967.

*G. Turnbull*

Class V2 2-6-2 No. 60931 accelerates out of Millerhill Yard in the early 1960s with a Millerhill and Aberdeen express freight.

*S. Sellar*

A J38 Class 0-6-0 No. 65915 winds south out of Millerhill 'up' yard in the mid 1960s with a local trip to the Dalkeith area.

*S. Sellar*

**Opposite:**
Mossend 'up' yard viewed from the south in 1972.

*C. Meacher/British Rail*

# Chapter 8

# Perth and Thornton

When the railways were nationalised in 1948, the Scottish Region found itself with an inheritance of 80 or so different marshalling yards. These were chiefly an endowment from the LMS and LNER, and even further back from pre-1923 companies. These marshalling yards were not only located in the wrong places from the operating point of view, but were also small and inadequately equipped. The railway management of the day was frustrated by the sight of so many small yards in Scotland when they viewed the progress at well-known yards south of the border, such as Toton, Hull and Whitemoor. Only four marshalling yards in Scotland had any gravitational aids and many had no reception sidings; some did not even have the incorporation of a shunting neck. Sidings were of inadequate length and predominantly single-ended. Added to these problems, poor telecommunications, ill-equipped administrative accommodation and time-expired trackwork made the freight-handling facilities in Scotland an ideal target for the 1955 Modernisation Plan.

**On 2nd May 1986, Class 20 No. 20224 arrives at the east end of Thornton Yard with the 6G01 trip from Methil Power Station; the empty wagons will be tripped later in the day to Westfield opencast site to pick up more coal.**

Nationalisation swept Scotland clear of old operating boundaries, and the Victorian practices of multiple wagon staging at large centres such as Glasgow or Perth could be abolished. Plans were laid to develop longer freight workings, reduce delays in transit and increase the mileage covered by fully-fitted freights. These plans envisaged the complete closure of many of Scotland's marshalling yards and, by 1956, twelve outdated yards and assembly points had already been closed. The full extent of the modernisation plan for Scotland can be appreciated when it is realised that the eventual plan was to concentrate on freight facilities at five new and ultra-modern yards in Scotland.

Forty six of the old marshalling yards were eventually to be closed with partial closure of a further thirteen. The sites for the five new yards were Thornton in Fife, Millerhill, near Edinburgh, Perth, Cadder, north of Glasgow, and Mossend, south of Glasgow. Only the first three yards were ever constructed, whilst the two to serve the Glasgow conurbation continued in their pre-nationalisation state. The sites for these five yards were chosen after close consultation with local industry, bearing in mind possible future developments in the area. New collieries, the erection of new electricity power stations and expansion of the iron and steel industry were important factors in their development. It is ironical to consider that the construction of the two Glasgow area yards was left until last because of the elaborate work involved in this congested railway area. Because of this delay, new yards were never constructed and, therefore, as the tide turned against the automated hump yard, the yards at Cadder and Mossend continued to flourish when compared to their more modern Scottish partners. In 1986, the main yard in Scotland was Mossend, near Glasgow, which was chosen not only because of its close links with local industry and commerce, but because of the absence of the modern hump shunting facilities present in several of its neighbouring yards.

In 1955, a handful of small yards were retained and modernised where necessary. Mineral sidings at Oakley and Kelty were refitted and a small new yard was constructed at Alloa. The spearhead of the modernisation programme was, however, the concentration of all freight traffic on the five ultra-modern yards.

**The new yard at Thornton had six secondary retarders, four of which are visible in this view of the sorting sidings. In November 1958, the yard is host to mainly coal wagons.**
*C. Meacher/British Rail*

# Thornton Yard

The new yard was laid out in open country, west of Thornton Junction on the 'down' side of the double track main line from Dunfermline. The principal reason behind the choice of this site was the shift in coal producing from the west to the east of Scotland. This, allied to the increasing industrial demands for coal in the west of the country, brought about the need for a marshalling yard to sort traffic from the Fife Coalfield destined for further afield in Scotland. The progressive exhaustion of coal seams in the Lanarkshire coalfield was off-set by big developments in Fifeshire. Seventeen pits and an opencast site were opened in the Cowdenbeath area with a further eleven pits and one opencast site around Thornton. In the late 1950s, the NCB were busily exploring further expansion in Fife. Two new pits were being developed at Bowhill and Dundonald and the country's biggest opencast site was being exploited at Westfield on the line to Kelty.

A large undersea pit at Seafield, near Kircaldy, had an output of 5,000 tonnes of coal a day, as did the Westfield opencast site. The largest development in the area was, however, in close proximity to Thornton Yard itself. A new pit was developed at Rothes with an expected output of 6,000 tonnes of coal a day, bringing the tonnage of new coal mined in the area of Thornton Yard to 15,000 tonnes each day. The justification for the new yard was therefore very clear cut. Whilst the developments at Seafield and Westfield were successful, the fate of the new Rothes pit was much less so. Before any coal was actually mined, underground flooding rendered the site useless and the derelict winding towers stand as a monument to the futile attempts to open a new mine at this site.

The additional workload that the increased coal traffic brought would have broken the back of the existing marshalling facilities in East Fife. In the early 1950s, all coal and goods traffic to or from East and Central Fife was handled in six yards near Thornton station. Four further yards at Burntisland, Townhill and Methil also aided in secondary sorting. Marshalling of freight was a slow business, hampered by double handling and a considerable amount of inter-yard staging. The combined output of these six groups of sidings was only about 900 wagons each day. The new coal traffic was expected to generate up to 3,000 wagons of traffic each day and the new central yard at Thornton was therefore sanctioned. In 1948, 78 acres of land were purchased, and in 1953 construction of the yard itself began.

Thornton Yard was unique in several ways. First, 'up' and 'down' traffic was dealt with in the same set of sidings. This was at variance with previous practice where a separate yard had always been provided for both 'up' and 'down' traffic. The new hump and retarder arrangements were somewhat different from those already in place at yards such as Toton. The hump was built higher than usual and this allowed

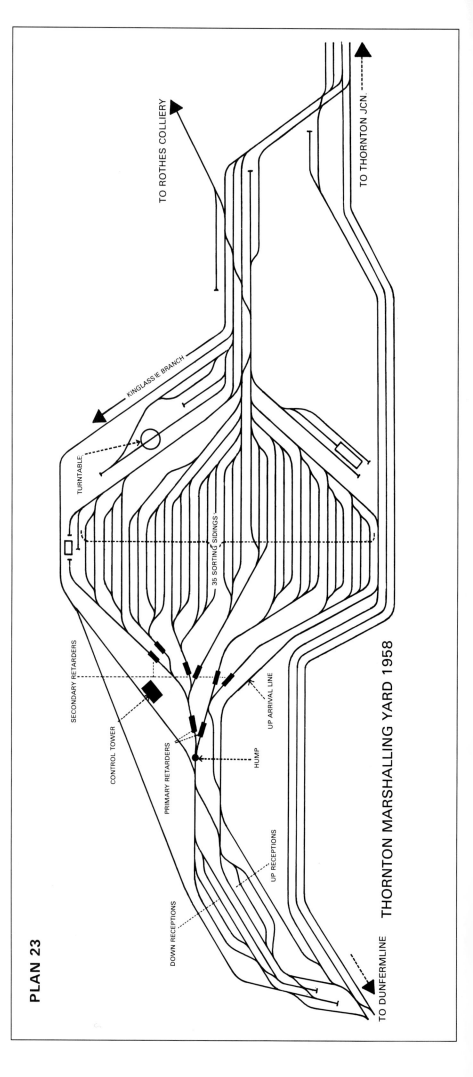

PLAN 23

THORNTON MARSHALLING YARD 1958

TO ROTHES COLLIERY

TO THORNTON JCN.

KINGLASSIE BRANCH

TURNTABLE

35 SORTING SIDINGS

SECONDARY RETARDERS

CONTROL TOWER

PRIMARY RETARDERS

UP ARRIVAL LINE

HUMP

UP RECEPTIONS

DOWN RECEPTIONS

TO DUNFERMLINE

In May 1986, Thornton Yard is pictured at sunrise. The control tower is disused and the retarders have been removed. Apart from stored MDV coal wagons there is very little traffic in the sidings, suggesting that further rationalisation may be on the way.

room for a longer stretch of down gradient at the requisite steepness. The extra length of slope meant that two sets of retarders were installed instead of the usual one. Two primary retarders were placed just below the 'King' points and a further six secondary retarders stood between 'Queen' points and the 'Jack' points where the tracks finally divided out into the sorting sidings. Thornton was also the first yard in which automatic hump shunting equipment, imported from the United States of America, was incorporated. Radar was employed for the first time to achieve a more precise control of the speed of wagons leaving the hump.

The layout of the yard consisted of reception sidings at the west end leading over the hump to 35 sorting sidings. The reception roads were divided into three for 'up' trains and three for 'down', whilst the sorting sidings were in two groups, a northern group controlled by four secondary retarders and a smaller southern group controlled by just two secondary retarders. Access to the 'down' reception sidings was

The 6B66 Speedlink feeder service from Perth to Millerhill winds into Thornton Yard, one hour early on 12th May 1986. The train, hauled by Class 47 No. 47377, will attach empty grain wagons returning from Cameron Bridge to East Anglia and empty china clay vehicles bound for St. Blazey.

controlled by Cluny Bridge signal box which stood at the western entrance to the yards. 'Up' trains had a more tortuous course, leaving the main line at Redford

**The power station at Methil Docks is specifically designed to burn slurry from the Westfield opencast site. In May 1986 Class 20 locomotives Nos 20221 and 20224 head out from the sidings at Westfield with the 6G02 freight to Thornton Yard.**

Junction, running along the southern edge of the sorting sidings on the 'up' arrival line, and finally coming to rest in the three southern reception roads. 'Up' and 'down' through goods lines were also provided which enabled freight trains to skirt the yard perimeter without interfering with marshalling.

As soon as a train arrived it was examined to isolate any wagons that were

defective or that could not be humped because of the nature of their cargo. Wagons with long wheelbases were also removed from the train because of their unsuitability to pass over the retarders. The shunter would then set off along the length of the train to uncouple the wagons and make out a cut card. This showed the number of the siding to which each wagon should be sorted. The cut card was made up

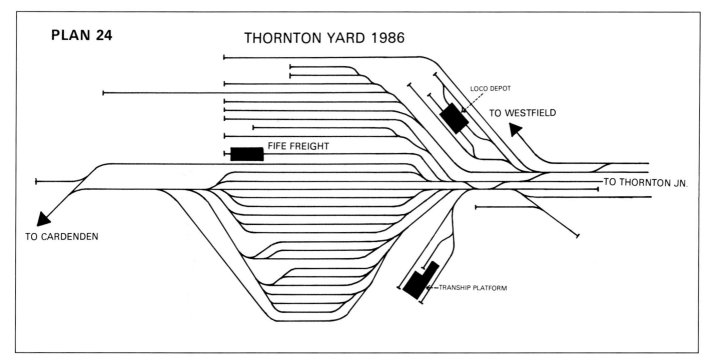

PLAN 24 · THORNTON YARD 1986

LOCO DEPOT
TO WESTFIELD
FIFE FREIGHT
TO THORNTON JN.
TO CARDENDEN
TRANSHIP PLATFORM

by the old-fashioned method of pencil and paper, unlike the American automated yards where shunters were equipped with portable tape recorders into which they dictated the siding numbers for each wagon. The Thornton shunter however, made out his cut card in duplicate and transmitted both copies from his 'Bothy' to the hump inspector's office by pneumatic tube. One copy was retained by the hump inspector so that he could check it against each wagon label as the train was humped, whilst the other copy was placed in the pneumatic tube which deposited it all but literally in the lap of the control tower operator.

Whilst this transfer of information was going on, an 0-6-0 diesel shunter, stationed at the yard's west end for humping, would be placed at the rear of the train. The control tower operator used the cut card to store a list of settings for the automatic shunting apparatus. This enabled 48 consecutive point settings to be operated in sequence as a train of wagons was propelled over the hump. The normal maximum length for a single cut of wagons was six, although the apparatus had the facility to deal with cuts up to a size of twelve wagons. Once the shunting sequence was stored, it was activated simply by depressing a switch and ran spontaneously from the moment the leading wagon of a train was propelled over the hump until the descent of the last vehicle in that train. Manual override was of course possible and a manual consul enabled false shunting movements to be corrected.

Control of hump shunting was effected by hump signals placed at 150 yard intervals along the reception sidings. These were doubled-fronted so that the driver of the shunting locomotive could view them from in front or behind. Three settings were displayed, a vertical line of white lights for hump at normal speed, a diagonal line for hump at low speed and a horizontal line for stop. In the event of any derailments or similar disasters, the hump inspector on the spot had an overriding emergency control

of these hump signals. As the wagons rolled off the hump down to the sorting sidings, their descent was controlled by the two sets of retarders already mentioned. The passage at each cut was translated into a pattern of flickering lights representing track circuits on the descent from the hump crest, and could therefore be followed by the yard controller in the hump panel. Further warning lights were provided to indicate when a siding was approaching capacity and a threatened blockage of a 'Jack' point had to be averted.

At the location of each pair of retarders on the diagram, there were yellow, four-position switches. The four settings were 'A' for automatic, 'O' for open, 'L' for light and 'H' for heavy. Above each of these yellow switches were white six-position switches, again one representing each retarder. These enabled the selection of six leaving speeds ranging from 3mph to 8mph. This allowed the yard operator to assess the distance which a wagon was required to run before it met with wagons already in the siding, and select an appropriate speed. This speed was fed into a computing apparatus which also received information from a radar beam and a weight detector placed at track level. One further factor in the management of the descent of a wagon from the hump was its rollability. There was a wide difference in the freedom with which wagons, fitted with roller and plain bearings, would run and it was therefore necessary to allocate a value for rollability.

Some American marshalling yards installed radar apparatus that could assess rollability. Each siding was accorded its own rolling resistance value according to the gradients and curvature involved in reaching it. The wagon itself was followed by radar, which measured the acceleration rate of each cut. Combining this value with the siding of destination, an accurate assessment of rollability could be incorporated in the computation necessary to bring the wagon to a halt at the correct position in the sorting siding. The variable of rollability escaped accurate computation at

Thornton. This was predominantly because of the increased cost necessary to refine marshalling to this extent. The zenith of automation that was reached in the early 1960s was linked to a feeling that further developments could abolish human intervention in freight shunting altogether. These ideas were extremely expensive and enthusiasm for them waned as wagonload traffic could no longer justify such massive investment.

Although Thornton Yard was a great step forward in British marshalling technology, there were still serious problems in several different areas. The most important of these was the inability of the yard to deal effectively with vacuum-braked wagons. Because of the time taken to separate these wagons from each other and the lack of any automatic couplings which included brake connections, trains with such wagons were halted short of Thornton Yard at staging points. Here the brake connections were separated and the trains continued to the yard as unfitted loads. This was obviously time-consuming and expensive. Even so, remarkable economies were reaped by the new yard. The daily throughput of 900 wagons in the Thorton area was increased to 1,800 after the opening of Thornton Yard in November 1956. The planned maximum capacity of 3,000 wagons a day was never reached, and figures for 1958 indicate that a weekly throughput of 10,150 wagons was the average for that year.

The sorting sidings themselves had a capacity to hold 2,311 wagons and varied in length to 55 to 78 standard length units. Twelve of the sidings were allocated to westbound traffic, whilst the remainder dealt with eastbound freights. There were three principal traffic flows from the yard, each of roughly equal volume. These were to the great steelworks, to other large industries and to public utilities such as wayside depots. Departures ran to the west of the country, northward via the Tay Bridge to Dundee and Aberdeen, and north-westward to Perth, Inverness and beyond.

Several other modern innovations made the yard such a major milestone in freight handling. A 70ft electrically-operated turntable and locomotive stabling point were incorporated purely for use by freight engines. Other modern technology, such as close circuit television and modern lighting masts, were also incorporated at Thornton.

A single 'Railfreight' Class 20, No. 20227, shunts at Cameron Bridge. The freight is the 6G04 trip which has already worked to Rosyth Dockyard and now brings CO2 tanks to the distillery at Cameron Bridge.

Both Perth and Thornton have suffered relatively severely under the rationalising arm of modernisation. The hump and reception sidings at Thornton were closed in the early 1970s, and by 1986 the freight services to the yard were very few in number. Whilst a large number of sidings are retained at Thornton, traffic through them is relatively sparse. The mining in-dustry of the area has, like that in the rest of the country, concentrated on major pits. After the miners' strike only two coal-producing locations were left in Fife. The opencast site at Westfield supplied coal for the power station at Methil. The only other coal-producing site at Seafield was served by merry-go-round trains which plied the route to Longannet Power Station. Other freight traffic using Thornton was brought to the area by either of two trips from Mossend Yard or two of the trunk Speedlink trains which called on their journey between England and Aberdeen.

Traffic was made up predominantly of polybulks containing grain for the distill-iery at Cameron Bridge. Other small con-signments included china clay from Corn-wall, which was staged at Thornton before being tripped to the paper mill at Auch-muty. A new flow of pulp from Scandinavia was being developed in 1986. Ships unloaded at Methil Docks from where wagons were tripped to Thornton Yard, before their final journey via Mossend to Corpach, in the Western Highlands. The MOD at Crombie and Rosyth Dockyard were able to connect their wagons with the Speedlink network at Thornton, as were local customers who used the Fife freight-handling depot built within the perimeter of the main marshalling yard. This variety of Speedlink traffic was handled by a triple-shifted trip locomotive which dealt with each of the local branch lines in succession. The yard pilot engine also tripped daily to Markinch.

Class 08 No. 08515 approaches the buffer stops at Auchmuty, near Markinch. The single wagon of china clay has come from St. Blazey in Cornwall. The Tullis paper mill used to receive up to 50 wagons each day carrying coal, grass, pulp and china clay. The railway now brings just eight PAA hoppers each week; no wonder traffic at the nearby Thornton Yard has fallen so substantially.

In addition to block loads of coal and wagonload traffic dealt with by Speedlink there were several ballast workings from the yard at Thornton. Regular trips were made to Inverkeithing and Ladybank. The modern locomotive stabling point saw an increase in traffic with the closure of Dunfermline (Townhill) depot. Now both freight locomotives and diesel multiple units used for local passenger services are serviced at Thornton Yard.

The massive expansion of coal pro-duction in Fifeshire in the 1950s lead to the construction of a new mechanised hump yard at Thornton. This yard was the first of its kind in the United Kingdom and the forerunner of the proposed modernisation plan for Scotland. It never handled more than 2,000 wagons daily, in spite of a design capacity for 3,000. The nearby Rothes pit, which would have provided much of the work at Thornton, was flooded before any coal was cut. The plethora of smaller pits around Fifeshire have gradually closed leaving only two coal-producing pits in the area. In parallel to this decline in coal traffic, wagonload traffic has also been seriously reduced. Although there has been a fall in freight traffic, a healthy network of branch lines still exists in the Thornton area and papermills, distilleries, collieries, power stations and the Ministry of Defence all benefit from their rail connections via Thornton Yard. Endeavours have been made to attract local customers to a new freight depot within the yard complex at Thornton, and a small amount of traffic will inevitably remain at this location. Many of the sidings still in situ at the yard are used for the storage of vacuum-fitted wagons, and it is probably fair to say that six sidings would be more than adequate to deal with the volume of freight traffic passing through the yard. Whether such further rationalisation will in fact take place is as yet unknown. The sidings at Thornton continue as an important secondary marshalling yard for Speedlink traffic, as well as playing an important role in the handling of block loads of coal.

# Perth

The Perth mechanised marshalling yard was opened on 12th March 1962 and was situated nearly two miles north of Perth station on the western or 'down' side of the main line to Aberdeen and Inverness. It replaced four yards at Perth itself and in addition, no freight was marshalled at Aviemore after the yard was opened, and there were reductions in the pilotage at Stirling as well as at Aviemore. Consider-able benefits were accrued from the closing of the former Perth yards and, as well as centralised marshalling facilities, wagon examination was much simplified at Perth. Freight trains were greatly speeded in their passage through the gateway to the Highlands.

## Layout and operation

The yard at Perth contained six through reception roads alongside the main line. To the west of these and parallel to them were 30 sorting sidings in five groups, each of six sidings. The reception roads had access to the 'up' and 'down' main lines at each end. All five groups of sorting sidings had access to the main lines of the south end of the yard, but at the north end only groups 'A' and 'B' had direct access to the main lines. These two groups of sidings were therefore used for the formation of 'down' or northbound trains. Groups 'C', 'D' and 'E' were used for 'up' or southbound traffic. There were also two small sets of secondary sorting sidings used to fine sort traffic for the 55 different destinations served by Perth Yard. The restrictions of the land available for the construction of Perth Yard meant that reception sidings and main sorting sidings were constructed adjacent to one another. Thus, a train arriving at a recep-tion road had to be drawn forward into the headshunt, which was a single line lying alongside the Almond Valley branch. From the headshunt the train was propelled back over the hump and into the sorting sidings.

The yard was fully mechanised using equipment supplied by the Westinghouse Velac Company. Complete automatic con-trol was exercised by two yard operators who worked in the main control tower. The first section in the control tower was called the signalling panel and all points and signals for movements in the yard, up to the time when the train was propelled over the hump, were controlled from here. The second section was called the humping panel and controlled movements from the top of the hump into the 30 sorting sidings. These were normally conducted automati-cally, but the operator in charge of the panel had an overriding control.

After arrival in the reception sidings a train was prepared for humping. The head shunter uncoupled any vacuum brake con-nections and loosened all screw couplings. A second shunter prepared the train's cut card in duplicate. Pneumatic tubes ran from three points along the reception roads to the yard inspector's office at the hump summit. Cut cards were forwarded to here and the yard inspector kept one copy before sending the second copy, again by pneuma-tic tube, to the yard control tower. Whilst this was underway, the train proceeded into the headshunt, where the final uncoupling of cuts was undertaken. The cut card in the control tower was translated into a perfo-rated paper tape, which was then fed into a tape reader. This programmed the point work for a sequence of different route settings. The whole yard from hump to the far end of the sidings was divided into sections, governed by rail circuits, and not the traditional track circuits. The difference was that the occupation of a rail circuit caused its relay to be energised and picked up, whereas the occupation of a track circuit caused its relay to become de-energised and drop. Rail circuit relays responded more quickly and this was an advantage as cuts were coming down the yard in rapid succession.

There was one primary retarder just below the hump and above the 'King' point, and there were five secondary retard-ers, one for each group of sidings. Each had its own computer and the six separate computers were fed with the following information:

(1) The rollability of each cut on the straight track between the hump and the primary retarder.

131

(2) The rollability of each cut on the curved tracks leading to the secondary retarder. These two measurements were assessed by radar, working on the Doppler principle.

(3) The weight of each cut.

(4) The number of wagons already in the destined siding.

These four readings were used to compute a 'target-buffering speed'. The prescribed speed over the hump was $1\frac{1}{4}$mph. The speed with which a cut made contact with wagons already in the siding was in the region of 4mph. It was of paramount importance that this speed should not be exceeded as a large amount of whisky was marshalled at the yard. To try to avoid variation in the target-buffering speed, a special control board was installed to cope with changing weather conditions. Frost, wet rails and wind speeds were all accounted for and each siding had a separate indicator. This showed the speed at which wagons were moving down it, so that minute to minute adjustments to the retardation of wagons could be made.

The panel on the humping side of the control tower was an illuminated diagram, which showed the progress of various cuts and the position of the points from the 'King' switch onwards. Above the panel were various indicators; one showed the destined siding for the first five cuts coming

over the hump, and another indicated the number of wagons already occupying each siding. There was even a facility for correcting siding occupation when a wagon stopped short of the other vehicles in the siding. Perth was one of the most sophisticated yards of its day. Signalling was of a conventional nature with position light signals which indicated three instructions, 'stop humping', 'approach the hump', and 'hump'. The pilot engine also had cab signals which worked in correspondence with the hump signalling. These were worked by induction from an aerial wire with four different frequencies available for transmission. Lighting at the yard was mounted on five 150ft steel lattice towers. This was supplemented in the wagon repair area by two 55ft towers, carrying single floodlights.

The yard at Perth was unusual in its layout and the adjacent construction of reception sidings and sorting sidings was a considerable disadvantage at the yard. Up to ten minutes was added to each shunting movement by the necessity to draw trains from the reception siding into the headshunt before they could be sorted. Even so, the yard was handling 1,300 wagons a day in 1962. It was anticipated that a further increase to 1,500 each day would arise when the working at Aviemore and Stirling had been altered. An important surge in traffic occurred in the seed potato

season. This brought in up to 250 extra wagons each day. The timetable of 1962 records 58 scheduled arrivals and 54 departures, quite a contrast to the Perth Yard of the 1980s. The various branch lines around Perth have all been closed. The main line to Aberdeen closed in the 1960s and the remnant of this line to Forfar was closed in the early 1980s. Perth Yard thereby lost its rail connections with the large Central Scottish hinterland and acted simply to connect local traffic to the Speedlink network. The Inveralmond Distillery, adjacent to the yard, still forwards some of its whisky by rail. There are other local customers like Perth goods depot as well as larger freight customers such as Shell, who have an oil distribution point at Perth. Daily freights from both Inverness and Aberdeen to Mossend Yard both call at Perth. There is also an afternoon Perth to Millerhill Speedlink feeder service. These three freight services and their return workings provide a stark contrast to the early 1960s, when over 100 trains a day utilised Perth marshalling yard. The retention of a recognisable marshalling yard at Perth must be under review given the decrease of freight traffic in the area. Perth Yard has however rendered 20 years of active service to the Scottish Region and, like its partner at Thornton, led the way for many of the larger English yards built later in the 1960s.

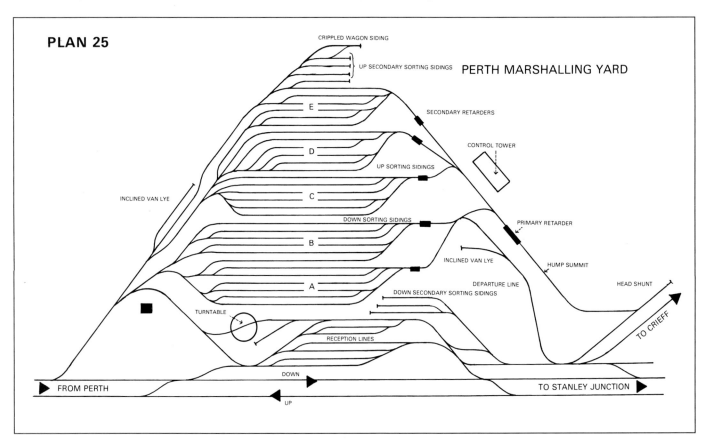

PLAN 25

PERTH MARSHALLING YARD

# Chapter 9

# Tyne Yard

Tyne Yard, at Lamesley near Newcastle upon Tyne, was built as part of the North Eastern Region modernisation plan. It was completed in 1963 and took over the work formerly carried out in nine small shunting yards all of which were virtually unchanged since their construction 50 years earlier. It was scarcely surprising that the North Eastern Region should pursue the improvement of its freight-handling facilities as approximately three-quarters of its total revenue was generated by the haulage of freight. There were 75 separate marshalling yards within the North Eastern Region, and such a large number of separate shunting yards brought about heavy delays for traffic travelling more than the shortest of journeys.

The marshalling yard modernisation plan had four clear aims:

1. An improvement in the transit times for individual wagons by drastically reducing the number of yards in which they had to be marshalled.
2. The development of a new pattern of sectionalised train working. This new scheme enabled groups of wagons to travel in a formation which aided the easy removal of sections at other main marshalling yards. The benefits of such a system were greatly improved transit times from the main north eastern yards to all parts of the country.
3. The provision of staging sidings which was a new feature in marshalling yards. These roads would allow the re-crewing and changing of locomotives on through freight services within the perimeter of the marshalling yard.
4. The provision of easy access to express through freights, whether block or sectionalised, for urgent and perishable shipments. This was regarded as an important development which would allow the railway to cater for the increase in short-term industrial ordering.

The three yards at Tyne, in Newcastle, Tees, near Middlesbrough and Healey Mills, near Wakefield, were built with these four aims in view. They all had extensive connections with the surrounding hinterland and a complex network of local services to collect traffic for trunk trains. Local yards and factories were served up to three times a day when the volume of traffic warranted. The yard at Tyne took over the work of the smaller sidings at Heaton, Blaydon, Low Fell, Park Lane, West Dunston, Addison and Tyne Dock. Thus all the freight traffic from both heavy and light industries on Tyneside and Wearside was marshalled at one central yard. Whereas prior to 1963 there had been four evening freights from Tyne & Wear bound for York (Dringhouses) 'Up' Yard, there was now only one from Tyne. In a similar fashion, all trunk freight services from the region were considerably rationalised. Tyne Yard made up trains bound for King's Cross, Whitemoor, Healey Mills, Hull, Glasgow, Carlisle, York, Darlington, Edinburgh, Tees and Doncaster. Further connections were available to more distant destinations by means of the train sections already mentioned. Thus a portion of wagons destined for Washwood Heath, Mottram, Bristol, Cardiff, Birkenhead, Liverpool, or Doncaster could be despatched on a trunk service to Dringhouses where rapid transfer to another main line freight was available.

Obviously such radical reallocation of freight services had effects throughout the North Eastern Region. Not only were local yards in Tyne & Wear closed, but major yards further afield at both Darlington and Shildon found their workload considerably reduced. The sidings at Shildon, which were reopened during World War II because of an increase in freight traffic, had handled 1,500 wagons daily. The concentration of East Coast Main Line freight services on York (Dringhouses) Yard had brought about a gradual reduction in the number of wagons shunted at Shildon. With the opening of Tyne Yard, this figure fell to only 300 wagons each day and Shildon was removed from the main freight network. The Croft Yard at Darlington was similarly affected and relegated to a secondary yard, dealing only with local traffic.

## Construction and Layout of Tyne Yard

The new Tyne Yard occupied a 135 acre site at Lamesley, four miles to the south of Newcastle upon Tyne. It was constructed on the west side of the main line and adjacent to the Team Valley Trading Estate. The area of land upon which the yard was constructed contained ten coal seams and although these were relatively thin, mining of the deposits would have caused up to 7ft of subsidence. A guarantee that they would not be mined was therefore extracted from the National Coal Board. The site was low-lying, and no less than 2,250,000 cubic yards of filling material had to be imported to level out the area. Most of this material was brought from adjacent colliery tips but 300,000 cubic yards came from Corbridge on the Newcastle to Carlisle line. Here an elderly tunnel was converted into a railway cutting and the soil from the site taken to Lamesley. A new cutting to the north of Durham yielded a similar tonnage of soil for the project. Construction work at the yard itself began in December 1959 and this tackled the diversion of the River Team to the west of the yard, along with the re-routing of the East Coast Main Line (ECML), to the east of the marshalling yard.

Local roads were diverted around the yard and five new bridges were constructed to carry the railway tracks in the area of the hump over the main link road from the A1 to the Team Valley. To the north of the yard a new road overbridge was constructed. It stretched a total of 435ft across 22 running lines and carried the local road known as Smithy Lane. Three further bridges were also required to carry the tracks over the National Coal Board's Bowes Colliery Waggonway. The yard itself was designed to handle between 3,000 and 4,000 wagons daily. Both 'up' and 'down' traffic were dealt with over a single hump at the south end of the complex. Altogether the yard contained 104 sidings comprising 54 miles of track. At the south end there were 14 reception sidings leading to the main hump. From here there radiated 48 sorting sidings into eight separate fans. A small secondary hump at the northern end of the yard controlled the access to 21 secondary sorting sidings; these were used for fine shunting of local traffic.

Twelve departure sidings were divided into two groups; six for northbound traffic and six for southbound. In line with the North Eastern Region freight handling policy, an additional nine staging sidings were provided within the yard perimeter. Four of these were for southbound traffic and five for northbound. Trains could arrive in the reception sidings from both north and south. 'Down' arrivals ran straight into the reception roads from the 'down' goods line, whereas 'up' arrivals traversed a long flyover from the 'up' goods line. This structure was 2,660ft long and provided access to the five eastern reception roads. The gradient profile of the yard was a conventional one with a maximum grade of 1 in 16 over the main hump. The wagon retarding equipment consisted of two fully automatic primary retarders, each 68ft 6in long. Beyond these were eight semi-automatic secondary retarders, each 78ft 6in long.

The new yard was controlled by two separate signalling installations. These were both housed in the control tower at the south end of the sorting sidings. The main

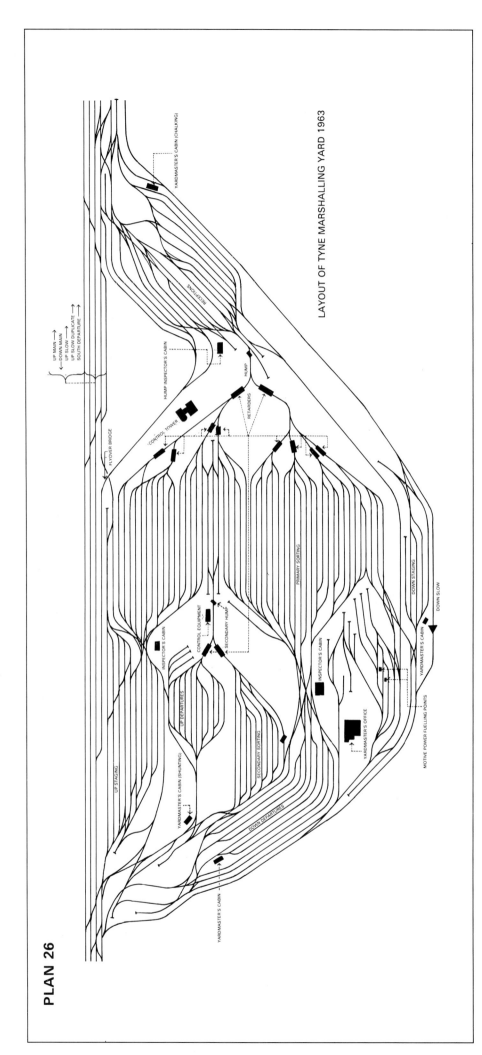

**PLAN 26**

LAYOUT OF TYNE MARSHALLING YARD 1963

UP MAIN →
← DOWN MAIN
UP SLOW →
UP SLOW DUPLICATE →
SOUTH DEPARTURE →

FLYOVER BRIDGE

YARDMASTER'S CABIN (CHALKING)

HUMP INSPECTOR'S CABIN

RECEPTIONS

HUMP

'CONTROL TOWER'

RETARDERS

INSPECTOR'S CABIN

CONTROL EQUIPMENT

SECONDARY HUMP

PRIMARY SORTING

INSPECTOR'S CABIN

UP DEPARTURES

SECONDARY SORTING

YARDMASTER'S OFFICE

YARDMASTER'S CABIN (SHUNTING)

UP STAGING

DOWN DEPARTURES

YARDMASTER'S CABIN

DOWN STAGING

DOWN SLOW

YARDMASTER'S CABIN

MOTIVE POWER FUELLING POINTS

signal room dealt with entry into and egress from the yard, as well as the adjacent main line. In the north the fringe boxes were at Gateshead and Norwood whilst in the south trains were handed on to Newton Hall and South Pelaw signal boxes. This area contained thirteen route miles of track which were resignalled with modern colour-light posts and power-operated points. Although such a power signal box is regarded as small by today's standards, the installation was considered to be exceedingly complex in the early 1960s. It controlled 70 main colour-light signals and 80 subsidiary ground signals as well as 101 pairs of points. In the other half of the control tower was the signalling panel for the marshalling yard itself.

The approach to the hump was controlled by an elevated, three-aspect, double-sided, lunar, white shunt signal. This could display three indications of 'stop', 'slow' or 'fast'. The second subsidiary signal controlled the release of train engines after their arrival in the reception sidings. Additional ground signals were provided to deal with shunting movements within the reception roads. The signalman in charge of the yard tower also controlled 64 electro-pneumatically operated points. The cylinders in the yard compressor generated air at a pressure of 35 psi. This was then distributed throughout the hump area in $1^{1}/_{2}$in plastic pipes. At each set of points a diaphragm valve controlled the access of air to the point motor. These valves were operated by switches at a voltage of 24 volts dc.

**March 1963, and the North Eastern Yard at Tyne is nearing completion. Only the administrative block and the 'down' recessing sidings are still to be completed.**

*British Rail (Eastern Region)*

Illumination of the yard at Tyne was provided by eight 150ft high steel lighting towers. Banks of 1,500 watt lamps arranged at the top of each tower guaranteed a light intensity throughout the yard of approximately one lumen per square foot. All external lighting was automatically extinguished in daylight hours by means of a light sensitive relay. The central office was built at the north west end of the yard, adjacent to a small diesel servicing depot. The new yard not only utilised the latest construction techniques of the day, but incorporated a considerable amount of second-hand material recovered from abandoned lines elsewhere around the country. Seventy five per cent of the trackwork came from closed lines, whilst the steel girders used for the main span of the flyover came from a bridge on an abandoned line near Selby.

## Operation and Traffic

The Tyne Yard, like most other major marshalling yards, received trains of wagons and sorted them into groups for particular destinations. Maximum efficiency was achieved when each arriving wagon was connected with the first available forward service. As each train arrived in

the reception sidings, its consist was recorded by a member of the yard staff and transferred to the hump tower on a cut card. This enabled up to 50 separate cuts to be stored and then automatically executed in the proper sequence.

In 1963, there were five 350hp shunting locomotives used for humping. A smaller 204hp locomotive was used in the secondary sorting sidings. Communication between the control tower and the shunting locomotive was possible using three different systems. The traditional colour-light signals were supplemented by a loudspeaker network which allowed communication with most parts of the yard. Provision was also made for a unique system of inductive radio telephone communication. A display of the hump signal was repeated in miniature inside the locomotive cab, in addition to which the controller had traditional radio communication with the driver of the shunting locomotive. Such innovations were particularly helpful when shunting had to be undertaken in adverse weather conditions.

The progress of shunting was monitored by staff in the control tower using two separate charts. The reception planning chart listed the arrivals, and their consist and enabled the yard controller to select the order in which arriving trains were to be sorted. The second, a sorting area chart, provided an up to date record of the siding occupancy beyond the hump. Entry into the sidings themselves was controlled by two sets of retarders. The first fully automatic pair of rail-brakes were controlled by both a rail weighbridge and radio equipment which assessed the rollability of wagons.

The secondary retarders were designated as semi-automatic. The yard controller was able to select one of six leaving speeds after having assessed rollability, weight and siding occupation. The main sorting sidings were somewhat shorter than elsewhere in the country and restricted to 50 standard length units.

The north east was a heavy industrial area, and during the early 1960s up to 26 million tonnes of coal were forwarded annually from Tyneside. The shipyards on the Tyne and Wear were the largest in the world and generated considerable rail-hauled traffic. The large steelworks at Consett, together with smaller plants on Tyneside, were also heavy rail users. Because Tyneside was an industrial area which received raw materials and dispatched finished products, there was a

heavier flow of freight trains into the area. The raw materials were more easily transported by rail, whilst finished products left the area by both road and rail. Most raw materials were purchased from suppliers in England and Wales and the freight movements from the south were therefore heavier than those from the north. The yard was accordingly laid out to favour this flow of traffic; the reception sidings being at the south end of the yard.

**By May 1963, the last touches were being applied to the track and turnouts in the hump area at Tyne Yard.**

*British Rail (Eastern Region)*

In 1963, a new freight depot at Gateshead was opened by Dr Beeching. This, the Tyneside Central Freight Depot, stood on a 22 acre site formally occupied by Park Lane Marshalling Yard and Borough Gardens Motive Power Depot. Smalls and sundries were collected from an area of 700 square miles. The new depot at Gateshead took over the work of ten older establishments at Newcastle (Forth), Gateshead (Eldon Street), Anfield Plain, Birtley, Blyth, Blaydon, Chester-le-Street, Consett, Fencehouses and South Shields. Thirty four sidings saw an average weekday traffic amounting to 500 wagon loads of smalls, and up to 200 wagons of full loads traffic. Many of these wagons were tripped to Tyne Yard where they were able to join long-haul services. Tyne Yard, however, never operated at its full design capacity. Even with considerable steel and coal traffic as well as the large volume of local smalls and wagonload freight, the number of vehicles passing over the hump each day rarely reached 3,000. A document of the day records optimistically that, "after the radical improvement of shipbuilding, steel and other industries in the North East that is hoped for, Tyne Yard will be handling its maximum daily throughput of 4,000 wagons". This optimistic industrial forecast was never realised, and the industries cited for improvement continued to decline.

**In June 1963 a container van is retarded in the primaries at Tyne.**

*British Rail (Eastern Region)*

# 1970 to 1985

During this fifteen-year period there were four major changes which brought about a drastic decrease in traffic at Tyne Yard. Coal shipment from the Durham and Northumberland coalfields was legendary but also inefficient. The 1970s saw the modernisation and the rationalisation of this operation. Smaller staithes served by wagonload traffic were discarded in favour of new coal terminals designed to deal with merry-go-round trains. This allowed an increase in colliery to terminal working and a concomitant decrease in coal wagons passing through Tyne Yard. Shipbuilding yards along the Tyne and Wear were also closing. The work that remained was sporadic and the supply of raw materials increasingly road-handled. The heavy flow of smalls and wagonload traffic from the

**Table 20**
**Tyne Yard Primary Sorting Siding Allocation**

| | | Capacity Wagons |
|---|---|---|
| 1. | Carlisle Fitted | 54 |
| 2. | Carlisle Unfitted | 54 |
| 3. | Tweedmouth | 45 |
| 4. | Millerhill Fitted | 42 |
| 5. | Millerhill Unfitted | 43 |
| 6. | Millerhill Class 8 | 48 |
| 7. | Fruit, Fish and Meat empties | 59 |
| 8. | Cripples | 52 |
| 9. | Blaydon | 45 |
| 10. | Hoppers | 51 |
| 11. | Med/C. flats/Highs/Lows/Lowfits | 57 |
| 12. | Vans/Vanfits/Palvans | 56 |
| 13. | Hawks | 52 |
| 14. | Gateshead Freight Terminal | 56 |
| 15. | Wearmouth and South Dock | 60 |
| 16. | West Hartlepool | 70 |
| 17. | S.B's - D.B'S - B.B's: Plates-Pipes-Tubes | 30 |
| 18. | Tees Up (Class 8 South) | 69 |
| 19. | Tees Down | 70 |
| 20. | Empties Other than those shown | 58 |
| 21. | Alnmouth | 53 |
| 22. | Morpeth | 58 |
| 23. | Forth-Elswick-Scotswood | 61 |
| 24. | Heaton | 51 |
| 25. | New Bridge St. and Trafalgar | 48 |
| 26. | X.P.O.s and Minfits | 47 |
| 27. | Hebburn | 57 |
| 28. | Jarrow | 58 |
| 29. | Tyne Dock | 50 |
| 30. | High Shields | 45 |
| 31. | Secondary Sort | 39 |

**Engine Line**

| | | Capacity Wagons |
|---|---|---|
| 32. | Secondary Sort | 43 |
| 33. | Brakevans | 47 |
| 34. | Doncaster Fitted | 55 |
| 35. | Doncaster Unfitted | 49 |
| 36. | King's Cross Proper | 51 |
| 37. | Mirfield Unfitted | 56 |
| 38. | Normanton Unfitted | 55 |
| 39. | York Fitted | 51 |
| 40. | York Unfitted | 57 |
| 41. | Dringhouses Fitted | 57 |
| 42. | Washwood Heath and Normanton Mid. Fitted | 62 |
| 43. | Whitemoor Fitted | 67 |
| 44. | | 66 |
| 45. | Hull and Leeds Fitted | 62 |
| 46. | Darlington | 56 |
| 47. | Ferryhill and Coxhoe Containers | 51 |
| 48. | Consett | 59 |

**Tyne Yard Secondary Sorting Siding Allocation**

| | | Capacity Wagons |
|---|---|---|
| S.1 | To Weigh | 14 |
| S.2 | Brake Vans | 19 |
| S.3 | Special Wagons | 21 |
| (S.4/1 | Felling Pelaw | 25 |
| (S.4/2 | Cadbury Fry | |
| S.5 | West Jesmond | 24 |
| (S.6/1 | T.V.T.E and B.R.S Low Fell | 26 |
| (S.6/2 | D.E. Storeyard Low Fell | |
| S.7 | Forwarded braked traffic to Gateshead Freight Terminal | 28 |
| | S7/1 King's Cross via (Ferme Park) | |
| | S7/2 Mirfield LNW | |
| | S7/3 Normanton L&Y | |
| (S.8/1 | Lanchester | |
| (S.8/2 | Bishop Aukland | 33 |
| S.9 | Riding Hills via North Wylam | 32 | Cont. |

| **Tyne Yard Secondary Sorting Siding Allocation continued** | | |
|---|---|---|
| S.10 | Hexham | 42 |
| S.11 | Haltwhistle | 41 |
| S.12/1&3 | Ponteland | 37 |
| S.12/2 | Rowntree's Siding | |
| S.13 | West Dunston | |
| S.14 | Washington, Durham via leamside | 40 |
| S.15/1&2 | Riverside Branch | 42 |
| (S.16/2 | Monkseaton | 47 |
| S.16/2 | Tynemouth & North Shields | |
| S.17 | Parcy Main & Albert Edward Dock | 41 |
| S.18 | Blyth & Tyne | 57 |
| (S19/1 | Birtley & Chester le Street | 32 |
| (S19/2 | Kimblesworth & Annfield Plain | |
| S.20 | Spare | 20 |
| S.21 | Not to Go | 16 |

Tyneside Central Freight Depot was short-lived. In line with British Railways policy, a move away from such traffic to block trains meant that many customers abandoned the railway for road haulage firms. Recent investment in Speedlink freight handling has won back some wagonload customers, and the old freight depot at Gateshead now handles traffic from several local customers. This traffic is dispatched on two daily Speedlink departures, neither of which requires marshalling at Tyne Yard. The steel industry in the north east was vitiated by the closure of Consett steel-

**This rather splendid aerial view, dating from September 1963, shows the yard fully completed and operational. Even the diesel servicing shed has been erected, although no trackwork is yet laid.**

*British Rail (Eastern Region)*

works in 1980. This further reduced traffic at Tyne Yard and with the closure of the Consett branch in 1983 came the closure of the hump at Tyne.

In 1977, there were 266,039 wagons humped at Tyne Yard. These arrived on 11,480 trains and gave a weekly average of 5,000 wagons over the hump; that is 1,000 each day. The total annual train throughput at Tyne was however 22,114.

**J27 class 0-6-0 No. 65796 embarks on the climb along the flyover leading to the reception sidings at the south end of Tyne Yard in about 1964.**

*M. Dunnett*

These trains conveyed 505,731 wagons, and it can thus be seen that only 50 per cent of the wagons arriving at Tyne Yard in 1977 were sorted by using the hump. In 1983, the number of trains arriving at Tyne Yard was 16,903; only 2,701 of these were sorted by propelling over the hump. Thus, from a total of 309,240 wagons to enter the yard, only 56,474 were dealt with over the hump. The absolute decline in traffic as well as the move away from hump-shunting for the more modern air-brake wagons brought about the closure of the hump at Tyne Yard. Subsequent rationalisation has meant the complete closure of the reception sidings and a considerable reduction in the number of sorting sidings available for traffic. Shunting is conducted from the north end of the sidings of which there are still 34. Twenty one roads at the western side of the sorting sidings are used for Speedlink traffic while the others are used for storage of spare and condemned wagons. The 'up' departure sidings and the secondary sorting sidings have been allocated to the Regional Civil Engineer. The 'up' staging sidings are heavily used by southbound Speedlink traffic, whereas northbound traffic uses the sorting sidings as mentioned previously.

In 1985, a selection of local customers provided rail traffic to connect with the Speedlink network at Tyne Yard. Fresh fruit and vegetables were supplied to the greenmarket at Low Fell, and chocolate was dispatched by rail from the Rowntree factory at Coxlodge. ICI supplied explosives for the National Coal Board via their sidings at Callerton. Further chemical traffic was transported to the Ciba Geigy plant at Hexham.

The shipyards at both Wallsend and Sunderland were supplied by rail. Local scrap dealers at Blaydon, Dunston, St. Peters and Sunderland availed themselves of the rail network. As well as the Tyneside Central Freight Depot at Gateshead, Redland Tiles utilised an adjacent siding to receive bricks from around the county using Speedlink wagons. A large tonnage of aggregates and lime were dispatched from the various companies operating from the quarries around Ferryhill. Blue Circle Cement had a terminal at Heaton which was rail-served each morning. Further customers included National Smokeless Fuels at Derwenthaugh, Jobling Purser at Elswick, British Steel Corporation at Jarrow and the MAT Car Company at Gateshead. A total of nine local feeder

### Table 21
### Tyne Yard Departure Pattern
### (Including Main Line and Local Freight Trains)
#### 1963

| Time | WTT or Class | Days | To | From | Notes | |
|---|---|---|---|---|---|---|
| 12.05 | 4E.13 | MX | Doncaster | Millerhill | Up staging Tripped ex Borough Gardens. Att. to through train (up staging) | M |
| 12.05 | L.27 | MYSU | Consett | | | M |
| 12.10 | 7 | MX | Carlisle | | | M |
| 12.30 | 7 | MX | Tees | | | M |
| 12.30 | L.16 | MX | Heaton and West Jesmond | | 11 & S.5 | M&S |
| 12.40 | 4E.37 | WO | Stratford | Dundee | Up staging | |
| 12.45 | 8 | MXSU | Tees via Pelaw | | | M |
| 12.55 | 4S.05 | MX | Millerhill | Whitemoor | Down staging | M |
| 1.00 | 9T.85 | MX | Percy Main | | S.16/1 S.17/ | S |
| 2.30 | L.15 | MO | Heaton | | 11 | M |
| 2.45 | 7D.37 | MX | Darlington | | | M |
| 3.15 | 9T.61 | MX | B. & T. Line | | S.18 | S |
| 3.30 | 4G.98 | MX | New Bridge Street | York | Det. x through train down staging | M |
| 3.40 | 7 | MX | Carlisle | | | M |
| 3.45 | 4S.07 | MX | Millerhill | Whitemoor | Down staging | M |
| 4.00 | L.15 | MO | Tynemouth and North Shields | | S.16/2 | S |
| 4.10 | L.18 | | Argyle Street SX and Morpeth | | | M |
| 4.30 | L.29 | | Borough Gardens | | | M |
| 4.45 | 4S.30 | MX | Whitemoor | Millerhill | Att. to through train Up staging | M |
| 4.55 | 7B.62 | MX | York Yard | | | M |
| 5.00 | L.10 | | Bishop Auckland (& Lanchester SX) | | S.8 | S |
| 5.00 | 9T.85 | MX | Tynemouth and North Shields | | S.16/2 | S |
| 5.00 | 7 | | Carlisle | | | M |
| 5.10 | 6D.77 | | Tees | | | M |
| 5.15 | L.11 | SX | Durham Goods | | S.14 | S |
| 5.25 | 4S.09 | TO | Millerhill | Burton | Down staging | M |
| 5.25 | L.20 | | New Bridge Street (SO & Rowntrees (SX) | | S.12/2 (SX) | S.O.(M) SX S |
| 5.35 | 6S.11 | | Millerhill | | | M |
| 5.40 | L.1 | SX | I.C.I. and Hexham | | S.10 | S |
| 5.45 | L.4 | | Hebburn to South Shields & Tyne Dock (Q) | | | M |
| 5.50 | 4G.99 | MX | New Bridge Street | York | Det. x through train down staging | M |

Cont.

## Tyne Yard Departure Pattern 1963 continued

| Time | Train | Code | Destination | | Notes | |
|------|-------|------|-------------|---|-------|---|
| 6.00 | 9P.28 | MX | Wearmouth to South Dock | | | M |
| 6.00 | 4E.01 | MX | King's Cross | Millerhill | Up staging | M |
| 6.00 | L.21 | | Team Valley T.E. and Low Fell Store Yard (SX) | S.6/1&2 SX | S.6 / S.6/1 (SO) | S |
| 6.00 | L.9 | | Kimtlesworth P.O. | | S.19 | S |
| 6.00 | L.6 | SX | Chaytons Bank & Pelaw | | S.4 | S |
| 6.15 | L.5 | | Jarrow and Tyne Dock | | | M |
| 6.15 | L.29 | | Hawks Yard | | | M |
| 6.20 | L.17 | SX | Ponteland P.U. | | S.12 except /2 | S |
| 6.30 | 4N.32 | MTFX | Dringhouses   Millerhill | | Att. rear x through train | |
| 6.50 | 4N.32 | TFO | Dringhouses | | Up staging | M |
| 6.40 | 7S.00 | MXQ | Upall | Ollerton | Down staging | M |
| 7.00 | 8S.23 | | Millerhill | | | M |
| 7.00 | L.21 | | Blaydon Station Yard | | | M |
| 7.05 | 7 | | Mirfield | | | M |
| 7.20 | 7 | MO | Carlisle | | | M |
| 7.30 | 4S.16 | MX | Millerhill | Victoria Dock | Att. to through train Down staging | M |
| 7.40 | L.28 | SX | West Dunston and Dunston Factories | | S.13 All (Rough) | S |
| 7.45 | L.16 | MX | | | Empties ex M. (G) for Washington | |
| 7.55 | 4E.33 | MX | Whitemoor | Millerhill | Att. to through train Up staging | M |
| 8.00 | L.15 | MO | | | Empties ex M. (G) for Washington | |
| 8.15 | L.24 | | Consett | | | M |
| 8.15 | 7 | MX | Carlisle | | | M |
| 8.15 | L.29 | | Forth Elswick and Scotswood | | | M |
| 8.30 | L.20 | | Borough Gardens and Cadbury/Fry | | S.4/5 | M&S |
| 8.45 | L.21 | | Heaton | | | M |
| 9.00 | L.2 | SX | Newburn and Riding Mill | | S.9 | S |
| 9.00 | L.14 | | Riverside P/U | | S.15 | S |
| 9.30 | 8 | | Tees (via Pelaw) | | | M |
| 9.30 | L.3 | SX | Stations Hexham to Haltwhistle | | S.11 | S |
| 9.30 | L.5 | | Tyne Dock | | | M |
| 9.40 | L.6 | | New Bridge Street | | | M |
| 9.45 | 40.92 | | Holborough | Uddingston | Up staging | M |
| 10.00 | 9T.78 | | Percy Main | | S.17 inc. traffic off 4G.37 | S |
| 10.30 | L.19 | SO | B. & T. & Morpeth | | S.18 | S |
| 10.40 | L.4 | | Hawks Yard | | | M |
| 10.45 | 6E.70 | | Ollerton | Millerhill | Upstaged | M |
| 10.50 | 4S.19 | MX | Millerhill | King's Cross | Down staged | M |
| 11.00 | 4S.21 | MX | Millerhill | Whitemoor | Att. to through train Down staged | M |
| 11.10 | L.29 | | Forth | | | M |
| 11.15 | L.7 | SX | Hebburn and Jarrow | | | M |
| 11.40 | L.6 | | Borough Gardens | | | M |
| 11.55 | 7L.24 | | Normanton | | | M |
| 12.05pm | L.23 | SX | Hawks Yard | | | M |
| 12.30 | L.5 | SO | West Dunston | | S.13 Rough | S |
| 12.40 | 6B.63 | | Dringhouses | | | M |
| 12.45 | L.13 | SX | Birtley and Chester P/U S.19/1 | | | S |
| 12.45 | 4N.28 | MX | Carlisle | Whitemoor | Att. to through train Down staged | M |
| 12.50 | L.20 | SX | Durham Goods P.U. | | S.14 | S |
| 13.00 | 8 | | Tees (via Pelaw) | | | M |
| 13.00 | L.19 | SX | B&T and Morpeth | | S.18 Only | S |
| 13.45 | L.23 | SX | Team Valley T.E. and Felling (Cad/Fry) | | S.6/1 & S.4/2 (ex 6G.24 H.Mills) | S |
| 13.15 | 7 | | Carlisle | | | M |
| 13.30 | 7 | | Doncaster | | | M |
| 13.45 | 7 | | West Hartlepool | | | M |
| 14.00 | 8 | | Darlington | | | M |
| 14.05 | | | West Hartlepool | | | M |
| 14.05 | 4S.37 | SX | Uddingston | Cliffe | Down staged | M |
| 14.10 | 7S.02 | MX | Uphall | Gainsboro' | Down staged | M |
| 14.15 | L.14 | | Borough Gardens | | | M |
| 14.30 | 8S.27 | | Millerhill | | | M |
| 14.30 | 9T82 | SO | Percy Main | | S.15/2 van & S.15/1 van | S |
| 14.15 | L.22 | SX | Rowntrees att. vanfits | | S.12/2 | S |
| 14.45 | L.7 | SX | Hawks and Washington | | S.12/2 | S |
| 14.45 | L.7 | SX | Hawks and Washington | | | M |
| 15.00 | L.8 | SX | Jarrow and High Shields | | | M |
| 15.15 | 7 | | Carlisle | | | M |

services from Tyne Yard provided connections for all of these local industries.

*Table 22* shows the 17 main Speedlink services which were marshalled at Tyne Yard in 1985. Most activity took place in the yard between 17.00 and 02.30. This uneven distribution of services brought many to suggest that re-timetabling could considerably reduce the number of sidings required at Tyne Yard. This idea has been actively incorporated in the plans to rationalize Tyne Yard as part of the East Coast Main Line electrification project.

## 1986 and the Future

In 1986, the number of Speedlinks using the yard had increased to 23 each day, reflecting a nationwide boom in Speedlink services. The local trip workings remained essentially unchanged, the only alteration being a new trip to Austin and Pickersgill Shipbuilders in Sunderland. 'Down' Speedlink traffic was handled in 15 roads that were part of the old primary sorting sidings. These varied in length to 50 to 60 standard wagon lengths (SWL) and provided more than adequate facilities for northbound Speedlink traffic. The 'up' traffic was dealt with in a variety of sidings; four 'up' staging roads averaged 85 SWL in capacity, six 'up' departure roads, and four of the old primary sorting sidings were also used for 'up' traffic. The secondary sorting sidings were used by the Civil Engineer. The 21 roads in this yard average between 20 and 30 SWLs in capacity. The wagon throughput for Speedlink traffic had increased somewhat to 700 wagons daily, whilst the Engineer's yard saw four booked trains per shift with men signed on for two shifts per day. The weekend however, saw as many as 20 trains using the civil engineering yard. Block loads of coal and steel, as well as chemicals, were also staged and re-manned in the sidings at Tyne Yard.

The future requirements of the Railfreight network must include a yard at Tyne. A provisional plan envisages eight 120 SWL capacity sidings at Tyne Yard. These would be electrified throughout and handle all Speedlink traffic for the Newcastle area. A budget of £1,000,000 has been allocated to concentrate freight facilities on the 'up' staging sidings and access to these roads will be improved by knocking out several supports from the old flyover at Tyne Yard to allow both 'up' and 'down' traffic direct lines into the new yard. The engineering sidings are likely to remain and may well expand to include the old 'down' departure sidings.

The locomotive stabling point is likely to become the main diesel depot on Tyneside should plans to close Gateshead by May 1988 come to fruition. Further attempts to concentrate Railfreight facilities at Tyne Yard are centred around the installation of a rapid loading bunker for mgr coal services. This would have replaced existing facilities at the nearby Swallwell Coal Disposal Point. After considerable discussion the decision was made to construct a new coal collection point at Wardley on the site of the old NCB workshops and not at Tyne Yard. The capacity of the new site to

| Time | WTT | Days | Destination | | Staging | Class |
|---|---|---|---|---|---|---|
| 15.20 | 40.93 | WFO | Holborough | Uddingston | Up staging | M |
| 16.30 | L.25 | SX | Consett | | | M |
| 17.10 | 7 | | Carlisle | | | M |
| 17.15 | L.13 | SX | Forth and New Bridge Street | | | M |
| 17.30 | | | Tees (via Pelaw) | | | M |
| 17.35 | 7S30 | | Millerhill | | | M |
| 18.00 | L.30 | | Borough Gardens | | | M |
| 18.15 | 4B.66 | SX | Dringhouses (1. Provincial Fish. 2. Peterboro 3. King's Cross Fish & Goods. 4. Leeds and Bradford Tobb. 5. Dringhouses ex Washington) | | | M |
| 18.30 | L.31 | | Borough Gardens | | | S |
| 18.30 | 9P.36 | SX | Wearmouth and South Dock | | | S |
| 18.50 | 4B.49 | | Dringhouses | | | M |
| 18.55 | 6S.29 | | Millerhill | | | M |
| 19.00 | 9T.82 | | Percy Main | | S.15/1 | S |
| 19.05 | 4E37 | Th.SO. | Stratford | Dundee | Up staging | M |
| 19.40 | L.8 | SX | Tyne Dock | | | M |
| 20.05 | 4E.36 | | Whitemoor (1. Lincoln. 2. Spalding 3. Whitemoor) | | | M |
| 20.15 | L.26 | SX | Consett | | | M |
| 20.25 | 7 | | Carlisle (L. Rd.) | | (Block Load) | M |
| 20.30 | 9T.83 | SX | Percy Main | | S.15/2 | S |
| 21.00 | 8 | | Tees (via Pelaw) | | | M |
| 21.00 | L.30 | | Borough Gardens | | | M |
| 21.10 | 4S.35 | | Aberdeen | King's Cross | Down staged | M |
| 21.15 | 4E.04 | | King's Cross | Millerhill | Up staged | M |
| 21.20 | 5B.68 | | York Yard | | | M |
| 21.25 | 4S.39 | T.Th.O | Uddingston | Cliffe | Down staged | M |
| 21.30 | 6K.27 | | Morpeth and Alnmouth | | | N |
| 21.50 | 5K.26 | | Tweedmouth | | | M |
| 22.00 | L.31 | | Borough Gardens | | | S |
| 22.40 | 4N.34 | | Dringhouses | Millerhill | Down staged | M |
| 25.00 | 4H.09 | | Hull (1. Hull 2. Leeds 3. Dringhouses) | | | M |
| 23.00 | 8 | | West Hartlepool | | | N |
| 23.10 | 4S01 | SX | Millerhill | Ferme Park | Att. to through train Down staging | N |
| 23.25 | 7 | | Carlisle | | | M |
| 23.30 | 8 | SX | Tees (via Wearmouth) | | | N |
| 23.45 | 4S.00 | | High Street | Hull | Att. to through train Down staging | M |
| 23.55 | 4S.04 | | Millerhill | King's X | Att. to through train Down staging | N |

**Key**

| | | |
|---|---|---|
| WTT | = | Working Timetable (Where no WTT headcode is quoted these trains run on as-required basis, ie if there was traffic.) |
| Class | = | Class of Freight |
| L | = | Local Tripper. In 1966 these became 8 or 9/P |
| M | = | Main Sorting Sidings |
| S | = | Secondary Sorting Sidings |
| Days | = | Runs Monday to Saturday unless stated. |
| From | = | Runs from Tyne Yard unless stated. |

**Table 22**
**Tyne Freight – May 1985**

**Speedlink**

| Code | From | To | Arr. | Dep. |
|---|---|---|---|---|
| 6E84 | Stranraer | Scunthorpe | 00.14 | 02.40 |
| 6N64 | Duxford | Tyne | 00.22 | |
| 6S71 | Whitemoor | Mossend | 01.08 | 02.00 |
| 7S59 | Tees | Stranraer | 01.48 | 04.16 |
| 4S39 | Dagenham | Millerhill | 02.25 | 02.50 |
| 6E95 | Stranraer | Tyne | 03.23 | |
| 6E53 | Hoo Junction | Tyne | 07.45 | |
| 7E63 | Carlisle | Tyne | 16.45 | |
| 6S53 | Tyne | Dundee | 17.45 | |
| 6S63 | Scunthorpe | Aberdeen | 18.24 | 19.55 |
| 6S66 | Tees | Stranraer | 19.15 | 21.50 |
| 6E96 | Stranraer | Tyne | 21.00 | |
| 6S92 | York | Aberdeen | 21.01 | 22.50 |
| 6E87 | Millerhill | Parkeston | 21.06 | 21.50 |
| 6E89 | Aberdeen | Immingham | 22.36 | 00.01 |
| 6S81 | Tyne | Mossend | | 23.05 |
| 6E86 | Mossend | Parkeston | 23.41 | 00.48 |
| 6S96 | Parkeston | Mossend | 23.50 | 01.41 |

load five merry-go-round trains each day will generate over £100,000 each week for British Rail in the North East. Such important revenue is crucial to the continued success of Railfreight.

There is also potential for further increase in local traffic around Tyneside. The possibility of delivering domestic coal to Follingsby is being explored. This would be transported north in FPA container wagons, similar to those used on the Anglo-Scottish coal trains. A new block train of dolomite from Ferryhill in County Durham travels via Tyne Yard to Gartcosh in Glasgow. This, along with the other aggregates traffic from Ferryhill, is an important arm of Speedlink operation in the county. The carriage of both food and drink to Tyneside Central Freight Depot in Gateshead has increased considerably in the last two years, and it is hoped that this increase will continue. A total of thirteen men on each shift operate the sidings at Tyne Yard, and when the new and compact Speedlink yard is opened in conjunction with the East Coast Main Line electrification, this staff may be further reduced, creating a highly efficient, high capacity, modern Speedlink yard.

My thanks to Mr K. Dickins, the Acting Area Operations Manager, Mr Walter Anderson, Mr Trevor Scott, the Area Freight Assistant at Tyne Yard and Mr Ken Groundwater, also of Tyne Yard.

**Trip Freights**

| Code | Destination | Dep. |
|------|-------------|------|
| 9P02 | Belford, Tweedmouth, Berwick | 05.30 |
| 9P03 | Heaton, Coxlodge, Callerton | 06.15 |
| 9P04 | TCFD, Jarrow, Simonside | 06.45 |
| 9P06 | Riverside, Ferryhill | 08.50 |
| 9P08 | Greenmarket, Dunston, Hexham | 08.50 |
| 9P10 | Simonside, Tyne Dock, Morpeth | 11.00 |
| 9P11 | Heaton, Coxlodge, TCFD | 11.30 |
| 9P13 | Elswick, Heaton | 23.15 |

In addition, five turns numbered 9J91 to 9J95 existed to carry local mineral traffic as required.

**Right:**
The hump was devoid of trackwork when this picture was taken in February 1986. The few remaining sorting sidings can be seen in the background.

Two views of the secondary sorting sidings at Tyne which show very little change in the track layout in this part of the yard. In 1974, however, the sidings are filled with

revenue-earning rolling stock as Class 40 No. 40006 heads north with a ballast working. By 1986, a similar engineering freight, hauled by Class 47 No. 47335, finds only engineer's vehicles in the background.

*T. Heavyside and Author*

**Right:**
Class 08 No. 08578 passes the TOPS office in the main administrative block at Tyne Yard. Behind it lies the Civil Engineer's yard and, beyond that, the 'up' Speedlink sidings.

142

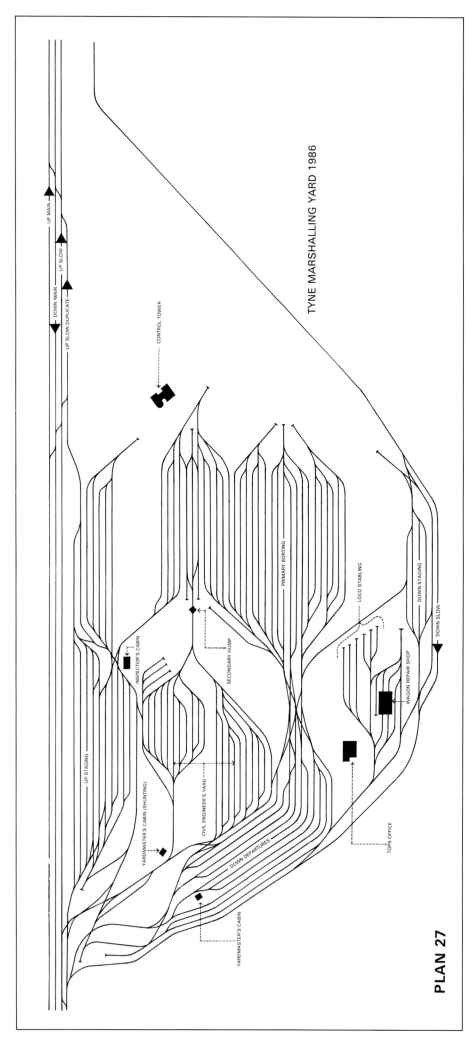

**TYNE MARSHALLING YARD 1986**

UP MAIN

DOWN MAIN

UP SLOW

UP SLOW DUPLICATE

CONTROL TOWER

PRIMARY SORTING

LOCO STABLING

DOWN STAGING

DOWN SLOW

INSPECTOR'S CABIN

SECONDARY HUMP

WAGON REPAIR SHOP

UP STAGING

YARDMASTER'S CABIN (SHUNTING)

CIVIL ENGINEER'S YARD

DOWN DEPARTURES

TOPS OFFICE

YARDMASTER'S CABIN

**PLAN 27**

'Down' Speedlink traffic at Tyne Yard uses two fans of the old sorting sidings on the western fringe of the yard. On 12th June 1986, Class 08 No. 08578 shunts PCA cement wagons from Eastgate cement works. They are bound for Carlisle and will travel forward on the 6M26 Speedlink working later in evening.

**Tyne Freight**

In May 1970, Class 17 No. D8594 leaves Pallion with the afternoon trip freight to Tyne Yard. The train is seen here passing Millfield.

*I. Carr*

Opposite:
An early morning freight from Tyne Yard approaches Belmont Junction on its way to Durham Gilesgate goods depot. On 15th April 1966, Class 24 No. D5105 has mainly coal in tow as it trundles past with its short trip freight.

*I. Carr*

The 9P12 trip freight from Tyne Yard pauses at Newcastle (Central) station on 4th May 1970. Class 17 No. D8597 hauls just two cattle wagons which are probably bound for rural Northumberland.

*I. Carr*

The 9P03 trip freight from Jarrow to Tyne Yard passes Pelaw behind Class 17 No. D8590 on 21st July 1969.

*I. Carr*

A mixed freight from Tyne Yard to Doncaster (Belmont) passes Penshaw North Junction on the Leamside line on 18th August 1967. In pouring rain, Class 20s Nos D8310 and D8315 from York shed are followed by construction materials and then coal in unfitted mineral wagons.

*I. Carr*

Opposite:
Even in the late 1960s, considerable tonnages of freight traffic began to travel as block loads which avoided re-marshalling in the major hump yards. This view at South Pelaw in 1969 shows two such loads. Class 24s Nos D5102 and D5108 pass with a train of iron ore for Consett as a block load of coal empties heads for Tyneside.

*I. Carr*

The 6E97, Mossend to Ripple Lane Speedlink passes Low Fell behind Class 37 No. 37146 on its approach to Tyne Yard.

Cement from the Blue Circle works at Eastgate is sent as a block load to Tyne Yard from where individual wagons are distributed throughout the North of England and Scotland on Speedlink services. Class 37 No. 37059 arrives at Tyne with the 6N31 from Eastgate, in 1985.

Another block load to avail itself of the sidings at Tyne to pause for re-manning is the evening oil train from Jarrow to Stanlow. On 12th June 1986, Class 56 No. 56045 pauses as Class 08 No. 08577 busies itself with 'up' Speedlink traffic.

Opposite:
The ubiquitous Class 37 locomotive remains the same, but all other aspects of Tyne freight have changed. The 6S63 Scunthorpe to Aberdeen Speedlink passes Low Fell on 11th June 1986, and behind Class 37 No. 37209 are 17 air-braked wagons. The rear half of the formation conveys sand from the Thrislington Quarry to Montrose, in Scotland.

An aerial view, taken in October 1962, shows the 'up' and 'down' yards at Thornaby nearing completion, whilst the old Newport yards have all but disappeared.

*British Rail (Eastern Region)*

Looking more like a model railway than part of Britain's largest capacity yard, the tracks from the 'down' hump to the sorting sidings are laid out in June 1962.

*British Rail (Eastern Region)*

# Chapter 10
# Tees Yard

Teesside is Britain's largest industrial area and it was because of massive post-war development around the Tees that the marshalling yard at Thornaby was built. The yard had the distinction of a capacity to sort 7,500 wagons each day, making it the largest marshalling yard in Europe. Construction began in 1959 and was completed for the official opening on 21st May 1963.

In 1963 the rail freight carriage from Teesside totalled 5.5 million tons; an alarming drop from the 1959 figure of 9 million tons. Because of this fall in rail traffic many branded the yard a 'white elephant' from its first day. However, freight tonnages rallied in the mid 1960s to reach 6.5 million tons in 1965. As a result the yard was well-used for the first five years of its existence. Whilst the freight traffic on Teesside thrived in the mid 1960s, the yard's future seemed secure. The yard was, however, doomed from the day of its opening. This can be seen from official British Rail policy of the day, which, speaking of block trainload working said: "This pattern of freight working the railway studiously encourages and is developing". Official policy was to move towards block trains, but it was always acknowledged that there would be 'substantial quantities' of less than block trainload dimensions. Today such traffic is handled by the modern Speedlink system.

After considering the planning and construction of the yard, this chapter will trace the changes in its fortunes as they relate to the changes in local industry and the pattern of local freight train operation.

## Planning and Construction

As already mentioned, the massive increase in heavy industry on Teesside created many difficulties for British Railways in the 1950s. The steel and chemical plants on both sides of the river generated vast amounts of freight traffic. Bulk raw materials including coal, coke, limestone and iron ore were all rail-borne on their journeys into the area. Coal originated from the pits in Durham and Northumberland, whilst coke was produced at several north eastern coking plants. Iron ore was imported at South Bank and carried to local blast furnaces as well as along the coast to Skinningrove. 'Exports' from the area were equally numerous. Against the backbone of finished steel, a plethora of bulk liquids and powders were conveyed from ICI plants in the area. The collected annual tonnage of these products, (excluding coal and coke), was 9 million tons. All this traffic had to be marshalled in the Newport yards constructed in 1910. The Newport complex consisted of two 'up' and two 'down' yards, unchanged since their initial construction 50 years earlier. Traffic could be delayed for days at this bottleneck — indeed, wagons could be lost for weeks!

In the light of such operating difficulties, two solutions were implemented. The first was the construction of Tees Yard to 'unclog' the bottleneck, and the second was the development of block trainload working. This continues today (see later).

The site chosen for the yard, to the south of the River Tees, two miles upstream from Middlesbrough, was already occupied by the four Newport yards. Thus a step-wise construction plan was needed to avoid too much disruption to the freight services already using these yards. In addition to the area covered by the Newport yards, extra land to both the north and south was needed to fit the much larger Tees Yard on to the south bank of the river. The main line from Darlington to Middlesbrough was diverted south around the site in two stages. In 1958 it was moved south of Thornaby motive power depot, and then in 1959 the southerly diversion was extended east, along the side of the main Thornaby to Middlesbrough road. Much of the northern edge of the 200 acre site, bounded by the River Tees, was marshy ground. To raise the level of this area, 250,000 tons of filling material were deposited along the river bank. In addition to these major earthworks, a tributary of the Tees (Stainsby Beck), had to be rechannelled and bridged by seven separate rail bridges.

The Tees Yard complex was made up of the 'up' and the 'down' yards. These were almost identical and functioned as separate yards. Trip freights ran between the two, allowing traffic to change direction. The combined yards contained 66 miles of track, 75 per cent of which was reclaimed from closed lines. Even two footbridges, which allowed access to the yard across the main line, were taken from closed stations. The entire complex was constructed with a view to possible future overhead electrification, and as such the clearance of all overbridges was higher than in other yards.

The siding layout was of a traditional pattern with arrival, sorting and departure sidings. In the 'up' yard twelve reception sidings led to a single hump, from which 40 main sorting sidings radiated. At the west end of the yard there were twelve 'up' departure roads which were also used as 'up' staging roads for block trains requiring a crew change. The 'down' yard, whilst similar, had a couple of structural differences to cater for a rather different flow of traffic. Twelve reception sidings here led onto a main hump, but the three most northerly roads also had access to a smaller secondary hump. From here wagons could enter roads 2 to 8 in 'A' fan. This arrangement was to allow two trains to 'hump' simultaneously; the secondary hump dealing with the stream of empty wagons returning from all over the country to Teesside. Empty wagons, being obviously lighter, only one retarder (the secondary retarder of 'A' fan) controlled their descent into the main sorting sidings. At the east end of the 'down' yard there were eight departure sidings, whilst six 'down' staging sidings were provided at the western entrance to the yard.

In addition to the complex trackwork, three new signalling installations were built to control the yard and its environs. One box controlled the 'up' yard whilst the other had two panels; one for the 'down' yard and a second for the main line from Bowesfield to Middlesbrough West. In each yard the signalling comprised a fixed three-aspect signal, ('stop', 'approach', 'hump'), with additional two-aspect ground signals for 'engine release' and the return of shunting engines into the reception sidings. All points were electro-pneumatically controlled, air being pumped along plastic pipes by a compressor located next to each of the two main signal boxes. It is interesting to reflect that the comparatively small 'panel' for the main line replaced four manually-operated boxes which between them contained 375 mechanical levers. These were Thornaby East, Old River, Foreshore and Newport East boxes.

Communication between the yard controllers could be effected in one of three ways. As well as an internal telephone system a loudspeaker network was installed throughout the yard. Thirdly an inductive radio-telephone communication allowed visual and audible instructions to be sent directly to the cab of the shunting engines. This was particularly important when fog enshrouded the yard, obscuring the shunting signal from a driver's view. Illumination and communication are of equal importance in the operation of a modern marshalling yard. At Tees, eleven 150ft lighting masts were arranged to provide a light intensity of not less than 0.6ft candles throughout the yard. (Very bright moonlight, sufficient to read by, is 0.4ft candles.) To do this banks of 1,500 watt bulbs topped the masts. These were automatically extinguished during daylight by means of light-sensitive relays.

**Overleaf:**
**By June 1963, the yards at Thornaby were fully completed and operational, as this picture from one of the lighting masts illustrates. It was at approximately this point that the A19 road bridge was constructed over the yard in the 1970s.**

*British Rail (Eastern Region)*

152

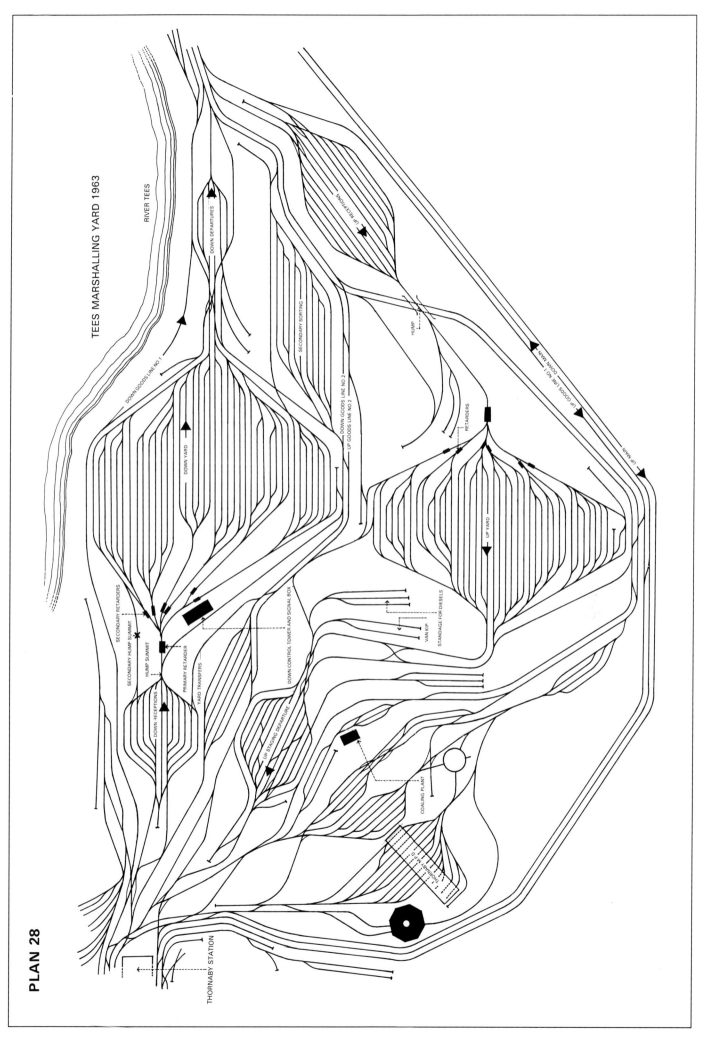

**PLAN 28**

TEES MARSHALLING YARD 1963

153

# Operation

The yard was a 'semi-automatic' install-ation. This means that whilst the primary retarders were fully automatic, the secon-dary ones were manually-operated by the signalman. He was able to select one of six leaving speeds for a wagon. This was done by combining the weight and rollability with an 'eyeball' assessment of its speed off the hump. One drawback of such a system is the problem of fog although this is a relatively rare occurrence in the area.

Freight trains were assembled in the traditional way; all wagons bound for a particular destination being directed into one siding. From here, timetabled services would depart, regardless of their load. Thus a train to Tyne Yard might consist of anything from one to sixty wagons; indeed some wagons might be delayed by as much as twenty four hours if the siding for Tyne was filled before they were sorted. Two charts to monitor wagon flow were kept in the control tower. The Reception Planning chart enabled the yard controller to select the order in which incoming trains should be sorted so that the maximum number of wagons were connected with imminent departures. This system often fell down because of the necessity to shunt whole

**In March 1963, the signalmen in the 'down' control tower concentrate as wagons are sorted over the hump.**

British Rail (Eastern Region)

trains to 'sort out' as few as one or two wagons which were urgently required for an approaching departure. This factor highlights one of the fundamental operating difficulties faced with the 'hump' method of shunting — "The inability to superimpose a 'business' priority on a system which is primarily geographically organised."

The second chart was a Sorting Area chart. This contained details of the accumu-lating wagons in each siding. Not only were these charts an operating aid, but their data was used to alter the freight timetable to avoid any recurrent overcrowding in the yard.

Each individual arrival was inspected by a 'checker' who recorded the various wagons on 'cut cards'. The details of these were forwarded to the control tower, where the signalman could pre-set as many as 50 consecutive route settings. These would be executed automatically by a 'feedback' from the track circuits. This ensured that each set of wagons was safely into its siding before the next route was set. The steepest gradient in the yard was 1 in 16 on the 'down' yard secondary hump (empty wagons). In spite of this gradient, all humps were negotiable by main line diesel locomo-tives of Type 3 and below.

As previously stated, the yard at Tees was, in its heyday, the largest marshalling yard in Europe. While its nominal capacity was to sort 7,500 wagons each twenty four hours, it very rarely had to deal with such a level of traffic. However, it is of interest to note that the record number of wagons dealt with in one shift in the 'down' yard was 2,000. Mr Noble, an Area Supervisor at Tees, recalls the day when technical prob-lems prevented 'humping' in the 'down' yard for eight hours. The backlog that resulted meant that 35 trains, containing a total of more than 2,000 wagons, were dealt with over the two humps of the 'down' yard within the eight-hour shift that followed. Quite a record for the 1960s when one considers that Europe's largest marshalling yard, Hamburg Maschen, has a capacity of 11,000 wagons each day, but with 128 primary sorting sidings.

# Changes in the 1960s and 1970s

Why has the yard at Tees been rationalised so radically? The answers are to be found in two main areas. Firstly in the changes within local industry, and secondly within national railway operating practice.

As mentioned earlier, the industry of Teesside generated 9 million tons of freight traffic each year in the late 1950s. Nearly all of this traffic was routed through the new Tees Yard. Much of it was carried in wagons grossing less than 15 tons and constructed of wood. The majority of wagons were unbraked and restricted to a maximum speed of 30 or 40mph. However, as industry changed, so too did the railway.

Collieries in County Durham have closed in their dozens during the last 25 years. The National Coal Board pursued a policy of concentrating on 'super pits' with profitable coal seams and a long-life expectancy. In a similar fashion the railway has streamlined its operation. Life-expired and small-capacity wagons have been gradually replaced by, first the HTV 21 ton coal hopper, and then the 32 ton HAA hopper. Not only have the wagon loads become heavier but the trains larger. No longer does a trip engine trundle up the branch to a colliery and pick up a couple of 16 ton mineral wagons, which then join their fellow wagons in the melee of the marshalling yard. Coal is carried to customers in bulk loads of 1,000 tons and more. Wagons are unloaded in half an hour and are then returned to pick up more coal and thus earn more money for the railways.

Coal usage on Teesside has also changed substantially. Whilst all ICI complexes were coal-fired in 1960, they were completely oil-fired by the late 1970s. The pendulum has swung back towards coal with a recent announcement that ICI Wilton is returning to coal firing. The works will receive 10,000 tons of coal each week via two daily merry-go-round trains. The export of coal from Tees Dock declined in the 1960s and 1970s and has turned full circle with the recent import of Polish coal at the Redcar mineral terminal. Thus another large flow of rail traffic has disappeared.

The steel industry has also changed beyond recognition. The plethora of furnaces and foundries which stretched east from Middlesbrough have closed. This leaves the high capacity blast furnace at Redcar as the only steel-producing works in the area. The steel industry of Teesside used to produce a wide variety of semi-finished products which were forwarded by rail to hundreds of small customers, but now the pattern has changed. Large volumes of unfinished steel leave the yard at Lackenby for secondary plants at Workington, Stoke, and Corby. Railway operation has changed to fit this situation. In the early 1960s, all traffic from the steelworks was carried in unfitted, low-capacity wagons. With the introduction of vacuum-braked steel wagons it was possible to start running 'block loads' of steel and thus avoid Tees Yard. At first, vacuum-fitted SPV wagons were marshalled into trains of 500 tons but, as the reader will be aware, such a train is small when compared with the 2,000 ton 'Steel-liner' from Lackenby to Corby.

As well as coal and steel, iron ore was an important commodity in the area. Imports of the mineral through Cargo Fleet were rail-borne on their journey to the local blast furnaces. In the 1970s, the high capacity ore terminal at Redcar was constructed. From here iron ore was transported by conveyor belt to BSC Lackenby. British Railways were however responsible for the carriage of ore to Consett (8), Workington (3), and Hartlepool (2) — figures in parenthesis being the number of trains each day. As steel making ceased at each of these locations, so too did the rail traffic.

The area in which the carriage of freight has been most radically altered is mixed goods, or 'smalls'. A sketch of the situation as it stood in the 1960s is helpful in understanding the important changes which have occurred in the last 25 years. Small goods stations around the region were closed in the 1950s in order to concentrate traffic on larger terminals at Stockton, Middlesbrough, Darlington and Bishop Aukland. Each evening, approximately 50 wagons would be dispatched from a goods yard like Stockton. They would be bound for destinations as widespread as King's Cross, Edinburgh and Cardiff. After remarshalling at Tees Yard, they would head off into the night on one of the overnight express freights. Similarly, many large companies in the area would dispatch finished goods to small customers by rail. ICI Haverton Hill used to ship bagged fertiliser out in 12 ton five-plank open wagons. Farmers, both locally and indeed throughout the country, would pick up their fertiliser at the local goods station, be it Whitby or Welshpool. In order to maintain this service, British Railways had to spend large amounts of capital for the upkeep of a grossly underused and decaying infrastructure. The subsequent changes in both terminals and wagons are well documented elsewhere. The important changes are best summarised as "a move towards privately-owned rail terminals and the efficient, computer-controlled, use of modern high-capacity freight stock".

When considering the demise of Tees Yard, the important factors are thus both local and national. In the particular case of Tees the change in local railway practices can be gauged very simply. In the 1986 freight timetable five block loads of steel and one block load of limestone travelled from Lackenby Yard every twenty four hours. The average tonnage of each train was 1,500 tons. In 1960 this traffic would have all been carried in wagons of, on average, one fifth the capacity of today's air-braked fleet. These wagons would have been remarshalled at Tees Yard. A quick calculation (using 15 tons as the average capacity of a wagon in 1960) leads to a figure of 600 for the number of wagons diverted from the Tees Yard of the 1960s, because of this modernisation in both wagon fleet and operating practice. The carriage of County Durham coal to Drax Power Station accounts for a similar number of wagons. Thus whilst the tonnage of freight traffic in the area has undoubtedly declined substantially from the mid 1960s peak of 6.5 million tons, modernisation has also had its impact, bringing a disproportionate fall in traffic at major marshalling yards such as Tees Yard.

# The 1980s

Whilst rail-borne freight declined steadily during the 1960s and 1970s, it was not until 1981 that major changes were made to the layout of Tees marshalling yard. First the 'up' reception sidings and hump were closed, leaving a single-ended yard shunted from the west end. Hump shunting continued in the 'down' yard for a further four years, until in 1985 both reception sidings and hump were closed there too. During the summer of 1985, only three or four trains were 'humped' each day. With all Speedlink working concentrated on the 'up' yard, and wagon throughput well below 1,000 each day, the need for a hump yard had gone. British Rail is left with two single-ended flat yards at Tees. Between them these contain 80 sorting sidings whose allocation is shown in Table 23.

In order to plan the Tees Yard of the future, the area management team has taken careful stock, both of current and expected freight traffic. Any arrangement of sidings must cater for Speedlink marshalling, civil engineering traffic and the stabling or re-manning of through freights.

Speedlink traffic in the area is closely linked to both ICI and BSC. ICI forward large volumes of chemicals from both Haverton Hill and Wilton. BSC Lackenby and the Redcar mineral terminal deal with a substantial tonnage of rail-borne goods, and the works at Hartlepool South and Skinningrove are served by Speedlink trips (Table 25). A varied selection of commodities are handled at the recently-modernised Middlesbrough goods depot, and they are connected with the national Speedlink network via Tees Yard. In addition to the main goods yard at Middlesbrough, several customers in the area, including Thomson's at Stockton and Stockton Haulage at Cargo Fleet, have smaller private sidings. The total number of wagons involved daily in these trip freights is around 200. To marshal these wagons into the nine main Speedlink departures from Tees Yard would require 20 sidings; ie approximately half the 'up' yard.

Whilst Speedlink wagons are delayed as little as possible in a marshalling yard, quite the reverse is true of wagons belonging to the Area Maintenance and Civil Engineers. Most engineering work takes place at weekends, thus during the week the vast array of ballast and track wagons must be stabled somewhere. Herein lies a major conflict of interest between Speedlink and the engineering departments of British Railways. It is thought that the Area Maintenance Engineer may be allocated ten sidings in the 'up' yard, whilst his colleagues in civil engineering will be allowed to occupy as much of the 'down' yard as is necessary. Thus, both engineering departments could be catered for in the Tees Yard of the future.

Through freight trains are not a major problem at Tees Yard. Most 'block loads' of steel originate in Lackenby Yard and pose no operational problem at Tees. Several oil trains from Jarrow to Stanlow reverse in the yard and are simultaneously re-manned. Meanwhile, both coal and stone wagons are stabled overnight and at weekends in the yard. The twelve 'up' departure roads and six 'down' staging tracks are used for this purpose. Consequently, the Tees Yard of the future would see the 'down' primary sorting sidings used by civil engineering traffic. The 'up' primary sorting sidings would be divided between Speedlink and the Area Maintenance Engineer (AME). To allow 'bi-directional' working in the 'up' yard it may be possible to connect roads 1 to 6 to the 'down' goods line by a new spur at the east end of the yard. Speedlink traffic

Table 23
Siding allocation in Tees Yard, April 1986

| 'Up' Yard | | 'Down' Yard | |
|---|---|---|---|
| 2 | Permanent Way | 2 | Skinningrove |
| 3 | " | 3 | " |
| 6 | " | 4 | BDA Tees Yard/Lackenby |
| 7 | " | 5 | " |
| 8 | " | 6 | SPA Tees Yard |
| 9 | Scunthorpe | 7 | RRA Tees Yard/Lackenby |
| 10 | Bescot | 8 | " |
| 11 | Doncaster & STJ | 9 | no allocation |
| 12 | Millerhill | 10 | Lackenby AB |
| 13 | Carlisle | 11 | Lackenby vac. |
| 14 | Mossend | 12 | Wilton |
| 15 | Stranraer | 13 | no allocation |
| 16 | Tyne | 14 | empty MCV/MXV |
| 17 | Healey Mills | 15 | " |
| 18 | Tinsley | 16 | Lackenby AB |
| 19 | Toton | 17 | empty BCW/BDW |
| 20 | Duxford | 18 | Tees Yard barrier wagons |
| 21 | York | 19 | Cripples |
| 22 | Darlington | 20 | Tees Dock |
| 23 | Eastgate | 21 | Lackenby |
| 24 | Scunthorpe (vac.) | 22 | Etherley tip |
| 25 | Tees wagon shops | 23 | Middlesbrough Goods |
| 26 | " | 24 | Hartlepool S. Works |
| 27 | " | 25 | Haverton Hill |
| 28 | Tees wheel lathe | 26 | Hartlepool and Newburn |
| 29 | Tees wagon shops | 27 | spare |
| 30 | spare | 28 | Eastgate |
| 31 | Tees shops | 29 | spare |
| 32 | " | 30 | Darlington |
| 33 | " | 31 | Tyne |
| 34 | " | 32 | spare |
| 35 | Dinsdale | 33 | Healey Mills |
| 36 | ex-Fishburn | 34 | York |
| 37 | no allocation | 35 | Scunthorpe |
| 38 | – | 36 | spare |
| 39 | " | 37 | Port Clarence |
| 40 | " | 38 | Permanent Way |
| 41 | 'Down' yard transfers | 39 | Dinsdale |
| 42 | " | 40 | Eaglescliffe/Dowmac |
| | | 41 | Stockton |
| | | 42 | Brake vans/Speedlinks |

**Notes**
1. In the 'up' yard roads Nos 9 to 21 are used by Speedlink traffic.
2. In the 'down' yard the fan, made up of roads Nos 2 to 8, closed in April 1986.
3. The only sidings which 'earn' money for British Rail are those which handle freight from customers other than BR itself. Over 90% of such traffic travels by Speedlink. Thus only 20 or so roads are profitable within the yard.

**Table 24**
**Trip Freights from Tees Yard, April 1986**

| Trip | Tees Yard Depart | Arrive | Destination or destinations | Traffic |
|---|---|---|---|---|
| 9P81 | 04.20 | 09.22 | Haverton Hill, Darlington FLT, Stockton FLT | Freightliner plus chem. |
| 6P85 | 05.49 | 13.04 | Lackenby, Hartlepool South, Middlesbrough Goods. | steel/mixed |
| 6P72 | 06.02 | 12.02 | Lackenby, Skinningrove | steel |
| 9P83 | 06.13 | 10.33 | Lackenby, Tees Dock | steel |
| 9P68 | 06.57 | 14.30 | Newburn | |
| 6P63 | 07.40 | 14.44 | L.E. from Thornaby to trip in Ferryhill area | aggregates |
| 9P77 | 07.57 | 14.52 | Thomsons, Lackenby, Dowmac | scrap, aggregates |
| 9P75 | 08.07 | 15.30 | Middlesbrough Goods | mixed |

would be shunted into the longer and straighter roads in the centre of the yard (Nos 11 to 30) and the AME would use roads 31 to 40. Any eastbound trip workings would be shunted into roads 1 to 6, allowing easy access to the 'down' goods line. Both 'up' departure and 'down' staging sidings would play an important role in train stabling and Speedlink shunting. The future seems stable on Teesside. The TOPS computer has helped to maximise wagon usage and allows rapid reallocation of wagons if a special trainload of goods arrives unexpectedly. The year 1986 saw many examples of TOPS gaining custom and saving time. The most notable was the provision of a rake of 'cartics' for imported cars which landed at Tees Dock. Within twenty four hours of the initial telephone call to the Area Freight Assistant (AFA), the block load of cars was on its way to distribution depots around the country. As Mr McVay, the Area Operations Manager, pointed out, "We can provide the mobile platform and there is a lot of traffic up for grabs".

The Channel Tunnel will have far-reaching effects throughout the rail network. The main impact on Teesside is likely to be seen in an increase of container traffic from Stockton Freightliner Terminal. Large increases in wagonload traffic may follow if the aggressive marketing of Railfreight continues. At the moment, steel from Skinningrove to Parkeston travels more quickly than the first class post. The completion of the Channel Tunnel will mean that railways can compete effectively for large volumes of traffic, such as the flow between Teesport and the Europort at Rotterdam. A conservative estimate envisages a three-fold increase in 'continental' rail traffic when the tunnel is completed. It seems likely that considerably more traffic may be won for the railways as the link becomes established.

What then is the future of marshalling yards like Tees? In the 1960s they were often busy for the wrong reasons. With the changes in railway operating and local industry, Tees Yard has been drastically rationalised. Will the envisaged upturn in rail traffic necessitate the construction of a new hump yard at Tees? It seems unlikely. With axle loading restricted to a maximum of 26 tons, the size of wagons cannot rise beyond 100 tons. Any growth in traffic will probably manifest itself in an increase in the number of wagons heading for a given destination, rather than a proliferation of new terminals and sidings. This will mean increasing the length and tonnage of Speedlink trains rather than the complexity of their marshalling. It has been suggested that marshalling yard planning should reflect this anticipated change and that sidings should be from 80 to 120 standard wagon lengths (SWL) in capacity. Today 60 SWL is the average siding length at most marshalling yards. In spite of these careful considerations, it is the author's opinion that Railfreight may be underestimating the need for marshalling yards in their future planning. Whilst cautious rationalisation is indeed wise in the current climate, it may prove difficult to accommodate any

| | | | | |
|---|---|---|---|---|
| 9P79 | 07.52 | 14.00 | ICI Wilton | chemicals |
| 6P82 | 08.16 | 13.52 | L.E. from Thornaby to trip between Boulby and Skinningrove. | steel or potash |
| 9P61 | 11.12 | 18.12 | Skinningrove | steel |
| 9P84 | 12.37 | 14.07 | Lackenby, Tees Dock | steel |
| 9P73 | 13.05 | 17.40 | Lackenby, Wilton, Stockton | steel, chemicals, scrap. |
| 9P64 | 15.52 | 22.52 | Lackenby, Hartlepool | steel |
| 6P69 | 14.47 | 20.32 | Lackenby, Skinningrove | steel |
| 9P80 | 17.57 | 00.12 | Tees Dock, Lackenby, Haverton Hill | steel, chemicals |
| 6P62 | 07.25 | 14.45 | Cemetry North, Thrislington returns to Thornaby L.E. | aggregates |
| 6N33 | 01.43 | 08.17 | Horden to York mgr | coal |
| 6N38 | 09.26 | 16.05 | Horden to York mgr | coal |
| 6G72 | 14.05 | 21.50 | Horden to York mgr | coal |
| 6N39 | 18.02 | 00.54 | Horden to York mgr | coal |
| 6P90 | 23.59 | 05.59 | L.E. from Thornaby to trip between Middlesbrough Goods and Boulby | aggregate (potash) |
| 6P65 | 04.22 | 09.57 | Boulby, Middlesbrough Goods | aggregates mixed |
| 6P68 | 07.20 | 14.05 | Boulby, Tees Dock | aggregates |
| 6P66 | 10.14 | 16.19 | Boulby, Middlesbrough Goods, Tees Dock | aggregates |
| 6P67 | 16.36 | 21.21 | Boulby, Tees Dock | aggregates |
| 6P70 | 15.45 | 23.55 | L.E. from Thornaby to trip between Boulby, Tees Dock and Middlesbrough Goods | aggregates |
| 6N69 | 03.30 | 10.52 | Easington to York mgr | coal |
| 6N67 | 07.10 | 14.35 | Easington to York mgr | coal |
| 6N70 | 11.22 | 18.50 | Easington to York mgr | coal |
| 6N68 | 15.15 | 22.38 | Easington to York mgr | coal |
| 6N71 | 19.25 | 02.30 | Easington to York mgr | coal |
| 6N66 | 23.31 | 06.40 | Easington to York mgr | coal |

**Notes**

1. MGR services from Horden and Easington start with empty wagons in Tees Yard and return to Tees Yard with empties. These services will decrease in number as the new 'super-pit' at Gascoine Wood increases its production during the next two years.

2. After leaving Thornaby or Tees Yard, each trip may travel to one or all of the destinations listed. Furthermore it may travel to one location several times. The exact movements of the train are determined by traffic requirements.

**Table 25**
**Speedlink Services from Tees Yard (April 1986)**

| | | | |
|---|---|---|---|
| 7L53 | 12.36 | Healey Mills | Portions for Healey Mills, York, Temple Mills and Barking |
| 6F83 | 15.25 | Parkeston | Portions for Doncaster, Severn Tunnel, Whitemoor, Ipswich and Parkeston |

Cont.

increase in traffic within the current infrastructure.

In concluding this chapter, I would like to thank the area management team at Zetland House, Middlesbrough, and particularly Messrs Stamp, McVay, Noble and Adams, for their invaluable assistance.

## Speedlink Services From Tees Yard (April 1963) continued

| | | | |
|---|---|---|---|
| 6O49 | 17.25 | Eastleigh | Portions for Temple Mills, Hoo Junction, Eastleigh, Oxford, Severn Tunnel, Bescot |
| 7S66 | 17.50 | Stranraer | Portions for Stranraer, Falkland Junction, Carlisle, Mossend, Millerhill, Aberdeen and Tyne |
| 6V66 | 18.35 | Stoke Gifford | Portions for York and Stoke Gifford |
| 6M85 | 19.34 | Bescot | Portions for Tinsley, Bescot, and Wolverhampton |
| 6M64 | 20.05 | Warrington | Portions for Warrington and Healey Mills |
| 6H85 | 21.55 | Duxford | Portions for Whitemoor, Ipswich, Parkeston, Cambridge and Duxford |
| 7S59 | 00.20 | Stranraer | Portions for Stranraer, Falkland Junction, Carlisle and Tyne |

A rag-bag of wagons stands in the 'down' recessing sidings at Tees Yard on 26th March 1986. The train is a General Utility Service or GUS from York (North) Yard to Tees, and is hauled by Class 37 Nos 37063 and 37079.

Class 47 No. 47198 arrives in the old 'up' departure sidings at Tees Yard with the 6O49, Haverton Hill to Eastleigh freight. Within minutes, Class 08 No. 08506 has attached to the end of the train to remove wagons bound for other Speedlink trains. Class 47s Nos 47302 and 47360 both await other evening Speedlink departures.

# PLAN 29

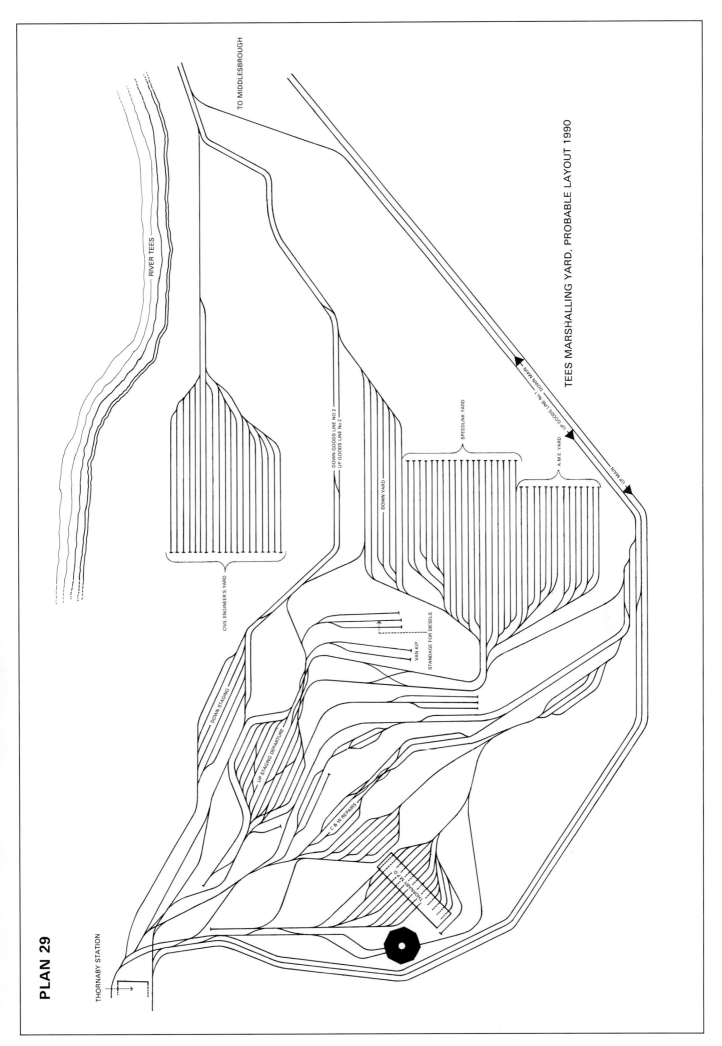

THORNABY STATION

RIVER TEES

TO MIDDLESBROUGH

CIVIL ENGINEER'S YARD

DOWN GOODS LINE No 2
UP GOODS LINE No 2

DOWN YARD

SPEEDLINK YARD

A M E YARD

UP GOODS LINE No 1 / DOWN MAIN

UP MAIN

TEES MARSHALLING YARD, PROBABLE LAYOUT 1990

DOWN STAGING

UP STAGING DEPARTURE

VAN KIP

STANDAGE FOR DIESELS

C & W REPAIRS

THORNABY M.P.D.

159

Another busy scene in the old 'up' departure roads on 7th March 1986 shows Class 31 No. 31317 arriving with the 9P61 from Skinningrove. The trip freight has dropped steel for export at Teesport and now brings empty BDA bogie-bolsters from the port into Tees Yard. Class 37 No. 37008 has just arrived from Stockton and Class 08 No. 08295 was one of the yard pilots on this day.

Opposite:
In March 1986, the 'down' reception sidings stand empty after their closure at the end of 1985.

Two ZRA vans stand on the 'down' hump at Tees to collect material being salvaged from the 'down' control tower. They will then travel by Speedlink freight to BREL York Works.

As the sun sets in October 1983, so the fan of sorting sidings radiating from the 'down' hump at Tees is highlighted. Such dramatic scenes will soon be a sight of the past as Britain's major hump yards are all now closed or rationalised.

The 'up' sorting sidings at Tees Yard were transformed by rationalisation. In 1980 vacuum-fitted Covhops are seen descending from the hump, whereas by 1983 the yard was reduced in capacity and shunted from the west end as a flat yard.

## Tees Freight

A Worsdell-designed Class J26, 0-6-0 No. 65776, passes Cargo Fleet with a freight bound for the old Newport yards at Thornaby. This view, taken in the late 1950s, shows the variety of low-capacity mineral wagons still in traffic at this time.

*Author's Collection (photographer unknown)*

The extensive sidings at South Bank are shunted by a Class 08 diesel, in 1972, whilst a Class 17 passes with a rake of steel wagons for the Lackenby plant.

*M. Dunnett*

In 1972, a Class 24 passes through the industrial gloom surrounding the South Bank area. The train conveys finished steel and a string of empty mineral hoppers.

*M. Dunnett*

Again in 1972, freights cross at Cargo Fleet. Large numbers of steel company sidings along the Middlesbrough to Redcar route generated much of the traffic handled at Tees Yard.

*J. Cooper-Smith*

Photographed from the same point but looking in the other direction, the changes in the steel industry and railway network are striking. On 22nd July 1986, Class 37 No. 37077 passes with a train of steel from Lackenby to Tees Yard; the Cargo Fleet steelworks have been demolished, the main line reduced to two tracks, semaphore signalling replaced, and all the many local sidings closed.

In June 1980, a Class 37, No. 37045, passes South Bank with a short trip freight from Lackenby to Tees Yard. Such freight operations are also a sight of the past, most minerals for industrial concerns such as BSC Redcar being conveyed as block loads.

# Chapter 11
# Healey Mills

Healey Mills, four miles west of Wakefield was a natural concentration point for east-west flows of freight traffic. It linked the industrial West Riding with the east coast ports of Hull and Goole, and the industrial areas of Lancashire and the Merseyside ports. It was also a convenient 'half-way house' between the heavy industrial area of north east England and Lancashire. As part of the North Eastern Region's freight modernisation plans, a new bi-directional hump yard was constructed at Healey Mills. This had a daily capacity to sort 4,000 to 4,500 wagons on its 140 acre site. Well over half of the traffic handled at Healey Mills was coal from the West Riding and empty coal wagons returning from Lancashire and beyond. Opened in 1963,

**A magnificent overall view of Healey Mills, taken from one of the 150ft lighting masts, shows the hump from which 50 sorting sidings radiated.**

*British Rail (Eastern Region)*

the yard rendered 20 years of service, until in November 1984 the hump was closed and the layout considerably rationalised. Further reorganisation of Railfreight in Yorkshire led to a much smaller role for Healey Mills in the marshalling of Speedlink and coal traffic.

## Planning and Construction

The 140 acre site occupied by Healey Mills was entirely underlain by a series of coal seams. The most profitable seams had been won, and subsequent agreement between British Railways and the National Coal Board meant that all coal working under the yard site was completed prior to 1962 when the levels for the main sidings had to be stabilised. Consequently, the sterilisation of coal was not as substantial as had been feared and was confined to thinner seams which might in any event not have been worked. The levelling of the site was a vast task; 298,000 cubic yards of filling material were generated by the construction of a cutting for the River Calder, but it was still necessary to bring a further 750,000 cubic yards of filling into the area. A total of 154,000 cubic yards came from a new railway cutting built at Stourton, 383,000 tonnes consisted of red shale from local colleries, whilst a further 230,000 tonnes were made up of ash for the bottom ballast. This came from various West Riding power stations and abandoned railway branch lines. The depth of filling material was 17ft over the reception area, and somewhat shallower in the main yard.

Preliminary work began in 1959 and started with the rebuilding of the Storrs Hill Road overbridge. A new bridge consisting of two spans measuring 90ft and 60ft was made of welded steel-plate girder and spanned the east end of the site. The River Calder had to be diverted into a new channel to the south of the yard. This involved the diversion of a length of stream totalling 1,030yds and was similar in essence to the diversion of the River Tees around the new Tees Yard. Several overhead high voltage electricity cables were rerouted underground, whilst, underground structures, including two high-pressure gas mains, had to be diverted from their old course which ran diagonally across the main site.

The Ossett Sewage Disposal Works was moved to a new site, and an old mill reservoir had to be filled in before the main yard control tower could be built. The poor beleaguered fish which it contained were moved to a short stretch of the old River Canal. A small private road was also diverted and three bridges were constructed to carry the railway tracks in the hump area over the River Calder. This initial site preparation was not without complications and, on 26th November 1960, shortly before the new river cut was completed, the River Calder rose in a considerable flood. It burst its banks and flooded part of the site, and damage was caused both to the site and the banks of the new river channel. Repairs were carried out and included a completely new and effective barrier against subsequent flooding.

Altogether, the yard contained 120 sidings, making up 57 miles of track. At the west end were 14 reception roads leading to the hump. From here there radiated 50 main sorting sidings with the provision of 25 secondary sorting sidings further west. Fifteen staging sidings were supplemented by thirteen departure roads, and there were three small sidings provided for internal services. The yard was classified as semi-automatic, and two fully-automatic primary retarders, each 65ft long, provided initial breaking for wagons leaving the hump. Eight, 75ft long semi-automatic secondary retarders were placed at the entrance to each of the fans of sorting sidings.

The main yard control tower contained two signalling installations. A new power-operated signal box controlled movement into, and out of, the yard and over $7\frac{1}{2}$ route miles of adjacent running line. This new box took over the work formerly done in seven separate manually-operated signal cabins. The fringe boxes to the west were Thornhill (London & North Western), Heckmondwike and Middlestown. To the east, Horbury Junction and Crigglestone West took over the control of trains. The panel at Healey Mills incorporated a route relay interlocking system with colour-light signalling and power-operated points. The control panel was fitted with miniature equipment including push-button indicators and thumb switches, and contained a geographically representative map of the area which it controlled. There were 464 different route settings possible, controlling 58 main colour-light signals and 81 position light ground subsidiaries. One hundred and twenty electro-pneumatically-operated points were connected by 50 miles of multi-core control cable. On the other side of the signal cabin was the control room for yard shunting. The immediate hump area came under the supervision of the operators in this part of the signal cabin.

The approach to the hump was controlled by an elevated, three-aspect, double-sided lunar white hump signal. This could display three indications, 'stop', 'slow' and 'fast'. It was supplemented by two-aspect position light ground signals which controlled the release of locomotives from the reception sidings and also the return of shunting engines into the reception area. There were 68 electro-pneumatically-operated points in the hump area and these were usually switched in accordance with a programme set by cut cards. This method of hump operation was the standard of the day and will be described later in the chapter.

## Operation

The yard at Healey Mills had a design capacity to handle 4,000 wagons a day, but its throughput was often in excess of 4,500 in any twenty four hour period. Well over half this traffic was made up of huge quantities of coal passing from the Yorkshire Coalfield to the factories of the West Riding and Lancashire. Smaller quantities travelled to power stations and ports all over the north of England. The rest of the wagons conveyed a great variety of basic materials and industrial products ranging from wool to wines, and textiles to timber. Much of the coal began to move in trainloads direct from the point of origin to the point of consumption, and as such needed no intermediate sorting. However, many coal trains were made up of unbraked 16 ton mineral wagons and these required sorting at the new yard. Superimposed on the trainloads of coal sorted at Healey Mills was a pattern of Class 4 fitted freight services connecting the yard with the rest of the country. Most of these trains operated along the east-west axis but, in addition, freight services between the North West and the North East, which had been previously

167

**PLAN 30**

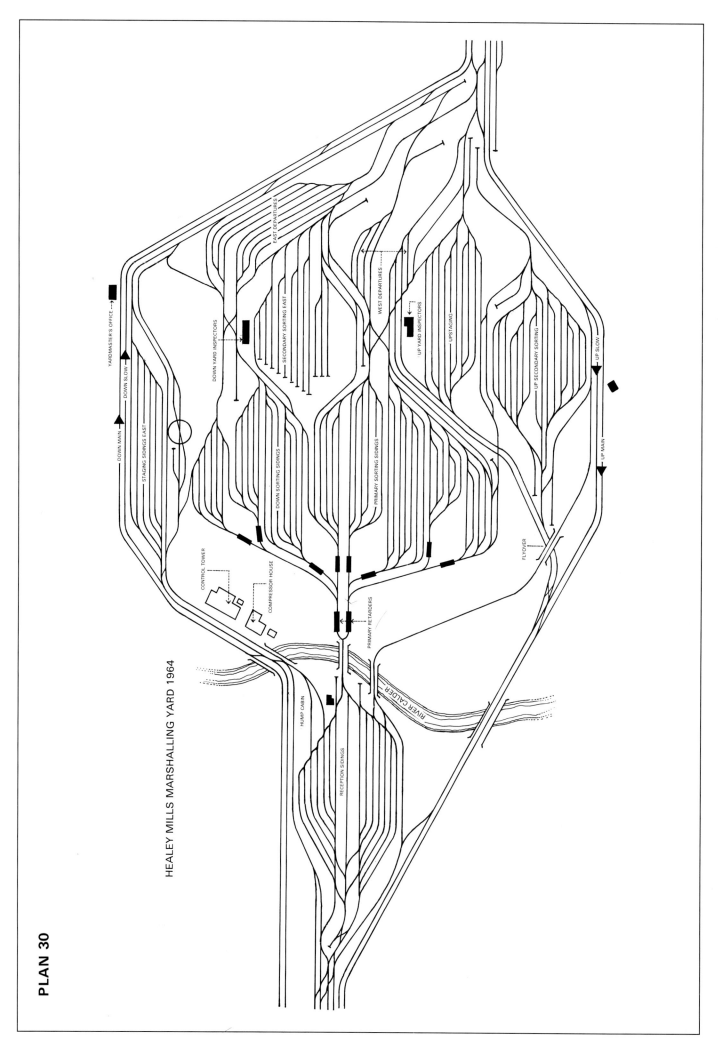

HEALEY MILLS MARSHALLING YARD 1964

marshalled at York, began to be sorted at Healey Mills. The marshalling of east-west traffic was formerly carried out in thirteen separate small shunting yards. Ten of these, at Mytholmroyd, Brighouse, Mirfield 'up' and 'down', Horbury Junction Sidings, Wakefield Exchange, New Withams, Turners Lane , Crofton Laden and Low Moor, were closed. Three further yards, Crofton Empty Sidings, Hillhouse and Copely Hill were retained, but operated with a reduced scale of activity. An example of the concentration of traffic at Healey Mills was the service from West Yorkshire to Rose Grove, near Burnley. In 1960, Rose Grove Yard received six trains daily from

**An aerial view of Healey Mills, taken in March 1963, shows that most of the sidings are complete and full of large numbers of mineral wagons.**

*British Rail (Eastern Region)*

the area around Wakefield. These freights were then remarshalled, and traffic for destinations further afield sorted out at Rose Grove. In 1963, after the new yard at Healey Mills was opened, only two daily services ran from the West Riding to Rose Grove and both of these contained traffic for the immediate Burnley area, whilst coal and sundries traffic, bound for destinations such as Blackburn or Accrington, proceeded directly from Healey Mills on identified services to other destinations. The initial timetable at Healey Mills followed the pattern of pre-Grouping freight services, but subsequent reorganisations made the freight timetable more simple by concentrating on only a couple of trans-Pennine routes.

*Fig.6* shows the routes feeding into and emanating from Healey Mills Yard. The numbers in circles represent trains arriving at the yard, whilst those in squares denote

departures from the marshalling complex. The 151 daily departures were divided almost equally between the east and west. Important coal flows to domestic customers, power stations and gasworks, as well as the west coast ports, were routed along the lines to Preston, Manchester and Liverpool. A particularly heavy flow of coal ran over Copy Pit to Burnley and the power stations along the valley to Preston. The yard received a similar number of arrivals (145), and it was interesting to note that there were eleven more arrivals from the east, suggesting a surplus of small trip freights from West Riding collieries, in contrast to long trains of empty mineral wagons approaching from the west.

The hump was operated in the traditional manner for 1963. A cut card was compiled for each arrival in the reception sidings and forwarded to the control tower. Here, up to 50 separate cuts could be recorded and

executed automatically as a train was propelled over the hump. The installation of 148 short rail circuits enabled such a programme to operate. The retarders were controlled by the standard technique, in that the automatic primary retarders assessed weight and rollability before applying an automatically-adjusted brake-force. The secondary retarders were manually-operated by the yard controller who could select one of six leaving speeds, depending upon his assessment of the rollability and weight of a cut. He was also able to take into account the occupation of the siding for which the wagons were destined. Arrivals from the east had access to the southerly reception sidings by means of a flyover, constructed from two lattice

Like a model railway under construction, the eight secondary retarders at Healey Mills fan from the hump. A Class 05 pushes a ballast wagon down into the sorting sidings whilst another rolls under gravity on a clear day in May 1963.

*British Rail (Eastern Region)*

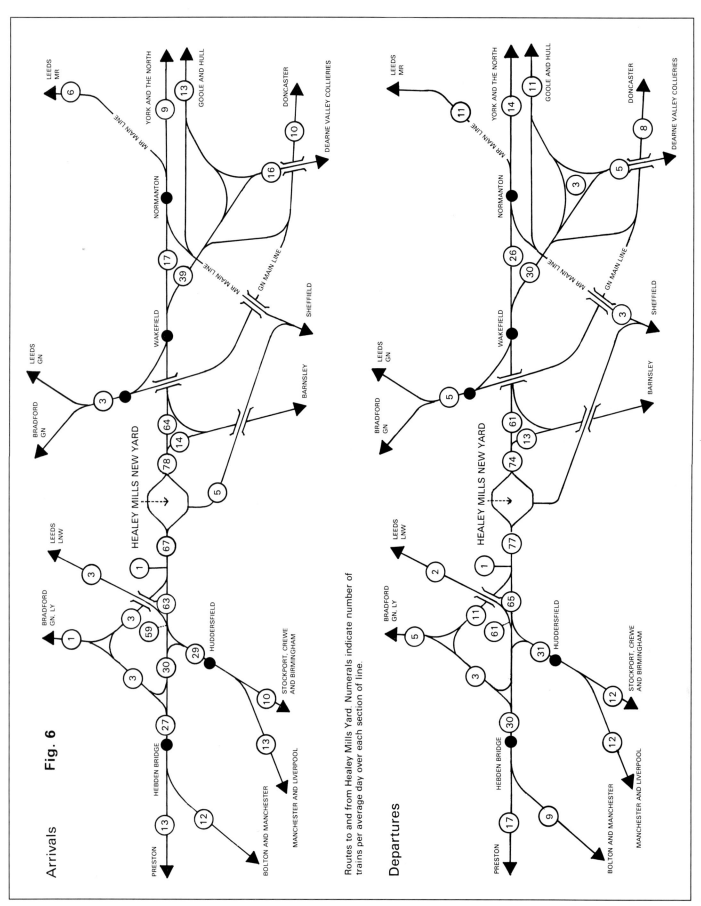

Fig. 6

Arrivals

Departures

HEALEY MILLS NEW YARD

Routes to and from Healey Mills Yard. Numerals indicate number of trains per average day over each section of line.

girders recovered from the bridge which formerly carried the main lines over the old mill reservoir. Arrivals from the west passed directly into the reception roads.

The 50 main sorting sidings were approached down an initial gradient of 1 in 16 from the hump. They were divided into eight separate fans, four for 'up' traffic and four for 'down' traffic. To the east of the main yard were the secondary sorting sidings; ten for 'up' traffic and sixteen for 'down'. Here, fitted heads for freight trains were assembled. The departure sidings were divided with seven for 'up' traffic and six for 'down' departures. One inconvenience of the bi-directional layout was that westbound departures could not receive their train engines as soon as they were marshalled, because this would have involved blocking the hump and interrupting marshalling to reverse the locomotive on to its load in the sorting sidings. It was therefore decided to employ two diesel shunters, purely to move sorted trains from the 'up' sorting sidings to the westbound departure tracks.

Good communications were paramount to the efficient functioning of the yard, particularly at peak periods when there was congestion at the site. Telephones were provided throughout the yard and a talk-back loudspeaker system enabled the controller and the yard inspectors to speak to yard staff at key points. Inductive radio-telephone communication between the control tower and shunting locomotives was also provided. In addition to these three modes of communication there were loud-speakers sited strategically throughout the shunting area. The yard was illuminated by eight 150ft high steel lighting towers which guaranteed a light intensity of approximately one lumen per square foot. The floodlights at the top of the towers contained 1,500 watt lamps and were arranged in banks. Five of the gantries had lighting on all four faces, whilst the remaining three had lights fitted to three faces only.

**The rails of the primary retarder at Healey Mills grip the wheels of an ex-LNER 21$^1$/$_2$ ton mineral wagon in June 1963.**
*British Rail (Eastern Region)*

Of the 57 miles of track used, 43 miles, or 75 per cent was serviceable track recovered from abandoned lines. The principle of something old and something new was also in evidence in the provision of a new footbridge linking the administrative buildings to the yard area. Serviceable lengths of lattice girders were recovered from an old 120ft span footbridge which formerly crossed the lines at the north end of Darlington station. A similar concession to the old methods of freight operation was made in the retention of a steam turntable at Healey Mills because of the large percentage of freight hauled by steam locomotives. The last steam depot on British Railways at Rose Grove, did not close until August 1968, and the last freight trains to be hauled by steam were between Healey Mills and Rose Grove. A diesel servicing point was built at Healey Mills but not until the yard had already been open for several years.

# Changes in traffic at Healey Mills

Up until 1975, the daily throughput of wagons at Healey Mills remained in excess of 4,000. By 1981, however, it had fallen considerably, and in the week ending 14th November 1981, 8,971 wagons arrived at the site in 357 separate freight trains. Of these vehicles, 7,759 were hump-shunted. This meant that an average of 1,500 wagons were passing over the hump on each working day. By November 1984, the weekly arrivals at Healey Mills had fallen to 114 trains. These contained 1,450 wagons of which only 491 were hump-shunted. This meant that an average of less than one hundred wagons each day were dealt with

by the expensive semi-automatic hump marshalling facility. In the same period from 1975 to 1985, dramatic changes had taken place in the number of block merry-go-round trains in the area. There were very few such services prior to 1975 but, by 1981, a weekly throughput of 94 trains containing 2,809 HAA 32$^1$/$_2$ tonne coal hoppers was recorded.

By March 1985, the reorganisation of coal shipment in the area and a drastic reduction in east-west flows of coal for power stations meant that only 18 trains were diagrammed to pass through Healey Mills each week. These contained 510 HAA coal hoppers. The number of mixed freight services arriving at Healey Mills in 1985 was 122, and this meant an input of 1,636 wagons each week and an output of 1,550. These freights were dealt with without a hump, and flat shunting was conducted in a new rationalised yard.

The key features of the rationalisation at Healey Mills were:
1.  The closure of the reception sidings as well as the hump and retarder area along with the abandonment of the east-west flyover. This meant that the yard was shunted from the east end, and access from the west end of the yard was no longer possible.
2.  The number of sorting sidings was

reduced by the removal of sidings numbered 1 to 7 and 34 to 50. Road No. 20 was also removed, leaving 22 primary sorting sidings.
3.  The 'down' secondary sorting sidings were also disconnected, whereas the 'up' secondary sorting sidings were used predominantly by the Civil Engineer.
4.  The 'up' staging sidings were an important re-manning and re-engining point for merry-go-round coal trains, whereas the west departure roads were used for both arrivals and departures from all directions, as well as for storage.

In May 1985 these reduced facilities *(Plan 31)* handled a combination of block and Speedlink freight traffic *(Table 26)*. The rationalisation of Healey Mills was not however complete. Further reorganisation of freight services in Yorkshire meant a reduction in trains using the yard and a redirection of many of the Speedlink freight services.

Marshalling expenses accounted for £16 million of Speedlink's total costs in 1984. There were four marshalling yards in Yorkshire, at Tinsley, Dringhouses, Doncaster and Healey Mills, all within a compact area where the workload could not justify such lavish provision for marshalling. It was therefore proposed that

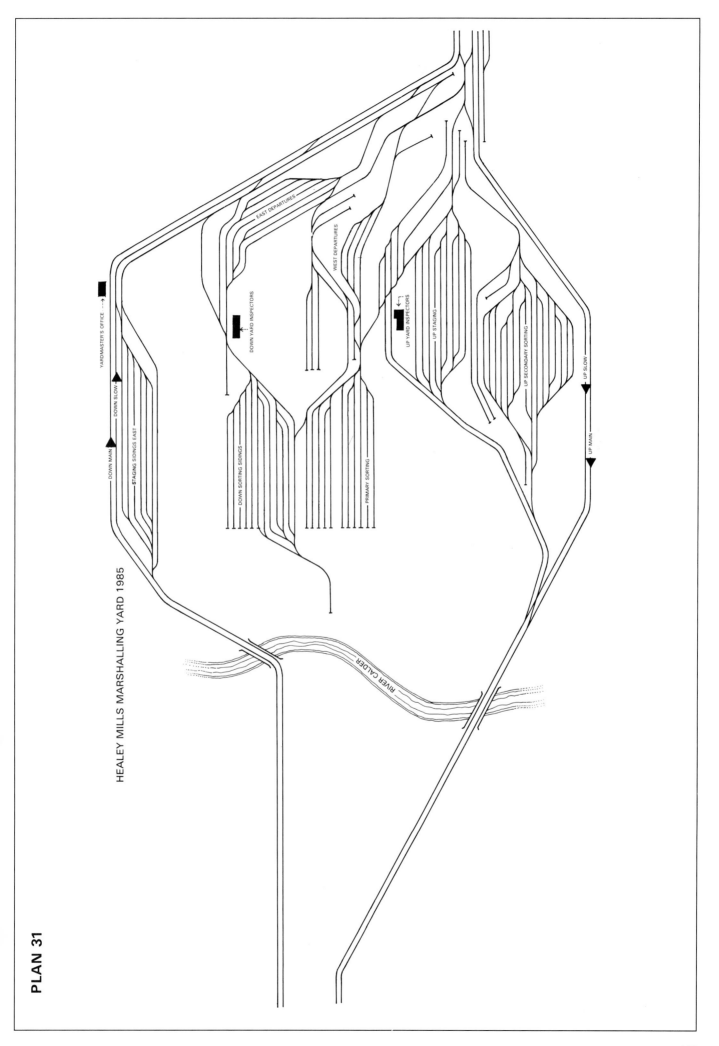

**PLAN 31**

HEALEY MILLS MARSHALLING YARD 1985

# Table 26

## Healey Mills Freight — May 1985

### EASTBOUND

| Train | From | To | Healey Mills Arr. | Dep. | Days |
|-------|------|-----|------|------|------|
| 6M17 | Barton on Humb. | Corcickle | 22.45 | 00.10 | TO |
| 6E77 | Warrington | Healey Mills | 00.13 | | MX |
| 6D66 | Healey Mills | Scunthorpe | | 00.15 | MX |
| 6E38 | Fiddlers Ferry | Healey Mills | 00.20 | | MX |
| 6E62 | Oakleigh | Healey Mills | 00.33 | | TFO |
| 7E26 | Folly Lane | Doncaster | 22.01 | 00.54 | MX |
| 6S67 | Healey Mills | Mossend | | 01.00 | MX |
| 9L01 | Healey Mills | Dringhouses | | 01.10 | MX |
| 6E50 | Stanlow | Torksey | 02.29 | 03.16 | WThFO |
| 6E65 | Corcickle | Barton on Humb. | 23.42 | 03.31 | FO |
| 6E50 | Stanlow | Torksey | 04.11 | 06.13 | MO |
| 6E27 | Stanlow | Dringhouses | 04.21 | 05.10 | MSX |
| 6E37 | Stanlow | Leeds | 04.59 | 05.17 | SuX |
| 7M75 | Healey Mills | Ribblehead | | 05.23 | SX |
| 6M37 | Immingham | Heysham | 04.44 | 05.42 | TFO |
| 6L17 | Healey Mills | Monkton | | 06.38 | TFO |
| 6E56 | Fiddlers Ferry | Healey Mills | 07.32 | | MX |
| 7D59 | Healey Mills | Scunthorpe | | 09.22 | |
| 6E18 | Stanlow | Jarrow | 07.46 | 10.24 | SX |
| 6E25 | Stanlow | Leeds | 09.16 | 09.37 | SX |
| 0J91 | Healey Mills | Crofton | | 10.02 | ThO |
| 7M72 | Healey Mills | Ribblehead | | 10.18 | TThO |
| 6E36 | Holyhead | Humber | 12.25 | 12.59 | ThO |
| 7M41 | Dewsbury | Earles | 12.57 | 13.17 | SX |
| 6E47 | Folly Lane | Seal Sands | 13.24 | 14.29 | SO |
| 7E60 | Preston | Lindsey | 13.31 | 14.15 | SX |
| 6E99 | Fiddlers Ferry | Healey Mills | 13.58 | | |
| 6E48 | Stanlow | Leeds | 14.41 | 14.43 | MWFO |
| 0M17 | Healey Mills | Monkton | | 14.50 | MThO |
| 6D84 | Healey Mills | Doncaster | | 15.07 | SX |
| 6E45 | Folly Lane | Seal Sands | 15.21 | 15.34 | SX |
| 6E20 | Glazebrook | Haverton Hill | 15.26 | 16.17 | MX |
| 9J28 | Healey Mills | Tinsley | | 15.40 | SX Y |
| 9D29 | Healey Mills | Doncaster | | 15.40 | SX Y |
| 6S46 | Healey Mills | Mossend | | 15.50 | SX |
| 6L44 | Healey Mills | Dringhouses | | 16.27 | SX |
| 6V06 | Healey Mills | Severn Tunnel | | 16.48 | SX |
| 6E97 | Heysham | Immingham | 15.35 | 16.53 | TWO |
| 6E70 | Oakleigh | Lindsey | 17.09 | 17.17 | SX |
| 6E31 | Weaste | Port Clarence | 17.15 | 17.35 | MWFO |
| 6E46 | Weaste | Lindsey | 17.15 | 17.35 | TO |
| 7D63 | Healey Mills | Worksop | | 17.49 | SX |
| 6E90 | Folly Lane | Grimsby | 19.03 | 19.05 | TThO |
| 6E17 | Folly Lane | Haverton Hill | 19.57 | 20.01 | SX |
| 9E27 | Ashburys | Healey Mills | 20.30 | | SX |
| 7D30 | Liversedge | Lindsey | 20.53 | 21.22 | FSX |
| 0L73 | Healey Mills | Crofton | | 22.38 | ThO |
| 7D53 | Healey Mills | Doncaster | | 22.45 | SX |
| 6L48 | Healey Mills | Wooley | | 22.50 | SX |
| 6E81 | Warrington | Haverton Hill | 22.11 | 23.54 | SX |
| 7E59 | Woolstanton | Healey Mills | 00.04 | | |

### WESTBOUND

| Train | From | To | Healey Mills Arr. | Dep. | Days |
|-------|------|-----|------|------|------|
| 6M84 | Healey Mills | Warrington | | 00.15 | MX |
| 6M76 | Healey Mills | Woolstanton | | 00.50 | MX |
| 7M26 | Healey Mills | Fiddlers Ferry | | 01.27 | MX |
| 6M27 | Immingham | Folly Lane | 01.14 | 01.40 | ThSO |
| 7M95 | Doncaster | Oakleigh | 23.10 | 01.45 | MX |
| 7L18 | Doncaster | Healey Mills | 02.11 | | MX |
| 6M60 | Scunthorpe | Monkshall | 03.25 | 05.15 | MO |
| 6L49 | Lindsey | Liversedge | 03.45 | 06.26 | MSX |
| 6M15 | Lindsey | Oakleigh | 04.05 | 04.14 | SX |
| 6M37 | Immingham | Heysham | 04.44 | 05.42 | TFO |
| 6M32 | Lindsey | Preston | 05.34 | 05.42 | SX |
| 6M08 | Haverton Hill | Glazebrook | 04.35 | 06.14 | MX |
| 6M26 | Haverton Hill | Folly Lane | 05.38 | 05.47 | SO |
| 7M32 | Healey Mills | Stanlow | | 06.09 | MO |
| 6M16 | Lindsey | Weaste | 06.26 | 09.26 | TO |
| 6M34 | Seal Sands | Folly Lane | 07.33 | 07.52 | MX |
| 7M47 | Healey Mills | Fiddlers Ferry | | 08.32 | |
| 6M49 | Port Clarence | Weaste | 09.14 | 09.26 | MWFO |
| 6M26 | Haverton Hill | Folly Lane | 11.06 | 11.37 | SX |
| 0M41 | Healey Mills | Dewsbury | | 11.45 | SX |
| 7M54 | Leeds | Stanlow | 12.14 | 12.16 | SuX |
| 6E60 | Mossend | Healey Mills | 12.19 | | SX |
| 6L76 | Scunthorpe | Healey Mills | 13.28 | | SX |

| | | | | | |
|---|---|---|---|---|---|
| 7E54 | Ribblehead | Healey Mills | 13.33 | | SX |
| 7M37 | Torksey | Stanlow | 13.58 | 14.29 | WThFO |
| 6L62 | Doncaster | Healey Mills | 14.03 | | SX |
| 9M27 | Healey Mills | Ashburys | | 14.56 | SX |
| 7L41 | Leeds | Healey Mills | 15.14 | | SX |
| 6E97 | Heysham | Immingham | 15.35 | 16.53 | TWO |
| 7L53 | Tees | Healey Mills | 15.42 | | SX |
| 7M35 | Leeds | Stanlow | 16.13 | 17.12 | SX |
| 7M37 | Torksey | Stanlow | 16.53 | 16.55 | MO |
| 6M17 | Monkton | Oakleigh | 16.48 | 17.52 | MThO |
| 7M43 | Jarrow | Stanlow | 17.06 | 17.45 | MO |
| 7M57 | Healey Mills | Fiddlers Ferry | | 18.33 | SX |
| 7M59 | Dringhouses | Stanlow | 18.58 | 19.21 | MSX |
| 6E57 | Earles | Healey Mills | 19.16 | | SX |
| 0D30 | Healey Mills | Liversedge | | 19.37 | FSX |
| 8E68 | Ribblehead | Healey Mills | | 19.42 | TThO |
| 9L29 | Doncaster | Healey Mills | | 19.50 | SX |
| 9L28 | Tinsley | Healey Mills | | 20.08 | SX |
| 7L60 | Worksop | Healey Mills | | 21.17 | SX |
| 6L54 | Scunthorpe | Healey Mills | | 21.32 | SX |
| 6E61 | Mossend | Healey Mills | | 21.37 | SX |
| 6M43 | Humber | Holyhead | 21.13 | 22.40 | TO |
| 6M82 | Leeds | Stanlow | 21.43 | 22.15 | MWFO |
| 6M64 | Haverton Hill | Arpley | 22.34 | 23.50 | SX |
| 9L01 | Dringhouses | Healey Mills | 23.21 | | SX |
| 6M17 | Barton on Humb. | Corcickle | 23.45 | 00.10 | MO |
| 7M42 | Jarrow | Stanlow | 23.57 | 23.59 | SX |

**Class 47 No. 47236 leaves Healey Mills Yard with 7D02, the 13.17 Healey Mills-Doncaster Belmont freight on 19th August 1988.**
*Paul D. Shannon*

Speedlink marshalling should be withdrawn from Healey Mills. Whilst the yard would remain as a centre of trainload and departmental activity, this would mean that the number of sidings and the number of staff could be reduced at Healey Mills. The proposed annual saving of such a reorganisation was in excess of £140,000 and involved a reduction in the freight services using the yard from 63 to 25 each day. No major changes were proposed for the operation of block trains in the area, many of which were staged and re-manned at the yard. There were many objections to this plan and its implementation has not been pursued to the full extent. There have,

however, been changes in the operation of less than trainload freights in the Yorkshire area which in summary involve a redistribution of several services away from Healey Mills. The yard retains a small Speedlink service but can no longer be classified as a network yard as it was originally, in 1975.

Whether the sidings at Healey Mills continue to sort wagonload traffic remains to be seen, but the yard will undoubtedly perform an important function in the staging of block trains en route between Lancashire and Yorkshire.

My thanks to the Area Manager at Healey Mills for his kind co-operation in this project.

The yard staff keep an eagle eye on shunting at Healey Mills in July 1963. By May 1985 a picture taken from exactly the same spot shows that the control panel for the hump has been removed and through the mist a row of buffers mark the end of the truncated sorting sidings.

*British Rail (Eastern Region) and Author*

At the east end of Healey Mills Yard Class 40 No. 40122 arrives with the 6L53 York to Healey Mills freight. In the rationalised yard all shunting was controlled from the small office which had acted as the 'up' departure Inspector's cabin.

The rain pours down on the rusting rails of the reception sidings at Healey Mills. The shunting signal was still standing in May 1985, although some of the supporting wire had cut loose.

## Healey Mills Freight

Class 56 No. 56023 stands in the 'down' recessing sidings at Healey Mills with an empty mgr train from Fiddler's Ferry Power Station in June 1986.

A vacuum-fitted freight, the 7L53 Tees to Healey Mills, arrives at the east end of the yard behind Class 31 No. 31189 on 20th June 1986.

A block oil train from Torkesley to Stanlow approaches Healey Mills on 16th March 1982. Class 40 No. 40141 heads the 6M37 working, one of a procession of block freights which are re-manned at the yard. The future of Healey Mills as a freight centre may depend upon such trans-Pennine block workings.

On 23rd August 1972 a rake of ballast empties, coded the 9B26, passes Copy Pit Summit on its way from East Lancashire to

Healey Mills. Class 25 No. 7654 will probably return later in the day with a train of coal for the power stations of East Lancashire
*T. Heavyside*

In the summer of 1977 there were still considerable numbers of unfitted mineral wagons in traffic in the Yorkshire area. A rake of such vehicles leaves Healey Mills for one of the local pits behind Class 40 No. 40169.

Class 47 No. 47282 accelerates away from Healey Mills at the head of the 6VO6 Speedlink service to Severn Tunnel Junction.

# Chapter 12

# Yorkshire and Humberside

The 1955 Modernisation Plan envisaged four major yards in Yorkshire. The three at Tinsley, Healey Mills and Dringhouses were built whilst the fourth at Leeds (Stourton) was never constructed. There was, however, a modern hump marshalling yard at Hull some 20 years before these other yards were even planned — the Hull Inward Yard at Hessle. In contrast, the

**Hull Inward Yard. This picture taken in 1962, shows a rake of mineral wagons descending into the sorting sidings at Hessle Yard. A further expanse of sorting sidings can be seen to the right of the yard control tower. By 1984 just six sidings served the freight needs of the port of Kingston upon Hull.**
*British Rail (Eastern Region)*

Belmont Yards at Doncaster were only opened in the late 1970s and are some of the most recent marshalling yards to be built by British Railways. As Speedlink concentrates its marshalling on the Belmont Yards at Doncaster, so the importance of the other yards in Yorkshire decreases. The yards at Hull and Scunthorpe are already classified as secondary, whilst both Dringhouses and Healey Mills will lose a lot of their importance as traffic is concentrated at Doncaster.

**Scunthorpe Hump Yard: In 1980 there was already a preponderance of air-braked steel wagons in the Scunthorpe West Yard. The small but busy yard at Scunthorpe was the third in Britain to benefit from the installation of a Dowty retarder system, and is the only location where the retarders are still in operation.**

## Hull

Opened in December 1935, the Hull Inward Yard was an extensive installation made up of six reception roads, thirty primary sorting sidings, and four departure roads. Four hydraulic rail brakes were incorporated to retard wagons descending from the hump. A roughly symmetrical outward yard was also built at Hessle. The subsequent fate of these installations reflects not only the change in the fortunes of North Humberside, but also the changes in railway operation over the 50 years since their construction. Initially, yards such as Hessle were regarded as the forerunners of the trouble-free, automated, hump marshalling yard, epitomised by Tinsley. As wagonload traffic decreased and the utopian dream of automated hump shunting began to crack and crumble, both the

**Rolling wagons blur as they pass the hump controllers panel at Scunthorpe Yard in 1972.**
*British Rail (Eastern Region)*

expense and inefficiency of yards like Hessle meant that their closure was only a matter of time. The root cause of the demise of Hessle lay in the refusal of Hull's dockers to accept containerisation in the 1960s. Much of the lucrative dock traffic moved to the south bank of the Humber, and Immingham Docks subsequently expanded. As shipping at Immingham increased, so too did the importance of the railway yards in the area.

Hull Yard, completed in 1935, was the forerunner of Dringhouses, Healey Mills and Tinsley, completed in the early 1960s. Marshalling yard construction in Yorkshire did not halt here as it did in the rest of Britain. Two yards in the county were 'born out of due time'. Both Scunthorpe New Yard and Doncaster Belmont Yard were completed in the 1970s.

## Scunthorpe

In the summer of 1962, the Minister of Transport approved the remodelling of Trent Yard at Scunthorpe. In 1964, an interim report suggested that the 'new wagon retardation equipment' promised such increased efficiency that the Trent Yard could be completely redesigned. It was suggested that hump earthworks could be reduced or even abolished by using the new Dowty Wagon Control System. The plan for the new Trent Yard was ready by mid-1966 — it was, however, never executed. A decreased throughput of wagons and increased 'block load' working made it impossible to justify the plan. A smaller

scheme was accepted and Scunthorpe New Yard (West Yard) was commissioned in 1971. Grant and Lyon Co. Ltd constructed a traditional hump yard containing 19 primary sidings, 7 miles of track, 40 turnouts, and 40,000 tons of sand to build the hump. The closure of the old Trent Yard was announced in 1986 leaving the Scunthorpe New Yard as the main marshalling yard on South Humberside.

## Doncaster

The rationalisation and reconstruction of the yards at Doncaster Decoy and Belmont was undertaken during the resignalling of Doncaster in the late 1970s; these yards being the most recently constructed major marshalling facilities in Great Britain. As the Railfreight network has come to mirror the InterCity network more closely, so the importance of a marshalling yard at Doncaster has increased. The Speedlink plans laid in the late 1970s envisaged three 'network yards' in Yorkshire. These were Dringhouses, Healey Mills and Doncaster. The yards at Tinsley, Scunthorpe and Immingham were classified as secondary yards, whilst marshalling facilities at Hull were reduced to a bare minimum (six sidings).

Doncaster has the advantage of being well situated at the junction of the East Coast Main Line (ECML), and the east to west lines from Hull and Grimsby to Manchester and Liverpool. The North East/South West corridor also passes

The multiple small jacks of the Dowty system are visible beside the running rails in this telephoto view of Scunthorpe West Yard. Class 47 No. 47217 stands at the head of a Doncaster-bound Speedlink feeder service whilst two Class 08s busy themselves shunting the yard.

Another general view of Scunthorpe West, or Hump, Yard shows the control tower on the far left, with the hump itself in the centre of the picture.

Plans in the 1960s suggested that a new hump yard should be constructed on the site of Scunthorpe Trent Yard, to the east of Scunthorpe. Here, in August 1986, the yard stands closed; its 23 sidings used for the storage of surplus steel wagons.

through Doncaster. In addition to its geographical situation, electrification of the ECML may reap further benefits for trunk freight services. Because of these advantages, a gradual transfer of traffic to Doncaster Belmont Yard is underway.

Unnecessary duplication of services in Yorkshire may be avoided by transferring all trunk Speedlink trains to Doncaster Yard and reducing Railfreight activities at Healey Mills and Dringhouses. This process is discussed in detail later in the chapter.

Thus the modern hump marshalling yard made its debut in 1935 at Hull, saw considerable proliferation during the 1950s and 1960s, and finally faded into obsolescence in the 1980s.

On 29th September 1986, the sidings at Immingham were closed as a Speedlink yard. On 3rd October 1986 there was very little work for Class 08s Nos 08508 and 08405, but the yard layout is a reminder of the lavish provision for freight traffic at ports like Immingham. Coal exported through the docks now uses the rapid unloader behind the second pylon on the left, and there is no longer any need for rows of parallel sidings cluttered with low-capacity mineral wagons loaded with coal awaiting shipment.

The 'down' yard at Doncaster Belmont betrays its past as part of a hump yard in the layout of its eight sorting sidings, which are seen here radiating from the site of the old hump at Belmont.

The 'up' yard at Belmont contains just six single-ended sorting sidings. The yard was shunted by Class 08 No. 08903 on 2nd June 1986 and contained only air-braked rolling stock.

The Decoy yards at Doncaster are used mainly by merry-go-round trains such as this one hauled by Class 58 No. 58035, seen departing from the south of the yard on 18th December 1985. Reorganisation of coal movements in Yorkshire may mean that these sidings could be used by Speedlink traffic in the future.

The Decoy 'down' yard is shared between block coal trains and crippled wagons awaiting repair at BREL Doncaster Works. Class 08 No. 08562 *The Doncaster Postman*, indulges in a little shunting in December 1985.

# Hull Yard

Hull Yard was not a single yard, but rather a collection of yards on a site to the north of the main line at Hessle. The Hull Inward Yard, opened on 9th December 1935, has already been mentioned. It allowed all goods traffic for Hull to be sorted at one modern yard. Entrance to the yard was controlled by Hessle Haven signal box. From here, trains could enter the six reception roads from the 'down' main and 'down' slow lines. Trains arriving from the east had access to the two most southerly reception roads; the yard was therefore 'bi-directional' although called the Inward Yard. Thirty sorting sidings and an engine release road radiated from the hump summit. At the east end of the yard there were four departure roads, each available for traffic from any of the 30 sorting sidings. The gradient profile from reception roads to departure was conventional with a maximum of 1 in 18 from the hump top to the first set of points ('King' points). Control of shunting movements was effected by a searchlight signal at the hump top. This could display three indications; red for stop, yellow for ordinary shunting speed and green for quick motion. In addition to the main signal a repeating signal was provided in the reception sidings 200yds from the hump. If weather conditions rendered these signals invisible, then a system of loud-sounding bells was used to transmit messages to the shunters.

The Inward Yard was only one of the yards at Hull. There was a similar Outward Yard as well as Loaded Mineral Yard, Priory, Drypool and Springhead yards. The Inward Yard was, however, the most

modern and consequently the most busy at Hull. The reception roads varied in length from 92 to 102 SWL, whilst the sorting sidings ranged from 437yds to 536yds long.

A total siding length of 10¼ miles had the capacity to hold 2,120 wagons. With a capacity to shunt 1,000 wagons each shift, the turn-round time for a wagon within the yard averaged twenty four hours. The operation of both points and retarders was manually executed according to the pattern provided by a 'cut card'. The head shunter was able to set the electro-pneumatically-controlled points into the sorting sidings by pressing a button at the bottom of the panel bearing the siding number. If, however, a wagon 'cut' was greater than six SWL long, the points had to be set individually because of the short track circuits on the hump. The four retarders at the yard were of the Fröhlich pattern made by Rail Brakes Ltd. Each retarder was 75ft long and weighed 55 tons, and, as the *Railway Gazette* of January 1936 points out, "had dealt sucess-

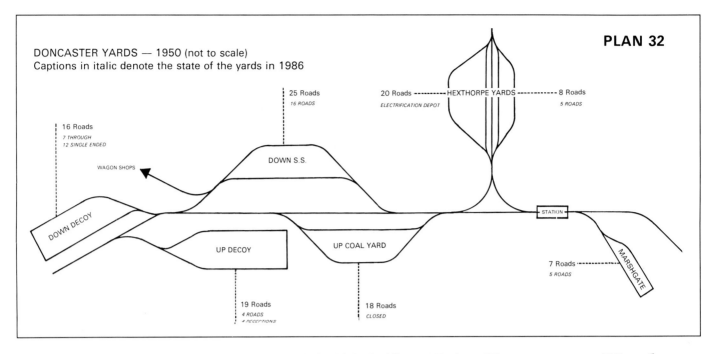

DONCASTER YARDS — 1950 (not to scale)
Captions in italic denote the state of the yards in 1986

PLAN 32

25 Roads
*16 ROADS*

20 Roads -------- HEXTHORPE YARDS -------- 8 Roads
*ELECTRIFICATION DEPOT*                      *5 ROADS*

16 Roads
*7 THROUGH*
*12 SINGLE ENDED*

WAGON SHOPS

DOWN S.S.

DOWN DECOY

UP DECOY

UP COAL YARD

STATION

MARSHGATE

7 Roads -------
*5 ROADS*

19 Roads
*4 ROADS*
*4 RECEPTIONS*

18 Roads
*CLOSED*

---

fully with a cut of 47 loaded coal wagons". A quaint note in the official description of the yard records: "On Mondays, Wednesdays and Fridays, the rails from the hump top to the fouling point of each siding are 'swept' by the Engineer's Department to ensure the track circuits functioning".

So much for the west end of the yard. At the east end all points were hand points and no such mechanisation existed. The departure roads held 55 to 65 wagons and were complemented by six secondary sorting sidings holding up to 24 wagons. In 1956, two diesel shunting pilots and a total of 15 staff were responsible for the smooth running of the Inward Yard. This staff included one lad porter to release the wagon brakes, another lad porter designated as a telephone attendant, and three 'chasers' who were responsible for taking wagons not suitable for retardation safely down into the yard. At this time the yard was still in full operation, and the list of 'road allocations' in *Table 27* will remind the reader of the drastic changes that have taken place in the last 30 years. Many of the stations listed are closed or have lost their goods yards. The carriage of fish and coal in the area has almost vanished; a reflection of the decreased activities of the port of Hull. Fish now travels by road, and coal exports travel via Immingham on the south bank of the Humber. By 1976, a major rationalisation had reduced one of the largest freight yard complexes in Britain to the Hull New Yard. This was built on the site of the old loaded mineral yard at Hessle and contained 23 double-ended roads. There was provision for future expansion to a total of 40 double-ended, flat-shunted, roads. The Hull New Yard TOPS office regulated the movement of 1,500 wagons each day. These travelled on 19 trip freights and pilot workings, or one of the six trunk freight trains to leave the yard each day (Dringhouses 2, Healey Mills, Tinsley, Doncaster, Scunthorpe). The last ten years have seen a drastic reduction of wagonload traffic in Hull. Rather than the planned expansion of Hull New Yard, it has been closed. The entire marshalling capacity in

the city is dealt with in six sidings at Hessle. Block loads apart, the yard has three 'trunk freights' each day; one to Toton and two to York (Dringhouses). Whether there will be future expansion of Railfreight in Hull is not clear. The neighbouring ports of Goole and Immingham remain relatively busy when compared with the total collapse of wagonload freight withing the city of Hull. It remains to be seen whether Speedlink can win traffic back after 30 years of steady decline.

# Doncaster Yard

## Pre-1980

There were several marshalling yards within the Doncaster area. Yards at Decoy, Belmont, Hexthorpe and Marshgate handled the freight of the town. In 1950 *(Plan 32)*, these yards contained a total of 113 sidings, and much of their capacity was taken up with 5,000 crippled wagons stored

**Table 27**

**Hull Inward Yard Siding Allocation 1957**

*Siding*

| | |
|---|---|
| 1 | Fish Empties Insul. |
| 2 | Fish (Main) |
| 3 | Bolsters |
| 4 | Common Users |
| 5 | Common Users |
| 6 | Vans |
| 7 | Vanfits |
| 8 | Chalk Lane |
| 9 | Fish kits, Goods, South Side, St. Andrews Dock |
| 10 | Outward Yards |
| 11 | Hull and Barnsley traffic for Springhead and Neptune Street |
| 13 | Hull |
| 12 | New Yards and Shipping |
| 14 | Spare road |
| 15 | Salt End tanks |
| 16 | Wilmington |
| 17 | Drypools |
| 18 | Stepney |
| 19 | King George Dock |
| 20 | Alexandra Dock |
| 21 | Shops |
| 22 | Coal for Mineral |
| 23 | Coal Empties |
| 24 | Beverleys |
| 25 | Hornsea |
| 26 | Paragon |
| 27 | Driffields |
| 28 | Stations Nafferton to Carnaby inclusive, Bridlington, Bankers, (Flamborough to Seamer) and Scarborough |
| 29 | Radiator |
| 30 | Withernsea |

In May 1977, Class 31 No. 31236 arrives at Doncaster Carr Yard with a trip freight from one of the local glass works. To the left of the train lies the 'up' coal yard which was closed during the Doncaster modernisation scheme of the late 1970s.

*L. Nixon*

in the area, pending their repair at Doncaster Works. By 1972 a few minor alterations had taken place; nine roads in the 'up' coal yard had been closed and a road taken out of use at Hexthorpe 'down' Yard. The layout of Doncaster's yards remained essentially unchanged.

The traffic at Doncaster could be divided into two types. First, the merry-go-round coal trains from local pits to Aire Valley power stations which did not require marshalling, but often needed stabling in the Doncaster area. The second arm of

freight operation in the 1970s was mixed goods. This traffic was carried on a mixture of vacuum and unfitted trains departing from both Belmont and Decoy yards. *Table 28* lists the arrivals and departures of the 1972 timetable. Today's timetable follows a similar pattern to that of 1972. However the superficial similarities in the pattern of services hides the great advances which have been made by Railfreight in the last 14 years. In 1972 a total of 37 'up' and 35 'down' trains were marshalled in the 44 sidings at Doncaster Decoy and Belmont. Of these, twelve were Class 6 trains, which had a maximum speed of 45mph — the rest more predominantly Class 8 and Class 9 with restrictions of 30mph placed upon them. Forty of the 72 services were truly mixed traffic whilst the rest carried block loads of grain, sand, steel or coal. Five of the trains were entirely devoted to the

carriage of cripples into the Doncaster area. This marshalling was handled by seven Class 08 pilot locomotives and a workforce of about 30 men.

When Doncaster was modernised in the late 1970s, all wagonload traffic (Speedlink) was concentrated on the Belmont Yard. Rebuilding enabled both 'up' and 'down' traffic to be dealt with on the west side of the ECML. The Belmont Yards (*Plan 33* contain six 'up' and eight 'down' sorting sidings; a reduction of 30 sidings from the 1972 total of 44. Not only are there fewer sidings, but their average length of 55 SWL is considerably shorter than their 1972 equivalents. The number of staff needed to deal with the marshalling at Doncaster (Belmont) totals only ten. Obviously the operation of the yard over the twenty four hour day means that approximately four times this number of men are employed at

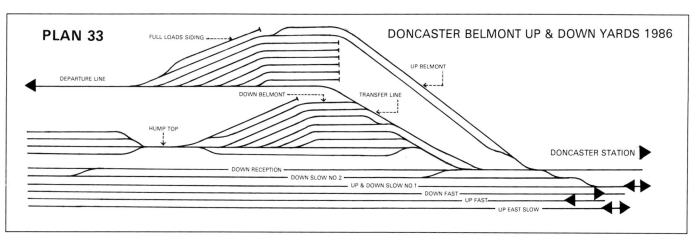

PLAN 33                     FULL LOADS SIDING ----                                    DONCASTER BELMONT UP & DOWN YARDS 1986

UP BELMONT

DEPARTURE LINE

DOWN BELMONT ----           TRANSFER LINE

HUMP TOP                                                                              DONCASTER STATION ▶

DOWN RECEPTION
DOWN SLOW NO.2
UP & DOWN SLOW NO.1
DOWN FAST
UP FAST
UP EAST SLOW

# Table 28

## Decoy Up Yard

| | | | | Traffic carried |
|---|---|---|---|---|
| 8M27 | | 06.45 | Decoy to Toton | mandatory mixed freight |
| 7T06 | | 07.09 | Decoy to Gainsborough | mandatory mixed freight |
| 9T14 | | 06.38 | Decoy to Rossington | loaded traffic for the coalite plant |
| 8D78 | | 07.00 | Scunthorpe to Decoy | steel traffic for the 7P71, 8P47, and 7P63 |
| 6E38 | | 09.50 | arrival from Burghead | empty grain wagons returning to East Anglia |
| 8D43 | | 09.30 | Tinsley to Decoy | 'rough' traffic including cripples for BREL |
| 6E64 | | 12.25 | arrival from Dufftown | empty grain wagons for East Anglia |
| 8E46 | | 13.40 | arrival from Warrington | mandatory mixed freight, traffic for 8P47 |
| 7P71 | SX | 14.40 | Decoy to Whitemoor | empty grain wagons for Ancaster, Sleaford and East Anglia |
| 8D58 | | 14.25 | Decoy to Lincoln | mandatory empty grain wagons for Ancaster |
| 9P10 | | 14.45 | Decoy to Whitemoor | all Whitemoor traffic less than 35mph |
| 8P18 | SX | 12.40 | Tees to Whitemoor | change engine and examine train |
| 8B18 | | 13.50 | Tees to New England (Peterborough) | attach and detach portions, mandatory mixed freight |
| 9T32 | | 15.12 | Decoy to Rossington | empty wagons to be loaded with coalite at Rossington |
| 9T02 | | 18.00 | Rockware glass to Decoy | sand empties for 8P53, gun powder vans for 7J06 and 6N66 |
| 9T28 | | | transfer to Belmont | |
| 9T02 | | 19.05 | Decoy to Bentley colliery | picks up coal from Bentley colliery |
| 8D12 | SO | 15.55 | York to Decoy | sand empties for 8P55 |
| 8P53 | SX | 18.11 | York to Whitemoor | mandatory mixed freight, calls to attach sand empties ex-9T02 and 8D12 |
| 8P53 | SO | 19.10 | Decoy to Kings Lynn | sand empties ex-8D12 and 9T02 |
| 8P47 | | 12.35 | Tyne to Whitemoor | mandatory mixed freight, calls to attach grain wagons ex-8E46 |
| 8P67 | SX | 18.40 | Healey Mills to Whitemoor | mandatory mixed freight, calls to attach and detach traffic |
| 7P61 | SX | 19.10 | Tyne to Whitemoor | mandatory mixed freight, calls to attach toric gas at Decoy |
| 8D93 | | 20.32 | Scunthorpe to Decoy | steel for Kings Cross and Grimsby (6E65 and 8D07) |
| 7P63 | SX | 21.48 | Healey Mills to Whitemoor | mandatory mixed freight, detach Temple Mills traffic, all loose loads to East Anglia to be attached |
| 8D38 | SX | 19.50 | Healey Mills to Decoy | sand empties for 8P43 |
| 6P65 | | 23.05 | York to Whitemoor | mandatory mixed freight, attach and detach traffic, forward as Class 7 |
| 8D41 | | 21.55 | Tinsley to Decoy | traffic to connect with 6E65 |
| 6C62 | | 20.15 | Tyne to Temple Mills | mandatory mixed freight, attach Temple Mills traffic, detach King X |
| 8P67 | SX | 18.40 | Healey Mills to Whitemoor | calls to attach and detach traffic (mixed) |
| 6E65 | | 18.25 | Millerhill to Kings Cross | mandatory mixed freight, attach traffic ex-6 C62, 8D93 and 8D41 |
| 6E87 | SX | 18.00 | Glasgow to Whitemoor | attach air-piped ferry wagons. |
| 9D67 | | 00.34 | Hull to Decoy | traffic for 8M27, 9D90, 9T06, and 8P43 |
| 8D07 | | 04.45 | Decoy to Grimsby | carries traffic ex-6D28 from 'down' side |
| 9D82 | MX | 02.55 | Healey Mills to Decoy | detach traffic for 8D07, 8P43 and 8M27 |
| 8D90 | | 05.05 | Decoy to Grantham | takes traffic from 6N66 and 6D28 |
| 8D42 | | 03.35 | Tinsley to Decoy | 'rough traffic' |
| 8P43 | | 05.20 | Decoy to Whitemoor | must take traffic ex-8D38 |

## Belmont Down Yard

| | | | | Traffic carried |
|---|---|---|---|---|
| 8T02 | | 05.55 | Belmont to Rockware glass | Sand from Kings Lynn |
| 8L05 | MO | 06.00 | Belmont to Healey Mills | Mandatory traffic ex-Whitemoor |
| 9T15 | | 06.13 | Belmont to BREL | Stores vans for Doncaster Works |
| 9J16 | MO | 06.42 | Belmont to Tinsley | Mandatory traffic ex-Whitemoor |
| 8L00 | | 03.15 | Whitemoor to Healey Mills | calls to detach and attach portions |
| 8L19 | MO | 07.43 | Belmont to Knottingley | sand from Kings Lynn |
| 9T15 | | 08.07 | Belmont to Hexthorpe | condemned vehicles and cripples to stable |
| 8L08 | | 06.13 | Whitemoor (Norwood) to York | conditional freight, calls to detach and attach portions |
| 9D86 | | 0.8.00 | Whitemoor to Belmont | grain for Scotland from East Anglia |
| 9D58 | | 07.30 | Whitemoor to Belmont | conditional grain train |
| 8D98 | SO | 08.35 | Grantham to Belmont | mandatory service (mixed) |
| 6S43 | | 14.15 | Belmont to Dufftown/Keith/Muir of Ord | grain in BGV wagons to Scottish distilleries |
| 6S40 | SX | 15.15 | Belmont to Burghead | grain in BGV wagons to Scottish distilleries |
| 7N29 | | 17.15 | Belmont to Tyne via Eaglescliffe | mandatory freight (mixed) |
| 8D12 | SO | 12.50 | Kings Lynn to Belmont | sand from Kings Lynn to Rockware Glass |
| 7N27 | SO | 18.25 | Belmont to Tees | conditional service |
| 7N27 | SX | 12.42 | Whitemoor to Tees | mandatory service (mixed) |
| 7J66 | SX | 17.50 | Grimsby to Tinsley | mandatory mixed freight, attach Derby and Crewe works stores vans |
| 7J06 | SX | 15.45 | Grantham to Tinsley | calls to detach and attach portions |
| 6S72 | SX | 14.55 | Parkeston Quay to Glasgow | calls to detach and attach portions, attach portions from Beverley and Newark to Aberdeen |
| 8L24 | SX | 17.14 | Whitemoor to York | detach sand traffic for Mexborough |
| 8D29 | SX | 18.58 | Whitemoor to Belmont | conditional freight service (mixed) |
| 9D05 | MX | 00.25 | Belmont to Scunthorpe | empty steel wagons returning to Scunthorpe |
| 6D28 | SX | 20.20 | Kings Cross to Belmont | portions for forwarding to Grimsby, Tyne, York, Tinsley, Healey Mills, Leeds, Hull, Newark and Grantham (mixed) |
| 8D69 | MX | 04.11 | Belmont to Scunthorpe | ICI explosives |
| 6N66 | SX | 20.23 | Temple Mills to Gateshead | mandatory mixed freight |
| 6L63 | SX | 23.26 | Whitemoor to Healey Mills | calls to detach and attach portions |
| 7J16 | W- | | | |
| | SX | 03.05 | Belmont to Tinsley | mixed traffic ex-6N66, 6D28 and 9T02 |
| 6L65 | MX | 03.35 | Belmont to Hunslet | mixed traffic ex-6D28 and 6L63 |
| 7D21 | MX | 04.50 | Belmont to Hull | mixed traffic ex-9T15, 6D28, 6L63 and 6N66 |
| 8N81 | | 00.10 | Whitemoor to Tees | calls for examination only |
| 8L74 | MX | 02.55 | Whitemoor (Norwood) to Monk Bretton | detach sand for Monk Bretton, attach sand for Cudworth |
| 7S68 | MX | 01.24 | Whitemoor to Millerhill | attach portion and examination of train |
| 7L06 | | 21.10 | Kings Lynn to Knottingley | detach Rockware sand |

Belmont. A direct comparison with the workforce of 1972 shows a two-thirds reduction, similar to the reduction in siding capacity. In the light of such sweeping changes in both material and human resources one might expect a great reduction in the traffic handled. *Table 29* reveals the very real increase in efficiency at Doncaster as reflected by the total of 75 freights passing through the yard on an average weekday. Not only is there a marginal increase in the number of trains utilising the yard, but a much higher percentage of the wagons are in revenue-earning service. It has not been possible to compare either the tonnage of or revenue from the freight services of 1972 and 1986, but staff at Doncaster have suggested that the length of trains in the two eras is roughly comparable. Thus a two-thirds reduction in manpower and trackwork has been effected alongside a considerable increase in the importance of Doncaster (Belmont) as a Speedlink marshalling yard.

The 6S63 Scunthorpe to Aberdeen freight arrives at Doncaster Belmont Yard after running round to the south of Doncaster. The train was routed via the freight-only line around the east of Doncaster to avoid any potential congestion in the station area. Class 37 No. 37004 will add some HEA coal hoppers to its load of Scunthorpe steel before departing north to its next stop at Tyne Yard. The train standing to the right of the 6S63 is a General Utility Service from March Whitemoor: this conveys wagons not suitable for Speedlink trains.

## Table 29
### Belmont 'Up' Yard From 12/05/86

| WTT | Time | Day-run | From | To | Arr. | Dep. | |
|-----|------|---------|------|----|------|------|-|
| 6E61 | 1630 | MX | Mossend | Belmont | 0046 | – | |
| 6E38 | 2121 | SX | Bescot | Belmont | 0142– | | |
| 6E26 | 2155 | SX | Warrington | Belmont | 0233 | – | |
| 6D87 | 0155 | MX | Scunthorpe | Belmont | 0243 | – | |
| 6E89 | 1435 | SX | Aberdeen | Immingham | 0318 | 0446 | |
| 6E86 | 1920 | SX | Mossend | P. Quay | 0330 | 0426 | |
| 6D62 | 0640 | SX | Belmont | Boston | – | 0640 | |
| 8T02 | 0619 | SO | Belmont | Askern/Markham | – | 0619 | |
| 6T08 | 0630 | MO | Belmont | T.Marsh/Colly. | – | 0630 | |
| 6T02 | 0724 | SX | Rockware | Belmont | 0826 | – | |
| 8T02 | 0845 | SX | Belmont | Askern/Markham | – | 0845 | |
| 6E94 | 0125 | MX | Severn Tnl. Jc. | Belmont | 1005 | – | |
| 4R40 | 0914 | SX | Wrenthorpe | Dagenham | 0953 | 1040 | |
| 6D72 | 1055 | EWD | Belmont | Immingham | – | 1055 | |
| 6D88 | 1123 | SX | Belmont | Boston | – | 1123 | |
| 4D92 | 1040 | MX | Wrenthorpe | Belmont | 1154 | – | |
| 6E60 | D408 | SX | Mossend | Belmont | 1239 | – | |
| 7D02 | 1330 | SX | Healey Mills | Belmont | 1408 | – | |
| 6T13 | 1420 | SX | Belmont | Worksop | – | 1420 | |
| 7R43 | 1305 | TTHO | Kilnhurst | Ripple Lane | 1428 | 1430 | Crew Rl. |
| 9H09 | 1528 | SX | Belmont | Peterborough | – | 1528 | |
| 6T02 | 1457 | SX | Rockware | Belmont | 1556 | – | |
| 6D81 | 1437 | SX | Hunslet | Belmont | 1553 | | |
| 6R82 | 1205 | SX | T.C.F.D | Ripple Lane | 1611 | 1655 | |
| 9D29 | 1540 | SX | Healey Mills | Belmont | 1654 | – | |
| 6D49 | 1610 | SX | Healey Mills | Belmont | 1712 | – | |
| 6D78 | 1500 | SX | Immingham | Belmont | 1734 | – | |
| 6T17 | | SX | Collieries | Belmont | 1810 | – | |
| 7D77 | 1745 | SX | Scunthorpe | Belmont | 1849 | – | |
| 6F83 | 1527 | SX | Tees | P.Quay | 1907 | 2210 | |
| 6O44 | 1605 | SX | T.C.F.D | Paddock Wood | 2028 | 2117 | |
| 9D09 | 2000 | SX | Scunthorpe | Belmont | 2105 | – | |
| 6E33 | 1925 | THO | Toton | Belmont | 2131 | – | |
| 6T02 | 2014 | MWFO | Rockware | Belmont | 2147 | – | |
| 9D71 | 2030 | SX | Tinsley | Belmont | 2140 | – | |
| 7D19 | 2144 | SX | Tinsley | Belmont | 2231 | – | |
| 6T12 | 2330 | SX | Belmont | Worksop | – | 2330 | |
| 6H39 | 1930 | SX | Monk Bretton | March Yard | 2100 | 0002 | |
| 9D01 | 2245 | SX | York | Belmont | 2350 | – | |

### Belmont 'Down' Yard From 12/05/86

| WTT. | Time | Day-run | From | To | Arr. | Dep. | |
|------|------|---------|------|----|------|------|-|
| 7J29 | 0046 | MX | Belmont | Tinsley | – | 0046 | |
| 9L02 | 0147 | MX | Belmont | York | – | 0147 | |
| 6N90 | 1850 | SX | P.Quay | Tees | 0133 | 0207 | |
| 6E53 | 1138 | SX | Dover | Tyne | 0222 | 0257 | |
| 6S67 | 0343 | MX | Belmont | Mossend | – | 0343 | |
| 4L30 | 0352 | MX | Belmont | Wrenthorpe | – | 0352 | |
| 7D36 | 0409 | MX | Belmont | Scunthorpe | – | 0409 | |
| 6L55 | 0508 | MX | Belmont | Hunslet | – | 0508 | |
| 6T02 | 0619 | SX | Belmont | Rockware | – | 0619 | |
| 6T93 | 0630 | SX | Belmont | Collieries | – | 0630 | |
| 6L43 | 0808 | SX | Belmont | Healey Mills | – | 0808 | |
| 8T02 | | EWD | Askern/Markham | Belmont | 1203 | – | |
| 6T08 | – | MO | Askern/Markham | Belmont | 1213 | – | |
| 7M37 | 1020 | WFO | Torksey | Stanlow | 1215 | 1425 | C&W Fxam |
| 6T17 | 1227 | SX | Belmont | Collieries | – | 1227 | |
| 6T13 | 1205 | SX | Worksop | Belmont | 1320 | – | |
| 6D63 | 1058 | SX | Boston | Belmont | 1343 | – | |
| 0T02 | 1407 | SX | Carr Loco | Stainforth | – | 1407 | |
| 6T93 | 1430 | SX | Belmont | Collieries | – | 1430 | |
| 7M37 | 1202 | MO | Torksey | Stanlow | 1405 | 1425 | C&W Fxam |
| 6L74 | 1115 | SX | Middleton Twrs | Monk Bretton | 1442 | 1505 | ('Down' Decoy) |
| 6S63 | 1330 | SX | Scunthorpe | Aberdeen | 1455 | 1553 | |
| 6S46 | 1558 | SX | Belmont | Mossend | – | 1558 | |
| 9D09 | 1624 | SX | Belmont | Scunthorpe | – | 1624 | |
| 9J71 | 1625 | SX | Belmont | Tinsley | – | 1625 | |
| 6T02 | 1635 | SX | Belmont | Rockware | – | 1635 | |
| 6D89 | 1432 | SX | Boston | Belmont | 1822 | – | |
| 9L29 | 1825 | SX | Belmont | Healey Mills | – | 1825 | |
| 7L09 | 1912 | SX | Belmont | Healey Mills | – | 1912 | |
| 6D86 | 1939 | SX | Belmont | Scunthorpe | – | 1939 | |
| 6M80 | 2004 | SX | Belmont | Bescot | – | 2004 | |
| 6V81 | 2018 | SX | Belmont | Severn Tnl. Jt. | – | 2018 | |
| 6M84 | 2110 | SX | Belmont | Warrington | – | 2110 | |
| 6S96 | 1345 | SX | P.Quay | Mossend | 2038 | 2118 | |
| 6T12 | 2119 | SX | Worksop | Belmont | 2222 | – | |
| 9D09 | 1924 | SX | Peterborough | Belmont | 2226 | – | |
| 6D42 | 1635 | SX | P. Quay | Belmont | 2244 | – | |
| 7M31 | 2301 | THO | Belmont | Toton | – | 2301 | |
| 4S39 | 1935 | SX | Dagenham | Millerhill | 0001 | 0053 | |

## 1980s

Before describing the work of Belmont Yard in detail, mention must be made of the considerable tonnage of coal stabled in the Doncaster area. Although the majority of this coal is not marshalled at Doncaster, an average of 40 merry-go-round services each day use the single reversible line from Doncaster station to Belmont Yard.

This single line is the only northern access into the Speedlink yard. The capacity of the yard is therefore limited by both siding capacity and access from the main line. To compound the problem of access, the headshunt for the 'down' yard crosses the main entrance to the yard. Thus any shunting precludes arrival or departure from the yard.

**York Dringhouses Yard. A busy scene in June 1986 belied the possibility of closure at Dringhouses. Class 47 No. 47319 has just arrived with the 6O49 Haverton Hill to Eastleigh, whilst to its right, Class 47 No. 47007 is waiting for the traffic which will form the 6O44 Tyneside Central Freight Depot to Paddock Wood, to be reassembled by the Class 08 seen shunting in the background.**

The congestion around Belmont Yard is the result of an outdated operating agreement. This stipulates that only Knottingley-based drivers may operate trains into the Aire Valley power stations of Drax, Eggborough and Ferrybridge. Thus coal trains from the Doncaster area must be re-manned in the yards at 'up' and 'down' Decoy before proceeding to the Aire Valley. This re-manning involves 100 trains each week, carrying a total of 100,000 tons of coal. This volume of traffic means that an average of five loaded trains are to be found waiting in the Decoy Yards and a 'bad day' may see as many as thirteen trains blocking the sidings at 'up' and 'down' Decoy as well as Hexthorpe Yard. British Railways are putting forward several ideas to alleviate this congestion. The keystone to these plans is an arrangement in which Knottingley crews service the pits at Bentley and Manvers. This would remove 60 trains each week from the Belmont and Decoy area. If the anticipated increase in production at Gascoine Wood is realised, the remaining Doncaster coal may be directed to West Burton Power Station on the River Trent. Thus the remaining coal trains from Doncaster will not need stabling in the yards at Decoy.

**Class 37 No. 37031 stands in the 'down' yard at Belmont with its load of coal. The train is the 6S46 Doncaster to Mossend, and on 2nd June 1986 it was loaded to maximum capacity. Later that day the locomotive failed at Thirsk on its way north because of 'hot water' in the boiler.**

This lengthy 'side-track' is important because it shows how the different sectors of Railfreight are closely interdependant. Operating changes in one area may have far-reaching effects throughout the rail network, and its various departments. The 'tinkering' with merry-go-round services linked to minor track alterations (*Plan 33*)

will greatly increase the capacity and efficiency of the Belmont Yards.

The Belmont of the 1980s is flat-shunted, using two Class 08 locomotives. The yard has two main functions:

1. The collection of Speedlink traffic from customers throughout Lincolnshire, South Humberside and South Yorkshire.
2. To attach and detach sections from long-haul Speedlink trains and to exchange sections between them.

The first activity involves a combination of 'trip' freights and Speedlink 'feeder' services. Local collieries are predominantly served by merry-go-round trains which link them to Yorkshire's power stations. A small percentage of their output, however, is designated as 'Speedlink coal' and travels to Belmont in HEA 32 ton hoppers and FPA container wagons. Markham Main Colliery is the busiest pit in the area with an output of twelve HEAs each day. Additional wagons also come from Brodsworth and Manvers Main pits. Apart from coal, the major local traffics are sand, potash and lime to the various glass works in Yorkshire. Monk Bretton, near Cudworth, receives its sand as a block load from King's Lynn. Jackson's at Knottingley takes in only lime and potash; this via the trunk trains to and from Warrington. Thus the only local trip freight from Doncaster is the 6T02 which services Barnby Dun three times each day. It carries sand from King's Lynn, lime from Hindlow, and soda ash from Northwich. A comparison with the services in 1972 shows the move away from the marshalling yard and a considerable reduction in trip working.

Whilst local industry receives relatively few goods by rail, the rural county of Lincolnshire is a growth area for Speedlink. Recent reorganisation of the freight services to the county, called 'Lincolnshire Green

Under the shadow of York Minster, Class 31 No. 31207 heads south with the 6F83, 15.25, Tees to Harwich Parkeston Quay Speedlink service.

In August 1985, the 6F83 Tees to Harwich Parkeston Quay Speedlink passes the yard at York North. The long parallel sidings of this yard make it an excellent candidate for

Fields', has resulted in two 'out and back' trips from Doncaster (Belmont). These serve ten customers including the docks at Boston and several grain terminals. Again the workload at Belmont has been increased, but considerable savings have been made at Lincoln and Peterborough. Unlike many trip freights of the past, these two trains are run on what management and drivers agree is 'split second timing'. A similar precision has come to rule at yards such as Belmont. The timetable is planned

to avoid congestion at the yard. As a result, feeder services from Healey Mills (2), Hunslet, Immingham, Scunthorpe (2), Worksop and Tinsley are evenly spaced throughout the twenty four hour day. Much of the traffic from Healey Mills and Worksop is 'Speedlink' coal, bound for Scotland. The traffic for Hunslet is mainly steel, bound for Whitehall Road goods depot, whilst the return trip brings scrap from Shipley and Laisterdyke on its way to Tinsley or Sheerness. The trips to and from

modernisation when the ECML is electrified, and it may become the Speedlink yard for York by the end of the decade.

Opposite:
An excellent example of a modern coal train is the 6S46 Doncaster to Mossend. Class 37 No. 37100 rounds the corner on to the freight avoiding line at York South with a consist of HEA hoppers and FPA container wagons, all passed to travel at 60mph.

An old-fashioned coal train passes York South on the freight avoiding line on 4th September 1972. The train of unfitted coal hoppers is hauled by Class 25 No. 7561 and emphasises the 'quiet' revolution in the Railfreight side of British Rail's operations.
*J. Cooper-Smith*

South Humberside carry a large volume of steel but also convey regular consignments of cement and fertilizers. Finally, much of the traffic on the Tinsley trip is scrap metal carried in POA wagons.

These varied trips and feeder services have booked connections with the trunk trains (*Table 29*) which call at Belmont. The trunk Speedlink network is divided into eleven major routes. Route 6, based around the East Coast Main Line, crosses Route 7, the trans-Pennine route at Doncaster. In addition, the north east/south west corridor, designated Route 2, has a couple of services routed via the Belmont Yards. The yard, therefore, has excellent connections to all points in the country.

One aspect of freight operation, unique to Doncaster, is the traffic generated by BRML and RFS Engineering at Doncaster. Not only are the works the major wagon repair centre in the country, but also an important supplier of spare parts for diesel maintenance depots. Crippled wagons were a major problem in the Doncaster yards. With as many as 5,000 wagons awaiting attention at the works, many of the sidings in Belmont and Decoy yards were 'blocked' by damaged rolling stock. Under the aegis of the 'cripple controller' at Derby, a more organised approach to wagon repairs has been instituted. This has cut the number of cripples awaiting attention from 5,000 to well under 500. The turnover of wagons at RFS Doncaster is around one hundred each week. This includes modifications, rebodying and rebuilding.

Thus if 30 HAA hoppers are to be rebuilt, the TOPS computer arranges for 30 wagons to arrive at Doncaster each week. The wagons arrive in Speedlink services, as most are classified as 'fit to run'. Any wagons which are more seriously damaged arrive on a 'GUS' or General Utility Service. Crippled wagons are however banned from the Belmont Yard because of their tendency to block the Speedlink roads for several days. They are therefore shunted to twelve roads in the 'down' Decoy Yard reserved for cripples. From here they are tripped, as required, to the wagon works. Even with such careful organisation, a mismatch between wagons arriving for repair and their entrance into the works could lead to a rapid overfilling of the 'down' Decoy Yard. A new system of 'contract repairs' should eliminate such mismatches. Contracts are arranged so that individual wagons are called for by number rather than as part of a batch. A wagon must arrive at Doncaster on a set day and be repaired within a pre-determined time span. Financial penalties may be incurred by either Railfreight or RFS if they fail to meet their deadline on any given wagon. This system is a very demanding one to operate but has further reduced the number of 'cripples' clogging the sidings around Doncaster.

The wagon repair traffic is only one arm of Speedlink's connection with BREL and RFS. The second arm is the dispatch of up to twelve ZRA vans each day; these contain urgent traffic for Canton, Laira and other large maintenance depots. These wagons are treated as normal Speedlink traffic;

BRML as a normal Speedlink customer. The stores department at BRML is under intense pressure because of British Railway's decision to purchase stores from the cheapest retailer rather than traditional suppliers. However a 'superstore' has now been set up by British Rail, on BRML property at Doncaster. This may lead to a dramatic increase in BRML-related Speedlink traffic. One estimate suggested that 50 ZRA stores vans would be dispatched each day!

## Future

It can be seen from the above discussion of trip and feeder services, together with local and regional changes, that Doncaster is becoming a very important marshalling yard. The freight operation around Doncaster is complex and the inter-relationships between block, Speedlink and other freights carefully balanced to obtain maximum usage of somewhat limited siding capacity. Future changes in merry-go-round coal operation and current improvements in the handling of 'cripples' have already been discussed. What then of the future of Speedlink at Doncaster? As mentioned earlier, current plans may see all Yorkshire's Speedlink marshalling concentrated in Doncaster.

## Healey Mills

The first stage of these plans, to concentrate Speedlink on Doncaster and initiated by the Speedlink manager as a cost-cutting exercise, has already taken place. The object of Stage 1 was a complete removal of Speedlink from Healey Mills. In the face of an alternative plan put forward by the NUR, and arbitration under the Worthing agreement, only a limited withdrawal from Healey Mills has been possible. Doncaster has gained three trips, two from Healey Mills and one from Hunslet, as well as two trunk services to Mossend. Trains to Warrington and Severn Tunnel still start at Healey Mills, and trips from the yard service the collieries at Grimethorpe and Kellingley. Long-term plans should foresee the closure of Healey Mills and a complete transfer of Speedlink traffic to Doncaster. In exchange Speedlink coal services were transferred to Healey Mills in July 1987 when the Discrete Coal Network was set up.

## Dringhouses

The third Speedlink yard in Yorkshire is Dringhouses. This is currently an important centre for the swopping of sections on long-haul Speedlinks. As the ECML is electrified, so the opportunity is being taken to streamline Railfreight's activity at York. The first step in a further concentration on Doncaster involves the transfer of both Hull and Goole feeder services to Belmont Yard. In addition some 'portion swopping' will take place at Doncaster. There are, however, considerable problems with the

track layout at Doncaster. Only the 'down' yard contains parallel through roads and even these are rather short.

Only two roads, Nos 5 and 6, are long enough to take a 60 SWL, long-haul, Speedlink train. It will therefore be necessary to transfer work to Tinsley and possibly as far south as Bescot. As electrification progresses, the yard at Dringhouses will close, and marshalling at York will be moved to York (North) Yard. This yard is currently used to stable coal trains on their way to the Aire Valley from the County Durham Coalfield. Minor track alterations and electrification will make the yard an ideal Speedlink marshalling point.

On 27th May 1964, an express freight from Park Lane Yard, in Gateshead, to York Dringhouses passes Fawcett Street in Sunderland. The Gateshead site was later redeveloped as the Tyneside Central Freight Terminal whilst Dringhouses continued as a Speedlink yard until closure in 1987. The train was classified as the 4B50, and hauled by Class 40 No. D357.

*I. Carr*

If the Speedlink system continues to expand, then York (North) Yard is an ideal site to handle the transfer of portions between the many long-distance freights along the ECML and NE/SW routes. Not only will it relieve congestion at Doncaster, but diesel-hauled trains from Teesside will benefit from an early change to electric motive power.

In the light of these changes, the already stretched facilities at Doncaster will see a gradual increase in traffic over the next two years. The changes in merry-go-round services, linked to minor track alterations, should enable the Belmont Yard to cope. If, at any stage, the predicted increases in traffic prove to be underestimates, then Railfreight may utilise the 'down' Decoy Yard for Speedlink marshalling. This yard is ideal for such work, its seven roads average 80 SWL, and are all through lines. Electrification is well underway at Doncaster; indeed through freight working may be possible well before October 1988. All the reception roads at Belmont will be electrified as well as the transfer line. In addition, two reception roads at the 'down' Decoy will come 'under the wires'. The 'up' and 'down' sorting sidings will all be electrified for their first ten SWL, and trains could be running under electric power by the end of 1988.

Predictions about the future beyond 1990 are difficult to make. The Channel Tunnel will be a major factor in the expansion of Railfreight. Not only the increase in traffic but also new ideas such as the 'U' bahn concept will shape the freight facilities of the future. This idea suggests that freight traffic from Lancashire to Yorkshire should travel via London! Most experienced railway managers do not seriously consider such plans as viable. However, electric haulage throughout, via the North London line, and new methods of accounting, have been used to justify such seemingly out-

An express freight from Dringhouses to Gateshead nears the end of its journey as it passes Pelaw Junction behind Class 40 No. D352, circa 1966. The first five wagons convey a traffic no longer handled by the railways — livestock.

*I. Carr*

The 6R82 Tyneside Freight Terminal to Ripple Lane approaches Doncaster behind Class 47 No. 47006 in 1984. Its load contains good examples of high-capacity grain and steel wagons.

*D. Allen*

Even back in 1970, considerable tonnages of coal had been transferred from wagonload haulage to modern air-braked merry-go-round trains. Here, Class 47 No. 1982 passes Doncaster on such a service in May 1970. The complete transfer of all power station coal to such block loads, along with much coal for big industrial users, was the death blow for many of Britain's marshalling yards.

*J. Cooper-Smith*

rageous ideas. In the light of such suggestions it is clear that the decisions about the future of marshalling yards may no longer be based upon traditional geographical and operating considerations. The future at Doncaster is bright, in spite of the limited facilities, and changes are afoot to make Belmont Yard one of only a handful of major marshalling yards left in Britain. Its evolution from a middle-sized traditional hump yard to a streamlined Speedlink yard

has been gradual. Changes at the yard have taken place predominantly as a response to changes in the freight trains it serves. Electrification, the Channel Tunnel and beyond, Railfreight has made a firm commitment to keep a modern marshalling yard at Doncaster.

My thanks go to the Area Manager's office at Doncaster, and particularly Mr Richard Tilsley (Traffic Manager, freight) and Keith Blount (ex-yard master) without

whose help this chapter could not have been written.

# Chapter 13

# Tinsley

Tinsley marshalling yard, between Sheffield and Rotherham, was the first yard in the world to be fully equipped with the Dowty Wagon Control System. It was opened on 29th October 1965 by Lord Beeching and the first yard manager was Mr Harry Whitehouse. Its capacity to handle 4,000 wagons daily was by no means the largest for a British marshalling yard, but the extent of automation at Tinsley did make it the most modern marshalling yard in the country at the time. It was the last major marshalling yard to be constructed in the wake of the 1955 Modernisation Plan, and served as a hump yard for only 19 years, for in December 1984 major rationalisation at the site included the closure of the hump and the reduction of shunting capacity at Tinsley.

## Historical Background

The first railway between Rotherham and Sheffield ran from Rotherham Westgate to Wicker and was opened in 1838. There followed a rapid proliferation of new railway lines in the area and further lines were opened as follows: 1840, Derby to Rotherham Masborough; 1845, Sheffield Bridgehouses to Manchester, via the Woodhead Tunnel; 1849, Sheffield Bridgehouses to Gainsborough, a new station being opened at Sheffield Victoria in 1851; 1864, Woodburn Junction to Rotherham and Masborough; 1870, Chesterfield to Attercliffe, including the Sheffield Midland station; 1900, Sheffield District Railway from Brightside Junction to Treeton Junction; 1903, City Goods Branch to Wharf Street. All these routes can be seen in *Fig.7*.

In 1923 the amalgamation of railway companies allocated the lines belonging to former Great Central Railway to the LNER, and the lines belonging to the old Midland Railway to the LMSR. Whilst some operating agreements to reduce the duplication of services were brought into practice at this time, no major alteration to the network took place. Nationalisation in 1948 and the Transport Act of 1947 provided the first opportunity to implement a cohesive rail transport plan for the Sheffield area. In 1950 the regional boundary changes brought the whole of Sheffield under the control of the Eastern Region of British Railways. Modernisation in the early 1950s included the completion of the electrification of the lines from Manchester to Sheffield and Wath. The freight service to Wath commenced in 1952 with passenger trains running to Sheffield Victoria by 1954, and freight continuing to Rotherwood exchange sidings in 1955.

In the mid-1950s, however, the network of railways and depots still remained much as it was at the turn of the century. The former LNER station at Sheffield Victoria had an accompanying main goods depot for small consignments at Bridgehouses, a coal depot at Harvest Lane, fruit and perishables at Blast Lane, and wagonload traffic at Park Sidings, Attercliffe and West Tinsley. Added to this were a carriage and wagon workshop at Neepsend and motive power

**Tinsley Yard. In 1965 the yard was nearing completion and in this view the diesel refuelling point and the yard control tower are clearly seen.**

*British Rail*

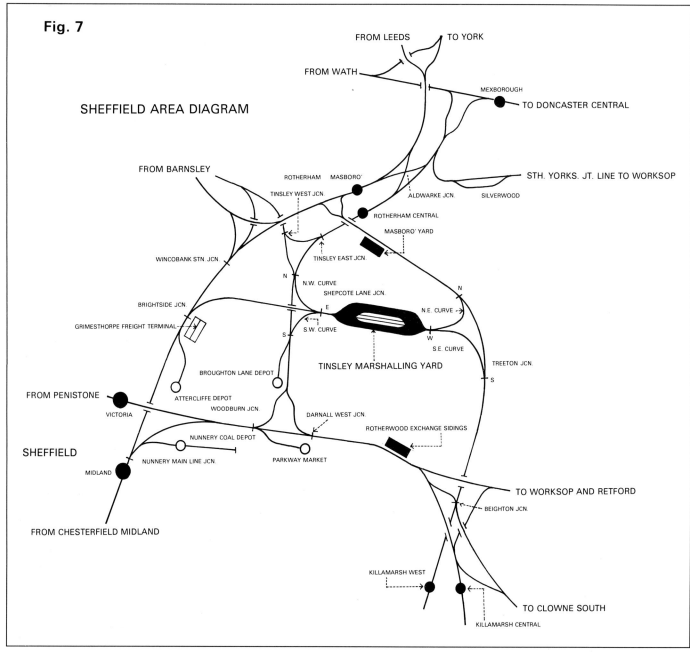

**Fig. 7**

SHEFFIELD AREA DIAGRAM

FROM LEEDS · TO YORK

FROM WATH

MEXBOROUGH

TO DONCASTER CENTRAL

FROM BARNSLEY

ROTHERHAM · MASBORO'

TINSLEY WEST JCN.

STH. YORKS. JT. LINE TO WORKSOP

ALDWARKE JCN. · SILVERWOOD

ROTHERHAM CENTRAL

MASBORO' YARD

WINCOBANK STN. JCN.

TINSLEY EAST JCN.

N.W. CURVE

SHEPCOTE LANE JCN.

N · N

BRIGHTSIDE JCN.

E · N.E. CURVE →

GRIMESTHORPE FREIGHT TERMINAL

S · S.W. CURVE

W

S.E. CURVE

TINSLEY MARSHALLING YARD

TREETON JCN.

S

BROUGHTON LANE DEPOT

ATTERCLIFFE DEPOT

FROM PENISTONE

WOODBURN JCN.

VICTORIA

DARNALL WEST JCN.

ROTHERWOOD EXCHANGE SIDINGS

NUNNERY COAL DEPOT

SHEFFIELD

MIDLAND

NUNNERY MAIN LINE JCN. · PARKWAY MARKET

TO WORKSOP AND RETFORD

BEIGHTON JCN.

FROM CHESTERFIELD MIDLAND

KILLAMARSH WEST

TO CLOWNE SOUTH

KILLAMARSH CENTRAL

depots at Darnall and Masborough. The major ex-LNER marshalling yard at Bernard Road was complemented by further yards at Broughton Lane, Ickles and Rotherham Road. The former LMSR passenger station was Sheffield Midland, and there were an even greater multiplicity of yards and depots associated with the LMSR network.

Goods depots at Wicker and Queens Road were complemented by coal depots at Healey and Nunnery. Perishable traffic was dealt with at Wharf Street and wagonloads at Healey, Ponds Street, Brightside Wharf and Upwell Street Wharf. Carriage and wagon repairs were carried out at Grimesthorpe, where there was also a motive power depot. Further engine sheds were provided at Millhouses and Canklow. The main marshalling yards were at Masborough and Woodhouse Mill, with secondary yards at Grimesthorpe, Engine Shed Sidings, Wincobank, Roundwood and Cardigan. All the passenger and freight-handling facilities around Sheffield were out of date, cramped, lacking in mechanical aides, and expensive to run. Their number

was far beyond the real need of the new circumstances brought about by nationalisation and the complexity of working between them induced consequent delays and an increase in the costs of handling traffic.

*Fig.7* illustrates the position as it stood in 1957 when the Sheffield District was formed. Not only was the railway network of Britain being reorganised to follow geographical considerations rather than inter-railway competition, but steam motive power was being replaced by diesel traction, and mechanisation was being applied to many areas of railway traffic handling. The basic requirements for the Sheffield area were one marshalling yard, one freight terminal and one diesel locomotive maintenance depot. The choice of sites for these new facilities presented considerable difficulty, because of the essential requirement that the marshalling yard, freight terminal, and diesel locomotive depot should be readily accessible to both former LNER and former LMS railway lines. Ideally it was hoped that these three facilities could be placed in close proximity

to one another. A site was selected half-way along the Sheffield District Railway. Here there lay an extensive area of undeveloped ground. Whilst the topography of this ground was most unfavourable, it was the only site large enough to take a modern marshalling yard within easy access of Sheffield and Rotherham.

By providing new connections to the Sheffield District line and a new north to east curve to the Midland main line at Treeton, access could be obtained from every direction. It was decided to build the diesel depot on adjacent ground and to site the goods depot at Grimesthorpe, displacing the motive power depot, carriage and wagon works, Grimesthorpe Sidings and T.W. Ward's Charlton Sidings. The rationalisation proposals were submitted to the British Transport Commission in 1960 and approved by the Ministry of Transport in 1961. Not only did they include the provision of a marshalling yard, freight terminal and diesel maintenance depot, but also several alterations to the railway network in the environs of Sheffield. A new scissors junction was to be provided at

Class 13 No. D4582 stands on the hump crest at Tinsley in March 1966. It is interesting to note that the two shunters are coupled the 'wrong' way round. Problems with visibility led to early alterations to these master and slave units. The locomotive stabling point is host to several diesel locomotives and a Stanier 8F 2-8-0.

*L. Nixon*

Another view of Tinsley taken in 1966 shows a rake of coke hoppers descending from the hump as two Class 31s and a Class 20, No. D8066, await attention at the refuelling point.

*British Rail*

Aldwarke, connecting Great Central and Midland main lines. The railway layout at Masborough was considerably simplified and a new curve at Nunnery allowed passenger services to be concentrated at Sheffield Midland station.

It was also suggested that the Manchester, Sheffield and Wath electrification scheme should be extended from Darnall to the new Tinsley marshalling yard. A final proposal to build a wagon repair shop at Woodhouse Mill was retracted and part of the Darnall motive power depot was converted for this use. These schemes were accepted and work began in 1961.

# Construction and Operation of Tinsley Yard

The new yard at Tinsley was the centrepiece of the rationalisation of railway facilities in the Sheffield area. It was designed to deal with traffic to and from the Sheffield industrial region and, over 70 per cent of

traffic was of local origin or destination. Some 80 per cent of this was handled by private sidings in the area. By its very nature such traffic was unsuitable for conveyance by freightliners and insufficient in volume to justify through train loads. The remaining 30 per cent of traffic handled at Tinsley was made up of wagons staged at the yard, whilst in transit. The site at Tinsley occupied 145 acres, 115 of which had to be purchased from twelve different owners. This was relatively simple, except in the case of one landowner, who had developed plans for a foundry extension on part of the area required for the yard. This vendor had to be found replacement land before the yard could be sanctioned. Some alteration in the course of the Sheffield to Leeds motorway was also necessary in order to fit the large new marshalling

complex into the land available. Because of the uneven nature of the site, considerable earthworks were carried out before construction could begin. In all, some 1.75 million tons of earth had to be moved. It is interesting to note that the diesel depot is built on top of a tunnel, which existed on the old Sheffield District Railway, whilst the adjacent reception sidings were laid at a level 60ft below that of the original ground.

In view of the fact that traffic would arrive and depart in all directions, separate 'up' and 'down' yards were undesirable. A large bi-directional hump yard was therefore decided upon. The multiplicity of divisions required by the complex of private sidings in the area made it necessary to construct not only 53 primary sorting sidings, but a secondary yard to cater for local private siding traffic. There were

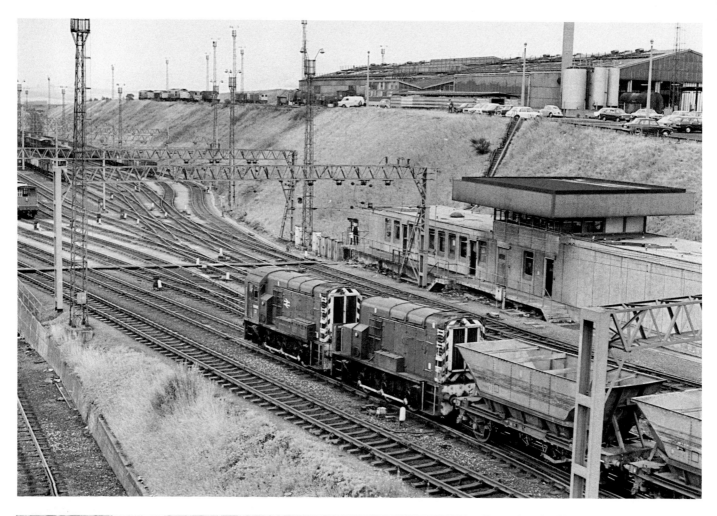

Renumbered Class 13 No. 13003 passes Tinsley Yard signal box as it propels a rake of HAA coal hoppers over the hump in July 1976.

*T.Heavyside*

A horizontal bar on the shunting signal indicates that Class 13 No. 13003 should stop on the hump at Tinsley. In January 1978 the yard is full of vacuum and unfitted rolling stock.

eleven reception roads with capacity of between 63 and 74 SWL. A hump engine return line and an engine return line also ran parallel with the reception sidings. Trains arriving from the south west along the arrival line had access to reception lines 6 to 11. These were electrified on the 1,500 volt dc Manchester to Sheffield system. In the main yard there were 53 sorting sidings in eight groups. Their lengths varied from 53 to 77 standard length units, and together they had the capacity to hold 3,690 wagons. Departures from sidings Nos 16 to 48 were via the western departure lines — these were electrified. Eastbound services departed from sidings 1 to 15 and were generally drawn back into the express freight yard or the departure sidings before leaving in an easterly direction. This avoided conflicting movements over the hump and possible delay in hump shunting. The western extremities of sidings 34 to 46 were all electrified to facilitate through freight operation along the Sheffield to Manchester, Woodhead route.

On 15th May 1972, Class 31 No. 5560 arrives
with the 8G50 trip freight, whilst the shunting
signal shows a vertical bar, or 'all clear', for
the Class 13 locomotive propelling SPV steel
wagons over the hump at Tinsley.

*J. Cooper-Smith*

Overleaf:
The short headway between consecutive cuts
is clearly illustrated in this picture taken at
Tinsley in 1977.

*L. Nixon*

**PLAN 34**

SHEFFIELD — TINSLEY MARSHALLING YARD 1966

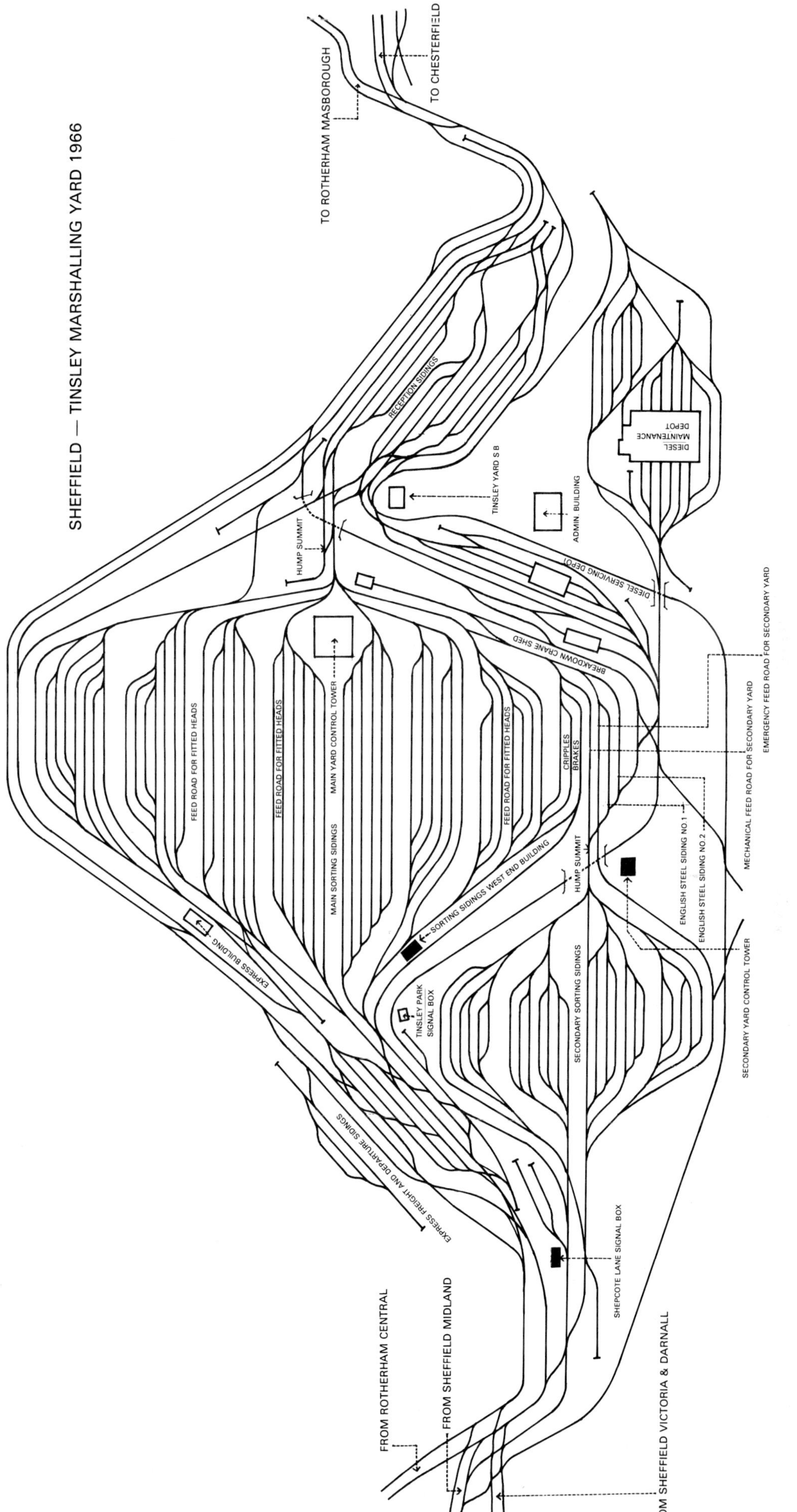

TO ROTHERHAM MASBOROUGH

TO CHESTERFIELD

RECEPTION SIDINGS

HUMP SUMMIT

TINSLEY YARD S B

ADMIN. BUILDING

DIESEL MAINTENANCE DEPOT

DIESEL SERVICING DEPOT

BREAKDOWN CRANE SHED

FEED ROAD FOR FITTED HEADS

FEED ROAD FOR FITTED HEADS

MAIN YARD CONTROL TOWER

MAIN SORTING SIDINGS

FEED ROAD FOR FITTED HEADS

CRIPPLES BRAKES

EMERGENCY FEED ROAD FOR SECONDARY YARD

MECHANICAL FEED ROAD FOR SECONDARY YARD

SORTING SIDINGS WEST END BUILDING

HUMP SUMMIT

ENGLISH STEEL SIDING NO. 1

ENGLISH STEEL SIDING NO 2

SECONDARY YARD CONTROL TOWER

SECONDARY SORTING SIDINGS

EXPRESS BUILDING

TINSLEY PARK SIGNAL BOX

EXPRESS FREIGHT AND DEPARTURE SIDINGS

SHEPCOTE LANE SIGNAL BOX

FROM ROTHERHAM CENTRAL

FROM SHEFFIELD MIDLAND

FROM SHEFFIELD VICTORIA & DARNALL

203

There were 25 secondary sorting sidings, numbered from 60 to 84. These were divided into four groups and had a capacity to hold between 31 and 46 standard wagons; the total standage of the yard being 964 wagons. These sidings were used mainly for traffic bound for local destinations in the vicinity of Sheffield. All traffic routed into this yard travelled directly from the hump and was thus subject to primary sorting in the same way as traffic dealt with in the main yard. The express freight yard was in many ways the forerunner of modern Speedlink yards in that it was designed to accommodate through express freight trains detaching or attaching wagons at Tinsley. Here five sidings were wired throughout for electric traction and each had the capacity to hold 76 SWL. The modern Speedlink network operates on the ideal that such minimum marshalling of express through freights can be conducted in small efficient yards, allowing rapid transit times for urgent freight consignments.

Three new approaches were built to make access to the yard more easy. At the west end of the site a curve to the south, which ran towards Darnall and Sheffield, was complemented by a new curve to the north, which connected the former Great Central line to Masborough with the Tinsley Yard. At the eastern end of the yard a new curve was built to the north, which joined the former Midland main line to Rotherham. The construction of the two curves at the western end of the yard involved the diversion of a length at the Sheffield and South Yorkshire Canal. It was also necessary to construct a new double lift canal lock and enlarge the canal basin, further increasing the cost of the new connections to Tinsley Yard.

# Dowty Wagon Control System

In a large hump marshalling yard a wagon has to run between a quarter and half a mile from leaving the hump until it reaches the other wagons already in the sorting sidings. The marshalling yards of the early 1960s were equipped with two stages of retarders which braked the wagons by gripping the tyres in a vice-like action. In earlier installations, such as March and Toton, the amount of braking applied was controlled by the retarder operator. Later, electronic equipment was used to measure the weight of each wagon and its rolling resistance. This information was fed into a computer which determined a suitable speed for the wagon and operated the retarder automatically to achieve the desired amount of braking. The limitations of such a mechanism meant that damage to both wagons and cargo was frequent in the major marshalling yards. It was impossible for the computer to predict how the wagon would run over the quarter of a mile or more beyond the last retarder.

The Dowty system of wagon control, which was used for the first time at Tinsley, avoided the need for predicting the wagon's resistance. This was done by using a large

number of small Dowty units, spaced out along the track. Each unit contained a speed-sensing device which detected whether the wagon was going too quickly or too slowly, compared to the design speed. The retarder unit was actuated and then responded by either braking or accelerating the wagon passing over it. Each Dowty unit consisted of a small hydraulic ram. This was bolted vertically to the inside of the rail. The head of the ram stood above the rail and was pushed down by the flange of an approaching wheel. As the wheel passed over the ram the head returned to its normal position. Two different types of units were installed; the simplest was the retarder which only had an effect on a wagon which was exceeding the required speed.

The second type was a booster/retarder, which was capable of accelerating a slow wagon as well as retarding a fast wagon. This dual action required an external source of energy, which was supplied by high pressure hydraulic pumps and piped along the track.

If a wagon approached the retarder at above its speed setting, the first part of the down stroke induced a pressure high enough to close an internal valve so that the remainder of the down stroke was made against high pressure in the oil; this resistance slowed the wagon down slightly. On the other hand, a wagon approaching a retarder at lower than its setting speed had no effect on the internal valve and passed the retarder with minimal loss of momentum. If such a wagon approached a booster retarder at below its speed setting, the internal valves allowed oil to escape to the low pressure return pipe on the down stroke, and admitted oil at high pressure on the up stroke which propelled the wagon forwards. Trip levers ensured that any wagon moving in the wrong direction was retarded and not boosted back to the hump. The speed profile was carefully mapped out from the hump summit to the sorting sidings.

First, as the wagon passed over the hump, it was accelerated from the humping speed of about 2ft per second to 12ft per second. This was achieved by a combination of gravity and 12ft per second booster/retarders which completed the acceleration of slow wagons and reduced the speed of any wagon which exceeded the required velocity. A few 0ft per second retarders were installed at the hump summit to ensure that wagons separated cleanly from the train. Secondly, through the switching area, all wagons were kept, as near as possible, at 12ft per second by a combination of booster/retarders and plain retarders.

Provided the speed was maintained, the space between successive wagons or rakes of wagons was sufficient for the points to be moved between them, so that they could be routed into their correct sidings. After passing the last turnout, and as they entered the sorting sidings, wagons were slowed down to a safe buffering speed. This was achieved by a belt of 8ft per second retarders followed by a combination of 5ft per second retarders and 4ft per second booster/retarders. Finally, along the sorting

sidings, a combination of 4ft per second booster/retarders and 5ft per second retarders were provided to keep wagons rolling gently toward those already in the sidings. It was expected that low wagon speeds in the sidings would prevent any possibility of damage to wagons and their contents, whilst the continuous control of wagons through the switching area permitted a high rate of working without loss of time for pushing down short-runners or correcting mis-shunts. Furthermore, at Tinsley, the saving of a diesel shunting locomotive resulted from the installation of Dowty units all the way along the mechanical feed road from the main yard hump to the secondary yard. Wagons approached and passed over the secondary yard hump after being propelled by Dowty 12ft per second units from the primary hump.

A total of 23,500 Dowty units were installed at Tinsley, and it was necessary to devise a means of testing them and identifying faulty units. A test machine was constructed in the form of a two-wheeled trolley which was pulled by a locomotive over the units at controlled speeds just above or below their operating setting. Equipment on the trolley recorded whether the unit retarded, boosted or failed to operate. A continuous tape enabled defective units to be identified immediately, thus facilitating maintenance or if necessary, replacement.

**The only yard to remain in operation in the Sheffield Division after the construction of Tinsley was at Wath. The traffic passing through Wath was predominantly coal from a plethora of local pits. Here, Class 20s Nos 20144 and 20145 depart with a rake of mineral wagons, in April 1979. The yard at Wath was eventually closed in May 1986 as wagonload coal in South Yorkshire had all but disappeared.**

*L. Nixon*

# Signalling and Communication

Two control towers were provided, one at the entrance to the main sorting sidings and one at the entrance to the secondary sorting yard. The main control tower was a four-storey building, comprising a relay room, staff accommodation, a signal engineering workshop and, on the top floor, a control room. The secondary yard control tower was a two-storey building with a relay room on the ground floor and an operating room on the second level. In addition to two control towers there were three new power-operated signal boxes built in the yard area. Shepcote Lane and Tinsley Park were at the western end of the complex whereas Tinsley Yard signal box was situated at the western end of the reception lines, in the shadow of the locomotive depot. A new signal cabin was also constructed at Brightside Junction, and this controlled access on to the former Sheffield District Railway from the Midland main line.

As with any such large installation, communication between employees on the site was of paramount importance. An automatic telephone exchange served the

yard area for traffic and administrative purposes. This also had connections to the GPO national telephone network and special lines to local steelworks, Sheffield Midland station switchboard and signal boxes in the area. Two-way loudspeaker circuits connected the main yard control tower and Tinsley Park signal box. A similar two-way system was installed between Tinsley Park signal box and the Express Freight Yard Inspector. In addition, one-way loudspeaker amplified circuits were provided from the main control tower to the reception sidings and the eastern end of the main yard. Tinsley

Park signal box had a similar arrangement with loudspeakers distributed around the western end of the main yard.

On arrival of a train in the reception sidings, a cutter examined the wagons and recorded details in a code on a cut card. At the same time the wagons were uncoupled according to route and destination. The cut card showed the intended sorting siding into which the cut would go, the number of wagons in each cut and the presence of any long wagons. The information was then sent to the control tower by means of the Ado Data Transmission System. During transmission all details were printed in the same form as they appeared on the cut card, and thus could be easily checked by the cutter. The receiving instrument in the control tower also printed the information in this same format. It also produced a punched tape in five-hole binary code for feeding into the point-setting control machine. This machine automatically set the points for each cut in both the main and secondary sorting sidings.

Mounted on the hump inspector's desk was a siding fullness indicator which recorded by electro-mechanical counters and fed automatically from information from the punched tape the number of wagons in each siding. After a departure, when the wagons were removed from the siding, the counters had to be adjusted manually by the switches on the panel. Individual point switch panels were also provided in both main and secondary hump control rooms to allow the operators to take over control in the event of a failure of the automatic route setting equipment. An additional unique feature to Tinsley Yard was the 'Selecto-board'. This comprised rows of horizontally and vertically-numbered holes in which pins were inserted, each row corresponding to one siding, thus a pin in the hole corresponding to No. 35 horizontally and vertically, denoted siding No. 35. If, however, the inspector wished to route traffic normally destined for this siding into another siding, perhaps because it was already full, then he merely moved the pin in the vertical column 35 to another hole, above or below. Therefore, if a pin was placed in the vertical column 35, but in the horizontal row No. 40, then the route-setting equipment would automatically send wagons destined for siding 35 on the punch card into siding 40. If route alterations were needed on one cut, only the hump operator could alter the route by using cancel buttons and setting the route manually, as the details of the given cut appeared in the first aperture of his control panel.

There were three shunting engines allocated to the yard. Each unit consisted of two standard 350hp diesel-electric locomotives permanently coupled together. They were modified by adding extra ballast to bring the total weight of the locomotive to 120 tons producing a 20 ton axle load. They were also fitted with cab signalling apparatus, precision speedometers and two-way radio-telephones. The cab signals were able to considerably speed movement in the reception siding. They were controlled through signals transmitted along the rails from suitable points and could indicate a different instruction from the fixed ground signals. Thus, the signalman at Tinsley Park could instruct a driver of a shunting engine to propel his train to the hump top by giving him the "all clear' on the cab signalling, whilst the fixed signal at the end of the reception siding remained on danger. The train would then propel to within a few feet of the fixed ground signal at which point a trigger would turn the cab signalling to danger. This reduced to a minimum the time interval between the humping of consecutive trains.

## Traffic at Tinsley

The new marshalling yard at Tinsley was the concentration point of traffic originating and terminating within the area bounded by Penistone in the West, Swinton and Masborough to the north, and Chesterfield to the south. The total volume of freight traffic in 1966 exceeded 24 million tons per annum. The bulk of this emanated from the 150 private sidings located within the relatively small area of the Sheffield Division. The first stage in the transfer of freight traffic to Tinsley involved those freights dealt with in ex-Midland Railway yards. Through loads were made up for Toton, Norton Junction, Washwood Heath, Healey Mills, Chaddesden, Leeds, Stanton Gate, Frodingham, Mottram, St. Pancras, Gowhole, Leicester, Brent and Port Talbot. Additional outlets to Hunslet, Nottingham, Carlisle, York and Glasgow, were provided by through freight services calling at Tinsley.

In October 1965, the new winter timetable involved the absorption of traffic dealt with at former Great Central yards, and additional through trains were made up for Lincoln, New England, Hull, Birkenhead, Liverpool Brunswick, Colwick, Doncaster, Whitemoor, King's Cross, Ferme Park and Worksop. These new operating arrangements brought a total of 3,000 wagons to Tinsley each day. The expected capacity of the yard was 4,000 wagons and, in the light of an apparent shortfall in freight trains at the yard, it was decided to transfer additional work from Masborough sorting sidings and further afield, as this became appropriate.

## Tinsley Diesel Locomotive Maintenance Depot

This was completed in January 1964 and daily servicing of locomotives commenced in April of the same year, when all maintenance work was transferred from Darnall depot. The allocation of diesel locomotives was brought up to a full complement of 190 main line engines and 80 shunting engines by 1966. The new shed was designed with six tracks at each end, providing accommodation for a total of 24 main line locomotives, and all diesel locomotives in the Sheffield Division were maintained at Tinsley. A separate servicing shed was situated to the south west of the main hump. This contained two, 2-berth, through lines with facilities for refuelling, lubricating, examining and sanding the locomotives. Secondary servicing depots were also located at Wath, Shirebrook and Barrow Hill.

## Sheffield Freight Terminal

This new terminal was constructed on the site of the old Grimesthorpe motive power depot and was designed to play a major role in the British Railways National Sundries Plan. It received small consignments from the entire Sheffield Division including Barnsley, Rotherham and Chesterfield. The goods shed was 920ft long, covering an area of 25,000sq yds. Capacity existed for dealing with over 600 tonnes of sundry traffic each day and berths were provided for 90 road vehicles. Alongside the sundry shed was a warehouse with 15,000sq yds of floor space. Outside, there was accommodation in the yard for 200 wagons in position for loading or unloading and standage for 56 wagons beneath a Goliath crane. This new freight terminal meant that warehouses at Bridgehouses, Wicker, Queens Road and Wharf Street were closed. Sundries traffic did dwindle in the late 1960s and early 1970s but Sheffield Freight Terminal remained open until it was burnt to the ground in 1984.

A freight terminal remains on the site and handles small consignments of steel for local customers as well as larger loads for the main companies in the area.

## Rationalisation at Tinsley

After nearly 20 years of service as an important freight centre, the yard at Tinsley was considerably rationalised in December 1984. In March of the same year the weekly throughput of wagons had totalled just over 5,000, of which 3,000 traversed the hump. The disruption to Railfreight traffic by the miners' strike meant that by November of 1984 the weekly throughput had fallen to 3,000 wagons, and only 1,500 of these traversed the hump. The yearly averages for 1984 revealed a mean of 356 wagons dealt with daily at the express freight yard compared with only 429 wagons hump-shunted each day. This gave a total average throughput of 785 wagons a day. It was in the light of such a sharp fall-off in traffic that the rationalisation of Tinsley was pursued. It is interesting to note that the five roads in the express freight yard handled nearly as many wagons during the year as the extensive array of sorting sidings radiating from the hump. Such statistics revealed the heavy losses being made by the expensive infrastructure installed at Tinsley, and pointed towards the future shape of marshalling yards which would be ideally small installations with long parallel sorting sidings.

The reasons for the drastic reductions in size at Tinsley and other yards are indeed many. Whilst the miners' strike undoubtedly precipitated many changes in the Railfreight infrastructure, they are changes that, for the most part, would have been pursued without the dispute, albeit more slowly. For the complex equipment in the

Dowty Wagon Control System which was installed at Tinsley to justify its retention, it had to be continuously utilised. The reduction of freight traffic carried by the railways is clearly documented, but this alone does not account for the recent changes in freight train marshalling. Several other important factors are involved in the turn away from the large and expensive hump yards. In May 1985 the TOPS computer at Tinsley listed a total of 6,000 wagons on hand in the Tinsley area. Of these, something over 3,000 were employed carrying freight traffic in the Tinsley region. At the same time the yard at Tinsley was turning only 750 of these wagons each day. Merry-go-round coal working was one important area where the marshalling yard had been bypassed. Additionally, steel travelled directly between Scunthorpe and the BSC plants at Aldwarke and Templeborough. Further loads of steel were dispatched directly from the BSC Tinsley Park plant to Lackenby, Dover and the east coast ports. Furthermore, oil was carried increasingly in block loads, thus avoiding stops in the yard between the refinery and the customer.

Tinsley was not designated one of the twelve network yards in the Speedlink timetable. In 1985 it was served by several long-haul Speedlink trains, whereas, the neighbouring Doncaster and Healey Mills yards were considerably more important, nationally. Traffic on the Speedlink Route 6, which runs from London and east coast ports, called at Doncaster on its way to Scotland. Trans-Pennine traffic, on Route 7, was directed predominantly to Healey Mills after the closure of the Woodhead route. The end of 1985 saw further re-arrangement in the Speedlink working patterns within Yorkshire and much of the traffic dealt with at Healey Mills was transferred to Doncaster. Whilst not a network yard, Tinsley remained a very important secondary yard with connections to trunk Speedlink trains.

The handling of Speedlink wagons is not suited to the hump-shunting method. As well as damage to cargo by insufficient retardation off the hump, many wagon control systems do not function correctly with long wheelbase wagons, eg VDA. This difficulty was partially overcome by the Dowty Wagon Control System at Tinsley. However, problems with long wheelbase wagons were experienced because of the length of track circuits on the descent from the hump, and special manual operation of the train sorting system had to be instituted when such wagons had to be shunted. This involved loss of time and money in the shunting process and made it hard to justify the retention of an outdated system when increasingly large numbers of long wheelbase wagons were brought into service.

Another fundamental change in freight train operation was the method of putting a selection of wagons together to make up a train. In the days of the hump, every wagon bound for a certain destination, for example Whitemoor, was shunted into the requisite siding. Once the siding was full, the yardmaster would direct all wagons for Whitemoor into another siding. At fixed times a freight would leave for March (Whitemoor) — if the load was light, so be it. If there were too many wagons the overspill would wait for the next booked departure for Whitemoor. An obvious flaw in the system was the customer whose goods missed the train and were therefore delayed twenty four hours. To avoid this problem British Rail has developed 'Speedlink Space Reservation Mandates' whereby customers are able to inform BR of their cargo and reserve space for it on the relevant Speedlink trains. Whilst this is excellent in theory, difficulties have been experienced because of persistent over-booking on certain trains. This provided a major headache for the operating department who had to try to arrange special additional services. Ironically the Sheffield area has been troubled by the success of Speedlink, particularly in the carriage of scrap. Resources have been stretched to the full and both POA scrap wagons and HEA

## Table 30
### A comparison of siding allocation in Tinsley Yard 1965 & 1985

| Siding No. | 1965 | 1985 |
| --- | --- | --- |
| 1 | Toton (UF) | spare POAs |
| 2 | Toton (F) | spare 16 ton minerals |
| 3 | Barnsley (I) | minerals |
| 4 | Norton Jn. (F) | Scunthorpe |
| 5 | Norton Jn. (UF) | SPA + Aldwarke |
| 6 | Masborough S.S. | Deepcar + spare BBA & BDAs |
| 7 | Rawmarsh | Scunthorpe (empty BDAs) |
| 8 | Barrow Hill | Sheffield F.T. |
| 9 | Washwood Heath (UF) | Engine line |
| 10 | Washwood Heath (F) | Speedlink South |
| 11 | Treeton/Orgreaves | Speedlink South |
| 12 | Healey Mills (F) | Reception |
| 13 | Healey Mills (UF) | Reception |
| 14 | Chaddesden (UF) | Deepcar |
| 15 | Stourton (UF) | New site |
| 16 | Feed road* | Speedlink North |
| 17 | Spare Hyfits | Speedlink North |
| 18 | Lincoln | Empty POAs |
| 19 | Hull (F) | Reception |
| 20 | Hull (M) | Reception |
| 21 | York (M) | Transfer |
| 22 | York (F) | Beighton |
| 23 | Feed road† | Darnall |
| 24 | St. Pancras (I) | (N) |
| 25 | New England (UF) | spare BDAs |
| 26 | Frodingham (UF) | (N) |
| 27 | Rotherham Road (I) | (N) |
| 28 | Spare Vanfits | spare STVs |
| 29 | Spare steel wagons | (N) |
| 30 | Spare mineral wags | (N) |
| 31 | Oughty Bridge | Smithywood |
| 32 | S.F.T. sundries | Treeton |
| 33 | S.F.T. full wagons | Barrow Hill |
| 34 | Barnsley Junction | Marple & Gillott |
| 35 | South Wales | Cripples |
| 36 | Deepcar | (N) |
| 37 | Wadsley Bridge | Tinsley misc |
| 38 | Darnall C & W | Darnall |
| 39 | Mottram (F) | Marple & Gillott |
| 40 | Mottram (UF) | (N) |
| 41 | Birkenhead (I) | (N) |
| 42 | Brunswick | (N) |
| 43 | Feed road° | Cripples for grading |
| 44 | Colwick (UF) | Cripples |
| 45 | Smithywood (I) | Cripples |
| 46 | Ickles | Grading siding |
| 47 | Doncaster (UF) | Grading siding |
| 48 | Whitemoor (UF) | Grading siding |
| 49 | Brake vans | Grading siding |
| 50 | Mechanical feed | (R) |
| 51 | Emergency feed | (R) |
| 52 | English Steel scrap | (R) |
| 53 | English Steel other | (R) |

Key
(UF) — un-fitted traffic
(F) — fitted traffic
(I) — also traffic for intermediate destinations
(M) — minerals
(N) — no siding allocation has yet been fixed
(R) — road removed
* — Traffic for Derby St. Marys, Chaddesden (F) and Stourton (F) is fed from here to the EF yard.
† — Traffic from here is bound for Lincoln (F), New England (F), Frodingham (F) and Goole via the EF yard.
° — Traffic which is fitted with and bound for Doncaster, Colwick and Whitemoor passes from here to the EF yard.

Footnote:- The secondary yard also had an allocation of various destinations for its 25 sidings. This yard was converted into a storage yard for condemned BR stock containing blue asbestos.

coal hoppers have occasionally been found to be in short supply.

The alterations undertaken at Tinsley in 1984 were the first step to achieving the goal of a yard designed to handle 400 wagons each day. In addition to this traffic, considerable numbers of stored and condemned wagons passed through the yard. It was hoped that as British Rail's time-expired rolling stock was disposed of, this traffic flow would diminish. *Plan 35* shows the layout as it stood in 1985. Both primary and secondary yards were retained and all shunting concentrated at the west end of the complex. The old reception sidings had been removed, as had the hump. The old express freight yard was used for the storage of block loads and also as the arrival sidings for roads numbered 1 to 19 in the main yard. Traffic could also arrive in any of the sidings' designated reception roads in the main yard, these being Nos 12, 13, 19 and 20. In the main yard roads

**After rationalisation in 1984, the hump at Tinsley was closed. Most shunting was conducted from the west end of the yard, but some trip freights still reversed into the sorting sidings from the east end. Here, just such a manoeuvre is conducted by Class 20s Nos 20054 and 20112, backing the 6T34 Aldwarke to Tinsley trip freight into the through sorting sidings at the yard on 9th July 1986.**

numbered 9 to 21 were retained as through sidings; all other tracks were severed from the old hump at the east end. It was envisaged that the yard would consist of sidings numbered 6 to 33 only, however, the southerly part of the yard (Nos 34 to 49) was retained to stable the large number of condemned wagons in transit to Sheffield scrap merchants. The entire secondary yard had been taken over by coaching stock containing blue asbestos. After British Rail has completed disposal of this stock, the secondary yard will close. In summary, the planned yard as envisaged in 1985 will contain the express freight sidings and roads numbered 6 to 33 of the main yard.

**In July 1976, Class 20s Nos 20130 and 20211 arrive from the west and enter the reception roads at Tinsley; hump shunting continues uninterrupted.**

*T. Heavyside*

The locomotive servicing depot at Tinsley was intended to fulfil a similar role to Carlisle New Yard servicing point, that is the refuelling and minor repairs of locomotives between their duties. Such refuelling was transferred to the main Tinsley shed, but the servicing depot found a new role looking after Sheffield's diesel multiple unit fleet. Rather than going to Darnall depot, dmus travel to Tinsley, where between 22.00 and 06.00, 2-car dmu sets are serviced and washed. The main depot at Tinsley was the regional maintenance centre in 1985 for an area that bordered with Thornaby in the north, Immingham in the east and Toton in the south. Its long-term future seemed secure.

From the facilities at Tinsley, we move to a survey of the traffic handled in 1985. In terms of cargoes this was mainly steel and

scrap for the Sheffield area. In addition there were small loads such as bananas to Parkway Market and commodities to the fire-damaged freight terminal. The wagons involved in this traffic were divided into 'pools' which were found employment by a contract manager. A pool of 60 BDA steel wagons might operate on the Cardiff circuit. Owing to the five day turn-around this took 50 wagons each week to convey steel bars from Yorkshire to the Allied Steel & Wire Company in Cardiffs' docklands. The ten remaining wagons filled in on trips from BSC Templeborough or BSC Aldwarke during the week. A similar pool of 181 POA scrap wagons existed and they were supplemented in their duties by 2,000 MXV scrap-carrying vehicles. The smaller MXV wagon could not operate on Speedlink trains because it did not convey

an air brake, and various plans were put forward to replace these wagons with a fleet of MDA type scrap wagons. This would have involved rebraking 400 MDV coal wagons, thus enabling scrap carriage to be fully integrated into the Speedlink network. Unfortunately, it was thought this investment could not be justifed and the project was temporarily shelved at the end of 1985.

At any point in time Tinsley Yard contained up to 2,000 wagons, but approximately 1,800 of these were cripples. This required a full-time grading inspector to evaluate the future of each wagon. The remaining 200 wagons were Speedlink wagons in transit and, as such, spent a minimum amount of time sitting in the yard. The shorter the turn-around time for a wagon, the more loads it could carry each week, and the more revenue it brought

---

## Table 31

### The trip workings from Tinsley Yard – 1985

| Loco | Trip No | Time/Times of Departure | Destination |
|---|---|---|---|
| 2x20 | T30 | 06.18, 09.46, 13.55, 17.19 | Deepcar |
| 08 | T32 | 06.50 | Broughton Lane & Meadow Hall |
| 08 | T33 | 10.20 | S.F.T. |
| 31 | T34 | 08.22 | Meadow Hall, Templeborough, Aldwarke 11" mill. |
| | | 15.08, 18.02, | Aldwarke New Site |
| 2x20 | T35 | 07.09, 10.02, 20.08, 04.02 | Aldwarke New Site |
| | | 17.35 | Darnall C & W |
| | | 22.54 | Wath Yard |
| 2x20 | T36 | 06.11 | Parkway market |
| | | 09.50 | Beighton CCE |
| | | 13.03 | Meadow Hall, Smithywood |
| | | 03.44 | Deepcar |
| 08 | T38 | 08.35—16.55 | Rotherham steel terminal |
| 08 | T39 | 06.15, 13.39 | S.F.T. pilot |
| 08 | T41 | 07.12, 13.57 | Templeborough pilot, trips to Aldwarke 11" mill. |
| 20 | T42 | 06.50 | Masboro S.S. |
| 2x37 | T54 | Dodworth MGRs | |
| 56 | T56 | Local MGRs | |
| 31 | T57 | ballast working as required | |
| 2x20 | T58 | No. 1 ballast working | |
| 31 | T59 | No. 2 ballast working | |
| 08 | T60 | 06.35, 14.10, 22.10 | Wath pilot, trips Manvers |

Exlanation: The departure times are from Tinsley Main Yard. A given trip, e.g. T35, may be in and out of the yard all day and in this case each departure from the main yard is listed together with the destination or destinations to be served before it returns to the yard.

---

## Table 32

### Tinsley, Non-Speedlink Arrivals and Departures – 1985

| Code | Time | Days | From | To | Arr. | Dep. |
|---|---|---|---|---|---|---|
| 6E49 | 20.45 | FSX | Stanlow | Tinsley | 23.57 | |
| 9J71 | 23.10 | SX-Y | Doncaster | Tinsley | 00.07 | |
| 9J70 | 00.08 | MX-Y | Dringhouses | Tinsley | 01.49 | |
| 7M68 | 02.07 | MSX | Tinsley | Stanlow | | 02.07 |
| 6J45 | 00.43 | MX | Immingham | Tinsley | 02.46 | |
| 8M81 | 07.52 | MSX | Tinsley | Derby | | 07.52 |
| 6L46 | 08.32 | SX | Tinsley | Goole | | 08.32 |
| 6M97 | 08.22 | SX | Tinsley | Wolverhampton | | 08.22 |
| 8O55 | 12.30 | M-TThO | Tinsley | Betteshanger | | 12.30 |
| 9D44 | 14.28 | SX-Y | Tinsley | Scunthorpe | | 14.28 |
| 6J25 | 18.45 | SX-Y | Scunthorpe | Tinsley | 20.09 | |
| 9J28 | 15.40 | SX-Y | Healey Mills | Tinsley | 17.12 | |
| 6E68 | 14.16 | SX | Wolverhampton | Tinsley | 17.39 | |
| 9L28 | 18.34 | SX | Tinsley | Healey Mills | | 18.34 |
| 9D71 | 20.30 | SX-Y | Tinsley | Doncaster | | 20.30 |
| 9L70 | 21.13 | SX-Y | Tinsley | York | | 21.13 |
| 7D32 | 20.45 | MFO | Tinsley | Immingham | | 20.45 |

Key
Y = to run as required

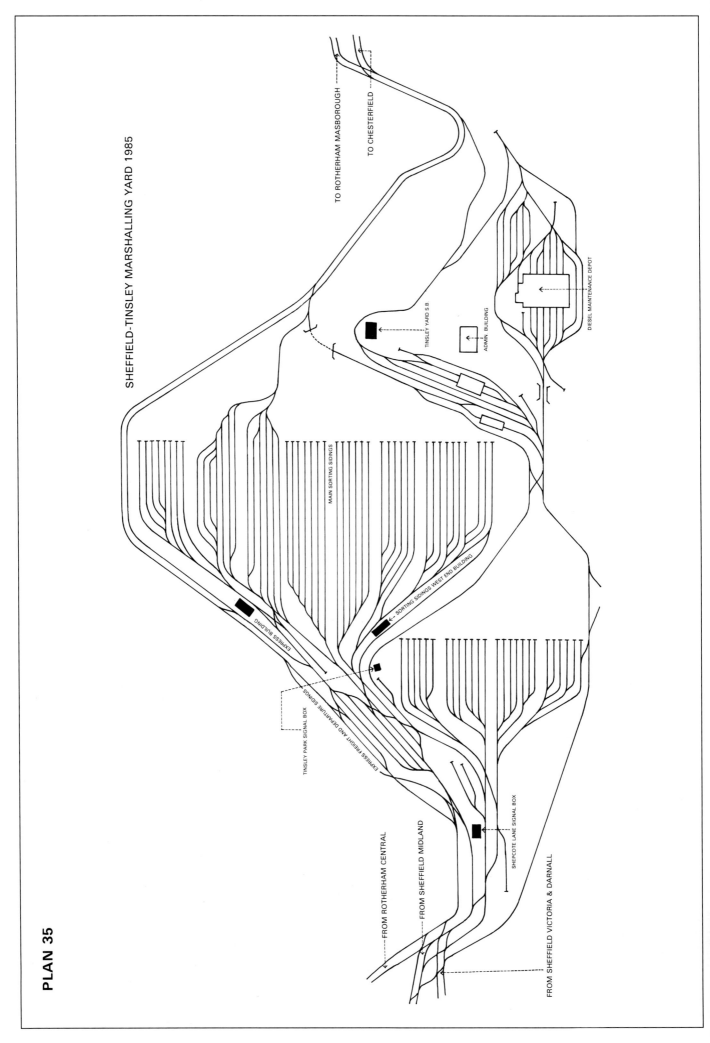

SHEFFIELD-TINSLEY MARSHALLING YARD 1985

TO ROTHERHAM MASBOROUGH

TO CHESTERFIELD

TINSLEY YARD S B

ADMIN BUILDING

DIESEL MAINTENANCE DEPOT

MAIN SORTING SIDINGS

SORTING SIDINGS WEST END BUILDING

EXPRESS BUILDING

TINSLEY PARK SIGNAL BOX

EXPRESS FREIGHT AND DEPARTURE SIDINGS

SHEPCOTE LANE SIGNAL BOX

FROM ROTHERHAM CENTRAL

FROM SHEFFIELD MIDLAND

FROM SHEFFIELD VICTORIA & DARNALL

British Railways. The varied steel and mixed traffic at Tinsley was conveyed in a combination of long-haul and short-haul Speedlink services which are listed in *Table 33*.

# The Future of Tinsley

All of Britain's major marshalling yards have been rationalised in the last 20 years. Some have closed and disappeared completely; others like Tinsley remain in a truncated and hopefully more efficient form. What then, of the future of freight

**Class 76s Nos 76022 and 76013 pass Shepcote Lane at the head of the 8E11 from Dewsnap Sidings in Manchester to either Tinsley or Rotherwood. On 23rd September 1980, the train was routed to Tinsley.**

### Table 33

### Tinsley Speedlink Arrivals and Departures – 1985

| Code | Time | Days | From | To | Arr. | Tinsley Dep. |
|------|------|------|------|------|------|--------------|
| 6V85 | 20.18 | SX | Tees | Bescot | 23.31 | 00.18 |
| 7J29 | 00.46 | MX | Doncaster | Tinsley | 01.33 | |
| 6E64 | 19.15 | SX | Severn Tnl. | Hav. Hill | 00.28 | 01.51 |
| 6E38 | 21.33 | SX | Bescot | Doncaster | 00.17 | 01.02 |
| 6J62 | 20.26 | SX | Parkeston | Tinsley | 03.37 | |
| 7M88 | 01.27 | MX | Dringhouses | Derby St. Marys | 02.56 | 03.50 |
| 6L81 | 04.10 | MX | Tinsley | Hull | | 04.10 |
| 6E75 | 21.24 | SX | Willesden | Hunslet | 04.36 | 05.16 |
| 6E63 | 02.12 | MX | Warrington | Tinsley | | 05.33 |
| 6J60 | 06.30 | SX | Tinsley | Barrow Hill | | 06.30 |
| 6J61 | 15.11 | SX | Barrow Hill | Tinsley | 13.34 | |
| 6V06 | 16.48 | SX | Healey Mills | Severn Tnl. | 17.54 | 18.41 |
| 7E49 | 15.14 | SX | Bescot | Dringhouses | 18.38 | 19.34 |
| 7L60 | 18.00 | SX | Worksop | Healey Mills | 18.40 | 20.05 |
| 7D63 | 17.49 | SX | Healey Mills | Worksop | 19.05 | 20.40 |
| 6H91 | 20.55 | SX | Tinsley | Whitemoor | | 20.55 |
| 7D19 | 21.44 | SX | Tinsley | Doncaster | | 21.44 |
| 6M70 | 21.56 | SX | Tinsley | Warrington | | 21.56 |

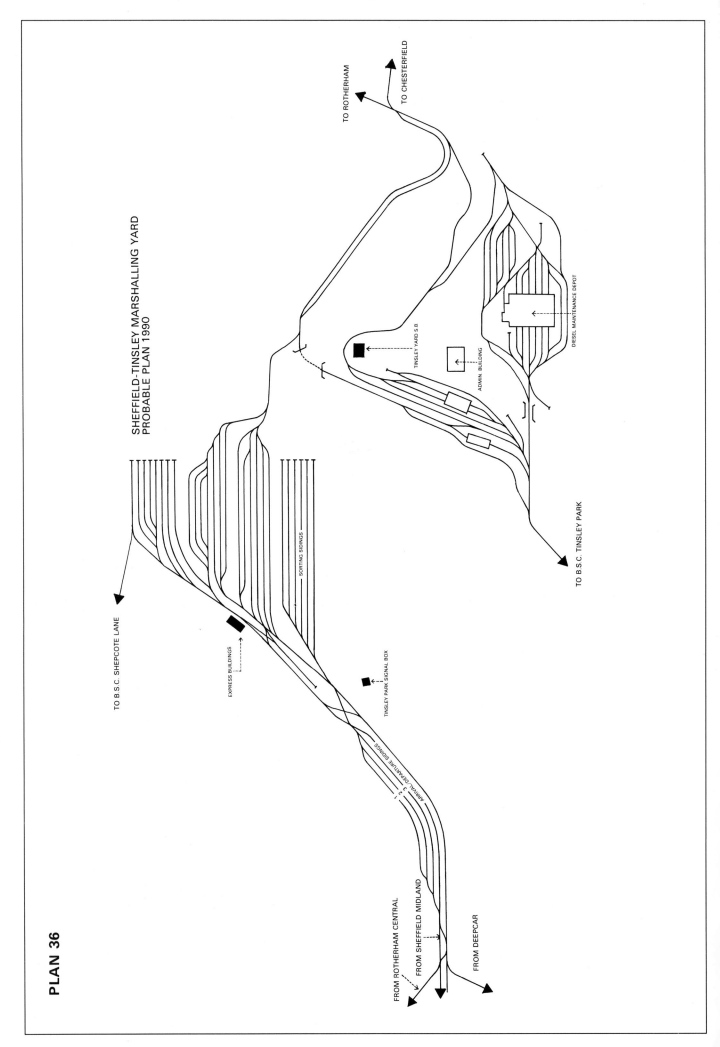

**PLAN 36**

SHEFFIELD-TINSLEY MARSHALLING YARD
PROBABLE PLAN 1990

TO ROTHERHAM

TO CHESTERFIELD

TINSLEY YARD S.B.

ADMIN. BUILDING

DIESEL MAINTENANCE DEPOT

TO B.S.C. TINSLEY PARK

TO B.S.C. SHEPCOTE LANE

EXPRESS BUILDINGS

SORTING SIDINGS

TINSLEY PARK SIGNAL BOX

ARRIVAL DEPARTURE SIDINGS

FROM ROTHERHAM CENTRAL

FROM SHEFFIELD MIDLAND

FROM DEEPCAR

train marshalling at Tinsley? The necessity for some marshalling facilities to service the Sheffield area is acknowledged by cynics who have dubbed the new Tinsley Yard as a glorified scrap siding. Far from this, the contracted layout is an important secondary marshalling point for the large tonnage of steel traffic generated within the Sheffield

The west end of Tinsley has become the focus of Railfreight activity in the Sheffield yard. In May 1985, the signalman at Tinsley Park signal box looks out over four freight trains. Class 47 No. 47314 departs with the 8T48, Tinsley to Frodingham trip, whilst Class 08 No. 08878 stands in the old express freight yard with the T32 from Broughton Lane. Next to it are Class 20s Nos 20064 and 20015 with the 6T35 from Aldwarke, and on the far right are Nos 20176 and 20098 at the head of the 6T30 from Deepcar.

Division. With all shunting concentrated at the west end of the yard, there is a possibility that the eastern approaches will be closed. Further economies could be made by singling the main line from Beighton Junction to Masborough Station South Junction.

With the Holmes Chord scheme very much in mind, further resignalling might extend from the Great Central lines through Rotherham to Tinsley Yard. This would involve the replacement of Shepcote Lane, Tinsley Park and Tinsley Yard boxes.

The residual sidings at Tinsley should consist of sidings 1 to 27 in the main yard with three new reception roads laid on the site of Tinsley Park box. The rest of the main yard, secondary yard and express yard could then be lifted. Whatever the future decisions about Tinsley, it is far more than a glorified scrap siding and continues to render valuable service in the marshalling of Speedlink and block load trains for dispatch around the country.

In conclusion I would like to thank the Area Manager and Mr White, the Area

Although Tinsley is not a major Speedlink yard, several long-haul Speedlink trains do call there. On 9th July 1986, the 6V06 Healey Mills to Severn Tunnel Junction approaches the yard from the east behind Class 47 No. 47355. Future concentration of traffic at the west end of the yard complex may lead to the closure of this connection with the Midland line from Chesterfield and Rotherham.

Freight Assistant, for their time and expertise, and also Mr Portlock for showing me around the yard.

Opposite:
On 16th July 1976 a single 'Tommy' traverses the electrified approach road to the reception sidings at Tinsley. Class 76 No. 76057 hauls a rake of empty coal hoppers and 16½ ton mineral wagons.

*T.Heavyside*

The long, parallel sidings of the Express Freight yard at Tinsley are clearly seen in this picture of Class 08 No. 08880 at the head of the T39 from Sheffield Freight Terminal at Tinsley. The train of MDV wagons conveys scrap for the BSC Stocksbridge plant at Deepcar.

In July 1986, a pair of Class 20s, Nos 20098 and 20153 pass the abandoned reception sidings at Tinsley with the 6T91 Barrow Hill to Tinsley trip freight.

Opposite:
A large volume of scrap metal from Teesside winds its way into Tinsley from the east behind Class 45 No. 45039 *The Manchester Regiment*. The train is an old-fashioned long-haul freight, most of the wagons having no airbrakes. It is the 8J12, 09.25, Tees to Tinsley.

215

# Chapter 14
# Toton Yard

Toton Sidings were originally developed in about 1850 as the most convenient point to the south of the Nottinghamshire and Derbyshire coalfields at which coal trains could be remarshalled for dispatch to London and the south. By 1871, coal traffic from the Nottinghamshire area had considerably increased and 25 miles of new sidings were laid out by the Midland Railway at Toton. Gradual expansion continued over the next 50 years until, in 1930, there were 65 miles of sidings in and

**Toton Yard South. Two views from the same footbridge to the south of Toton compare the scenes in 1955 and 1980. The wagon repair shops remain unchanged, whilst the semaphore signals have disappeared and the track layout has been simplified. Class 37 No. 37283 is seen hauling a train of empty ballast wagons south in the latter view.**

*British Rail and Author*

around Toton. In 1939, the 'down' yard at Toton was mechanised. Alterations to the hump included the provision of four automatic rail brakes. After World War II, in 1948, the rebuilding of Toton 'up' yard was started. This side of the marshalling complex at Toton was completely rebuilt and opened at the end of 1950. After a little more than 25 years of service, the rationalisation of Toton began in 1978 with the closure of the 'down' hump. A further reduction in traffic suitable for hump-shunting brought about the closure of the 'up' hump and yard in 1984. By 1986, the marshalling facilities at Toton had been reduced to a mere 28 sidings.

## Pre-1939

The Erewash Valley line from Trent to Mansfield was opened in 1845 and later extended from Highbridge Junction to join the Derby to Sheffield main line at Clay Cross. The first sidings at Toton were developed in 1850, and a locomotive depot was first established at Toton in the 1860s. It was, however, called a locomotive stable, hinting at the use of horses for shunting within the sidings.

In 1842, the Midland Counties Railway had a meeting with local coal owners, who were dissatisfied with having to pay 1½d per ton mile for the carriage of coal. They asked for, and got, a reduction in the price

**Contrasting views of the 'up' hump at Toton. In the early 1950s the sorting sidings are filled with coal wagons, whereas by 1986 the entire yard lies out of use; some condemned wagons are stored on the eastern side of the sidings otherwise only the weeds flourish where once thousands of wagons were sorted daily.**

*British Rail and Author*

of coal transport to 1d per ton mile. Auditors for the railway company were worried that this could bring about heavy losses for railway operators. A document at the time records that, "the whole emolument from this coal traffic was a very bagatelle". Similar difficulties were being experienced by the Liverpool & Manchester Railway who stated that, unless coal paid 2d per ton mile it was not worth having. By the 1870s, however, the railway companies had discovered that 1d per ton mile rendered a handsome profit in the carriage of coal, and by 1871 coal traffic in the Nottinghamshire and Derbyshire areas had increased beyond all expectations.

Shipley Colliery in the Erewash Valley was producing 400,000 tonnes of coal per annum and, in view of such tonnages, the Midland Railway built their first major yard at Toton. The 25 miles of sidings handled most traffic from South Yorkshire and the Erewash Valley to London. The shunting in this early yard was undertaken by horses, and this practice was continued well into the twentieth century, but as traffic increased, however, the shunting movements were taken over by steam locomotives. The locomotive depot at Toton became the largest freight engine shed on the London, Midland & Scottish Railway. The combined throughput of 'up' and 'down' sidings at Toton was often in excess of 10,000 wagons a day. The daily throughput of 140 arrivals and 140 departures made Toton one of the busiest yards

in the world. In 1927, long-haul coal trains were dealt with by two tender engines and restricted to 90 loaded coal wagons or 100 empties.

As with most other major marshalling yards in the country, there were considerable delays and difficulties with the complex and ramshackle arrangements at Toton. A document of the day describes the yard as bearing a closer resemblance to a leg of mutton than a satisfactory wagon sorting and marshalling facility. Thus, in 1939, the 'down' sidings at Toton were modernised, this being the first step in the eventual modernisation of the entire complex.

## Toton 'Down' Yard

The 'down' yard at Toton handled a variety of traffic, the largest percentage of which was made up by coal and coke. There was, however, considerable mixed traffic passing over the hump. In 1910 the new high-level arrival lines enabled all trains from the south to pass straight up to the hump. Previously, arrivals from the south had often had to reverse up to the hump for shunting. The yard consisted of 35 sorting sidings and was operated in the traditional manner. This entailed the hand operation of points and the hand pinning down of brakes on the wagons rolling off the hump. In 1939 alterations to the hump and points area brought about the automation of this process. All points radiating from the hump were electro-mechanically-operated and four Fröhlich-type retarders were installed beyond the hump apex. After a train's

arrival in one of the two 'down' arrival lines the wagons were chalked with the number of the siding for which they were destined. The train was propelled over the hump at a speed of 1.75mph and, as a wagon or cut of wagons approached the apex, an operator in the hump room set the route for a particular siding by depressing the appropriate button. He also depressed a button on a small bank of switches to indicate the number of vehicles in the cut. The settings made by the hump room operator were transmitted simultaneously by a teletypewriter to the control tower; from here both the rail brakes and points beyond the 'Jack' points were controlled. The fall in gradient in the 'down' yard was steep at 1 in 18; this was because of the large number of empty wagons passing through the sidings.

Sixty per cent of traffic was made up of coal and coke empties returning to the local collieries. Other heavy flows of traffic included scrap metal to the local ironworks at Stanton, iron ore and limestone to customers in Lancashire, and manufactured goods to all parts of the country. The yard was open continuously for six days of the week. The 70 daily arrivals brought an average of 3,500 wagons to the hump. These were sorted with an average cut size of three vehicles. During World War II, however, up to 5,000 wagons a day were marshalled, and from 1939 to 1951 the yard never dealt with less than 1,000,000 wagons a year.

**In 1955 a cut of six coke hoppers are retarded at Toton 'up' yard.**

*British Rail*

## Toton 'Up' Yard

The old 'up' sidings at Toton were completely rebuilt between 1948 and 1950. A combination of factors made the construction of a new yard on the east side of the main line imperative. The old Toton 'up' yard had short arrival lines and, with the introduction of longer coal trains, these were of insufficient length to accommodate complete trains. The introduction of Beyer-Garratt locomotives had meant that longer trains were running from Toton. Nineteen of these engines were allocated to Toton Depot whilst eleven worked from Wellingborough and three from Westhouses. Similarly, the introduction of Stanier 8F class 2-8-0s meant an increase in the average size of freights. Difficulties were also experienced at the hump. The old manually-operated hump had a gradient of only 1 in 54. Whilst suitable for old-fashioned grease-lubricated axle boxes, this was not steep enough to cope with newer, heavier wagons with oil-lubricated axles. After careful consideration of all the requirements for a new yard, it was decided that 100 per cent remodelling of the 'up' sidings was the only answer.

## Construction

The preparation of the modernisation scheme had only just been completed by the London, Midland & Scottish Railway, when Nationalisation of the railways came into effect. The work was sanctioned by

British Railways (London Midland Region) and construction commenced in 1948. A piecemeal rebuilding was completed on 4th September 1950, and at no time during the three years work on the yard were the sidings completely closed to traffic. For two years relief had to be given, and this was done by diverting trains to other yards and re-timetabling those still using the Toton 'up' sidings.

About 430,000 cubic yards of earth were involved in the readjusting of the old levels and enlarging the yard. The entrance to the reception sidings was 300yds further north. This enabled an extension of the sidings providing ten roads, each capable of holding 75 wagons, together with a locomotive and guard's van. The old layout had consisted of ten arrival lines but one had always been left clear so that the humping engine could run from the hump before proceeding behind a train. This had meant that, in effect, only nine sidings were available as reception lines. The new yard, therefore, included an eleventh road, numbered six, and used exclusively for the run-round of hump engines. A total of 37 sorting sidings were provided in four fans. These were divided into two separate yards, the West Yard and the East Yard. West Yard lay adjacent to the main line and comprised 18 sidings, which varied in length from 63 to 79 standard length units. Progress from this part of the yard was directly onto the main line and was controlled by Toton Junction signal box. The East Yard contained 19 sidings which were considerably longer than those in the West Yard. The shortest had the capacity to hold 82 wagons whilst the longest could accommodate 110.

Departure from the East Yard was via a new bridge over the River Erewash and controlled by Toton East Junction signal box. Because of the spacious layout at the south end of the East Yard, secondary shunting could take place in these sidings. Three roads in the most easterly fan were accessible only from the south end of the yard. In addition to these three sidings seven further tracks, called the Chillwell Sidings, were used to deal with traffic bound for destinations other than those dealt with in the main yard. Seven short dead-end sidings, just south of the River Erewash, were used for minor wagon repairs; they were duly placed 18ft apart to allow access to both sides of a wagon.

From the hump apex wagons accelerated down the initial gradient of 1 in 20 which flattened to 1 in 80 over the rail brakes. Each rail brake set weighed approximately 45 tonnes and comprised a bedplate on which were mounted two, 62ft long braking rails. These were hydraulically raised to grip the wheels of passing wagons. Under the 'up' yard modernisation scheme the opportunity was taken to acquire a spare retarder in order that a programme could be arranged for carrying out major repairs on the retarders in rotation. This avoided the necessity to close one fan in either the 'up' or 'down' sidings whenever important maintenance to a retarder had to be undertaken. Day to day alterations to the retarders were made by means of a tunnel under the hump. This enabled minor

repairs to be conducted without interrupting the shunting at the yard concerned.

# Operation

Trains arrived from the north under the control of the signalman at Stapleford & Sandiacre signal box. The signalman directed the train into one of the arrival lines and then indicated the road as blocked. The train locomotive was released and departed south along the hump avoiding line from where it could return to the locomotive depot, or take another freight train from the yard. The head shunter examined the train to look for cripples, and then labelled each wagon with a chalk number denoting the siding into which it was to be sorted. The train was then propelled over the hump by an 0-6-0 diesel shunting locomotive. The control of shunting was executed via colour-light signals. The old 'up' yard had only one humping signal of the semaphore type. This was often difficult to see from the northern end of the arrival sidings and had only two positions — stop and go. A new type of lunar white humping signal was incorporated at Toton Yard. These were placed between arrival lines and repeated at 680ft intervals. They displayed three shunting indications of 'stop', 'hump slow', and 'hump normal' and a horizontal bar showed which siding was to be shunted.

At the apex of the hump was the hump room from where several duties were carried out. Train engines were liberated and humping operations controlled, and the cutting of wagons into the sorting sidings was set and this data was transmitted to the control tower by means of a teletyper. Shunting performance was recorded, and liaison of movements within the rest of the yard was made through the hump room. The control tower, situated to the east side of the hump, was an ideal position for the observation of the behaviour of the cuts. From here, corrective action was taken in the case of wrong sorting, the wagon speeds were regulated using the rail brakes, and cuts were prevented from overtaking each other. Eighty per cent of the traffic handled in the 'up' yard was coal and coke bound for London and the south. Other smaller tonnages included iron ore and oil tanks, but very little ordinary traffic passed through the 'up' sidings. Each of the 37 sorting sidings handled traffic bound for a particular destination (Table 34).

Trains bound for London often grossed over 1,500 tons and were hauled by Beyer-Garratt locomotives. Both domestic coal and coal for gasworks left the yard for the conurbations of London and Birmingham. A block train of 16, 40 ton, fully-fitted, hopper wagons left thrice weekly for the power station at Stonebridge Park, whilst other local power stations were serviced by unfitted wagons. The 'up' yard saw a daily throughput of between 3,000 and 4,000 wagons, making an annual total in 1953 of 996,871 wagons. The cut size at the 'up' sidings was, on average, 2.15 wagons, whilst the record number of wagons sorted in an eight-hour turn of duty was 1,549. The normal yard working on the 'up' side required five 350hp diesel-electric

shunting locomotives. Two of these worked at the hump end whilst a third operated at the south end of the West Yard; the fourth operated at the south end of the East Yard and the final locomotive shunted the Chillwell Sidings. The locomotives were manned by a driver only in the yard itself, but movements across the main line required the provision of a second man.

The freight locomotive depot at Toton comprised three roundhouses which took an allocation of 154 locomotives. These consisted mainly of Beyer-Garratt articulated locomotives, Stanier 8F 2-8-0 steam engines and various smaller 0-6-0 locomotives. The yardmaster appointed in 1950 was Mr W.D. Lander who had joined the Great Central Railway as a clerk in 1911 and moved to the Midland Railway at Wath in 1912. Subsequent appointments at Toton and Beeston culminated in his promotion to yardmaster at Toton in 1950. With a staff of 500, he was responsible for the two million wagons handled annually at Toton; 250 of his staff were railway guards and the remaining 250 were responsible for day-to-day operation at Toton Sidings. Thus an average of 60 people were employed per eight hour shift in the yard at Toton.

| | | Table 34 | |
| --- | --- | --- | --- |
| | | **Siding Allocation Toton up Yard 1948** | |
| Number of siding | Capacity. Wagons at 20 ft over buffers | Sidings classification | |
| | | **WEST SIDE** | |
| Fan 1 | | | |
| 1 | 79 | Long Eaton | |
| 2 | 79 | Foleshill Gasworks | |
| 3 | 73 | Birmingham, Windsor Street Gasworks | |
| 4 | 73 | Western Region via Gloucester | |
| 5 | 68 | Westerleigh, Bristol | |
| 6 | 68 | Via Wichnor, excluding Stafford & Salop | |
| 7 | 69 | Derby St. Mary's, Ripley & Wirksworth branches and stations to Darley Dale | |
| 8 | 69 | Chaddesden, Water Orton & N.S. line | |
| Fan 2 | | | |
| 9 | 66 | Holwell | |
| 10 | 65 | Birmingham, Nechells Gasworks | |
| 11 | 63 | Washwood Heath, front fan | |
| 12 | 63 | Beeston | |
| 13 | 69 | Washwood Heath, back fan | |
| 14 | 69 | Via Banbury | |
| 15 | 70 | Via Bordesley | |
| 16 | 70 | Birmingham, Saltley Gasworks | |
| 17 | 76 | Burton & Exchange | |
| 18 | 76 | Branston Exchange | |
| | | **EAST SIDE** | |
| Fan 3 | | | |
| 19 | 110 | District wagon repair shop | |
| 20 | 92 | Eastern Region via Nottingham | |
| 21 | 95 | Lloyds, Weldon & Corby | |
| 22 | 94 | Leicester Exchange | |
| 23 | 87 | Leicester Humberstone Road | |
| 24 | 87 | Leicester Aylestone Road Gasworks | |
| 25 | 88 | Wigston, including K.I. coke | |
| 26 | 86 | Toton Down yard | |
| 27 | 82 | Kettering Exchange, excluding K.I. coke | |
| 28 | 82 | Wellingboro' | |
| Fan 4 | | | |
| 29 | 89 | Lillie Bridge | |
| 30 | 89 | Bletchley Exchange | |
| 31 | 85 | Rugby Exchange | |
| 32 | 85 | Northampton Exchange | |
| 33 | 93 | Watford Exchange | |
| 34 | 93 | Willesden High Level | |
| 35 | 97 | Willesden Low Level | |
| 36 | 102 | Chillwell group for subsidiary shunting | |
| 37 | 102 | Eastern Region via Peterborough | |

In March 1980, hump-shunting progressed at Toton 'up' yard under the watchful eyes of a party from the Cambridge University Railway Club. A bogie-bolster, converted to carry timber, approaches the retarders.

# Rationalisation 1976 to 1986

The yard at Toton dealt predominantly with coal traffic and, as such, was hit less hard by the recession and the transfer of mixed goods to road haulage. Whilst many other yards were virtually closed during the 1970s, Toton continued to sort approximately 2,000 wagons each day over both 'down' and 'up' humps. Freight traffic in the Nottingham Division as a whole was buoyant during the 1970s. Whilst the introduction of North Sea gas brought about the closure of Britain's coalburning gasworks, a simultaneous increase in coal-fired electricity generating stations meant that many areas saw no decrease in the number of coal trains. Modernisation, however, brought about the introduction of block merry-go-round trains, and these bypassed the major marshalling yards.

Production from the 24 collieries and three opencast workings in the Nottingham Division accounted for 15 per cent of the national total in 1973. Of the 15.6 million tonnes of coal mined annually, 60 per cent moved directly from collieries to eight local coal-fired power stations. By 1978, the majority of power stations were equipped to receive merry-go-round coal trains, and the number of coal wagons passing through Toton was, therefore, greatly reduced. This decrease in traffic, along with the introduction of the TOPS computerised wagon processing system, led to the closure of the 'down' hump and Meadow Sidings at the end of 1978. The North Yard continued to be used for non-hump traffic, including Speedlink wagons to and from Derby and Nottingham. All hump traffic was concentrated on the 'up' yard.

The developments during the late 1970s and early 1980s indicate the further move away from large marshalling yards. In 1969 the Nottingham Division carried 854,000 tonnes of aggregates; this rose by 1974 to 2,000,000 tonnes per annum. This freight was conveyed directly from railheads at Barrow-on-Soar, Loughborough, Croft, Cliffe Hill, Mountsorrell, Draycott, Wichnor and Willington to specifically-designed terminals throughout the South of England. Trains were run as block loads and no marshalling of traffic was required. Whilst such bulk commodities were increasingly carried by rail, smaller loads of coal and steel, which required marshalling, were being lost. The closure of the steelworks at Corby in 1979, meant that 1,000,000 tonnes of rail-borne coke and coal disappeared overnight.

After all hump shunting was concentrated on the 'up' yard in 1978, the daily throughput averaged 2,500 wagons. A gradual decline in this figure was exacerbated by the miners' strike of 1984, and by October of that year there were only 200 wagons passing over the hump each day. The hump was therefore closed along with the East Yard, and Speedlink marshalling

Below and opposite:
The 'up' reception sidings in 1955 and 1986. By 1986 the shunting signals have been removed from their posts, the engine run-round line disconnected from the hump, and modern lighting installed along the sidings. These ten roads now constitute the major marshalling sidings at Toton and, on 24th February 1986, they are host to Class 56 No. 56085 at the head of the 7O34, Oxcroft Colliery to Ridham Dock.

*British Rail and Author*

In March 1980, Class 20s Nos 20152 and 20156 are released from their train which they have just deposited in the 'up' reception sidings. The characteristic design of the hump office is typical for British Railways buildings of the 1940s.

concentrated on the West Yard which was then shunted from the south end. A few sidings in the North Yard were retained to deal with 'down' traffic (Plan 38). After this, rationalisation the 'up' yard at Toton dealt with just over 40 arrivals daily and approximately the same number of departures (Table 35). The 'down' yard dealt with half this number of trains and these are also listed in Table 35. Of the 120 trains using 'up' and 'down' yards daily, only 28 were classified as Speedlink services. Most of the other trains conveyed block loads of coal or empty coal wagons, whilst several other services were simply recessed at Toton for re-manning or re-engining. The move away from the marshalling yard towards the block train is most graphically understood by consideration of the fact that in 1985 there were 70 daily block freight trains timetabled to run within the Toton Division, none of which came into contact with the marshalling yard.

Further rationalisation at Toton occurred in 1986. The 'up' yard was completely closed and all freight train marshalling concentrated on the ten arrival lines and thirteen sidings in the Old Bank Yard. The

facilities on the 'down' side of the main line were reduced to five sidings.

## The Current Position

Toton Yard was originally constructed to handle large flows of coal traffic from the Midlands to London and the South West. These domestic flows of coal have significantly reduced, to be replaced by heavy coal flows from collieries directly to power stations and some coal forwardings from local pits to coal concentration depots. The area around Toton never generated large

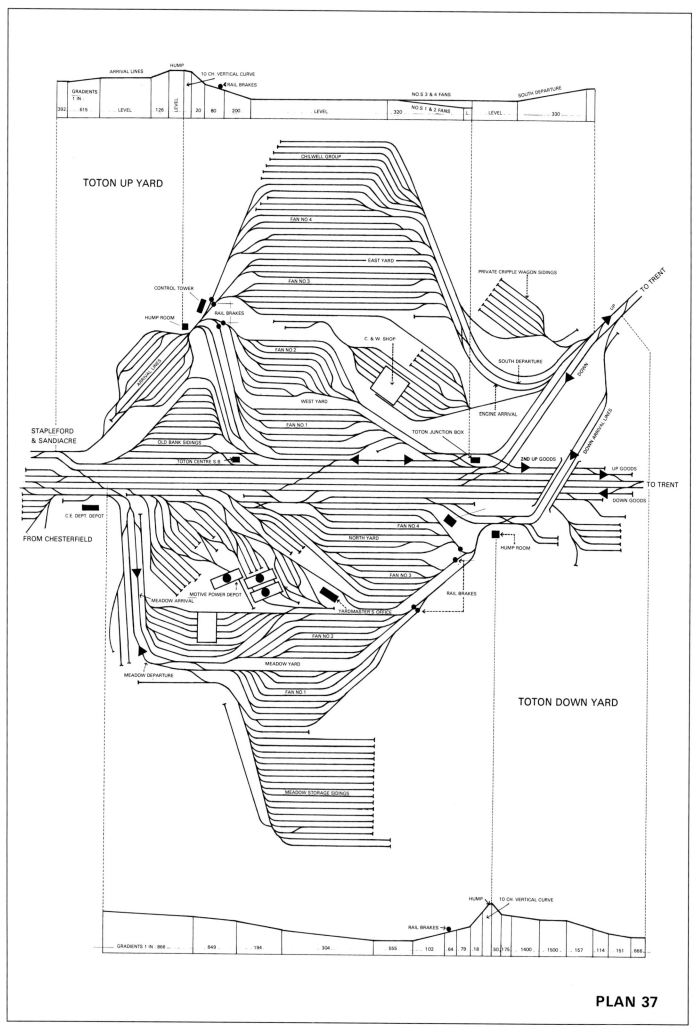

PLAN 37

222

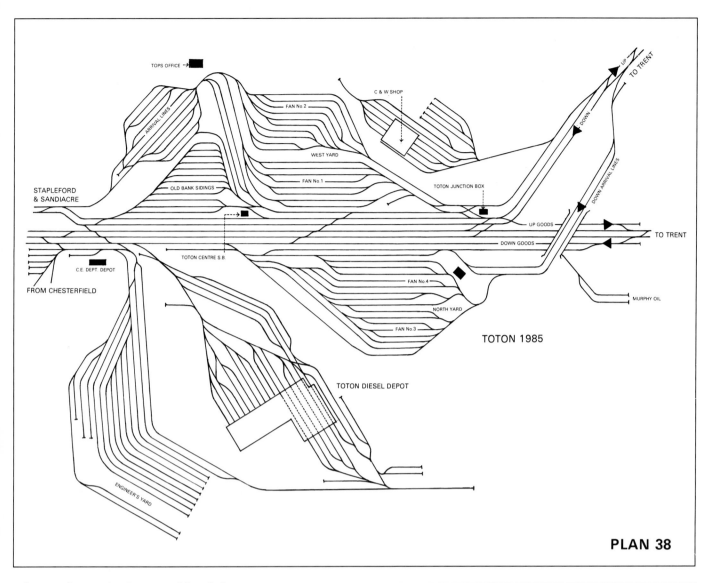

PLAN 38

volumes of wagonloads or sundries. It is therefore, not surprising that the local towns contribute little to the Speedlink merchandise network. Other than CEGB coal from the Leen Valley and Erewash Valley collieries, freight is conveyed in wagonloads on Speedlink services to customers around the country such as the output of Avenue coke works at Chesterfield. The only regular merchandise Speedlink customers include the Metal Box Company at Sutton-in-Ashfield, who receive tinplate from the BSC works at Trostre and Velindre in the South Wales. Others are McIntyres scrap merchants at Beeston, Blue Circle Cement, also at Beeston and Rugby Portland Cement at Sandiacre. In view of the relatively small number of Speedlink customers general Speedlink merchandise traffic was transferred from Toton Yard to Derby St. Mary's on 19th January 1987, to allow Toton Yard to concentrate on the development of the Speedlink Coal Network. Speedlink merchandise traffic is now tripped from Derby to the terminals described above.

## Table 35
## Toton Freight
## 1985

| 'UP' ARRIVALS | | | | 'UP' DEPARTURES | | | |
|---|---|---|---|---|---|---|---|
| Train | From | Arr. | Days | Train | To | Dep. | Days |
| 7D10 | Humberstone | 06.31 | MO | 7A84 | Willesden | 06.26 | SX |
| 6M81 | Worksop | 07.45 | SX | 9T64 | Ratcliffe | 06.35 | MO |
| 6T23 | Toton N Yd | 09.05 | MO | 9T71 | Beeston | 06.45 | SX |
| 6M56 | Westbury | 09.18 | SO | 6T23 | Spondon | 06.45 | SX |
| 6M94 | Barrow Hill | 09.41 | SX | 9T77 | Bestwood | 06.50 | SX |
| 7D56 | Bescot | 10.01 | SX | 9T75 | Gedling | 06.58 | SX |
| 7T50 | Silverhill | 10.55 | SX | 7V46 | Didcot | 07.02 | SX |
| 9M40 | Whitemoor | 11.35 | SX | 7F10 | Humberstone | 07.15 | SX |
| 7T23 | Derby | 11.55 | SX | 7M03 | Warrington | 08.43 | SX |
| 6T64 | Kirkby Summit | 12.30 | SX | 7P06 | Burton | 09.15 | SX |
| 7M20 | Ollerton | 12.58 | SX | 7F07 | Corby | 09.25 | SX |
| 9T77 | Bestwood | 13.05 | SX | 6E61 | Worksop | 09.30 | MO |
| 8055 | Treeton | 14.05 | MTThO | 6T23 | Derby | 09.35 | MO |
| 7M29 | Maltby | 14.30 | MWFO | 7F47 | Garston Dock | 10.44 | SX |
| 7T49 | Silverhill | 14.35 | SX | 6G47 | Three Spires | 12.05 | MWThO |
| 7034 | Oxcroft | 14.40 | SX | 7T23 | Derby | 12.20 | SX |
| 7T23 | Toton N Yd | 14.45 | SX | 6T68 | Colwick | 12.25 | SX |
| 6M47 | Lackenby | 15.13 | SX | 9E40 | Whitemoor | 12.35 | SX |
| 7M60 | Ashburys | 15.20 | SX | 7085 | Northfleet | 13.00 | SX |
| 7D09 | Burton | 15.32 | SX | 6T64 | Eggington | 13.20 | TThO |
| 9T71 | Bestwood Park | 15.31 | SX | 6T64 | Ilkeston | 13.20 | WFO |
| 6T64 | Eggington | 16.03 | SX | 9T77 | Bestwood | 13.40 | SX |
| 9T75 | Gedling | 16.12 | SX | 7M20 | Garston Dock | 13.40 | SX |
| 9T93 | Avenue | 17.00 | SX | 7V85 | Didcot | 14.22 | SX |
| 8M45 | Bescot | 18.02 | SX | 7M29 | Garston Dock | 15.02 | MWFO |
| 7D24 | Willesden | 17.41 | SX | 7T23 | Derby | 15.20 | SX |
| 9T68 | Beeston | 17.57 | SX | 6M47 | Corby | 15.33 | SX |
| 6M70 | Worksop | 18.57 | SX | 9T75 | Leyton | 17.45 | SX |
| 6M63 | Saltend | 19.00 | SX | 7034 | Ridham Dock | 18.03 | SX |
| 7D11 | Humberstone | 19.15 | SX | 8M45 | Ashburys | 19.17 | SX |
| 6T23 | Toton N Yd | 19.30 | SX | 7030 | Northfleet | 20.33 | SX |

The date of 19th January 1987, is significant in the history of Toton Yard as its commercial role is now exclusively dealing with coal traffic. Toton has become a focal point of the National Distributive Coal Market with a view to preserving rail involvement therein. The yard is the focal point for all East Midlands coal producing locations, and shunts, marshalls and prepares trunk trains in the Old Bank section of the yard for Scotland, Healey Mills, Washwood Heath, Didcot, Westbury and East Anglia. The yard complex also continues to be important for the recessing and crew changing of block coal trains. The layout which comprises eleven "up" sidings on the New Bank, ten roads in the Old Bank and the aforementioned "Down Yard" is ideal for such activities.

| 9T77 | Bestwood | 19.35 | SX | 6V56 | Westbury | 20.40 | SX |
|---|---|---|---|---|---|---|---|
| 6V06 | Healey Mills | 20.12 | SX | 6V06 | Severn Tunnel | 21.18 | SX |
| 8M33 | Worksop | 20.20 | MThO | 6A83 | Willesden | 21.25 | SX |
| 6O55 | Tyne | 20.45 | WFO | 8E36 | Worksop | 21.44 | MThO |
| 8E36 | Longport | 21.05 | MThO | 8M33 | Longport | 22.05 | TThO |
| 6M80 | Doncaster | 22.13 | SX | 8O55 | Betteshanger | 22.12 | SX |
| 6M61 | Didcot | 22.58 | SX | 6M80 | Bescot | 23.26 | SX |
| 6M31 | Doncaster | 23.58 | TWFO | 6E76 | Tinsley | 23.40 | SX |
| 6E95 | Warrington | 00.14 | SX | 7P07 | Burton | 00.48 | MSX |
| 7M75 | Whitemoor | 00.14 | SX | 7E35 | Foxton | 00.52 | MSX |
| 7E35 | Thoresby | 00.32 | FSX | 6O39 | Hoo Junc | 01.00 | MSX |
| 7D06 | Coalville | 01.39 | SX | 6O39 | Sheerness | 01.00 | SO |
| 6M29 | Lackenby | 03.18 | SX | 7E95 | Parkeston | 01.10 | SX |
| 6M87 | Tinsley | 03.58 | MX | 7E96 | Whitemoor | 01.48 | MX |
| 7M27 | Clipstone | 04.30 | MSX | 7P03 | Coalville | 03.25 | MX |
| 7M88 | Dringhouses | 05.19 | MX | 7M27 | Garston Dock | 05.03 | MSX |
| | | | | 6M29 | Corby | 05.15 | MSX |
| | | | | 6D23 | Corby | 05.22 | MO |
| | | | | 7P05 | Derby | 05.30 | MSX |
| | | | | 7P04 | Spondon | 05.30 | SO |

'DOWN' ARRIVALS        'DOWN' DEPARTURES

| Train | From | Arr. | Days | Train | To | Dep. | Days |
|---|---|---|---|---|---|---|---|
| 7D10 | Humberstone | 06.23 | MSX | 6E22 | Ollerton | 06.30 | MSX |
| 6M38 | Port Clarence | 07.32 | TFX | 6E94 | Doncaster | 07.17 | MX |
| 9T64 | Ratcliffe | 08.00 | MO | 6T64 | Kirkby Summit | 08.49 | SX |
| 6M32 | Northfleet | 08.12 | MX | 6E24 | Tyne | 08.53 | WFO |
| 8E24 | Cricklewood | 08.33 | WFO | 8E25 | Treeton | 08.53 | MTThO |
| 8E25 | Betteshanger | 08.33 | MWFO | 6T23 | Derby | 09.05 | SX |
| 6T23 | Derby | 08.40 | SX | 6T67 | Bennerley | 08.50 | SX |
| 6E61 | Westbury | 09.06 | MSX | 6E61 | Worksop | 09.35 | MSX |
| 6D25 | Garston Dock | 12.18 | MSX | 6E19 | Oxcroft | 09.55 | SX |
| 7T23 | Derby | 14.30 | SX | 6E98 | Barrow Hill | 11.13 | SX |
| 6T68 | Colwick | 15.50 | SX | 6T50 | Bentinck | 11.50 | SX |
| 6M56 | Didcot | 16.20 | SX | 6E50 | Port Clarence | 12.08 | TFX |
| 8D05 | Nuneaton | 16.53 | TO | 6E34 | Clipstone | 14.20 | FSX |
| 6E07 | Foxton | 17.22 | MSX | 6E34 | Ollerton | 14.20 | FO |
| 6D22 | Garston Dock | 17.55 | SX | 7T23 | Toton N Bank | 14.35 | SX |
| 6D48 | Three Spires | 18.19 | TWFO | 6T49 | Silverhill | 15.50 | SX |
| 7D11 | Humberstone | 18.46 | SX | 6E39 | Worksop | 16.00 | MWFO |
| 6T23 | Derby | 19.10 | SX | 7E49 | Dringhouses | 16.54 | SX |
| 6D26 | Garston Dock | 21.00 | SX | 6E07 | Thoresby | 17.42 | TWThO |
| 7M86 | Parkeston | 21.19 | SX | 6E07 | Shirebrook | 17.42 | FO |
| 6D81 | Bescot | 21.53 | SX | 7D11 | Toton N Bank | 18.56 | SX |
| 6D27 | Garston Dock | 22.34 | MWFO | 6T23 | Toton W Yd | 19.20 | SX |
| 6E30 | Eastleigh | 23.09 | SX | 6E62 | Worksop | 20.47 | SX |
| 6M95 | Dover | 01.11 | SX | 7M86 | Warrington | 22.00 | SX |
| 6E75 | Willesden | 01.46 | SX | 6E30 | Tyne | 23.55 | SX |
| 6M59 | Ridham Dock | 03.14 | SX | 6E33 | Doncaster | 01.35 | WThSO |
| 7D08 | Burton | 03.51 | MSX | 6E75 | Hunslet | 03.19 | MX |
| 6M52 | Northfleet | 04.05 | SX | | | | |
| 6T67 | Ratcliffe | 05.55 | MX | | | | |
| 6E94 | Severn Tunnel | 05.56 | SX | | | | |

Meadow storage at Toton is the remains of the two western fans of the 'down' yard. Nos 45038/042/072/075, 25287 and 45010 await their fate on 2nd July 1985. The sidings are now used to store condemned wagons.

The majority of roads are over 75 standard length units and therefore capable of accommodating the longest block trains currently run by British Rail. The traction maintenance depot at Toton however, remains the largest diesel servicing point in Europe. Locomotives now predominantly dedicated to the coal business are allocated to Toton. They operate throughout the London Midland Region and parts of the Eastern Region, returning to Toton only for major examinations. This side of the Toton complex continues to thrive and has a bright future. The future size of the yard itself, depends on how the Distributive Coal Market develops. There will always be a need for the recessing and crew changing for block coal trains to the power stations and a continuing role for the shunting out of mgr wagons for preventative maintenance.

My thanks in writing this chapter to John Grador (Area Manager Nottingham), Alan Peel (Area Manager Leicester) together with John Langford, Peter Arthur and Pat Hare at Toton.

**On 27th May 1988 Class 37 No. 37235** *The Coal Merchants' Association of Scotland* **arrives at Toton with a Speedlink coal working from Washwood Heath. Note there are both empty and loaded HEA wagons in the train. The empties are returning to Nottinghamshire pits from coal depots in the South, whilst the loaded wagons bring South Wales coal for remarshalling before departure to East Anglia.**

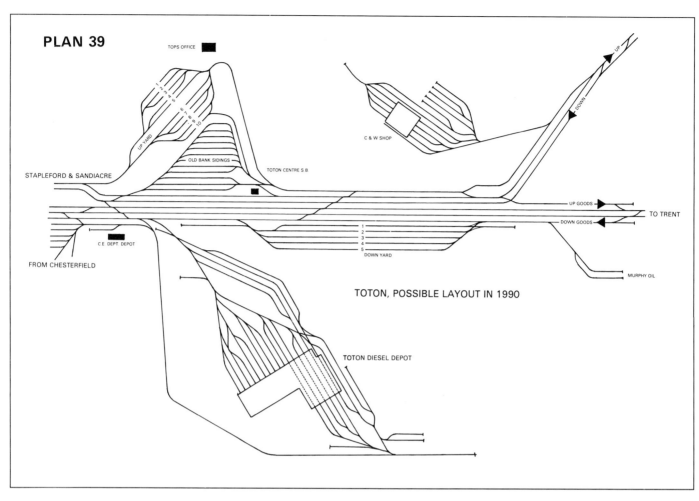

PLAN 39

TOPS OFFICE

UP YARD
1 2 3 4 5 6 7 8 9 10

C & W SHOP

UP

DOWN

OLD BANK SIDINGS

STAPLEFORD & SANDIACRE

TOTON CENTRE S B

UP GOODS

TO TRENT

DOWN GOODS

1
2
3
4
5
DOWN YARD

C E DEPT DEPOT

FROM CHESTERFIELD

MURPHY OIL

TOTON, POSSIBLE LAYOUT IN 1990

TOTON DIESEL DEPOT

**Opposite:**
In July 1985, the two eastern fans in the 'down' yard are still in use, albeit shunted from the north end. The yard control tower, retarders and most of the sorting sidings have stood disused since the closure of the 'down' hump in 1978.

**Above:**
A pair of Class 20s, Nos 20176 and 20086, accelerate north from Toton at the head of a rake of HEA coal hoppers. The train is the 6E34, 14.15, Toton to Clipstone Colliery, and is seen passing the Old Bank Yard on the left.

**Below:**
The Old Bank Yard at Toton remains to cater for Speedlink traffic. In July 1985, Class 31 No. 31102 departs from the Old Bank Yard with a Class 9 freight bound for March Whitemoor. The train conveys household coal for the concentration depots of East Anglia.

The diesel depot at Toton is the largest such installation in Western Europe. Class 25 No. 25205, passes the depot with a departure from the 'down' yard — the 6T64, Toton to Kirkby-in-Ashfield. The two VDA vans convey steel from South Wales bound for the Metal Box Company at Kirkby.

For a short period in the early 1980s, Speedlink traffic was shunted in the two western fans of the 'up' sorting sidings; this before their complete closure at the end of 1985. Here, Class 08 No. 08757 marshals a Speedlink freight under the watchful eye of the head shunter.

## Toton Freight

**Opposite top:**
Nottinghamshire coal takes the main line south to the Capital on 3rd October 1977 behind Class 44 No. 44008, *Penyghent*. A sea of coal wagons can be seen in Toton 'up' yard in the background.

*W. Chapman*

**Opposite:**
By December 1985, all freight marshalling on the 'up' side of the main line at Toton was dealt with in the sidings shown here; the 'up' reception roads and the Old Bank yard. Class 31 No. 31130 arrives with the 7D09 Burton to Toton trip freight.

**Above:**
Chemical tanks from Spondon near Derby, to Saltend are hauled past Toton on 3rd June 1981 by Class 37 No. 37290. The train is the 6E12, which departed from Spondon at 17.45.

**Below:**
A Toton to Brent Yard coal train passes Kibworth in April 1968. Class 44 No. D5 *Cross Fell* will take its load of 16$\frac{1}{2}$ ton mineral wagons to the Cricklewood Yard, from where they will be distributed to individual customers throughout London and the south east.

*J. Cooper-Smith*

**Opposite:**
A rake of coal empties winds into the 'up' reception sidings at Toton on 3rd June 1981 behind a brace of Class 20s, Nos 20165 and 20151. The Stapleford & Sandiacre signal box on the left controls the entrance to the 'up' yard.

Opposite:

Class 25 No. 25182 eases south along the south departure road from the 'up' yard at Toton. In the background is the East Yard and on the right the Chillwell Sidings. The train, made up of civil engineering stock, is bound for Nottingham.

Above:

The new order in coal carriage as Class 58 No. 58030 passes Stapleford box, to the north of Toton, on 18th December 1985.

The diesel depot at Toton mainly services freight locomotives. This 2nd July 1985 view shows Class 45s Nos 45150 and 45127 undergoing repair. On the right is No. 20008. The depot is now the major repair centre for all locomotives involved in the work of the trainload coal sector of Railfreight.

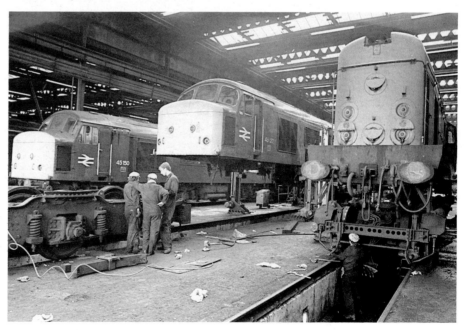

WHITEMOOR MARSHALLING YARDS 1933

PLAN 41

234

# Chapter 15

# March Whitemoor Yard

On 3rd March 1929, the LNER opened their new marshalling yard at March, in Cambridgeshire. This replaced a yard that had been on this site from the previous century *(Plan 40)*. This yard was the first in the United Kingdom to utilise the Fröhlich system of hydraulic rail brakes. An array of 43 sorting sidings provided accommodation for 4,000 wagons, and 350 separate destinations were served from the 'up' yard at March. Traffic for the eastern section of the LNER arrived from places to the north east and north west via Doncaster. Further freights from the collieries and yards of Nottinghamshire and Derbyshire travelled via Lincoln to the new yard at March *(Fig. 8)*.

In 1933, further expansion at Whitemoor involved the construction of a 'down' yard. *(Plan 41)*. This was similar to its partner on the 'up' side of the main line but contained only two sets of wagon retarders. At the start of World War II, in 1939, the yard complex at Whitemoor had a capacity to sort 8,000 wagons daily. The war placed heavy demands on the freight facilities at March and further expansion of the sidings was undertaken. The 'up' yard saw the addition of ten departure roads at its southern extremity. This enabled the departure of trains at an even rate without interference with shunting at the south end of the sorting sidings.

Freight at Whitemoor remained essentially unchanged until the mid 1960s when a reduction in branch lines and small goods stations was introduced by Dr Beeching. This lead to a concomitant decrease in the number of destinations served by the marshalling yards and therefore a decrease in the complexity of marshalling at the sidings. During the same period the sidings at Ferme Park on the Great Northern main line were closed, and all traffic south of Doncaster diverted to Whitemoor. The concentration of Eastern Region freight traffic on Whitemoor meant that both hump yards remained operational until the early 1970s. In 1972, the 'down' hump was closed and the 'down' sorting sidings were used for wagon storage. By October 1980, there was no longer enough traffic to justify the hump in the 'up' yard and the reception sidings at the northern end of the yard were closed.

Speedlink traffic has used Whitemoor since the inauguration of the network in 1975. Freight from both East Anglia and the Continent, via Harwich, is marshalled at Whitemoor before dispatch throughout the country. Since the closure of the 'up' hump in 1980 most marshalling has taken place in the 'up' departure sidings, and these ten roads now form the backbone of the marshalling facilities at Whitemoor.

## Early Yards Around March

March had always been an important railway junction controlling the flow of traffic from the north and west of the country into East Anglia and the eastern side of London. By the 1920s serious delays in the passage of freight traffic were being experienced. This was due to the very inadequate accommodation for reception, sorting and marshalling of trains at Whitemoor. Freights from the Midlands, Nottinghamshire and Derbyshire were staged at Peterborough. Often wagons had to be transferred from the Great Northern yards at New England to the Great Eastern yards further south of Peterborough. Such transfers brought about yet further delay

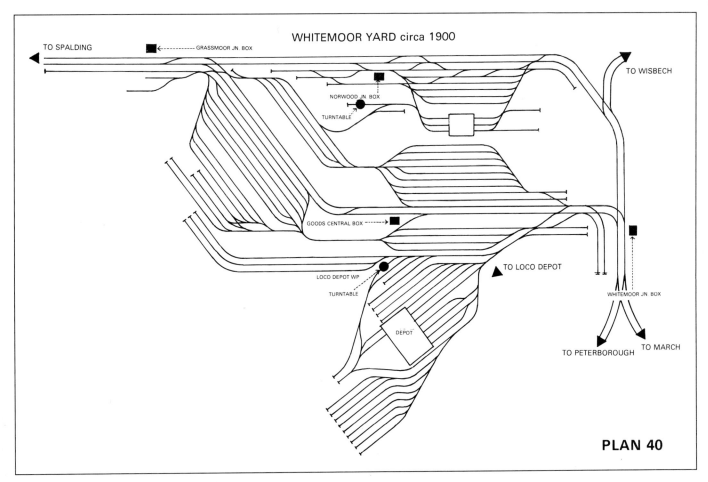

PLAN 40

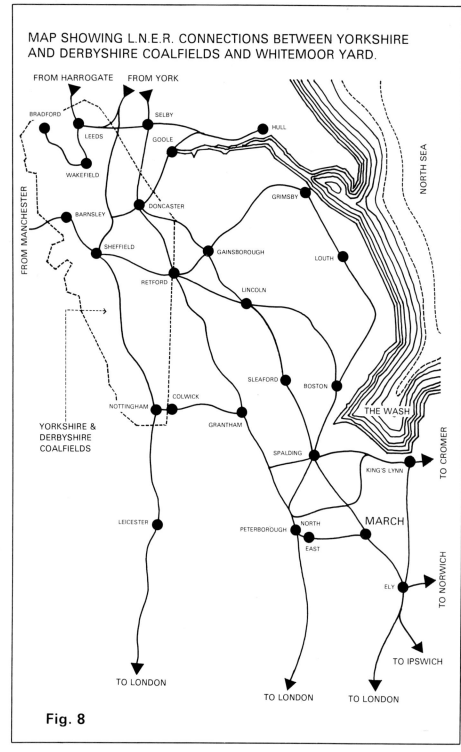

MAP SHOWING L.N.E.R. CONNECTIONS BETWEEN YORKSHIRE AND DERBYSHIRE COALFIELDS AND WHITEMOOR YARD.

**Fig. 8**

turnover at Whitemoor, along with a reduction in locomotive costs. 'Up' traffic was handled at the four separate yards already mentioned. Their total of 40 sidings had the capacity to hold 2,100 wagons. The flow of traffic into East Anglia and south to London was, however, erratic, because of the four separate starting points for freights bound for the south and east. Pathing problems south of Whitemoor were common and trains often had to wait for several hours after missing their booked path. These difficulties, along with the excess of trip workings around March,

made the provision of a new marshalling yard at Whitemoor an important priority for the LNER. Folklore recounts how Gerry Feinnes first conceived the modern bi-directional hump yard whilst taking a bath. Whatever the true origin of this design, the LNER was the first to build such a yard at March (Whitemoor). Its 40 sidings had the capacity to hold 3,311 wagons and the provision of ten reception roads, each of 80 standard wagon lengths, made it by far the largest single yard in Great Britain. When the yard was opened in 1929, trains from the Midlands ran directly from Colwick to Whitemoor via Sleaford; this a distance of 69 miles. Trains were allowed to load up to a maximum of 80 wagons along this route. The old passage for traffic from the Midlands had been from Colwick to New England Yard, and then forward by a trip freight to Peterborough East Yard from where trains were dispatched to March.

This route was shorter at only $64^{1/2}$ miles, but various loading restrictions meant that a maximum of 42 wagons could be transferred from New England to Peterborough East in any one train. The simplification of freight services from the Midlands to March is emphasised by a comparison of the paths available for freight trains into East Anglia before and after the opening of Whitemoor New Yard. In 1925, there were 34 paths daily into Peterborough from Colwick; from here trains had to be tripped twice to Peterborough East Yard and on to Whitemoor. In the same year there were 23 direct main line paths for trains into Whitemoor. With the introduction of the new service in 1929, there were 57 main line paths into Whitemoor and only seven to the old Great Northern Yard at Peterborough. This shows very clearly the facilitation of freight services brought about by the opening of March (Whitemoor) Yard.

for traffic travelling to East Anglia. The Great Eastern sidings in Peterborough were particularly cramped and unable to cope with the heavy demands that traffic from the Midlands to East Anglia put upon them. Freight trains from Northern England and Scotland were routed via the old GN and GE joint line into Whitemoor. The old Whitemoor yards were both on the west side of the joint line and access to them was controlled by the old Grassmoor Junction signal box. The 'up' yard had four reception sidings leading to nine sorting sidings and was hump shunted. The 'down' yard had a similar layout with the addition of four single ended sorting sidings on the western border of the yard; it was hump shunted. There was also a small 'up' yard called the Goods Yard at Whitemoor; this had just five sidings. The total of 24 sorting sidings

at Whitemoor had a standage capacity of 1,265 wagons. It is not surprising that the yards were overcrowded when a throughput in excess of 3,000 wagons per day was expected. The fourth yard which dealt with freight traffic entering East Anglia was east of March station. The 'up' sidings contained 13 roads with a capacity to hold 655 wagons and were level shunted.

The 'down' half of this yard was somewhat smaller with only ten sidings, and was also level-shunted. As well as the four main yards at Peterborough East, Whitemoor Coal Bank, Whitemoor Goods Yard and March, there were overflow sidings at Whittlesea. These were often needed during peak flows of traffic such as during the sugar beet season.

Analysis of freight flows through March revealed the need for a speedier wagon

# Operation of the New Yard at Whitemoor

Trains entered the ten reception sidings at the north end and, after being inspected and segregated, the wagons were pushed over the hump by shunting engines. The type of engine used at March was the North Eastern Railway 3-cylinder T1 tank which had a 4-8-0 wheel arrangement. These locomotives were capable of propelling a 72 wagon train over the hump at 2mph and were fitted with special low register speedometers to facilitate control whilst shunting. The hump at Whitemoor was constructed in order that wagons leaving the hump crest at 2mph gained sufficient momentum to reach the sorting sidings whilst not exceeding 16mph during their descent. The initial approach to the hump crest was level for 63yds. followed by a short ascent at 1 in 80. The first descent was for 50yds. at 1 in 18 followed by a 70yd. stretch at 1 in 60 where the pneumatic retarders were placed. After another level interval of 95yds. there was a gradual descent of 1 in 200 for 243yds. before a final level interval of 380yds.

After a train had arrived in one of the reception sidings, a shunter walked along the train, uncoupled the wagons and made out a cut card. This card indicated the number of wagons which had to be run off into the respective sorting sidings. When the card was completed it was sent by pneumatic tube to the control cabin from where the yard operator was able to pre-set up to 50 routes electrically. These route settings were transferred via a drum in the floor of the control cabin to the first seven sets of points in the yard. This meant that wagons were automatically guided into eight separate fans of five sidings. Beyond the first seven pairs of points the turnouts were manually-controlled.

A primitive system of track circuiting was installed and four-aspect colour-light signalling controlled the approach to the hump. The addition of claxon horns and a megaphone system were essential during foggy weather and when special instructions needed to be transmitted to shunting staff. The yard was illuminated by means of the 'Blaizolite' system which was supplied by Baxter & Caunter Ltd. The retarders were the first to be installed in Great Britain and were manufactured in West Germany in accordance with the patents of Doctor Fröhlich. The provision of four retarders, or rail brakes, brought a vast improvement in the capacity of Whitemoor Yard to sort wagons. A train of 70 wagons containing

from 40 to 50 separate cuts was shunted in seven minutes and the overall improvement meant that, in one eight-hour shift, 1,369 wagons were shunted, this involving 962 cuts.

Opposite:
The same Frölich retarders installed at Whitemoor in the 1920s were still in operation at yards like Oberhausen Osterfeld Süd in 1986. Even the signal cabin bears a striking resemblance to that at Whitemoor.

The Frölich rail brakes, or retarders, were in full operation by 1929 as this picture shows. A wooden mineral wagon is clasped in the metal rails of the retarder as it descends from the 'up' hump.

*British Rail*

The new yard at Whitemoor had 40 sorting sidings which were divided into three sections, that is the east, the middle or main section, and the west section. Each of these sections received wagons of a distinctive nature. The centre sidings, numbered 11 to 31 handled wagons bound for other major sorting or delivery yards in the Eastern Region, eg Norwich, Spittlefields, Ilford, Angel Road or Cambridge. Trains then left these sidings at regular intervals for the major yards of East Anglia and London. The east side of the yard was the home of country traffic; that is traffic for all small stations situated between Whitemoor and other large marshalling yards. Into the nine sidings numbered 32 to 40 traffic was shunted for the various stations on branch lines or sections of the main line. An example of this was the allocation of siding No. 35 for all stations between Wimblington and Histon. Siding No. 33 received traffic bound for stations between Great Chesterford and Stanstead, thus a train departing from one of these sidings might comprise wagons for ten or more separate destinations.

Opposite:
In 1928, the old 'down' yard at Whitemoor was still in use and it was not until 1933 that it was modernised. The new 'up' yard can just be seen in the background, with construction only in its early stages. This view dated 8th May 1928 was taken from the top of the coaling plant, looking north east.

*British Rail*

A Saturday afternoon in 1980 finds the hump very much as it must have looked in the 1930s; only the new lighting masts spoil an otherwise 'vintage' scene.

It was therefore important that wagons in the country yard were sorted so that the trip freight could detach wagons in the correct order. To enable secondary sorting of these wagons, the southern ends of these nine sidings were joined together to form a long shunting spur constructed over an auxiliary hump. This secondary hump was much smaller than the main hump at Whitemoor, and consisted of a 1 in 20 descent for 25yds. which gave a quick clearance of wagons, enabling rapid sorting of trip freights. In each twenty four hours, twelve to eighteen different trains were made up in the country side of the yard, and the provision of a secondary hump was essential for this traffic. The west side of the yard contained ten sidings numbered 1 to 10 and undertook more simple shunting. Trains on this side of the yard were made up in two sections, ie a Bury St. Edmunds train consisted of:
1. Bury town traffic next to the brake van and
2. Bury district traffic next to the engine.
Similarly, two-part trains were marshalled for all the major towns around East Anglia. The rear portions were shunted directly from the reception roads into the sidings allocated for each town, whilst the front portions were shunted into a common road, from where they could be drawn forward on to a shunting spur at the southern end of the yard, and then reversed back into the appropriate siding.

The old marshalling yards at March (Whitemoor) and Peterborough East distributed wagons to 350 different stations and depots. After freight marshalling was concentrated on the Whitemoor New Yard, all the old channels through which wagons had previously reached their destinations were reviewed. The 40 sorting sidings at the hump yard had a completely new range of destinations allocated to them, and it was of paramount importance that the staff at the hump should know into which of the sidings any given train should be shunted. The first attempt to communicate this information to the railway employees at Whitemoor was by means of a list of all destinations served by the yard, laid out in alphabetical order; the number of the siding being inserted opposite each destination. This was, however, unsatisfactory to the shunters at the departure end of the yard who needed to know exactly which destinations they would find in a given road. Consequently, the range of stations and destinations were reorganised into lists under siding numbers *(Table 36)*. The complexity of marshalling at the yard can be gauged by the fact that this information ran to a 58 page pocket pamphlet which was distributed to all staff at the yard.

At the southern end of the sorting sidings the 40 roads converged to form two departure lines. At this point there was an inclined brake siding or kip with connections to both departure roads. All brake vans off trains which arrived at the reception sidings were worked through the yard and placed as opportunity arose on to the kip. This could accommodate up to 15 vans. As a guard arrived in the yard, he was given the number of the locomotive that was to work his train and the particular brake van which was to be attached to the rear of it. He was also informed of the siding from which his train was to be drawn. His first duty was to examine the wagons in the appropriate siding and check that the correct number was present. The engine was coupled to the train as soon as it arrived from the locomotive shed, and at this stage the guard signalled to the shunter of the train that it was ready to be drawn forward into the departure road. As soon as the last wagon of the train was drawn clear of the brake-kip point, the brake van was released and ran on to the rear of the train. As this was taking place, the signalman controlling the outlet was advised of the approach of a departure; this facilitated rapid progress from the yard onto the main line.

Much traffic handled by the railways was designated as smalls; that is, goods that did not make up a full truck load. In conjunction with the 'up' yard at Whitemoor a new transhipment shed was constructed on the west side of the yard. This had three through roads with standing accommodation for up to 60 wagons. A rapid turnover of wagons was achieved and as many as 140 were loaded each day. Mandatory departures were afforded to nearly every depot on the Eastern Region, and this ensured delivery of goods the day after transhipment at Whitemoor. This was a vast improvement on the old system where transhipment at Whitemoor led to departure to further transhipment sheds around the country, rather than direct transit to goods depots. The LNER had also purchased 20 road vans to allow distribution of smalls to surrounding villages and towns

## Table 36

### March Whitemoor

| Station | Coal or Goods Only. | Siding No. |
|---|---|---|
| Noel Park and Wood Green | – | 12 |
| North Elmham | – | 1 |
| North London Line | Mineral | 15 |
| North London Line | Goods | 21 |
| North Walsham | – | 30 |
| North Weald | – | 17 |
| North Woolwich | Coal | 27 |
| North Woolwich | Goods | 21 |
| North Wootton | – | 5 |
| Norwich Thorpe | – | 30 |
| Norwich Victoria | – | 26 |
| Oakington | – | 35 |
| Old Hall Siding | – | 32 |
| Ongar | – | 17 |
| Orwell | – | 6 |
| Oulton Broad North | – | 30 |
| Oulton Broad South | – | 30 |
| Outwell Basin | – | 27 |
| Outwell Village | – | 27 |
| Overstrand | – | 30 |
| Padnal Siding | – | 36 |
| Palace Gates | – | 12 |
| Pamisford | – | 37 |
| Parham | – | 6 |
| Parkeston | – | 9 |

This, however, did not meet the requirements of the shunters at the depature end of the yard, who required to know exactly what destinations they would find in each road. Consequently, the whole range of stations applicable to each siding is now shown, again in alphabetical order, as follows:–

**Siding No. 11. Park (A).**
Althorne.
Angle Road (Goods).
Angel Road (Merchants Coal).
Battlesbridge.
Billericay.
Burnham-on-Crouch.
Cricksea Siding.
Down Hall Siding.
East London Line (Coal only).
Fambridge.
Hockley.
Hogwell Siding.
Mountness Siding.
New Cross Depot.
Park Yard.
Ramsden B Siding.

Rayleigh.
Rochford.
Southminster.
Tottenham.

Tufnell Park.
Wickford.
Woodham Ferrers.

**Siding No. 12. Park (B).**
Blackwall (Coal only).
Canning Town (Coal only).
Chingford (Locomotive coal only).
Clapton.
Hoe Street.
Noel Park.
Palace Gates.
Seven Sisters.
Thames Wharf (Coal only).
Victoria Docks (Coal only).
West Green.
Wood Street.
Walthamstow.
**Siding No. 13. Angel Road.**
Angel Road (Gas coal only).
**Siding No. 14. Goodmayes Down Yard.**
Chadwell Heath.
Chadwell Heath, Wills Siding.
Gidea Park.
Goodmayes (Engineers' traffic and slag).
Harold Wood.
Romford.
Romford Factory.

that were either not well-connected, or where the volume of traffic did not justify the use of a railway wagon.

# Retarders and Signalling

Overall control of marshalling at Whitemoor was effected from a central tower, located near the base of the hump. The top floor of this tower was surrounded by a window set at an angle so that an excellent view of the hump and yard was possible without reflections from either low sun or the lighting within the yard at night. Three men worked in the control tower; two were involved in actuating the two groups of retarders whilst a third manned the switchboard which controlled the electrically-operated points leading to the sorting sidings. On the middle floor of the control tower was an ingenious apparatus known as a collector drum locking frame.

This consisted of seven collector drums, one for each set of automatic points, an outer drum had a row of studs around it and these were able to record up to 50 consecutive movements for the pair of points which they controlled. An inner drum carried a switch arm which was operated by the studs on the outer drum. As a wagon, or group of wagons, passed down the hump, the inner drum was made to turn one notch as each wagon activated the track circuits on the hump. This would automatically set the points into the sorting sidings for the next wagon in the shunt. The first seven points from the hump crest were automatically controlled. Beyond this, whilst the turnouts were electrically-controlled, they had to be manually-operated by switches on the control board on the top floor of the control tower.

The yard was equipped with four hydraulic rail brakes which consisted of a table which could be raised or lowered by means of several hydraulic cylinders. Initially, each retarder was equipped with five such cylinders, but after several years of operation two of the retarders were lengthened and equipped with a total of seven cylinders. Each rail brake was mounted in a concrete pit and measured 50ft x 10ft 4in; hydraulic pressure was provided by a 25hp electric motor supplied by Crompton Parkinson.

**Many unpublicised minor mishaps occurred with the alteration of working practices at Britain's major hump marshalling yards. In 1981, the northern end of the 'up' sorting sidings at Whitemoor are littered with de-railed wagons; a direct result of the closure of the hump and the transfer of marshalling to the south end of the yard. Later investment in 'stop blocks' for the sidings avoided further mishaps!**

This enabled a maximum hydraulic pressure of 1400psi to be applied to the rail brakes, thus raising the parallel flanges of the retarder to grip either side of a wagon wheel. As pressure was increased, so the wagon was simply lifted from the running rail, wedged between the braking rails, and a maximum retarding effort was then applied. The system at Whitemoor was capable of raising the heaviest wagon from the running rails and thereby submitting it to the maximum retardation.

In June 1986, marshalling at Whitemoor was concentrated on a portion of the old 'up' sorting sidings, with most long-haul Speedlink trains being dealt with in the 'up' departure sidings. The wagon repair sidings for Whitemoor are on the left in this view of the yard, and in the middle-distance stands the disused Grassmoor Junction signal cabin. To the right of the array of sorting sidings is the brake van kip.

In the early stages of the yard's operation, there were problems with wagons fitted with old-fashioned wheels. These contained ring fastenings which projected beyond the tyre, and if allowed to progress through the retarders caused damage to both the wagon concerned and the rail brakes. To avoid this, wagons with riveted wheels were shunted without the use of the retarders. A detector was installed at the entrance to the reception sidings and once an old-fashioned wagon had been found it was shunted into road No. 31 passing over the retarder into the non-braking position.

Whitemoor Yard was not only the first yard to incorporate Fröhlich type rail brakes, but also the first marshalling installation to use track circuiting. This was installed from the hump crest to the run-off from the 'Jack' points. A total length of 38ft was considered adequate for each track circuit. This was divided into 13ft before the point tongue, and 23ft behind it. Thus any wagon which was longer than 38ft between the axles could not be hump-shunted as it would register as two separate vehicles passing down the hump. The system was extremely successful and led the way for many future marshalling yards which were, whilst much more complex essentially, the same in their mode of operation.

Two new signal boxes were erected to control the entrance and exit from the yard. The old box at Whitemoor Junction had contained 52 levers in 1883. In 1886 the west curve was opened and a new 86-lever box was provided. This was further updated in 1928 ready for the new Whitemoor 'up' yard and a 147-lever box was built. This was further extended to work the new 'up'

The 'up' departure sidings at Whitemoor make an ideal yard for portion swopping on long-distance air-braked freights. In June 1986, a rake of vans for Wisbech stands in the middle-distance whilst a train carrying concrete sleepers awaits departure for Cambridge via the permanent way yard at Chesterton.

departure sidings which were installed during World War II. The Grassmoor Junction box replaced two smaller signal cabins at Norwood Junction and Grassmoor. The 52-lever frame controlled the entrance to the tranship shed as well as the engine release road from the 'up' hump. A few years later, in 1933, it also controlled the departure end of the 'down' yard. A third box was also involved in the control of movements in and around Whitemoor Yard. This last signal box started life as Twenty Foot River Siding and controlled yet another wayside goods yard complete with brick-built goods shed. It had 25 levers and was sited 1½ miles north of the old Whitemoor Yards, next to a level crossing. When the new 'up' yard was opened in 1929, the box had been revamped with a 44-lever frame installed on 7th October 1928. The signal cabin had been extended to receive this and the join could clearly be seen even into the 1970s!

# 1930 to 1960

The benefits of the new 'up' yard at Whitemoor were very rapidly recognised and it was decided that the 'down' yard should be similarly remodelled. Ten reception sidings were built on the site of the old 'down' yards; these led over a single hump

to the 40 sorting sidings. The gradient into the yard was slightly steeper than in the 'up' yard at 1 in 17; this because of a heavy flow of empty wagons returning to the Midlands and the North. There were two rail brakes after the 'King' points rather than the four in the 'up' yard. The sidings were divided into central, western and eastern groups as in the 'up' yard, and the eastern group could be shunted from the north end. Five sidings for crippled wagons were also incorporated and a little-known narrow gauge railway installed to facilitate the removal of heavy parts from damaged wagons. Traffic passing through the 'down' yard was both empty wagons and agricultural produce from the large farming areas of East Anglia and Southern Lincolnshire.

With the start of World War II, an increased burden was placed on Britain's major marshalling yards because of the large volume of armaments and supplies which had to be moved rapidly around the country. It was partly because of this increased traffic that ten 'up' departure sidings were built at the southern end of the 'up' yard. These varied in length from 52 to 62 SWL and form the main marshalling point for modern Speedlink traffic in the 1980s and as such it remains one of Britain's busiest marshalling complexes. Throughout the post-war years, heavy trainloads of coal were sorted at Whitemoor before progressing to household coal depots around East Anglia, as well as major gasworks in East London. Agricultural produce was transported by railway through Whitemoor to retail centres throughout the country.

It will of course be remembered that the first automatic rail brakes or retarders were installed by a German company under the

patent of a German engineer named Dr Fröhlich. In view of the close working relationship with the German railways during the construction of Whitemoor Yard, it was certain that the Germans would know the exact location of this railway nerve centre when war broke out in 1939. Within ten years the countries of Great Britain and Germany had moved from close industrial co-operation to all-out war. It was obviously important that such a crucial freight-handling centre should remain unscathed by enemy bombing raids.

## Whitemoor Freight

**Only the roofs of the wagons which make up the 6H98 Cambridge to Whitemoor can be seen as the train passes March East behind Class 31 No. 31183. Traffic on 27th June 1986 included cement from Foxton, grain from Newmarket, and coal empties from Cambridge.**

This was achieved by an ingenious plan which involved the set-up of a mock marshalling yard some four miles to the west of Whitemoor. In order to do this, lighting masts were arranged in a pattern similar to a marshalling yard alongside derelict dykes and farmland. During air raids a blackout was observed at Whitemoor whilst the lights at the mock yard were left on. This idea ensured the protection of Whitemoor Yard during World War II.

In 1953, British Railways rationalised the Peterborough yards and all general freight traffic was transferred to March 'down' yard, which became a general classification yard. Norwood Yard, which occupied the

site of the old 'up' Whitemoor, dealt with coal empties returning to the various collieries in the Midlands as well as parcels and seasonal fruit specials. The 500 acre site with its 70 miles of track was dealing with up to 7,000 wagons daily at the end of the 1950s.

## 1960 to 1985

On a typical day in 1960, Whitemoor dealt with 126 arriving freight trains and dispatched 135 trains. The records from an average day revealed this was the equivalent to a throughput of between 4,500 and 4,800 wagons. The flow of minerals from the Midlands and the returning empties was an important part of traffic in Whitemoor, as was the marshalling of general freight traffic. Fruit and vegetable seasonal traffic was also received from East Anglia and Essex and despatch to market centres in the Midlands and the North. Up to 130 vans per day came with produce from the greenhouses in the Lea Valley and fruit-growing areas of Cambridgeshire and Suffolk. A similar heavy flow of van traffic was experienced during the sugar beet and seed potato seasons.

A complex series of connections were made at Whitemoor to most of the major yards around the country. A constant stream of fitted and non-fitted freights left

**Opposite:**
A mammoth Speedlink train passes Whitemoor Junction signal box as it departs from Whitemoor on 9th June 1982. The train is the 6S71, 18.21, Whitemoor to Paisley, headed by Class 47 No. 47239 and made up of 28 high-capacity air-braked wagons.

Class 37 No. 37003 approaches March station with the 6H90 from Norwich to Whitemoor on 27th June 1986.

**Opposite bottom:**
A typical East Anglian trip freight in the 1960s approaches Ipswich in the 'up' direction. British Thomson Houston locomotive No. D8242 hauls CPV cement wagons and MCV coal wagons; probably from the nearby Claydon cement works.

*J. Cooper-Smith*

Coal empties pass March East signal box in January 1961 behind Class 24 No. D5024. The March 'down' yard can be seen in the background with rows of stored wooden-sided wagons.

*J. Baker*

the yard bound for Doncaster, Niddrie, Newcastle upon Tyne and the North East, Manchester, Sheffield and the Midlands, Toton and Birmingham. Under the National Frieght Train Plan of 1966. British Railways concentrated marshalling at fewer major yards and freight was diverted from the East Coast Main Line on to the Joint line from Doncaster to March. Yards such as the New England Sidings at Peterborough were classified as primary yards, and forwarded their freight to the major or secondary yards which marshalled block trains for forwarding to other parts of the country. Immediately after this re-organisation in freight services, Whitemoor

became overloaded at peak times and, with reception roads full, trains were forced to seek refuge in sidings miles back along the Joint line and the Ely to Peterborough line. Train crews could spend a whole shift moving slowly forwards from loop to loop between Spalding and Whitemoor. This congestion was, however, short-lived. By the late 1960s, wagonload freight traffic had begun to decline. A once extensive distribution of household coal was in contraction.

Power stations in the South East were converted to oil-firing and smaller works were closed. As North Sea gas became available, coal-fired gasworks were also

closed, bringing further decreases in the demands for Midlands' coal. Whitemoor remained busy at times, particularly when the late autumn seasonal carryings of beet-pulp and seed potato traffic coincided with the pre-Christmas parcels rush. By 1970, however, British Rail proposed closing Whitemoor 'down' yard. Not only decrease in wagon load traffic but also the increase in block train working were cited as reasons for the closure. On the Eastern Region alone, block train working had increased from 70 per cent in 1970 to 80 per cent in 1978. Similar modernisation in the wagonload sector had brought the introduction of long wheelbase wagons, which were unsuitable when shunted over the short track circuits installed at Whitemoor in the 1920s and 1930s.

By 27th January 1972, freight traffic had declined to the extent that British Rail closed the 'down' yard. All marshalling at Whitemoor was concentrated on the 'up' yard with some 'down' traffic being transferred to the Norwood Yards. These had previously been opened for only one shift a day, but now worked for twenty four hours, and it was claimed that Norwood, with a good crew, could shunt over its small knuckle as much as could be achieved at the Whitemoor 'down' yard. The sidings in the 'down' yard remained in situ and were used for storage of out-of-season vans brought from a wide area of the country. During the mid 1970s, the first experiments with both Speedlink working and TOPS computer control of wagons were undertaken.

In October 1973, the Eastern Region's second trial air-braked Speedlink train was introduced between Parkston Quay and Edinburgh. A year later, in 1974, a TOPS computer was installed at Whitemoor. As the number of Speedlink services grew, so the need for complex marshalling decreased. By 1980, it became hard to justify the hump in the 'up' yard as any limited re-marshalling now necessary could be dealt with by flat-shunting. In October 1980, the 'up' hump was closed, and all freight marshalling was conducted from the south end of the 'up' yard. During the introduction of this alteration in working, most freight marshalling was transferred to March 'up' and 'down' yards to allow completion of track and signalling changes. The Whitemoor Junction signal box was altered at a cost of £100,000 and became single-manned. The 'up' yard was initially flat-shunted without track alteration at the northern end but this led to some unfortunate accidents as illustrated.

The temporary working arrangements at Whitemoor were far from satisfactory and it was not until November 1982, when the March to Spalding line closed, that complete rationalisation at Whitemoor was possible. The reception roads at Norwood Yard and Whitemoor 'up' yard were then closed and a line of condemned brake vans placed across the middle of the 'up' sorting sidings to form mobile buffer stops.

The pattern of working at Whitemoor was then set for the next five years. The 'up' departure sidings were used for arrival and departure of trunk Speedlink trains, whilst a selection of sorting sidings were used to sort local traffic connecting with the main

**Table 37**
**Whitemoor Freight Timetable — June 1986**

| Arrivals | | | | Departures | | | |
|---|---|---|---|---|---|---|---|
| Head | Code | From | Arr. Time | Head | Code | To | Dep. Time |
| 6H91 | SX | Tinsley | 00.13 | 6J62 | MX | Tinsley | 00.14 |
| 6E95 | MO | Ince | 00.28 | 7H92 | TO | Peterboro. | 00.33 |
| 6F83 | SX | Tees | 00.28 | 6E95 | MO | Braintree | 01.00 |
| 7E35 | FSX | Thoresby | 00.50 | 6F83 | MX | Parkeston | 01.30 |
| 6E97 | SX | Mossend | 01.38 | 6E97 | MX | R. Lane | 02.59 |
| 6H80 | SX | Hitchin | 01.52 | 6B93 | MX | Hitchin | 03.30 |
| 6E93 | SX | Birkenhead | 02.03 | 9H32 | MO | Wisbech | 03.35 |
| 6E80 | MX | Deanside | 02.11 | 9E80 | MSX | Wisbech | 03.35 |
| 6H39 | MX | Monkbretton | 02.24 | 6H93 | MX | Cambridge | 03.42 |
| 6H85 | MX | Tees | 02.30 | 6E95 | MX | Parkeston | 03.55 |
| 6E82 | MX | S.T.J. | 02.36 | 7E35 | MSX | Foxton | 04.08 |
| 6E95 | MX | Arpley | 03.25 | 6H41 | SX | K. Lynn | 04.48 |
| 6E87 | SX | Millerhill | 03.52 | 6E87 | MX | Parkeston | 05.04 |
| 6E94 | SX | Eastleigh | 04.34 | 6H85 | MSX | Duxford | 05.23 |
| 9H01 | SX | Wisbech | 05.45 | 6H85 | MO | Duxford | 04.37 |
| 6E88 | SX | Trostre | 06.50 | 7P81 | SX | Norwich | 05.28 |
| 6E86 | SX | Mossend | 07.16 | 6Y97 | SX | Bury | 06.25 |
| 9H83 | SX | Peterboro. | 11.36 | 8E50 | TFO S | K. Lynn | 06.50 |
| 9H76 | SX | Cambridge | 11.54 | 9C71 | SX Y | T. Mills | 08.11 |
| 9H35 | SX | Wisbech | 12.00 | 9P71 | SX Y | Norwich | 08.14 |
| 6H94 | SX | Bury | 12.27 | 9G40 | SX Y | Doncaster | 08.22 |
| 9H80 | SX Y | Ipswich | 13.39 | 9M40 | SX Y | Toton | 08.22 |
| 9H86 | SX Y | Norwich | 14.17 | 9H82 | SX Y | Peterboro. | 08.22 |
| 8E27 | SX | Mt. Sorrell | 14.34 | 9H34 | SX | Wisbech | 08.35 |
| 9H86 | SX Y | T. Mills | 15.39 | 7H85 | SX | K. Lynn | 08.50 |
| 9E40 | SX Y | Toton | 15.51 | 6E86 | MSX | Parkeston | 09.30 |
| 7H91 | SX | Peterboro. | 16.14 | 6E86 | SO | Parkeston | 09.12 |
| 6N84 | SX | Duxford | 16.19 | 6F85 | MO | Parkeston | 09.30 |
| 7H86 | SX | K. Lynn | 16.28 | 6P89 | SX | Norwich | 09.45 |
| 6S96 | SX | Parkeston | 16.50 | 7H90 | SX | Peterboro. | 09.54 |
| 6H90 | SX | Norwich | 17.00 | 9H77 | SX | Cambridge | 13.34 |
| 8E50 | MThOS | Derby St.M | 17.58 | 9H36 | SX | Wisbech | 13.40 |
| 7M86 | SX | Parkeston | 18.02 | 8Y81 | SX | Ipswich | 14.30 |
| 7R43 | TThO | Kilnhurst | 18.07 | 6N84 | SX | Tyne | 17.15 |
| 6H78 | MO | Braintree | 18.25 | 6S96 | SX | Mossend | 18.10 |
| 6H98 | SX | Cambridge | 18.30 | 7M86 | SX | Arpley | 18.52 |
| 9S93 | SX | Wisbech | 18.50 | 6S71 | SX | Mossend | 19.03 |
| 6D42 | SX | Parkeston | 19.37 | 6S93 | SX | Deanside | 19.15 |
| 6H95 | SX | Norwich | 19.43 | 7R43 | TThO | R. Lane | 19.43 |
| 6N90 | SX | Parkeston | 21.50 | 6V85 | SX | S.T.J. | 19.52 |
| 6J62 | SX | Parkeston | 23.25 | 6090 | SX | Eastleigh | 20.00 |
| | | | | 6D42 | SX | Doncaster | 20.22 |
| | | | | 6V14 | SX | S.T.J. | 21.15 |
| | | | | 6M90 | SX | Birkenhead | 22.25 |
| | | | | 6N90 | SX | Tees | 22.47 |
| | | | | 8E27 | SX | Leyton | 22.50 |

Speedlink network. During 1982, Whitemoor was dealing with 3,500 wagons weekly, the majority of which were air-braked and destined for Speedlink trains. Only eight brake vans were allocated to Whitemoor Yard by January 1983, and the transfer to fully air-braked freights was almost complete.

In 1960, there were over 2,000 men employed at Whitemoor depot and yards. By 1983, 300 remained at the locomotive depot of which 160 were drivers. Whitemoor Yard, in contrast, retained only 34 staff, a phenomenal reduction when compared with the hundreds of men employed at the old hump yards.

## The Future of Whitemoor Yard

In 1982, British Rail argued that it could save £628,000 if Whitemoor was closed, and all freight train marshalling transferred to Peterborough. Ironically, a large part of the New England yards at Peterborough had been sold off in the early 1970s, leaving only limited siding space at the East Coast Main Line station. The success of the Speedlink network and the considerable increases in

both grain and ferry traffic meant that Peterborough Yards did not have the necessary siding capacity. Not only were the sidings of inadequate length, but as the yards were on the 'up' side of the ECML, freight trains would have to cross this on the level when arriving at or leaving from the yard. Locomotive servicing facilities were very limited at Peterborough, with only a single track diesel refuelling shed. In contrast, land, siding capacity and locomotive facilities were more than adequate at Whitemoor, and it was therefore decided to retain a major marshalling yard there. Whitemoor is classified as one of twelve Speedlink network yards and as such has an important future in the development of British Rail's air-braked freight services.

The decade from 1972 to 1982 saw repeated rationalisation at Whitemoor in response to decreases in wagonload freight traffic. There was an inevitable time lag between alterations at Whitemoor and the changes in the economic climate. It was, therefore, ten years between the trough in wagonload freight, experienced in the early 1970s, and the completion of rationalisation at Whitemoor. During those ten years considerable gains were made by Railfreight, and the future prospects for wagonload freight in the March area are good. The main success story concerns the Wisbech line. In 1978 traffic was restricted to tinplate for the Metal Box Company along with a few wagons of coal for the Charringtons coal yard. The 1980s saw the introduction of the two-way traffic in Spillers canned pet food to Paisley, near Glasgow. The traffic generated by the

**Robinson 2-8-0 No. 63705 stands in the 'up' reception sidings at Whitemoor after arriving from the Joint line with a freight from the north April 1961.**

*J. Baker*

Spillers Company used up to twenty four high-capacity VGA wagons daily, and the branch has returned to relative prosperity. Railfreight has also won traffic from the Campbell's Soup Factory at King's Lynn and carries a considerable tonnage of grain from centres all over the East Anglia to Scottish distilleries and ports such as Barry and Birkenhead.

In 1986, further minor alterations to the layout at Whitemoor were undertaken. The ten departure roads in the 'up' yard remained unaltered and provide an important marshalling point with their average length of 60 SWL. The sorting sidings were reduced and Nos. 1 to 27 are still intact. The most westerly sidings, numbered 1 to 13, are very short with a maximum siding length of 20 SWL. The centre of the yard, roads Nos 13 to 27, provides sidings with a capacity of 30 SWL, and these are used for local Speedlink traffic, whereas the shorter roads are filled

with engineer's traffic.

The 1986 timetable *(Table 37)* contained 66 arrivals and departures with nine further conditional services. These brought up to 700 wagons each day to Whitemoor for marshalling, giving a weekly throughput of up to 3,500 wagons. This was easily dealt with in the new and much smaller Whitemoor Yard *(Plan 41)*. Development of the land vacated after closure of Whitemoor 'down' yard will complete the transformation of Britain's first automated, bi-directional hump yard. A 432-inmate category 'B' prison will be constructed at a cost of £18.5 million and should be completed by 1988. Post-industrial Britain, the philanthropists' dream, is replacing

symbols of the country's past hard work by evidences of a decaying society!

My thanks go to Michael Back who, both as BR Customer Service Officer, and as an enthusiast, helped greatly with this chapter. Acknowledgement is also due to Peter Waszak whose article about March was essential source material, and the staff at Whitemoor whose anecdotes and stories have been incorporated in this chapter.

**'Full of sound and fury', J15 class No. 65458 and J39 Class No. 64901 accelerate past Whitemoor Junction. Their train of empty mineral wagons is bound for the Midlands on this day in September 1960.**

*J. Baker*